Academic cognitive psychology can be characterized as the pursuit of deep philosophical questions with empirical means, and indeed the first professors of psychology were affiliated at philosophical faculties. Philosophy and psychology have parted ways since then, but this brave book tries to bring these two disciplines back again into closer touch. Not by going back in time, but by moving forward, not shying away from recent developments in neural plasticity, artificial intelligence, morality, and gender issues. This is not only courageous and timely, but also serving an important function in encountering the continuing fragmentation of our scientific disciplines by means of a bold integrative approach. Very well done indeed!

Bernhard Hommel
Technical University, Dresden

Cognitive Science is now over a half century old. Ramesh Kumar Mishra has written an up-to-date account of work on standard topics (like attention and consciousness) as well as ones rarely covered in texts (e.g., religion, morality, and gender). While reporting findings carefully, he also presents his own viewpoints.

Howard Gardner
Hobbs Research Professor of Cognition and Education
Harvard Graduate School of Education

In Cognitive Science, Dr. Ramesh Kumar Mishra provides a masterful introduction to several of the more fascinating (and contentious) topics in contemporary cognitive science. The well-written text is aimed at intermediate students, as well as scholars in other disciplines who are curious about this rapidly changing field of study. Mishra covers a wide-ranging but selective sample of major issues. He has a fine feel for historical and philosophical context and takes care to identify significant theories and summarize important experiments. Mishra does not shy away from difficult topics – he tackles both consciousness and gender, for example – and he does so in order to frame what cognitive science currently understands, what it hopes to be able to discover, and what may be beyond its reach.

Thomas Wynn
Distinguished Professor of Anthropology, Emeritus
University of Colorado

This is not a typical text on Cognitive Science, and this is this book's strength. If you want to find out about state-of-the-art research in language processing, vision science, neuroscience, learning, and computational approaches to cognition, you would be well-served by a more traditional text. But if you want to find out about morality, social interaction, gender identity, religion, AI, consciousness and their relationships to cognition and its evolution, then this book is for you. It is a taster of many aspects of cognitive behavior that are often left out from traditional texts or courses on Cognitive Science. Mishra is not afraid to tackle topics head-on that others have skirted around. And although he confesses to not being a reductionist (which many cognitive scientists are), his approach to these many topics is even-handed. Where the field is split between one view or another, he explains the alternatives; this book will educate, not indoctrinate. It will enrich its readers.

Gerry Altmann
Department of Psychological Sciences
University of Connecticut

Cognitive Science

This volume provides an overview of cognitive science and critically assesses areas within the topic that are evolving rapidly. Using multidisciplinary studies and rich empirical literature, discussions and demonstrations, this book:

- Discusses the evolution of cognition with reference to material records and the use of brain imaging
- Highlights emerging domains and novel themes within cognitive science such as transgender cognition, space cognition, cross-cultural cognition, futuristic artificial intelligence, social cognition and moral cognition
- Reflects on the status of cognition research in these emerging areas and critically evaluates their current progress
- Explores data both from behavioural and neuroimaging research literature, and sheds light on the potential effects of technological growth and changing habits on attention and cognitive abilities of humans
- Examines the effects of religious and meditative practices on its core cognitive science components
- Speculates research domains that would gain importance in the next few decades in cognitive science research

Finding commonalities in theoretical frameworks and models in upcoming areas in cognition research, this comprehensive study will be of interest to students, researchers and teachers of cognitive psychology, cognitive science, neuroscience, medical science, and computer science. It will also be helpful for academicians, psychologists, neuroscientists, mental health professionals, medical professionals, counsellors and those looking for an alternate perspective on the topic.

Ramesh Kumar Mishra is a cognitive scientist currently teaching at the University of Hyderabad. He has explored the dynamics of the human mind within the cognitive science framework. His most recent monographs have been on topics as diverse as bilingualism and the interaction of language with vision and attention. He is a fellow of the Psychonomic Society, USA, and is the editor-in-chief of the *International Journal of Cultural Cognitive Science* (Springer). He is deeply interested in the question of the mind, its evolution and its contemporary manifestation in different facets of life. The chapters of this book summarise his current thinking, which connects the mind to the world.

Cognitive Science
New Developments and Future Directions

Ramesh Kumar Mishra

R Routledge
Taylor & Francis Group

LONDON AND NEW YORK

Cover image: Getty Images

First published 2023
by Routledge
4 Park Square, Milton Park, Abingdon, Oxon OX14 4RN

and by Routledge
605 Third Avenue, New York, NY 10158

Routledge is an imprint of the Taylor & Francis Group, an informa business

British Library Cataloguing-in-Publication Data
A catalogue record for this book is available from the British Library

ISBN: 978-1-032-14765-9 (hbk)
ISBN: 978-1-032-32656-6 (pbk)
ISBN: 978-1-003-31605-3 (ebk)

DOI: 10.4324/9781003316053

Typeset in Sabon
by Apex CoVantage, LLC

To my mother

Contents

List of Figures

Preface

The enterprise of cognitive science can mean many things to many people. It depends on their backgrounds and also on what they think of the mind and the brain. However, most will agree that it is a multidisciplinary field in which chief concerns relate to the question of the mind: to who we are and our goal in a meaningless and indifferent universe. Beyond intelligent behaviour, as cognitive science is often defined in many textbooks, it is about us, social primates inhabiting a planet and projecting meaning onto it. This view takes away the easy mechanistic explanations of the issue and forces us to think of the human mind and cognition in very broad terms, that encompass all our activities. In writing this book, I aimed to write about a few important questions which I thought should be elaborated more. The old-style behaviourism couched in computational or neurologic terms and its claims of modernity representing a new science of the mind had been bothering me. The issues might have come up in seminars, in conference discussions, or during teaching courses and they needed to be explained. I started thinking of the book, or more specifically the topics, many years ago while teaching cognitive science to students both at the University of Allahabad and later at the University of Hyderabad. The book was not planned as a straight monograph on any one topic. My earlier two books have been monographs based on research in language-vison interactions and bilingualism. This was planned as a collection of chapters on both emerging and older areas with some new twists. It is aimed at students, teachers, and other enthusiasts who value cognitive science. I have been both opinionated and argumentative in many places. This was to show the problems as they are without appearing biased towards any particular theory. The chapters are pretty much stand-alone. Since I have devoted an entire first chapter to different issues related to the book and its structures, I won't repeat them here. The chapters contain both older and newer theories and focus on the debates that have shaped the field. Since cognitive science is still a new and growing multidisciplinary enterprise, my approach has been to show the reader the possibilities more than the certainties of discoveries. The book will benefit anyone with some basic knowledge of cognition but I don't assume any specific training.

However, it is important to note here, briefly, the main motivation behind the book. First and foremost, I wanted to examine somewhat non-mainstream topics. For instance, the question of gender or morality. Topics such as attention, Artificial Intelligence, or consciousness are more popular and find a place in many books. A few years ago, primarily through teaching various subjects to students of cognitive science, I became aware of the main undercurrents of cognitive science and the key historic conflicts, since the cognitive revolution has been centred on the mind-brain issues. How does cognition work? Secondly, I was interested in the diversity or individual difference question. This probably forms the main thread of the book that connects the chapters. How do different people cognise the world and what is cognition for? The selection of chapters was done with this in mind. Of course, there are still many other interesting topics that could have found a place. The coronavirus pandemic began when I was in the middle of this book, around March 2020. I completed many chapters while in full or partial lockdown, looking at the paused world from the windows in different places. It has been apparent to me that this virus and its spread is first and foremost an attack on the very heart of human social cognition. With social distancing and humans in masks, it's not clear what is the future of our mutually agreed-upon cognition. I spent the initial three months of lockdown at Rourkela, Orissa, the place where I had spent my dramatic boyhood and adolescence. A significant portion of the book was completed there. The care of my family gave me peace and comfort to write the book.

It is time to thank those who have helped in the preparation of this manuscript in many significant ways. Seema Prasad, my former student and currently Humboldt postdoctoral fellow at TU Dresden did much of the editing and making sure that the text is readable. Without that the manuscript would be suffering from lack of clarity in many ways. Her dedication and co-working attitude have been always helpful. I don't think it was possible to complete this in the time duration which I fixed for myself without that kind of support. I thank her for all these and wish her a bright career in cognitive science. My PhD student, Aswini Madhira, helped in the formatting of the chapters as per the publishers' demands. I thank her for her time and effort. I thank my other students Vaishnavi Mohite, Siddhima Gupta, Benaifer Fernandes, Manasa Padmanabhuni, and Sneha Kedia for valuable input during proofreading. The Centre for Neural and Cognitive Science, where I teach, has been the intellectual home for most of my activities. The University of Hyderabad has been very supportive of everything I have done in the last seven years. I would also like to point out that during the writing of the book, I received the prestigious iBrain, integrated track in brain and cognitive sciences, ERASMUS+ grant along with many other

International partners in Europe and India, that allowed me to conduct many seminars, workshops and intellectual activities. These activities and discussions therein helped me to try out my ideas before I wrote them out in the book. I also received the Indo-Shastri travel grant to visit Raymond Klein at Dalhousie University, and the DUO-India visiting fellowship to visit Niels Schiller at Leiden University, during various stages of revision of the book. Ideas exchanged with them helped in reformulating some of the narrative. Hesitantly I asked, sending the chapters of this book to scholars such as Bernhard Hommel, Howard Gardner, Thomas Wynn and Gerry Altmann, who have kindly provided blurbs and their opinions. I am thankful to all of them.

I am thankful to Ms. Irfan Lubna, the commissioning editor for this book from Routledge, who has been very helpful with this project. The comments of the reviewers helped substantially in revising the ideas and the manuscript as a whole. I hope this book achieves its aim of inviting the curious-minded to cognitive science. Finally, I thank Riya, my daughter, and my wife Bidisha, for their support in many ways, at different times. People don't write the books for you but they create that state of mind both in their presence and absence in which books are written.

1 Introduction

1. Cognition: A brief history

This book is about the mind and cognition. In contrast to ontological facts such as brains and Mt. Everest, words like "mind" and "cognition" are conceptual. They are epistemological projections that we have made which we are trying to understand. This circularity within a material world wherein everything is explained by science in causes and effects would naturally pose problems. Therefore, investigation of conceptual categories like the mind and mental states using current methods of science has not been easy. A book that claims to cover important topics of contemporary and futuristic relevance in cognitive science should first clarify these conceptual bottlenecks. Before it goes on to explain the mind's attributes and turns to the brain, it should ask, "Why do we even have minds?" This becomes a question of evolution of which we have a little knowledge. Since we do have minds, it then becomes our responsibility to understand them "scientifically." It is then reasonable to briefly review some critical philosophical foundations of this science before getting into more applied areas. The formal recognition that minds are real entities and need to be explained has been through a revolution popularly known as the cognition revolution.

It would take several books to track any reasonable history of cognitive science since the evolution of this discipline, as we know it today, stands on very long-running historical strands of multiple disciplines. More generally, scholars simplify this by designating the sixties as the time when cognitive revolution originated. An interdisciplinary enterprise began to study the human mind. Many have covered the drama and intrigue of this phase of development of this discipline (Gardner, 1987; Miller, 2003; Sperry, 1993). By reading these books and articles, the curious beginning student, who is interested in interdisciplinary ideas, comes in thinking cognitive science indeed began as a revolution. However, in what exact sense this was a revolution and what were its features has not been easy to track. The student ends up learning that there was a very strong reaction in multiple disciplines against materialistic psychology, which appeared meaningless to the human spirit and mind. This was true in some sense but many have reacted against

DOI: 10.4324/9781003316053-1

such a simple verdict (Watrin & Darwich, 2012). By this time, while "mind" had remained a philosophical concept for centuries, certain definite progress had happened in physiology and computer science. Such a climate was conducive for bringing in the "mind" as an explorable phenomenon within the ambit of science through objective methods and experiments.

Since "mind" is essentially a philosophical concept, the story should start with some philosophical history. In the 1960s, many analytical philosophers turned to the brain for seeking solutions to the mind-body problem. The mind-body problem had been an age-old perennial issue, at least more formally since the time of Descartes, that made a fundamental distinction between "mental" and "physical" stuff. The problem made it difficult to explain how something like the "mind" may exist in an utterly physical universe. Descartes accepted the mind as immaterial and as made of a different substance. The body was material, obeyed the laws of physics, and had visible and measurable properties. Importantly for Descartes, these two substances interacted in mysterious ways. Descartes thought that the mind did not arise because of external sense perceptions. The ultimate substance of the mind, after it has cleansed itself from sensory perceptions and acquired impressions, was important to Descartes. But for David Hume, the mind was a complex collection of many "bundles of perceptions" that arose from the environment (Armstrong, 2018). Perceptions or ideas were imprinted on the mind and connected to external reality. For Hume, mental perceptions or sense data interacted with the body or the physical strata. The innateness of the mind's attributes and the mind being a reflector of external impressions have remained conflicting dichotomies ever since. Behaviourists and other materialists, while rejecting the mind as a metaphysical concept unworthy of scientific attention, took behaviour that the organism displayed as a reaction to external sensations.

Psychology by the end of the nineteenth century under the influence of "logical positivism" had become materialistic. Under similar influences, analytical philosophers too had turned materialistic and aimed at explanations that satisfied the requirements of science. Both philosophers and psychologists either were indifferent or offered straight-forward rejection of words such as "mental," "subjectivity," and "consciousness." If methods of science with its rigid paradigms could not explain something, then the phenomenon may not exist. Gilbert Ryle's *The Concept of Mind* masterfully summed up this philosophy and set the trend for a materialist philosophy of mind (Ryle, 2009). Australian philosophers such as J. J. Smart and U. T. Place brought the brain to discussion, suggesting even if there is anything called mental, then it must be found in the brain (Place, 1970; Smart, 1970). Stronger versions of such theories equated mental states with hypothetical brain states. It was not the case that these philosophers had any actual ideas about the brain, since there was no brain imaging research then. Such proposals however made it a potential possibility that if brains are studied properly then one can learn about the mind. Any mental state that arises in anyone should have a corresponding neural state that should be trackable using scientific methods. After almost 50 years of Wundt's empirical and James's introspective psychology, every subjective qualitative mental state of whatever type was considered to be nothing but a certain neural state. Folk psychological statements about inner mental states were to be stated using the language of neurophysiology. Such an approach towards the mind and the brain appeared to have made the mind-body problem easier to tackle.

However, to others even within philosophy, the proposal that mental states are similar to brain states did not appear valid, since mental states are nothing like physical states and that is standard epistemology. Herbert Feigl, a student of Moritz Schlick, the founder of logical positivism, argued that mental states cannot be simply equated to brain states since they are not identical (Feigl, 1970). Very counterintuitively Schlick proposed that the mental and the physical are simply two different conceptual systems we use to refer to the same phenomenon. Therefore, both psychological and neural data refer to or describe the same phenomenon using different vocabularies, just as "morning star" and "evening star" both refer to Venus but they are not Venus. This "double language" use established multiple references over identity. Feigl's arguments sounded like some sort of monism. That is, there is only one type of stuff, either mental or physical. The two different conceptual systems refer to the same stuff. This way of putting the identity theory avoided the burden of equating the mental with the physical, at least temporarily.

Hilary Putnam's multiple realizability hypothesis questioned the one-to-one correspondence between brain states and mental states (Putnam, 1967). He argued that organisms could have different types of brains and thus eventually different kinds of minds. It is even possible that these brains may not always be biological in origin. For instance, it's also possible that the artificial agent will have brains made of silicon. How does one, then, ascribe any "mind" to such entities? Putnam's "functionalism" described mental states in functional terms without referring to any one-to-one correspondence with any particular neural hardware. Since it is very likely that different organisms may have the same mental states linked to the same or different neural processes. Therefore, it is unnecessary to assume that all types of mental states have a common brain state. This functionalist argument proved to be a potential challenge to the type-identity theories, but has not been proved to be empirically testable. Neural realisation refers to the exact neurobiological mechanisms that lead to certain specific psychological states. Putnam had claimed that similar realisers are behind the pain in mammals and molluscs. But they have very different brains. But, how can we know if the pain felt by molluscs is the same kind of pain that mammals feel? Current progress in comparative neuroscience does not support the multiple realisation theory (Polger & Shapiro, 2016).

Functionalism meant an emphasis on functions (Lewis, 1966). Functionalism wanted to avoid not only materialism and behaviourism but also dualism. Did it succeed? Functionalism succeeds in avoiding dualism since it does not treat the mental and the physical as two separate things. It does not seek their interactions. Mental states that may include all kinds of folk psychological belief structures are functionally realised in different physical systems through different means. States of computers that work on input and output models on symbols are of this type. We do not speak of the interaction of the hardware and the software. In its attempt to naturalise the mind, functionalism left out important stuff such as qualia, consciousness, and intentionality of agents. Mental states are functional states but mental states have qualia too. Agents know what it feels to be in such a state and that could be different from one to another. In spite of theoretical problems, Putnam's ideas led to functionalism, which still rules cognitive psychology (Churchland, 2005). All mental states are functions of the brains. Thus, the study of cognition is nothing but the study of functions of brains.

These critical insights have led to the investigation of the mind in connection to the brain. More particularly, psychological functions are seen as extensions of brain states, which can be tracked (Barrett, 2009). Therefore, cognitive science has accommodated findings from neuroscience in spite of many conceptual issues that are still unsolved. Today, we can map brain dynamics with reasonable temporal and spatial resolution and correlate them with apparent mental states of research participants. No one knows if this reduction is correct or not but it has become a standard part of many dominant paradigms in mind-brain sciences (Libet, 2006; Neisser, 2014).

Gilbert Ryle once gave an example to justify his claims of the non-existence of the mind (Ryle, 2009). Ryle said that if someone is watching cricket and observing each player doing something, i.e., batting, bowling, fielding, etc., and questions, "Where is cricket?" then this question results from a category mistake. The question is pointless since there is nothing called cricket on and above each individual who is playing. Similarly, his other example was if someone goes around Oxford University and comes across the many colleges, Chappell grounds, and so on, and finally asks, "Where is the university?" this is also a category mistake. Ryle was giving these examples to bring home his point that there is nothing on and above the workings of the brain that counts as behaviour. The so-called mind is behaviour. Similarly, if someone sees research activities in various fields such as neuroscience, psychology, computer science, anthropology, etc., and asks, "Where is cognitive science?" this is a category mistake. The very activities that are being conducted in some areas in some of these disciplines are cognitive science. There is no such thing called cognitive science on and above the individual activities. One might collect in a textbook various chapters from these topics and tell a student that this is cognitive science. However, it must be noted that all research activities within these participating disciplines are not to be called cognitive science but only some, just as not all the states produced by the brain are mental states that denote subjectivity, but only some.

I prefer the phrase "the science of cognition" compared to "cognitive science." This not only gives me a different feel about what I intend to describe but also takes away the existential pain of defining the boundaries of the discipline. The science of cognition is about cognition: the psychological and neurobiological phenomena that make us who we are. Cognition began within the emergence of life itself. For physicists, the Big Bang offers a mutually agreed-upon starting point for theory construction. There is no such thing for cognitive scientists. Therefore, it's important to define what cognition itself is and why it evolved in a material world. The field called cognitive science that took formal shape around the fifties has merely attempted to put all the pieces together. But it has never been easy to define cognition to our fullest satisfaction. Just as music did not begin with Beethoven or Chopin, cognitive science did not begin with a few radical scholars trying to see things differently and challenge the orthodoxy in the fifties. It began with the mind's awareness about itself in this material universe. The different chapters of this book reflect this underlying thinking beyond the data and experimental results.

2. The diversity of cognition

The question of cognitive diversity has become very important in recent decades. Naturally, this has social, economic, and cultural attributes along with growing consciousness of individual rights. Therefore, respecting this will need one to bring the diversity model to theories of human cognition. There cannot be a general theory of mind, cognition, and human nature that satisfies all, unlike what we see in physical sciences. Although the study of cognition has taken a materialistic turn in recent times that includes brain imaging, this data too clearly indicates massive individual difference (Barch et al., 2013). Each brain has its unique manner of correlating with specific cognitive functions of that agent. And, agents vary with regard to their experience, culture, lifestyle, and many other variables that we cognitive scientists hardly consider in everyday laboratory-based research. But theory construction can no longer neglect this because this may decide how fruitful cognitive science is to human needs in general. Considering this, the book includes a few chapters that are at the forefront of individual difference research as far as mind and brain are concerned. For example, the question of sexuality, gender, and cognition as well as the mysterious effects of religions on human consciousness.

The study of cognition now has moved on from the early obsession with the computer metaphor in which minds were looked at as nothing but problem-solving algorithms housed in human brains. Today, in multiple fields within the mind-brain sciences, mental states that belong to agents are holistically examined in connection to both the body and cultural forces. A new era of embodiment and cultural cognition that looks at the uniqueness of the human mind as an expression of historical forces and biology has begun (Herrmann & Tomasello, 2012; Qu et al., 2021). More recently the field of cultural neuroscience has visibly grown to expand experimental and theoretical approaches to this issue. Understanding how cultures affect neural functioning also has benefits for planning health policy and intervention (Chiao et al., 2013). Transcultural neuroimaging studies have shown that cultural forces shape how brain functions differ widely (Han & Northoff, 2008). These studies have revealed the fine-tuning of brain functions for selected psychological functions such as attention of memory. The narrative of many chapters in this book expresses this underlying thought.

In 2010, Henrich et al. (2010) published a paper slamming psychology for its biased approach to human research. They coined the phrase WEIRD (western, educated, industrial, rich, democratic) which has gained ever increasing popularity. The acronym speaks for itself and is very critical of the way psychology within cognitive science has developed. They alleged that since we have not studied a wide range of people from different cultures with different identities, we don't know much about them. The so-called mainstream theories based mostly on white population can't be universally applicable. This led to the examination of unique forms of cognition in diverse populations and developments of methodologies to deal with these challenges. More recently, Barrett (2020) has further clarified how and why cultural and individual difference research matters. According to him, we have to see cognition from the perspective of the individual, the interpersonal, and the societal. So far, mostly we have studied the individual cognitive processing in a small range of people. There has been some work at the interpersonal level, for example in emotion recognition or linguistic communication, but not much. Very little is known how cognition works at the societal level. At this level, one can study concepts such as religion, morality, and proximal behaviour of conflict management. When countries go to wars, this level of cognition matters as well as when people of a war-ravaged country gather the pieces and rebuild. In this book, I address at least one such group-level cognitive system that is religion. Thus, current and future investigations of the mind depend on how holistically we see the mind as a tool of human experience rather than a computational hub running on abstract symbols. Such a proposal does not seem as radical now as it was some time ago, since there is now widespread acceptance of such holistic theories of mind and cognition (Alessandroni, 2018; Núñez et al., 2019).

3. Contemporary cognitive science

Cognitive science is defined differently by its practitioners depending on their commitment to diverse conceptual foundations. For example, if you survey the websites of departments and research centres around the world that offer courses on cognitive science you will come across many variations in their description of cognitive science. Cognitive science developed in the sixties as a loose ensemble of like-minded scholars who wanted to pursue the question of the mind. However, today, cognitive science is more multidisciplinary and applied, and those who study it differ in their choice of theoretical positions. Further, some refer to it as "cognitive science" and others use "cognitive sciences." Some view it as a single unified discipline with its theories and methods while others think of it as a collection of disciplines in which much diversity exists. Rafael Núñez and colleagues wrote a provocative article titled "What happened to cognitive science?" (Núñez et al., 2019) in which they examined the state of the field in the current scenario. Their main argument was that over many decades cognitive science has not materialised into a coherent field but presents only a vague collection of ideas and disciplines without any unity. This could be taken both as good and bad depending on our theoretical commitments. It's only natural that over time many other disciplines interested in developing this field have emerged with their own questions about the mind in addition to the original ones. Núñez et al. further noted that the field has been heavily influenced by cognitive psychology and other fields are neglected. It's possible that the founding fathers viewed this field as a singular discipline that would explore the mind and create theories, but this may not be the case anymore. Contemporary cognitive science, therefore, has moved beyond its initial assumptions and includes many different fields such as cognitive science of religion and cognitive science of education, and indicates much diversity in methods and practices. The collection of chapters in this book provides the reader with this perspective that they can link with their own.

Cognition is about agents and their minds and what they do with those minds in the real world. Therefore, there is a practical angle to the problem of the mind and cognition that must be addressed within the discipline. While including the chapters I have kept this urgency in mind. For example, the question of religious belief or morality is personal to agents and they must be in a position to understand them more objectively. Similarly, we all experience states of attention and consciousness in our everyday lives and we should understand recent scientific progress on them. Those who are interested in computers and how AI is changing the world should also understand its consequences on the mind. Cognitive science today includes discussions and writings on all these aspects of human life that matter in the everyday world. More recently, Barret (2020) has proposed that cognitive science has to include the individual and cultural perspective without which it will remain a monolithic field. According to Barrett, the study of cognition in the wider world must be conducted at social, interpersonal, and individual levels to be holistic. So far, cognitive psychology, which has contributed the most to the field, has not considered these critical aspects of the human mind. We have to explain what actual people do in the world with their minds and their subjectivities and biases and develop theories to explain them. This raises a serious methodological question whether we are ever going to have one theory of the mind integrated into the biology that would be universal. That's a legitimate dream since cognitive science is an empirical field and therefore it must aspire for general theories that are invariant. However, cognition is about real people in the world and how they navigate its everyday complexity in diverse social, cultural, and geographic situations; it may not have a single theory. I have included a chapter on the cognition of gender and sexuality which falls within Barrett's classification of interpersonal cognition. The gender and sexuality of individuals influences how they experience cognition. Similarly, how individuals experience attention, consciousness, or even moral states depends on who they are and what cultural values they subscribe to. The diversity of chapters in this book demonstrates this idea more generally with many examples.

Paul Thagard defined cognitive science in this way:

> Cognitive science is the interdisciplinary study of mind and intelligence, embracing philosophy, psychology, artificial intelligence, neuroscience, linguistics, and anthropology. . . . The central hypothesis of cognitive science is that thinking can best be understood in terms of representational structures in the mind and computational procedures that operate on those structures.
>
> (Thagard, 2020, para 1, 11)

Figure 1.1 depicts the most famous picture of cognitive science and its original disciplines. The founding fathers believed these disciplines would be the ones that would legitimately study the nature of the mind in an interdisciplinary manner. According to Núñez as reviewed earlier, some of these disciplines have not played a big role in the development of cognitive science, such as anthropology. But there are ambiguities in Núñez's analysis. For example, on one hand, he aspires to see a more unified and coherent cognitive science with a rigid central theory; and on the other hand, he laments the takeover of the field by cognitive psychology. Gentner (2019) thinks that cognitive science is doing fine and more diversity in methods and approaches are being recognised. My aim in this volume was to include chapters that characterise that belief. Cognitive science is a human science and it has to align with the expectations and ethos of human diversity. Humans don't carry around a digital computer in their heads and therefore a single algorithm won't explain their behaviour. Subjects like anthropology, culture studies, evolution, and philosophy will play a greater role in putting the human being at the centre of this enterprise. This matters for the reader of this book since they would like to know what cognitive science is really about. They would like to know if there is a set of standard theories and procedures in cognitive science today that they can further apply to their desired needs. Unfortunately, there is none as of now, and it was also probably not designed to be so. Cognitive science has to be diverse and broad while maintaining some of its basic assumptions and has to be in tandem with the needs of the times. I will give an example that will further demonstrate the potential conflicts within the field and the assumptions.

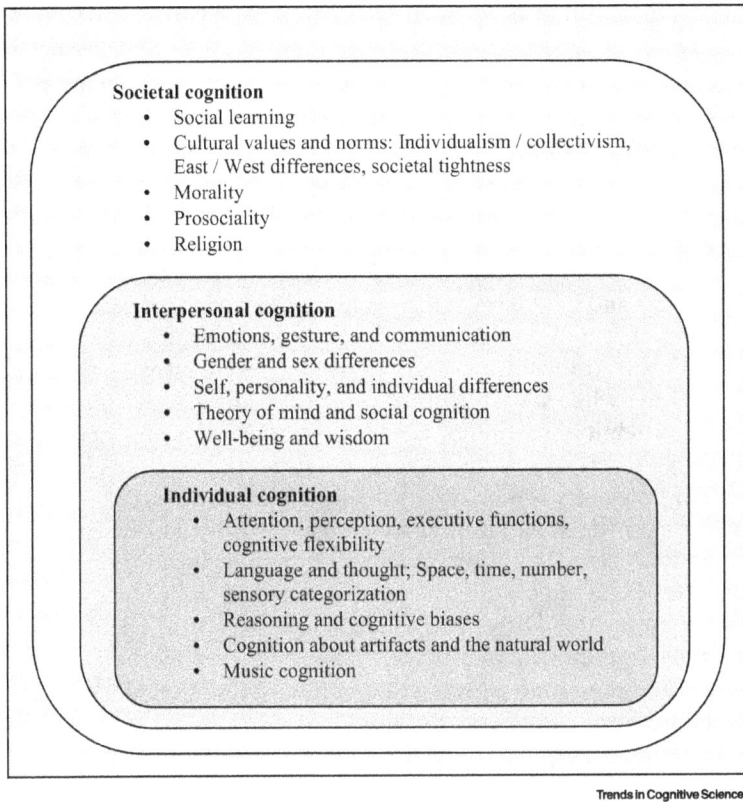

Figure 1.1 Newly developing areas within cross-cultural cognitive science that are moving beyond studying individual cognition.

Source: Reprinted from Trends in Cognitive Sciences, Vol 24, H. Clark Barrett, Towards a Cognitive Science of the Human: Cross-Cultural Approaches and Their Urgency, 620–638, 2020, with permission from Elsevier

This book has a chapter on attention and another one on consciousness. These topics involve the standard theories and experiments that every textbook usually has. However, attention is something that people use to do things in the real world. The study of attention in the sixties began as a laboratory enterprise and many fundamental discoveries of its nature and neural underpinnings were discovered (Posner, 1980). However, in the last several decades because of the rise in technology we live in a more connected world, particularly via social media. A standard narrative today is that social media is addictive and bad for your attention. One of its chief proponents of this narrative is the computer scientist Carl Newport (Newport, 2016). Newport argues that social media is just entertainment and can be very destructive to our mental health in the long term. Social media companies make their products and algorithms very addictive to hook people for later monetising. This is a popular argument as far as we are, in general, concerned about our psychological beings. But is there any standard theory that tells how humans must use their attention? There is none. All models and theories about attention in cognitive psychology are about the basic processing of stimuli. They are not about the actual use of attention in the real world by individuals. Does Carl Newport have a single theory of attention that predicts that all humans will equally suffer if they are hooked to the internet and social media most of the time? Even then we have to also define with empirical facts and have a predictive model of how much exact involvement with the internet will be damaging to our mental health creating a fragmented self. Unfortunately, we don't have any current research that predicts this. Therefore, while we can express concern about the individual capacity to use their attention, we do not have a general theory yet. It's possible that in parallel to social and technological evolution, humans are also evolving their biology to adapt to the new challenges. That is essentially the basis of neuroplasticity, which I address in a chapter in this book. There will always be people who can control their attention and produce meaningful work even if they spend time on social media and there will always be others who suffer from ADHD from its overuse. We have to therefore study the interpersonal and individual aspects of cognition shaping the mind in both its cultural and economic aspects to explain how attention works in the real world and how real people use it to do things. Therefore, theoretical discussion on attention is one thing and its actual manifestation in individuals who come with diverse biological and psychological dispositions is another. This is one example from current approaches to the mind in which there is a conflict between theory and applications. Social media companies are guilty of making their products more addictive with regard to attention, but can they also be more sensible in making them so that individuals are repelled from overusing them? Humans come with a limited capacity for processing information. Therefore, it is natural that addictive technologies will affect them more, creating mental illness. However, we are yet to uncover what could be the right scientific approach to the problem that considers the demands of the economy and the activities of the individual within it in a practical sense (Lane & Atchley, 2021).

4. Overview of chapters

In Chapter 2, the story of cognition begins at the beginning: how it all happened and came together, the astounding success of human cognition in the natural world. The story of evolution of the human mind is very complex and is the least discussed topic in mainstream cognitive science textbooks. The chapter explores how understanding our deep past could give us clues about our future. Disciplines like evolutionary archaeology and cognitive anthropology have been consistently discovering interesting facts on human evolution, particularly cognition. The chapter covers important findings about the brain's evolution as well as the mind's symbolic capacity. The dominant theory is that the production of symbolic art which started around fifty to sixty thousand years ago has been linked to the emergence of complex cognition. Together with language, production of symbolic art is indicative of higher cognition that includes intentionality and sense of agency. The chapter introduces the basic findings in cognitive archaeology which are relevant for a holistic study of cognition. I have also included data from contemporary neuroimaging science which has taken this field to newer heights. Since the brain is under biological laws of evolution, the mind has likely followed a similar trajectory. The chapter furthers the idea that true cognitive revolution in the *Homo sapiens* happened long ago in the sense that agents with autonomous minds started producing abstract art and tools in a fully self-conscious way. These achievements required a well-developed brain in terms of cognitive systems, many of which we even use now, albeit in a different context.

Among other participating disciplines, it is cognitive psychology which has driven the agenda of cognitive science enterprise since its appearance in the 1950s. Today it's a matured subject with well-integrated frameworks that span computational, behavioural, and neuroimaging sciences. Cognitive psychologists have examined and have proposed models of important cognitive systems that drive the various facets of cognition in specific tasks. Among these systems, attention has been the most studied for clear reasons. William James had turned to attention to empirically explain the mind and consciousness. Today, many researchers think that we can explain the contents of the mind and consciousness as a result of attention.

Chapter 3 introduces the reader to some basic concepts of attention and more importantly the ones that dominate current research in different fields within mind-brain sciences. The chapter makes the point that our capacity to attend is the most fundamental of cognitive functions that link intentional thinking, action, and its regulation. Even evolutionarily speaking, our achievements are mainly linked to our ability to attend to what we want to. Although the exact role of attention on contents of awareness and consciousness is still debatable, I have attempted to show that we need a very comprehensive understanding of this baffling mechanism. The chapter serves as a gateway for the later chapters since it sets the tone of the book.

Chapter 4 is on religion and its cognitive realisation in the human mind. Today, cognitive science of religion is an established field. However, not many textbooks cover its findings since religion is often considered way too abstract and mysterious for explanations. Religious belief stands in sharp contrast to our rational understanding of the world. Although the evolution of organised religions is more recent, the human mind has always sought some connection between the mystical and the objective reality. Many researchers have started to study religions in an interdisciplinary manner more recently within the mind/brain sciences. The discipline called cognitive science of religion investigates the functional links between religious practices and cognition. My attempt in this chapter has been to show that religions should be seen as collective practices that train different aspects of cognition and are part of the larger human culture. The practice of a certain type of religion has been shown to influence specific aspects of attention and control in the practitioner. Studying religions as collective cognitive events could expand the scope of cognitive science. I have also attempted to show that not all pious and good happens in the name of religions. The chapter considers some major theories of cognitive science of religion and demonstrates dominant findings in the field. Since most cognitive psychologists derive their conclusions from well-controlled laboratory-based studies, the results are not easily applicable to mass phenomena. The chapter builds on my conjecture that cognitive science has to explain everything that humans have been doing all along with their minds and religion is no exception. Therefore, empirical studies of religions within the mind and brain sciences have the potential to eradicate some misunderstandings between the objective and the subjective; the material and the non-material.

Exploration of the mind and mentality in non-biological systems has always remained a top priority among cognitive scientists. Certain philosophers of the mind also accept that minds could be found in any system with given properties and not just in the biological brains. Theories and concepts in AI have led to sophisticated robots that deliver help and participate in human affairs. Humans interact with them while they show concerns about their agency. The chapter aims to focus on some emerging trends within the broad field of artificial intelligence. One important point of debate centres on humans' inherent suspicion and non-acceptance of the AI in spite of its technological powers. Why can't humans accept the AI in any meaningful, satisfying manner? Humans have always displayed awe and fear of the artificial. In Chapter 5, I have attempted to focus on the philosophical and conceptual issues that do not allow humans to truly appreciate the artificially intelligent systems. The chapter covers issues related to ethics and morality on the human artificial interaction and problems herein.

Chapter 6 on neuroplasticity attempts to show how the idea of neuroplasticity has been used and developed in different fields. No one today doubts the concept of neuroplasticity, and it has multiple applications. The brain changes with regard to our actions and sometimes as a result of environmental demands. I have attempted to elaborate a few theories of neuroplasticity that are dominant in the field; particularly, the difference between the way neuroscientists and cognitive psychologists explain neuroplasticity. It's not yet clear how different deliberate practices change selective structures and functions of the brain. It's also not clear if such changes are permanent or temporary. Because of inherent difficulties, it has not always been possible to study neuroplasticity in humans at the level of the brain, unlike animal models. Studying neuroplasticity has great significance for understanding diseases and their potential eradication.

Just like religion, I have always been fascinated by the question of human morality. Why are humans moral agents? Often, they judge others as immoral with great perversity and certainty. We know very little about the appearance in our species and its continuation. Morality heavily influences our everyday decision making and colours our perception of reality. Apart from our consciousness, it's our moral self that is fundamental to our existence. In the last one or two decades, cognitive scientists have attempted to peek deep into our moral selves. Chapter 7 explores the current research into the moral self both from psychological and neuroscientific perspectives. Research reveals that our moral positions are transitory and not fixed. Different people take different moral positions based on how they perceive different situations. They also keep track of their benefits and losses in such decisions. The chapter shows that moral decisions are often biased and irrational. The chapter covers data from cognitive neuroscience and experimental psychology that show how neural systems implement our moral positions in the real world. It also covers new fascinating studies that show the use of language and expression of morality including decision making. The chapter offers a critical albeit futuristic overview of main tracks of current thinking in this area. One important question in this field is if moral decisions are conscious or unconscious. The chapter attempts to address this issue by taking cues from available studies.

The question of consciousness is critical for any theory of cognition and the mind. Current approaches include investigating consciousness using both cognitive psychological as well as brain imaging techniques. Of course, philosophers of the mind have been at it for the last two thousand years. There are extreme theoretical positions on the question of consciousness. For example, Ned Block and David Chalmers would say that there is no way we can investigate the phenomenal subjective part of consciousness. That is the hard problem. Eliminative materialists would completely discard the problem. Cognitive psychologists as usual link this with attention, and study using their regular paradigms. There is widespread reductionism in the question of consciousness in many fields. Chapter 8 offers a selective overview of the main questions and also current developments.

Chapter 9 focuses on the relationship between gender, sexuality, and the mind. Particularly, cognition of people who identify themselves as transgender assumes critical importance in this case. I have described some dominant theoretical frameworks that are being used to study both psychology and neurobiology of gender cognition. Unfortunately, the debates linking gender to cognition in its wider sense are mostly prominent in humanities and social sciences and not much in psychology or neuroscience. That might be because most natural scientists think of gender as something static and individuals may not have the rights to define it according to their convenience. However, that view is now being challenged both on the political and social justice front. I included this chapter intentionally to bring the debate to the tables of cognitive scientists since their research mostly assumes a strict binary model of gender. Expanding our definitions of gender may have consequences for the models.

Finally, in Chapter 10, I discuss the challenges that lie ahead for cognitive science as a multidisciplinary field in the twenty-first century. I discuss the mandate of cognitive revolution formulated in the 1960s and evaluate if contemporary cognitive science is fulfilling that mandate. There is discontent from several corners of the field that cognitive science is overly dominated by psychology and has failed at the overarching aim of being an interdisciplinary field. I will critically analyse these arguments and discuss potential ways to address these concerns. As one of the measures, researchers are now beginning to focus on topics – like cultural influences and individual differences – that have been ignored so far in mainstream cognitive science. I end the chapter by summarising the key questions of these emerging sub-disciplines and how the research paradigm can be different so as to arrive at a holistic understanding of the mind.

5. Unifying the themes

Thematic unity of chapters in any book depends on the underlying conceptual assumptions of the author. I too have my assumptions that run through the selection and exposition of facts in the chapters that are on different topics. It will be evident to the reader that I do not accept any reductive materialistic view of the mind although I don't disregard the scientific achievements so far. I also don't think cognitive science's progress so far can be only summed up in a computational or neural theory of mental functions. While the chapters mention current facts and models, they also present their limitations and my cynicism. For example, I show that we have not integrated knowledge from evolution into our approach to the question of the mind. Similarly, we have to also explain complicated themes of religion and gender identity. This cynicism also shows up when I discuss ethical issues in the domain of our approach to AI and our non-acceptance of non-human agents. We simply can't accept them as intentional moral agents in spite of their computational power. Thus, the book, in principle, shows the reader both what ideas about the mind we have successfully understood and more importantly what we have not.

This book is about cognitive science which arguably values the mind more than the brain. Although within a functionalist materialist tradition we are vulnerable when talking about the mind, I am of the firm opinion that the mind is certainly not the brain. More specifically, measuring activity from the brain won't tell us much about the mind of the agent in causal terms. For example, in the chapter on neuroplasticity, I discuss that we have not yet understood how training impacts the cognitive side of neuroplasticity more generally. A similar mind-brain distinction appears in the chapter on self and morality where it will be obvious that reducing conceptual and metaphysical terms to neural data is not satisfying. These conceptual anxieties reflect the problems in the field. Wherever possible, the chapters present both psychological and neural data but with a caveat on our inability to ground the mind in the brain despite methodological and analytical sophistication. We don't have causal theories of the mind that are grounded to matter. In the chapter on consciousness, I discuss the recent resurgence of panpsychism which also suggests the limitations of the physicalist enterprises. Both neuro-behaviourism and neuro-computationalism have conceptual limitations that have not allowed us any general theory of mind with robust explanatory power. The chapters are also written with the assumption that cognition can't be reduced to certain psychological functions that we conveniently measure today with instruments and propose models with brain data. The book raises the ultimate question of the rise of intentional agents with mysterious inner subjectivity and personal stances towards an indifferent and material universe. The book may not offer a ready solution to these issues but will convince the reader that any simple solutions are bound to be unsatisfactory.

There are two types of chapters in this book. Chapters on attention or consciousness are usual topics to be found in any book on the mind or cognitive science. The other kind is chapters dealing with evolution or morality. In this book, the two types of chapters feed into one another. For example, the empirical grounding of morality, however problematic it may be, is probably possible through the application of cognitive psychology. That's why we need to know how agents' attention and consciousness influence their moral selves. Similarly, we can ask when attention and consciousness evolved in our species since we know their attributes and what they do to us from the last several decades of research. By putting these chapters together, I have invited the reader to apply mechanistic theories to grand problems that are at the core of our existence as mental creatures. In this sense, the two kinds of chapters are unified since they both show empirical knowledge. We need to reduce complex issues to manageable proportions and their limitations. Most chapters introduce the major theories that are relevant with coverage of pertinent literature.

6. Scope of the book

Humans since their evolution have tried to understand their minds in the same the way they have been curious about the natural universe. Cognitive science interests everyone since it's natural to be curious about the mind. Beyond philosophical speculations, products of the mind have great practical significance. I have written the book with some very clear intentions which I will spell out now. I have already mentioned that it is not a straightforward textbook on cognitive science or psychology and therefore some usual topics that the reader can find in other books, such as language or neuropsychology, are skipped. My earlier two monographs on language (Mishra, 2015, 2018) should provide any interested reader with much information on recent developments. However, the interested reader will find topics in this book that such textbooks don't cover; for example, evolution, morality, or gender. The selection of topics, therefore, aims at expanding our current thinking on the mind and the potential future direction in which this may go. The stream of unifying thought is our current struggle between materialism and mentalism. The book's chapters as described earlier deal with some basic aspects of cognition such as attention or consciousness and also how we can put that knowledge into tackling bigger issues like religion or morality or even concerns about AI. In that sense, they equip the reader to go beyond the technicalities and confront more conceptual and epistemological issues. It would be impossible to accommodate every topic that is being researched in cognitive science today in any single volume. Therefore, for brevity, topics that represent more generally what is new and also my ideas about the past, present, and future of mind sciences were selected.

There are two types of readers of any technical book like this. The first category is the students, researchers, and academics who specialise in mind and brain sciences and would like to know the latest update on the theory and data of their field. Or, they may even be interested in how some old concerns have been reinterpreted by the author. The other type of readers is the practitioners such as neurologists, neuropsychologists, speech pathologists, computer scientists, cultural theorists, and others. These experts wish to know about theories of cognition and issues related to brain functions so that they can use those concepts in their practice. In 1999, Michael Posner edited a volume titled *Foundations of Cognitive Science* for which many influential practitioners of the field wrote chapters. In that edited volume, one could see the state of the field (Posner, 1989). The book included chapters on visual attention, language, and computation, but there was no mention of cultural influences or any topics on religion or morality. Today, it's almost impossible to talk of the foundation of cognition as merely computation carried out by an information processing system that is neurally realised. This was the exact view that Turing had proposed in his essay titled "Computing machinery and intelligence" in 1950 and which became the main theory of early cognitive scientists who proposed the information processing view of the mind. Today, the practitioners I referred to earlier would like to know more about crucial matters such as the influence of culture and environment on cognition, how individual faith and belief shape cognition, how brain activity is influenced by affective stimuli in the environment, etc. What was the foundation of cognitive science in 1998 is not the foundation now. That's why this science's influence or take-home message for the practitioners has to be very different. For example, the rapid rise in cognitive behavioural therapy and the use of humanoid robots are good examples. No longer does therapy involve the use of rigid psychometric tests and measurements of verbal and nonverbal IQ but concepts like fluid intelligence, multiple intelligence, social cognition, and even the use of virtual reality for training are part of the everyday activity of the therapist. Similarly, many neurologists do not view the brain as a collection of specialised neural tissues that have specific functions but the whole brain is both structurally and functionally connected even while achieving a simple task. These new developments have revolutionised the application of concepts and techniques of cognitive sciences in a wide range of fields. Decades ago, speech-language therapists did not view language functions dominated by attention or executive functions, but now they are invoked in their core understanding of the symptoms of the individual. This book, therefore, is an invitation to readers who want to update their knowledge of some main principles of cognitive science and who also wish to expand their horizons with new ideas that will probably soon be mainstream as far as applications are concerned. All this while acknowledging that principles of cognitive sciences as related to the mind may not directly translate into any practice.

In his hugely popular book *How the Mind Works*, Steven Pinker cites Noam Chomsky who had said that there are both mysteries and problems in any field of human inquiry. We identify those as problems that we can solve given our current knowledge and technical skills by applying known laws of science. However, many mysteries surround us and we don't know how to reasonably explain them. Given the explorative nature of humans, mysteries are converted into problems. This means that they are reduced to some manageable form so that their territories are mapped and then can be solved. Many chapters that are included in the present volume indicate both problems and mysteries. For example, we can now explain how to comprehend visually presented objects and memorise things by applying theories of cognitive psychology and in some instances mapping responses from the brain. Several computational models guide us in achieving that level of understanding. However, there are mysteries in human affairs that we don't know how to explain; for example, the origin and maintenance of religious belief in the age of rationality, the mysterious nature of phenomenal consciousness, the nature of morality, or even our fears of AI taking over us. They are currently in the domain of metaphysical speculation and subjective arguments. However, the chapters on these themes in this book do suggest that in the last few years many of them have been now converted into solvable problems; for example, the use of brain imaging and cognitive psychology to know the effect of religious belief or individual differences in it. From this point of view the students or the practitioners will realise that even if we don't know what the mind is, we can approach it with our current know-how as a problem. This can be computational, neurobiological, evolutionary, or cultural. These various frameworks and their interdisciplinary interactions will help us approach the mysteries. However, there will always be some unsolved issues that we may not ever fully understand. For example, we may now have mechanistic models of what consciousness does or its behavioural manifestation, but we do not know why even it evolved in the first place. Similarly, today we have psycholinguistic models to explain language behaviour but we do not know why language evolved. As Pinker noted in the preface of his book, he does not know what the mind is. I agree with him in saying so. We don't know what the mind is, but we certainly know what it does for us in our everyday waking life and what we can do to protect and improve it.

The best thing about writing a book on the mind and cognition is to accept with humility that we still don't know much. We may have some knowledge about the biology of the brain but the human brain has 80 billion neurons and we are merely able to simulate a few artificial neurons in our connectionist models. How the brain achieves many extraordinary feats of cognition is still outside our rational knowledge. In addition, we have the conceptual and metaphysical problem of reducing the mind to the physical strata. Therefore, to me, cognitive science is an ongoing multidisciplinary enterprise and is in its infancy. This is not true for other traditional disciplines such as chemistry, biology, or physics that support cognitive science exploration. This is what any reader of such a book has to keep in mind while evaluating the theoretical claims and the data. They are all a work in progress and much is yet to be known. Professionals who are new to cognitive science may get the flavour by reading the chapters.

There are many models and theoretical frameworks on each given topic than what can be covered in any book. But all theoretical proposals do not predict empirical results and therefore remain in the realm of metaphysical discussions. In the chapter on consciousness, I discuss several such theories that don't generate any data but are important. The student of cognitive science, therefore, has to have a theoretical inclination to understand what the mind may be, and also should learn techniques and methods to empirically ground some specific proposals and conduct experiments. That's how cognitive psychology or cognitive neuroscience operates. We can't yet be confident that with our latest computer-based simulations and knowledge of neurons we can develop a confident framework to explain the mind's emergence from such physical strata. Despite these limitations, anyone can ask what we are supposed to learn from these experimental data in cognitive psychology or facts about the brain. There is much to learn of course, and these limitations are based on some of our anxieties. One clear implication is to better understand brain-based diseases that affect millions and develop comprehensive therapies. In today's competitive world, one with a smart competing mind that's ready to adapt to challenging novel situations will have more success. That's why we have a variety of brain-training software or traditional methods like meditation that induce neuroplasticity. Human performance depends on such abilities and most of us would like to know how to go about that. Theories of cognitive science are valuable to successfully harness the benefits of such practices. Cognitive science theories are being applied to enhance educational practices. The key question is how to influence key cognitive systems that aid in learning and educational achievements. Then of course, we have the commercial side where computational algorithms are being created to mimic humans, to support them.

Thus, the scope of this book is broad. It is for students and researchers in cognitive science who can mostly identify the main concepts discussed in any chapter. It is also for the professional from another related field who can get a good introduction to the study of cognition. The reader will take away the core message that the study of the mind is both metaphysically and empirically complicated and we have no coherent theory yet. However, there are many readily available ideas for applications from already known facts. We want machines to be conscious since we accept it as an undeniable fact of our existence. We want to be smarter since it's economically and culturally useful. This indicates the intuitive level of understanding humans bring to the question of the mind and its applications. Although we create material things and develop technology harnessing natural laws, we live our lives phenomenally and cherish symbolic cultural products. Although we want to have a fully explained universe and ourselves included as biological entities, we are deeply incurable about giving up the notion of subjectivity. We yet don't fully comprehend how and why affective states arise that consume us although we know that they may not have a causal influence if we accept a strictly material view of our existence. We want machines to be intelligent with our qualities but we can't have them dominate us. We remain biased moral agents although we value our logical abilities. Finally, there are more mysterious questions which I described such as morality, self, consciousness, religion, and peace which we will try to understand in the future. The reader of this book gets a reasonable glimpse of current thinking on these topics and ideas that can be pursued further. Many of these questions have been addressed in this book although that may not be sufficient. This book asks more questions than it answers. This is bound to happen in any work in progress, which is the current state of cognitive science. A book on the mind and cognition is not a technical manual with a series of implementable facts. It is a book of ideas about us and our core nature that are currently being pursued by interdisciplinary scientists.

References

Alessandroni, N. (2018). Varieties of embodiment in cognitive science. *Theory & Psychology, 28*(2), 227–248.

Armstrong, D. M. (2018). *The mind-body problem: An opinionated introduction.* Routledge.

Barch, D. M., Burgess, G. C., Harms, M. P., Petersen, S. E., Schlaggar, B. L., Corbetta, M., Glasser, M. F., Curtiss, S., Dixit, S., Feldt, C., Nolan, D., Bryant, E., Hartley, T., Footer, O., Bjork, J. M., Poldrack, R., Smith, S., Johansen-Berg, H., Snyder, A. Z., & Van Essen, D. C. (2013). Function in the human connectome: Task-fMRI and individual differences in behavior. *Neuroimage, 80,* 169–189.

Barrett, H. C. (2020). Towards a cognitive science of the human: Cross-cultural approaches and their urgency. *Trends in Cognitive Sciences, 24*(8), 620–638.

Barrett, L. F. (2009). The future of psychology: Connecting mind to brain. *Perspectives on Psychological Science, 4*(4), 326–339.

Chiao, J. Y., Cheon, B. K., Pornpattananangkul, N., Mrazek, A. J., & Blizinsky, K. D. (2013). Cultural neuroscience: Progress and promise. *Psychological Inquiry, 24*(1), 119.

Churchland, P. M. (2005). Functionalism at forty: A critical retrospective. *The Journal of Philosophy, 102*(1), 33–50.

Feigl, H. (1970). Mind – body, not a pseudo-problem. In *The mind-brain identity theory* (pp. 33–41). Palgrave.

Gardner, H. (1987). *The mind's new science: A history of the cognitive revolution.* Basic Books.

Gentner, D. (2019). Cognitive science is and should be pluralistic. *Topics in Cognitive Science, 11*(4), 884–891.

Han, S., & Northoff, G. (2008). Culture-sensitive neural substrates of human cognition: A transcultural neuroimaging approach. *Nature Reviews Neuroscience, 9*(8), 646–654.

Henrich, J., Heine, S. J., & Norenzayan, A. (2010). The weirdest people in the world?. *Behavioral and Brain Sciences, 33*(2–3), 61–83.

Herrmann, E., & Tomasello, M. (2012). Human cultural cognition. In *The evolution of primate societies* (pp. 701–714). University of Chicago Press.

Lane, S. M., & Atchley, P. (Eds.). (2021). *Human capacity in the attention economy* (p. 223). American Psychological Association.

Lewis, D. K. (1966). An argument for the identity theory. *The Journal of Philosophy, 63*(1), 17–25.

Libet, B. (2006). Reflections on the interaction of the mind and brain. *Progress in Neurobiology, 8*(3–5), 322–326.

Miller, G. A. (2003). The cognitive revolution: A historical perspective. *Trends in Cognitive Sciences, 7*(3), 141–144.

Mishra, R. K. (2015). *Interaction between attention and language systems in humans.* Springer.

Mishra, R. K. (2018). *Bilingualism and cognitive control* (Vol. 6). Springer.

Neisser, U. (2014). *Cognitive psychology* (Classic ed.). Psychology Press.

Newport, C. (2016). *Deep work: Rules for focused success in a distracted world.* Hachette.

Núñez, R., Allen, M., Gao, R., Rigoli, C. M., Relaford-Doyle, J., & Semenuks, A. (2019). What happened to cognitive science?. *Nature Human Behaviour, 3*(8), 782–791.

Place, U. T. (1970). Is consciousness a brain process?. In *The mind-brain identity theory* (pp. 42–51). Palgrave.

Polger, T. W., & Shapiro, L. A. (2016). *The multiple realization book.* Oxford University Press.

Posner, M. I. (1980). Orienting of attention. *Quarterly Journal of Experimental Psychology, 32*(1), 3–25.

Posner, M. I. (Ed.). (1989). *Foundations of cognitive science* (pp. 183–197). MIT Press.

Putnam, H. (1967). The nature of mental states. *Art, Mind, and Religion,* 37–48.

Qu, Y., Jorgensen, N. A., & Telzer, E. H. (2021). A call for greater attention to culture in the study of brain and development. *Perspectives on Psychological Science, 16*(2), 275–293.

Ryle, G. (2009). *The concept of mind*. Routledge.

Smart, J. J. (1970). Sensations and brain processes. In *The mind-brain identity theory* (pp. 52–66). Palgrave.

Sperry, R. W. (1993). The impact and promise of the cognitive revolution. *American Psychologist*, 48(8), 878.

Thagard, P. (2020, Winter). Cognitive science. In E. N. Zalta (Ed.), *The Stanford encyclopedia of philosophy*. Stanford University Press.

Watrin, J. P., & Darwich, R. (2012). On behaviorism in the cognitive revolution: Myth and reactions. *Review of General Psychology*, 16(3), 269–282.

2   Evolution of Cognition

1. Cognitive evolution

Cognitive scientists generally don't worry about the evolution of cognition. The story of the origin of human cognition has not attracted much attention (Donald, 1991). A significant question however is when cognition evolved and why. Cognition here is loosely defined as intelligent, conscious, intentional behaviour produced by organisms. There are two main lines of thinking that separate scholars who study human evolution. One view is that we emerged from apes through millions of years of evolution as a continuous process. Darwin believed that the human mind differed from the non-human primate only quantitatively, not qualitatively. That is to say that human behaviour is only a sophisticated version of what apes do. This process has been shaped by the constant struggle between adaptation and forces of natural selection. If we want to understand the evolution of human cognition, then we just look back and connect the dots. The other group views evolution as discontinuous. Sophisticated cognitive skills evolved in our species suddenly for some reasons that we don't know yet. For example, Chomsky has suggested that human language could not have continuously evolved but emerged suddenly (Berwick & Chomsky, 2013), through a mutation. One can then similarly predict sudden emergence of other cognitive systems such as attention, perception, memory, and decision making.

The question of when cognition began in our species is dependent on our estimation of the time scale of evolution of *Homo sapiens* as a distinct species. Jean Jacques Hublin and colleagues discovered fossils in 2017 in Jebel Irhoud on the coasts of Morocco, which they claimed were the most ancient *Homo sapiens* from 300,000 years ago (Hublin et al., 2017). Similarly, the discovery of *Homo erectus* fossils in Diminisi in Georgia has challenged the out-of-Africa theory of human migration (Vekua et al., 2002). Most accounts suggest that anatomically modern *Homo sapiens* coexisted with Neanderthals, Denisovans, and others for a very long time, although evidence of symbolic art in these other hominins has been scanty and debatable. Some suggest that Denisovans and Neanderthals did have symbolic cognition that reflects in the use of tools and artefacts (Douka et al., 2019). There

DOI: 10.4324/9781003316053-2

is general agreement that, some 50,000 years ago, there was an unprecedented explosion of cultural activities by the *Homo sapiens*, in the form of cave paintings, sculptures, and other artefacts. Such extraordinary skills in symbol manipulation and creative imagination were not seen in previous or co-existent species such as the Neanderthals. The modern mind emerged with the capacity for agency, consciousness, intentionality, and aesthetics to produce symbolic artefacts. Such records, if studied well, could reveal the timeline of evolution of cognition in our species.

Human cultural evolution is broadly divided into three main phases, i.e., Lower, Middle, and Upper Palaeolithic. During the Middle and Upper Palaeolithic, symbolic culture of a sophisticated type emerged around 40,000 years ago. The art produced during this phase had a sense of symmetry, control, artistry, and aesthetics. The artefacts reflect higher mental abilities and general cognition of their creators (Coolidge & Wynn, 2018; Donald, 1991). The brain of the modern human had symbolic cognition, could hold large amounts of data in memory, could pay attention to details, could attribute agency like authors, and had the ability to think of effects of actions, theory of mind, aesthetics, and imagination including thoughts of posterity (Wynn & Coolidge, 2017). While it is difficult to say why such art was produced or its immediate relevance to the lives of those who created it, it indicated growing "consciousness" and emergence of a complex mind. These ancestors had minds that had intentionality and could entertain subjectivity. They could experience abstract thoughts and their art reflected this.

Tools indicate what agents can do with them. Thus, tools became proxies for cognition. Long before our ancestors painted the cave walls with emotional depiction of animals, the first artefacts were tools of everyday use. The making of these tools such as the hand axes required a very evolved brain and basic cognition. Stone Age industry of the Lower and Middle Palaeolithic periods lasted for a considerable amount of time. *Homo erectus*, the ancestor to both Neanderthals and *Homo sapiens*, belonged to this period. Louis Leakey first described the oldest stone tools found in the Olduvai Gorge in Tanzania. According to estimates, these were made by very early hominins some 2.5 million years ago. Paranthropus who might have made these early tools from stones were ape-men (Susman, 1991). These were simple tools made by smashing one stone against another to butcher animals and plants. The later Acheulean tools made by *Homo erectus* were much sharper stone hand axes with greater symmetry and complexity. This industry developed around 1.6 million years ago and served a much wider purpose than before. These bifacial tools required greater planning, hand coordination, and memory capacity to make. Cognitive development in the genus *Homo* took place during this period leading up to the final emergence of high-material culture in the Upper Palaeolithic (Wynn & Coolidge, 2017). These ancient hominids also made art using these tools on walls of caves or shells. They were rudimentary, but were intentional and indicated symbolic processing. The petroglyphs discovered at the caves of Bhimkhetta in Madhya Pradesh, India, are known to be the most ancient arts by members of genus *Homo* before the Acheulean period.

Cultural artefacts could be linked to the emergence of sophisticated cognition. Palaeolithic art created by anatomically modern *Homo sapiens* between 40,000 and 10,000 years ago is too varied in themes, motives, and materials used (Guthrie, 2005). The voluptuous *Venus of Hohle Fels* was found in a cave in Germany. It is dated to be around 40,000 years old. It's not clear why our ancestors thought of making a figurine of busty women with very strong and suggestive anatomical proportions. It was likely a dedication to women, fertility, and sex. The complex figure shows the metaphorical mapping of thoughts onto a material base. The very idea that it symbolises something in the immaterial world was the expression of consciousness. The second well-known artefact is the *lion man*, found again in Germany in 1939 (Figure 2.1). The sculpture has the head of a lion and the body of a man. Dated around the same time as that of the *Venus of*

Figure 2.1 Left (a): The reconstructed lion man found in Germany. This sculpture, which has the head of a lion and the body of a man, indicates the first appearance of figurative art.

Source: Wikipedia commons, by Hollmann

Figure 2.1 Right (b): The *Venus of Berekhat Ram* figurine made of volcanic rock dated 230,000 to 500,000 years ago.

Source: Wikipedia commons, by Cahana

Hohle Fels, this indicates the first appearance of figurative art. The oldest known cave art on the other hand, is the picture of a bull in Borneo, about 50,000 years ago (Aubert et al., 2018). The mapping of consciousness onto objects, the thoughts about posterity, the high symbolic thinking, and the subtlety of the art all indicate a kind of cognitive revolution. The *Venus of Berekhat Ram* was discovered in Israel in 2002. This is a tiny figurine made of volcanic rock dated 230,000 to 500,000 years. There is considerable debate whether this figurine was made by hand or if it were shaped by wind and natural forces (d'Errico, & Nowell, 2000). Considering the timeline in which this was allegedly made, there is a possibility that it was created by *Homo erectus* although cognitive symbolism has not been associated with *Homo erectus*. However, a shell found in Java had geometric engravings, apparently made by *Homo erectus*. The marks on this shell had a systematic pattern (Joordens et al., 2015). Abstract drawings found in the caves at

Blombos, South Africa, some 73,000 years old (Henshilwood et al., 2018) were also created by *Homo erectus*. Some scholars argue based on such evidence that such symbolic engravings indicate a much earlier evolution of abstract thinking, long before anatomically modern humans appeared on the scene (Joordens et al., 2015). There might not have been any sudden cognitive evolution in the *Homo sapiens*. It was slow and gradual (Finlayson et al., 2019). Why discuss art when our interest is in cognitive evolution? That is because these artefacts show the emergence of symbolic thinking and a superior consciousness. They also indicate subtle changes in the brain that led to the evolution of such cognitive functions.

2. Evolution, brains, and symbols

The evolution of the brain certainly played a key role in cognitive evolution. However, this purely biological view does not help in explaining the emergence of the rich symbolic products of that time. Nevertheless, there has been a sustained attempt to link the brain to the art of the Palaeolithic era through empirical studies involving modern techniques. The anatomically modern human's brain is not just significantly larger but is also globular in shape. Neubauer and colleagues compared data from *Homo sapiens* at three distinct time points in evolution. The shape of the brain has evolved gradually over 300,000 years and it reached its current form 100,000–35,000 years ago (Neubauer et al., 2018, Figure 2.2). This means there was no such event as a sudden cognitive revolution based on changes in the brain. This gradual adaptation took a very long time leading to full-blown behavioural manifestation in the Upper Palaeolithic era. The globular shape was primarily because of the enlargement of the parietal and temporal cortices. These areas are involved in spatial thinking, sensory-motor association, planning, and attention. Significant expansion of the parietal cortex also led to an increase in the praecuneus, which plays a vital role in cognition.

Tools, art, and other artefacts created by early modern *Homo sapiens* clearly indicate intentionality, consciousness, language, reasoning, goal planning and action control, etc. The art of the Upper Palaeolithic shows a species who were efficient users of symbols and had aesthetics. They probably also had theory of the mind which is an intrinsic understanding of others' mental states. Large brains also led to the evolution of social cognition (Pearce et al., 2013). They could work in groups to produce artefacts. Endowed with an exceptional brain, they could control their actions and complete goals. Most importantly, they had the imagination to map real-life experiences onto metaphorical thinking. They could produce symbolic artefacts for their own sake beyond everyday survival needs. One proposal suggests that the growth in the parietal lobe allowed them to enact situations and events as well as their actors in an inner virtual theatre in their minds (Pearce, 2018). The social cognition angle is important since cultural evolution did not happen in isolation but in groups.

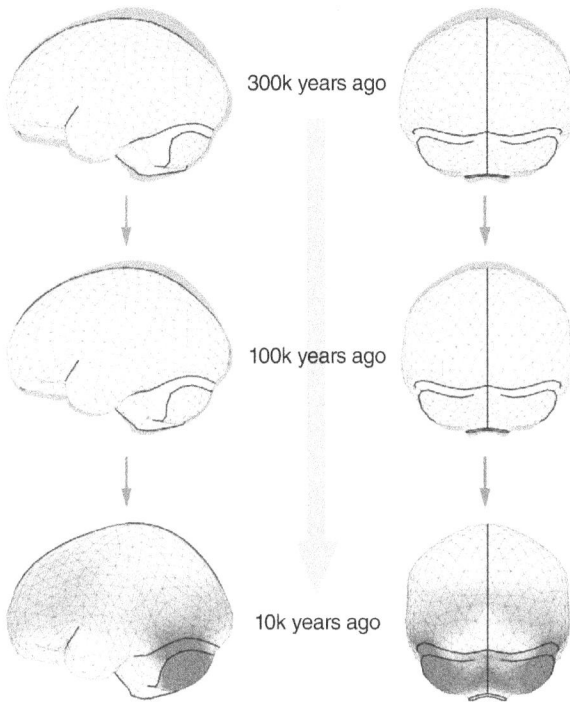

Figure 2.2 Changes in endocranial shape in *Homo sapiens*. Complex cognition has likely evolved from gradual changes in the brain over millions of years.

Source: From Neubauer et al. (2018)

Homo sapiens developed a large parietal cortex and intricate connections with the frontal lobe. Making artefacts such as the *Hohlenstein-Stadel Löwenmensch* figurine called for both visuospatial skills and control. The parietal lobe and frontal lobe working in harmony achieved this (Wynn et al., 2009). Mapping humans and lions together to create an abstract figurine called for considerable attention. In the absence of any models, the entire thing has to be executed slowly, retrieving information from both long-term and working memory. It was probably the first instance of feature conjunction in the mind which called for attention. Although grasping, holding, and motor control had developed long before, a fine executive control system that worked in tandem with attention emerged only then. This emergent aspect of cognition allowed fine control in giving external shapes to complex internal conceptual thoughts (Coolidge & Wynn, 2018). The *Hohlenstein-Stadel Löwenmensch* figurine was found at an isolated area in the back of the cave, away from more public areas. Maybe it was an object of worship. If it was made for a group of people to engage in collective esoteric practice, then this further indicates beginnings of religion. Art and shamanism could have thus evolved among ancient caveman (Wallis, 2019).

The transition from the *Oldowan* tools to the more refined *Acheulean* hand axes took 800,000 years. This transition could not have been achieved without the perfect handling of stone tools supported by an efficient brain. A vast array of the brain network that supports working memory, motor control, and visuospatial attention are involved when one makes these tools (Putt et al., 2017). Greater control and a fine-tuned mind operating on details were seen in the *Homo sapiens*, which was later selected by natural selection and became a dominant trait of their mental life (Miyagawa et al., 2018). Particularly, the integration of information from different domains was supported by an efficient working memory and executive control system. For the archaic artists, producing art required retrieving the memory traces of the emotions, ferocity, and gait, as well as postures of the animals in their absence. These artists retrieved multi-sensory information and translated them into a visual format.

A superior and diversified brain network supporting all such information helped achieve this (Mellet et al., 2018). Neuroimaging research shows that many areas in the visual cortex are active when contemporary humans look at these ancient drawings and engravings (Mellet et al., 2018). It is possible that neuronal changes led to the appearance of a more complex pattern of behaviour linked to symbolic art production (Hodgson, 2019). Neuroimaging methods have been applied to computer-generated models of brains created from endocasts of fossils. This allows insights into the brains of early *Homo sapiens* (Malafouris, 2010). One methodology currently in use is to train modern humans in such toolmaking and track the brain activity. The idea is to find brain areas that are active during learning of such a process and see how it might offer clues about neurocognition of early humans. When modern humans are trained to make *Acheulean* tools, their brain networks show a wide array of activity. Areas involved in auditory, visual, and memory networks show integration when people make these tools (Putt et al., 2017). While the *Oldowan* technique required just working memory, the *Acheulean* style called for a kind of recursivity seen in the language (Mahaney, 2015). Large scale production of sophisticated tools were a stronger sign of social innovation than technical (von Hippel & Suddendorf, 2018).

3. Working memory and fluid intelligence

Cognitive psychologists have proposed multiple models of working memory (e.g., Baddeley & Hitch, 1974; Engle, 2002) and attention (e.g., Broadbent, 1957; Treisman & Gelade, 1980). Often the brain networks for these systems overlap considerably. These systems also show tremendous variation and individual differences during the lifetime of an individual. Adding to this complexity is the notion of cognitive neuroplasticity induced by habits and environmental pressure. Working memory, visual perception, and attention change according to everyday habits. Therefore, it is not easy to pinpoint which systems evolved in ancient humans and at what point in time. It depends on the objective assessment of environmental demands for survival at that time, and such data is difficult to come by. Considerable debate exists among scholars on how these cognitive systems lead to higher cognition that give us consciousness, subjectivity, intentionality, and sense of agency. As a starting point, we can say that working memory was critical in the development of complex material culture. However, this won't be enough to comment on the development of aesthetics and symbolic thinking.

Coolidge and Wynn (2005) presented working memory as a key model to understand the tremendous rise in *Homo sapiens* cognition in the last 100,000 years. Not just better management and integration of information or its storage, the enhancement of the parietal cortex and related areas also led to the emergence of subjectivity and agency (Welshon, 2010). Working memory led to the rich cultural artefacts of the Upper Palaeolithic era. The enlargement in brain sizes was not due to the expansion of the parietal lobe, but was a result of increasing connections and expansion of the praecuneus. Integration of verbal and visuospatial information with the action control system could be possible with this expansion. Others think that many other cognitive systems apart from working memory were also necessary, and they were jointly responsible for producing such symbolic art. Kellogg and Evans (2019) proposed an ensemble hypothesis in which different cognitive systems or capacities that already existed entered into novel interactions. The total sum effect of this interaction was greater than what those components may have produced individually. These components could be language, working memory, the theory of the mind, inner speech, and episodic memory. Contemporary models of executive control, for example, are also multi-componential (Miyake et al., 2000). The ensemble hypothesis predicts that at some point in time these different systems came together and interacted dynamically, producing novel forms of cognition that were non-existent.

Sophisticated cognition requires fluid intelligence. Although it is a contemporary concept (Gray et al., 2003), it is possible to link this to our archaic artists. They were intelligent enough to know the power of symbolic art that transcends time and space. Fluid intelligence and executive control systems appear more suitable for evolutionary exploration (Geary, 2009). Fluid intelligence allows the agent to manipulate currently available information in the environment to anticipate dynamic changes and adapt to them. This cognitive flexibility includes selective attention, working memory, goal planning and monitoring, and control. Importantly, these abilities also lead to a sense of self and agency in the actors (Buss, 2015). There is now an overwhelming consensus that core psychological functions such as selective attention, control, and working memory give rise to higher subjectivity

(Kunzendorf, 2016). Fluid intelligence uses the prefrontal cortex and several regions of the surrounding areas (Gray et al., 2003). Fluid intelligence was essential for the development of theory of the mind and social cognition that was used in art creation (Ibanez et al., 2013). Research suggests that sociality, intelligence and language evolved together (Pinker, 2010). It was social intelligence, not instrumental intelligence, that made us who we have become (Donald, 1991). Evolutionary forces may have selected pro-sociality since it was necessary for survival at longer time scales (Hare, 2017).

4. Language and cognitive evolution

So far, the story of cognitive evolution told through cultural artefacts emphasises the rise of symbolic thought. Language might have evolved around the same time although we do not have any material evidence of it. Language after all uses abstract auditory-verbal symbols that refer to objects and ideas. Language evolved to reflect symbolic cognition in more abstract ways. It also manifested the growing computational powers of the mind. Language through its words expressed subjectivity and referred to things across time and space. Donald (1991) suggested a four-stage development of cognition in prehistory. These stages start with a symbol-mimicking stage and extend to a scientific stage with reasoning. To others, social cognition and sharing of symbols have played a key role in cognitive evolution (Tomasello, 2009). Language helped in this sharing of symbols in a meaningful way.

Tracking language evolution has been challenging in the absence of hard material evidence. We cannot say from cultural artefacts if the brain of the archaic human were language-ready. One of the reasons is the substantial time lag of millions of years between the first appearance of anatomically modern humans 300,000 years ago (Hublin et al., 2017) and the appearance of language 80,000 years ago (Berwick & Chomsky, 2013). The complexity of the Acheulean tools made by *Homo erectus* (Akhilesh et al., 2018) raises the possibility that they did have the ability to manipulate a range of symbols and communicate them. However, it has been controversial to make inferences about the timescale of the evolution of language from archaeological records. Language might have evolved out of long cultural transmission (Thomas & Kirby, 2018). Even bird songs could offer clues about human language's origin since they share some characteristics with language (Suzuki et al., 2019). Maybe music could also tell if language evolved from it (Ravignani et al., 2018). None of these ideas have given us much about language's mysterious emergence. When the brain's capacity to compute symbols reached some sophistication, language suddenly emerged (Berwick & Chomsky, 2013). Humans could only produce speech in rapid succession when the larynx was lowered (Lieberman, 1985). But language cannot be reduced to just speech. Speech is the external manifestation of language. Language arises from intentional thoughts that individuals think in their brains as agents. They want to communicate these thoughts to the members of their species. Unless we know when such conscious capacity for thoughts emerged in our species, we won't know about the anatomical changes in the brain that accommodated language. Language could also have evolved from grooming behaviour and our desire to gossip (Dunbar, 1998). Or language might have evolved to help our ancestors with deception and succeed in mate selection (Franks & Rigby, 2005). Taken together, one could have a biological, computational, or social theory of language evolution or a combination of these. There was no continuous evolution that we can track from some primitive form, since there is no parallel anywhere. While we can infer some things about the gradual evolution of culture from the cave paintings and other artefacts, there is no evidence for the emergence of language (Bickerton, 1995).

Language reflects the emergence of a computational mind that manipulates symbols. In an influential paper, Chomsky and colleagues proposed a mechanism of the evolution of the language faculty (Hauser et al., 2002, Figure 2.3). The language faculty has two main aspects to it – first is a broad faculty which will include two components: the sensory-motor and the conceptual-intentional system. Second is the narrow faculty which includes the linguistic computational system that produces syntax. The proposal singles out a phenomenon called "recursion" which is typical to human language. Recursion happens when infinite newer structures are produced from

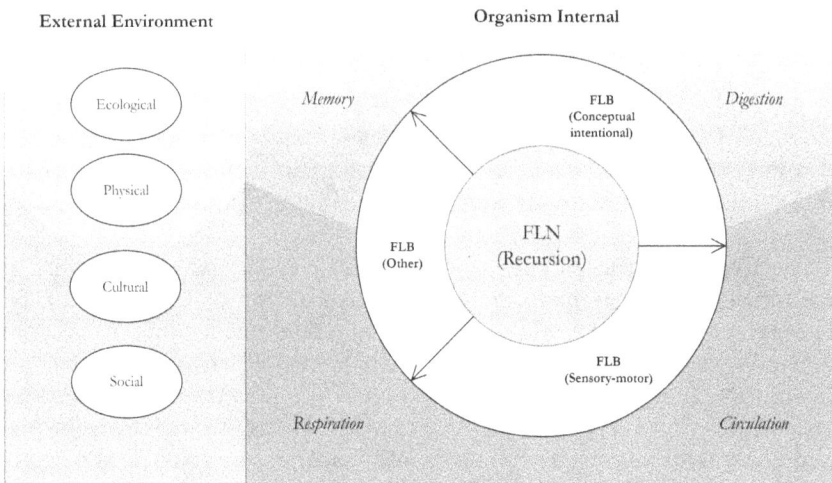

Figure 2.3 Distinction between faculty of language in the broad sense (FLB) and faculty of language in the narrow sense. FLB is the broader sensory-motor and conceptual apparatus which is shared by other animals. FLN is the uniquely human component involving recursion.

Source: Adapted from Hauser et al. (2002)

a few unique structures following some rules. According to Tattersall (Tattersall, 2019), archaeological proxies may show that anatomically modern humans did have material culture and produced artefacts in a skilled manner. But we should not infer that they were an outcome of symbolic thinking and computation of the sort that language uses. The conceptual-intentional system was internal to the mind, and it must be older. Its manifestation in speech could be a later evolution. Recursion has been found in the making of Acheulean tools (Hoffecker, 2007). Human children learn the language effortlessly since they come already with this computational capacity. Steven Pinker, in his book *The Language Instinct*, popularised this strong nativist view. However, Daniel Everett (Everett, 2007) found that in an Amazonian language, there is no recursion.

5. Emergence of the attending brain

Attention bridges external reality with inner phenomenology. It brings objects to consciousness. It is an umbrella term for a range of related systems in the brain (Posner & Peterson, 1990). It must have evolved to help visually forage the environment (Klein, 2000). It orients the mind's focus and helps in survival (Masataka et al., 2018). It guides selection of information for action (Allport, 1987) and is a part of complex cognition. Since we have discussed much about art, it is important to see if attention played a role there. Apart from its role in stimulus detection, attention amplifies affective cognition. For example, happy and sad faces hold attention differently (Bayliss et al., 2010). The Upper Palaeolithic artist used attention to focus and create art. It also helped in distinct perceptions that facilitated objective portrayal of figures. The carefully drawn art of animal forms in the Upper Palaeolithic era shows a very focused nature of attention to details of those animals – not merely to their environmental contexts and features but also to emotions (Mithen, 1988). Thus, the artists could select from available stimuli what to work on and then executed a series of actions leading to completion.

Selective and visuospatial attention evolved at different time points in our history since they had different purposes (Wynn & Coolidge, 2017). The archaic hominin's world was simple with fewer items; thus attentional demands were less. As time passed, with increasing environmental complexity, the brain dedicated more resources for attention. The temporo-parietal junction evolved to play a key role in selective attention. In one study, researchers compared humans and macaques on visual search tasks (Patel et al., 2015). The idea was to see if brain networks for attention are fundamentally different for the two species. The two species separated from a common ancestor some 25 million years ago. The imaging data showed that when humans pay selective attention, the temporo-parietal junction is active. No such area is seen active in the monkey brain. Further, there is a dynamic give-and-take between the dorsal attentional areas and the temporo-parietal junction activation in humans. Attention gave our ancestors both objective knowledge and conscious representations of the objects (Mole, 2008).

Can we infer from material records when our selective attention might have evolved? It is the chicken-and-egg problem. Robin Dunbar proposed that as the social group size increases, the brain size of individuals increases proportionately. The social brain hypothesis looks at cognitive evolution as a function of the brain's ability to negotiate within a group (Dunbar, 1998). It is possible that attention as a filtering mechanism evolved to select what was important within the group. Objects, animals, and interlocutors have to be constantly selected and then discarded for current goal fulfilment. As material complexity grew, the demands on attention and memory also grew (Overmann & Coolidge, 2019). Attention could be jointly deployed onto one object which led to theory of the mind. Construction of complex tools or artefacts required sustained joint attention for long spans of time. Joint attention and its evolution has been hailed as the most important evolutionary outcome which made us intelligent (Tomasello, 2019). According to Tomasello, our core human nature shows up during developmental years. Our pro-sociality, joint attention, and intentionality emerge by constantly learning from others and their interactions. These traits are not uniquely human but are seen in many primates and other animals. However, in complete contrast to joint attention in primates, humans can jointly focus on abstract concepts. The casual relationship between attention and working memory/language also led to more holistic development of the cognitive structure. Contemporary studies in cognitive neuro-archaeology with human participants reveal how some of these subsystems might have evolved to produce cultural artefacts on a mass scale. It is possible that these different functions or attributes of attention such as filtering, consciousness, selecting, and monitoring developed at different time points as the complexity of cognition grew.

Finally, attention emerged as a key mechanism for intentional control of behaviour. In that sense, attention binds consciousness and action control (Posner et al., 2004). Cognitive control was required to plan suitable actions or to terminate them if they were not needed. The dorsolateral prefrontal cortex and the anterior cingulate cortex play a key role in cognitive control (Miyake et al., 2000). In ancient humans, the prefrontal cortex and ventromedial prefrontal cortex jointly evolved to regulate cognitive functions (Stout, 2010). Thus, material records stand as proxies for such control. Attention's role in cognitive evolution both at the individual and group level was significant.

6. The emergence of consciousness

Although I have dedicated an entire chapter to consciousness in this book (Chapter 8), some discussion of it in an evolutionary sense is necessary.

Consciousness remains the most baffling phenomenon for mind-brain scientists today. Among many other aspects of consciousness, phenomenality and subjectivity are central (Phillips, 2018). These qualities make the mind self-reflective. When did the mind achieve self-reflective ability? Art, for instance, could not be produced without the artists having these abilities. Agents who have consciousness know who they are and can perform intentional actions. In this sense, our archaic artists were self-conscious and intentionally planned their actions. They also experienced the subjectivity that is a part of being conscious. From *Australopithecus afarensis* who appeared 3.5 million years ago to modern humans (Tattersall, 2011) the evolution of sentience has taken a long time. Agents who had such minds also experienced qualia and intentionality. Material objects that we are left with today reflect both objective and phenological aspects of agents who created them.

What are the conditions for the evolution of minimal consciousness in an organism? Fundamentally organisms must store stimuli-response information to execute actions at will. With "unlimited associative learning" (Bronfman et al., 2016), organisms become self-reflective. Organisms must be able to bind features of stimuli into a complex whole, to represent in memory. They should then have a self to embody this experience across time and space. Minimal consciousness that allowed goal-directed flexible learning evolved during the Cambrian explosion (Feinberg & Mallatt, 2016). John Eccles had proposed that consciousness emerged with the evolution of the neocortex. Reptiles do not have a neocortex but display fight or flee behaviour. Eccles guessed that consciousness should have evolved in the mammalian brain some 200 million years ago. The large pyramidal neurons that are known to drive higher mental functions formed large clusters called dendrons. Each dendron was linked to a psychon, which was conceptualised as a mental unit (McCulloch & Pitts, 1943).

Although we don't find any such specialised structures in the brain that give rise to consciousness in organisms, it is likely that the emergence of consciousness had to do with the increasing complexity of the nervous system. Different species thus evolved self-reflective consciousness to different degrees, depending on their cortex. There is no model that tracks evolution of consciousness from the very simple to the very complex organisms over the timeline of evolution. Consciousness may include but is not restricted to intelligent behaviour. Qualia and self-reflective mental states are different from intelligence. While we can track the evolution of intelligent behaviour to some extent from the material records, tracking the evolution of subjectivity is difficult. There is no evidence that rational behaviours, planning, and environmental monitoring are related to qualia and subjectivity. Subjectivity may include all of these, including the product of sensory processing. Phenomenality is beyond perception and intelligent behaviour. The subjective experience could be species-specific given their evolutionary history of experience. Do I see more of a ripe banana than the chimpanzee? There is no *a priori* rationale to claim that we have a much higher and better-developed phenomenality. It is again possible that all biological agents have some form of phenomenality (Klein & Barron, 2016).

W.T. Feinberg and Mallatt (2016) in their book *The Ancient Origins of Consciousness* try to explore the origin of consciousness using data from multiple fields. The Cambrian explosion that took place around 560 million years ago produced a range of complex creatures. These creatures have more complex nervous systems and developed even more complex behaviour. According to the proposal, which the authors dub neurobiological naturalism, these creatures not only developed the ability to process information through sense organs but also created inner imagery of such experience. This experience gradually was unified over time, and the complexity grew. All animals later developed this ability, and therefore, the origin of sentience is linked to the development of more complex nervous systems. The kind of inner mimicking of experience that was based on sensory processing of external stimuli, the authors' term "mapped exteroceptive consciousness." This allowed the animals to experience a subjectivity that was unique to them beyond mere reflexive stimuli processing.

With the increase in brain structure and complexity, the frontal areas overtook this function in many creatures. At this stage of evolutionary progress, the animals did have some inner knowledge of "what it means to be that animal." In the beginning, there was this sensory consciousness, which also has phenomenality. When we talk about consciousness in our species, we talk about higher consciousness. This has features such as "self-reflection," "self-awareness," "access consciousness," and "theory of Mind" (Feinberg & Mallatt, 2016). Sensory consciousness is different and is very basic, which all creatures have. It is a basic inner representation of the external stimuli. Following this proposal, one can say that self-reflective consciousness took much longer to evolve – while a basic form of sensory consciousness was parallel to the origin of life forms itself. Even though we accept this thesis, the evolution of "personal experiences" and "qualia" will remain unexplained.

Consciousness in organisms may give rise to sentience. It is the ability to experience subjectivity as a unique agent. Animals and other insects may have some form of sentience (Klein & Barron, 2016). A prokaryote is a single-celled organism that lacks specialised organelles. They show many properties like navigation, sensory processing, and some form of awareness of their environments. This means they are not just genetically programmed material but have sentience. For example, they show membrane excitability when there are changes to their environment. Some biologists believe that this is the very basis of the cell's awareness of its environment. These are signs of subjective awareness, however rudimentary, even at this level (Baluška & Reber, 2019). There is now an increasing body of literature that argues for subjectivity and sentience in non-human animals. Nevertheless, at a mechanistic level, one can try to find correlates of consciousness in lower animals that at least have a neocortex and are multicellular. Minimally biological systems that create consciousness show capability to integrate information, neural synchronisation, attention, and also emotion. For instance, ray-finned fish have sentience since they are aware of internal and external awareness, motivation, and some subjective experience (Woodruff, 2017). In this case, the pallium serves as the generator of consciousness. Such comparative analysis may look optimistic but we have to remember Nagel's bat example (Nagel, 1974). Even if lower animals have sentience or experience subjectivity, we are not privy to it since we are not them. If consciousness and phenomenal awareness evolved gradually, then it must have occurred according to the biology and needs of each species. Our ability to entertain subjectivity serves functions which may not be necessary or relevant for a fish.

7. Summary

The chapter reviewed some important themes related to the evolution of cognition. It is very clear that different disciplines have approached this question differently and there has not been much theoretical integration. Cognitive archaeologists like Coolidge and Wynn (2005) revealed how working memory evolved as a key mechanism in producing complex cultural artefacts. Cognitive psychologists have rarely paid any attention to the evolution question. That's why this question remains under-explored in many disciplines. There has to be more integration of methods and approaches across disciplines for us to crack the evolution-of-cognition question. While cultural artefacts can tell us one side of the story, much remains hidden. We don't know how and why higher-order consciousness evolved to make us adaptive to the ever-changing demands of the environment. It seems, even if we can have experimental proof of more objective attributes of consciousness, we may not grasp the nature and evolution of phenomenal consciousness. The chapter thus merely exposes important questions that are at the frontiers of the scientific quest today.

References

Akhilesh, K., Pappu, S., Rajapara, H. M., Gunnell, Y., Shukla, A. D., & Singhvi, A. K. (2018). Early middle palaeolithic culture in India around 385–172 ka reframes out of Africa models. *Nature, 554*(7690), 97.

Allport, A. (1987). Selection for action: Some behavioral and neurophysiological considerations of attention and action. *Perspectives on Perception and Action, 15*, 395–419.

Aubert, M., Setiawan, P., Oktaviana, A. A., Brumm, A., Sulistyarto, P. H., Saptomo, E. W., Istiawan, B., Ma'rifat, T. A., Wahyuono, V. N., Atmoko, F. T., & Zhao, J. X. (2018). Palaeolithic cave art in Borneo. *Nature, 564*(7735), 254.

Baddeley, A. D., & Hitch, G. (1974). Working memory. In *Psychology of learning and motivation* (Vol. 8, pp. 47–89). Academic Press.

Baluška, F., & Reber, A. (2019). Sentience and consciousness in single cells: How the first minds emerged in unicellular species. *BioEssays*, *41*(3), 1800229.

Bayliss, A. P., Schuch, S., & Tipper, S. P. (2010). Gaze cueing elicited by emotional faces is influenced by affective context. *Visual Cognition*, *18*(8), 1214–1232.

Berwick, R. C., & Chomsky, N. (2013). *Birdsong, speech, and language: Exploring the evolution of mind and brain*. MIT Press.

Bickerton, D. (1995). *Language and human behavior*. University Washington Press.

Broadbent, D. E. (1957). A mechanical model for human attention and immediate memory. *Psychological Review*, *64*(3), 205.

Bronfman, Z. Z., Ginsburg, S., & Jablonka, E. (2016). The transition to minimal consciousness through the evolution of associative learning. *Frontiers in Psychology*, *7*, 1954.

Buss, D. (2015). *Evolutionary psychology: The new science of the mind*. Psychology Press.

Coolidge, F. L., & Wynn, T. (2005). Working memory, its executive functions, and the emergence of modern thinking. *Cambridge Archaeological Journal*, *15*(1), 5–26.

Coolidge, F. L., & Wynn, T. (2018). *The rise of Homo sapiens: The evolution of modern thinking*. Oxford University Press.

d'Errico, F., & Nowell, A. (2000). A new look at the Berekhat Ram figurine: Implications for the origins of symbolism. *Cambridge Archaeological Journal*, *10*(1), 123–167.

Donald, M. (1991). *Origins of the modern mind: Three stages in the evolution of culture and cognition*. Harvard University Press.

Douka, K., Slon, V., Jacobs, Z., Ramsey, C. B., Shunkov, M. V., Derevianko, A. P., Mafessoni, F., Kozlikin, M. B., Li, B., Grün, R., & Comeskey, D. (2019). Age estimates for hominin fossils and the onset of the upper palaeolithic at Denisova Cave. *Nature*, *565*(7741), 640.

Dunbar, R. I. (1998). The social brain hypothesis. *Evolutionary Anthropology: Issues, News, and Reviews: Issues, News, and Reviews*, *6*(5), 178–190.

Engle, R. W. (2002). Working memory capacity as executive attention. *Current Directions in Psychological Science*, *11*(1), 19–23.

Everett, D. L. (2007). Challenging Chomskyan linguistics: The case of Pirahã. *Human Development*, *50*(6), 297.

Feinberg, T. E., & Mallatt, J. M. (2016). *The ancient origins of consciousness: How the brain created experience*. MIT Press.

Finlayson, S., Finlayson, G., Guzman, F. G., & Finlayson, C. (2019). Neanderthals and the cult of the sun bird. *Quaternary Science Reviews*, *217*, 217–224.

Franks, B., & Rigby, K. (2005). 10 Deception and mate selection: Some implications for relevance and the evolution of language. *Language Origins: Perspectives on Evolution*, 208.

Geary, D. C. (2009). The evolution of general fluid intelligence. *Foundations in Evolutionary Cognitive Neuroscience*, 22.

Gray, J. R., Chabris, C. F., & Braver, T. S. (2003). Neural mechanisms of general fluid intelligence. *Nature Neuroscience*, *6*(3), 316.

Guthrie, R. D. (2005). *The nature of Paleolithic art*. University of Chicago Press.

Hare, B. (2017). Survival of the friendliest: *Homo sapiens* evolved via selection for prosociality. *Annual Review of Psychology*, *68*, 155–186.

Hauser, M. D., Chomsky, N., & Fitch, W. T. (2002). The faculty of language: What is it, who has it, and how did it evolve?. *Science, 298*(5598), 1569–1579.

Henshilwood, C. S., d'Errico, F., van Niekerk, K. L., Dayet, L., Queffelec, A., & Pollarolo, L. (2018). An abstract drawing from the 73,000-year-old levels at Blombos Cave, South Africa. *Nature, 562*(7725), 115.

Hodgson, D. (2019). The origin, significance, and development of the earliest geometric patterns in the archaeological record. *Journal of Archaeological Science: Reports, 24*, 588–592.

Hoffecker, J. F. (2007). Representation and recursion in the archaeological record. *Journal of Archaeological Method and Theory, 14*(4), 359–387.

Hublin, J. J., Ben-Ncer, A., Bailey, S. E., Freidline, S. E., Neubauer, S., Skinner, M. M., Bergmann, I., Le Cabec, A., Benazzi, S., Harvati, K., & Gunz, P. (2017). New fossils from Jebel Irhoud, Morocco and the pan-African origin of *Homo sapiens*. *Nature, 546*(7657), 289.

Ibanez, A., Huepe, D., Gempp, R., Gutiérrez, V., Rivera-Rei, A., & Toledo, M. I. (2013). Empathy, sex and fluid intelligence as predictors of theory of mind. *Personality and Individual Differences, 54*(5), 616–621.

Joordens, J. C., d'Errico, F., Wesselingh, F. P., Munro, S., De Vos, J., Wallinga, J., Ankjærgaard, C., Reimann, T., Wijbrans, J. R., Kuiper, K. F., & Mücher, H. J. (2015). Homo erectus at Trinil on Java used shells for tool production and engraving. *Nature, 518*(7538), 228.

Kellogg, R. T., & Evans, L. (2019). The ensemble hypothesis of human cognitive evolution. *Evolutionary Psychological Science, 5*(1), 1–12.

Klein, C., & Barron, A. B. (2016). Insects have the capacity for subjective experience. *Animal Sentience, 1*(9), 1.

Klein, R. M. (2000). Inhibition of return. *Trends in Cognitive Sciences, 4*(4), 138–147.

Kunzendorf, R. G. (2016). *On the evolution of conscious sensation, conscious imagination, and consciousness of self.* Routledge.

Lieberman, P. (1985). On the evolution of human syntactic ability. Its pre-adaptive bases – motor control and speech. *Journal of Human Evolution, 14*(7), 657–668.

Mahaney, R. A. (2015). *Cognition and planning in paleolithic technology: Studies in experimental archaeology* [Doctoral dissertation, Indiana University].

Malafouris, L. (2010). The brain – artefact interface (BAI): A challenge for archaeology and cultural neuroscience. *Social Cognitive and Affective Neuroscience, 5*(2–3), 264–273.

Masataka, N., Koda, H., Atsumi, T., Satoh, M., & Lipp, O. V. (2018). Preferential attentional engagement drives attentional bias to snakes in Japanese macaques (Macaca fuscata) and humans (*Homo sapiens*). *Scientific Reports, 8*(1), 17773.

McCulloch, W. S., & Pitts, W. (1943). A logical calculus of the ideas immanent in nervous activity. *The Bulletin of Mathematical Biophysics, 5*(4), 115–133.

Mellet, E., Salagnon, M., Majkic, A., Cremona, S., Joliot, M., Jobard, G., Mazoyer, B., Tzourio Mazoyer, N., & d'Errico, F. (2018). Neuroimaging supports the representational nature of the earliest human engravings. *Royal Society Open Science, 6*(7), BioRxiv, 464784.

Mithen, S. J. (1988). Looking and learning: Upper Palaeolithic art and information gathering. *World Archaeology, 19*(3), 297–327.

Miyagawa, S., Lesure, C., & Nóbrega, V. A. (2018). Cross-modality information transfer: A hypothesis about the relationship among prehistoric cave paintings, symbolic thinking, and the emergence of language. *Frontiers in Psychology*, 9, 115.

Miyake, A., Friedman, N. P., Emerson, M. J., Witzki, A. H., Howerter, A., & Wager, T. D. (2000). The unity and diversity of executive functions and their contributions to complex "frontal lobe" tasks: A latent variable analysis. *Cognitive Psychology*, 41(1), 49–100.

Mole, C. (2008). Attention and consciousness. *Journal of Consciousness Studies*, 15(4), 86–104.

Nagel, T. (1974). What is it like to be a bat?. *The Philosophical Review*, 83(4), 435–450.

Neubauer, S., Hublin, J. J., & Gunz, P. (2018). The evolution of modern human brain shape. *Science Advances*, 4(1), eaao5961.

Overmann, K. A., & Coolidge, F. L. (Eds.). (2019). *Squeezing minds from stones: Cognitive archaeology and the evolution of the human mind*. Oxford University Press.

Patel, G. H., Yang, D., Jamerson, E. C., Snyder, L. H., Corbetta, M., & Ferrera, V. P. (2015). Functional evolution of new and expanded attention networks in humans. *Proceedings of the National Academy of Sciences*, 112(30), 9454–9459.

Pearce, E. (2018). Neanderthals and *Homo sapiens*: Cognitively different kinds of human? In Di Paolo, L.D., Di Vincenzo, F., De Petrillo, F. (Eds.) *Evolution of primate social cognition* (pp. 181–196). Interdisciplinary Evolution Research, vol 5. Springer, Cham.

Pearce, E., Stringer, C., & Dunbar, R. I. (2013). New insights into differences in brain organization between Neanderthals and anatomically modern humans. *Proceedings of the Royal Society B: Biological Sciences*, 280(1758), 20130168.

Phillips, I. (2018). The methodological puzzle of phenomenal consciousness. *Philosophical Transactions of the Royal Society B: Biological Sciences*, 373(1755), 20170347.

Pinker, S. (2010). The cognitive niche: Coevolution of intelligence, sociality, and language. *Proceedings of the National Academy of Sciences*, 107(Supplement 2), 8993–8999.

Posner, M. I., & Petersen, S. E. (1990). The attention system of the human brain. *Annual Review of Neuroscience*, 13(1), 25–42.

Posner, M. I., Snyder, C. R., & Solso, R. (2004). Attention and cognitive control. *Cognitive Psychology: Key Readings*, 205.

Putt, S. S., Wijeakumar, S., Franciscus, R. G., & Spencer, J. P. (2017). The functional brain networks that underlie early stone age tool manufacture. *Nature Human Behaviour*, 1(6), 0102.

Ravignani, A., Thompson, B., & Filippi, P. (2018). The evolution of musicality: What can be learned from language evolution research?. *Frontiers in Neuroscience*, 12, 20.

Stout, D. (2010). The evolution of cognitive control. *Topics in Cognitive Science*, 2(4), 614–630.

Susman, R. L. (1991). Who made the Oldowan tools? Fossil evidence for tool behavior in Plio-Pleistocene hominids. *Journal of Anthropological Research*, 47(2), 129–151.

Suzuki, T. N., Griesser, M., & Wheatcroft, D. (2019). Syntactic rules in avian vocal sequences as a window into the evolution of compositionality. *Animal Behaviour*, 151, 267–274.

Tattersall, I. (2011). Before the Neanderthals: Hominid evolution in middle Pleistocene Europe. In *Continuity and discontinuity in the peopling of Europe* (pp. 47–53). Dordrecht: Springer.

Tattersall, I. (2019). The minimalist program and the origin of language: A view from paleoanthropology. *Frontiers in Psychology, 10*.

Treisman, A. M., & Gelade, G. (1980). A feature-integration theory of attention. *Cognitive Psychology, 12*(1), 97–136.

Thomas, J., & Kirby, S. (2018). Self domestication and the evolution of language. *Biology & Philosophy, 33*(1–2), 9.

Tomasello, M. (2009). *The cultural origins of human cognition*. Harvard University Press.

Tomasello, M. (2019). *Becoming human: A theory of ontogeny*. Belknap Press.

Vekua, A., Lordkipanidze, D., Rightmire, G. P., Agusti, J., Ferring, R., Maisuradze, G., Mouskhelishvili, A., Nioradze, M., De Leon, M. P., Tappen, M., & Tvalchrelidze, M. (2002). A new skull of early Homo from Dmanisi, Georgia. *Science, 297*(5578), 85–89.

von Hippel, W., & Suddendorf, T. (2018). Did humans evolve to innovate with a social rather than technical orientation?. *New Ideas in Psychology, 51*, 34–39.

Wallis, R. J. (2019). Art and shamanism: From cave painting to the white cube. *Religions, 10*(1), 54.

Welshon, R. (2010). Working memory, neuroanatomy, and archaeology. *Current Anthropology, 51*(S1), S191–S199.

Woodruff, M. L. (2017). Consciousness in teleosts: There is something it feels like to be a fish. *Animal Sentience: An Interdisciplinary Journal on Animal Feeling, 2*(13), 1.

Wynn, T. G., & Coolidge, F. L. (Eds.). (2017). *Cognitive models in Palaeolithic archaeology*. Oxford University Press.

Wynn, T. G., Coolidge, F., & Bright, M. (2009). Hohlenstein-Stadel and the evolution of human conceptual thought. *Cambridge Archaeological Journal, 19*(1), 73–84.

3   Attention

1. Selective attention

Epicurious, the Greek Stoic philosopher, talked about attention. To him, attending was fundamental to our emotions. He said one experiences what one attends to. What one does not attend one does not experience. Lucretius linked attention to intentions and readiness to perceive. He recognised that the mind could voluntarily attend to things of interest in the environment. The greater the intention and the readiness is, the more focused attention to that object. However, attention only became an academic topic of inquiry in the seventeenth century. Chapters started appearing in books on attention, mostly from philosophical perspectives (Hatfield, 1998). A critical discussion of attention as an important mechanism in cognition appears in Wolff (1740). Wolff assumed that most focused attention is given only to a very small area of the visual field. It was probably the first time attention was visualised as a beam or a spotlight, which has remained very popular even now. Thus, the continuing orthodoxy is that the mind is what it attends to.

William James said that selective sustained attention is key to any genius. It is the ability to stay focused on something of interest for hours that leads to mastery of that very thing. James acknowledged that selective sustained attention comes in pulses and its nature is to wander. However, by willpower one can bring back attention to that very topic and keep it focused. Since the nature of attention is to keep drifting, the genius has to keep it renewed each time it wanders off. This continuous renewal is sustained focus. James thought that one can renew by creating interest in something that is linked to something that one already knows. Attention won't automatically renew on that same topic by itself. However, by willpower, it can be brought back to that point. James writes,

> Geniuses are commonly believed to excel other men in their power of sustained attention. In most of them, it is to be feared, the so-called 'power' is of the passive sort. Their ideas coruscate, every subject branches infinitely before their fertile minds, and so for hours they may be rapt. But it is their genius making them attentive, not their attention

DOI: 10.4324/9781003316053-3

making geniuses of them. And, when we come down to the root of the matter, we see that they differ from ordinary men less in the character of their attention than in the nature of the objects upon which it is successively bestowed.

(James et al., 1890, p. 423)

Attention intensifies memory representations. If little attention is paid to some idea or representation, then its memory representation is feeble. It fades away easily. James also noted that attention can enhance perceptual awareness of stimuli. This perceptual intensification is often experienced as clearer and more vivid. Consider the visual illusion in Figure 3.1. If you keep your eyes fixed at the centre white dot and orient your attention to any one of the circles, it appears darker than what it is. Attention can thus change the brightness of objects. It can enrich our conscious experience. This may mean attention amplifies reality more than what is. The illusion also shows that attentional deployment is not dependent on eye movements. One can focus attention on any object and gather more detailed information at will. Apart from illuminating things for cognition, attention first and foremost filters the relevant information.

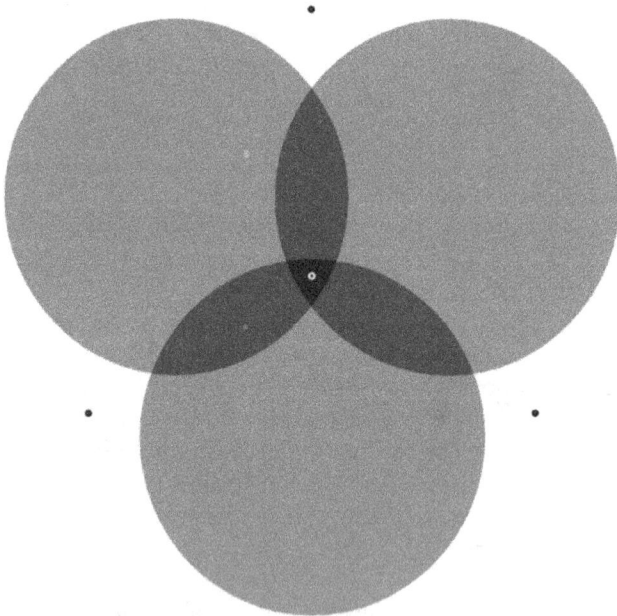

Figure 3.1 Illusion.

Source: Reprinted from *Vision Research*, Vol. 45, Peter U. Tse, Voluntary attention modulates the brightness of overlapping transparent surfaces, 1095–1098, 2005, with permission from Elsevier

Attention filters the most important information in the environment for further processing in the mind. Broadbent was an engineer interested in solutions to applied problems. Broadbent's *Perception and Communication* is a landmark book in the history of cognitive psychology and perception (Broadbent, 1958). An important problem during the post-Second World War military warfare was signal detection. How do people separate multiple channels of speech signals that are arriving at the same time? Broadbent wanted to sort out this problem by postulating a model that would work as a filter. Broadbent examined temporal selection of information from sensory stimulation onwards until higher-order semantic processing. He proposed that very early on, as soon as there is sensory stimulation, attention filters out the relevant from the irrelevant. This filtering happens soon after a brief period of maintenance of information pertaining to the physical features of stimuli in the short-term memory. At this stage, no semantic processing happens. After this brief analysis of the physical features of all stimuli, only a subset is allowed to enter into further semantic processing. Broadbent found that selective focusing and separation of channels is easy when they are different qualitatively.

Broadbent had predicted that selective attention would efficiently block out all such unattended information (Figure 3.2). In his 1954 experiment, Broadbent presented streams of digits to listeners in a dichotic listening task. He asked listeners to recall digits in the same sequence from each ear when instructed. Listeners had no trouble doing this separation, which he ascribed to selective attention. He proposed that even if information input is simultaneous in both the channels there must be a mechanism whereby focusing on each was occurring in a serial manner. That is, listeners could switch attention between channels in a serial manner – when attention is on one channel, the other channel is blocked out. Participants had some problems when the information was both visual and auditory. Attention filters information efficiently when it is fed through the same modality. In the same modality, people can easily separate qualitatively different information such as tones and digits (Broadbent & Gregory, 1963). This early experimental work established the mechanism of selective attention. Humans can selectively attend to what they are interested in by filtering out the rest.

Interestingly, the human mind is not so good at completely ignoring information that's not being attended to. Moray (1959) observed that people can recall their names being spoken even when they were attending to something else in another ear. High frequency and relevant words captured attention instantly in a bottom-up manner. Moray also did an experiment using galvanic currents attached to words delivered to participants. Strangely, people could recall those words which they had not attended to when the current was administered. This coupling of stimuli in an unconscious manner suggested that it's not always possible to ignore the unattended stimuli completely. It depends on the strength of the stimuli as well as the relationship of the stimuli to the current goals of the perceiver. If the strength of the

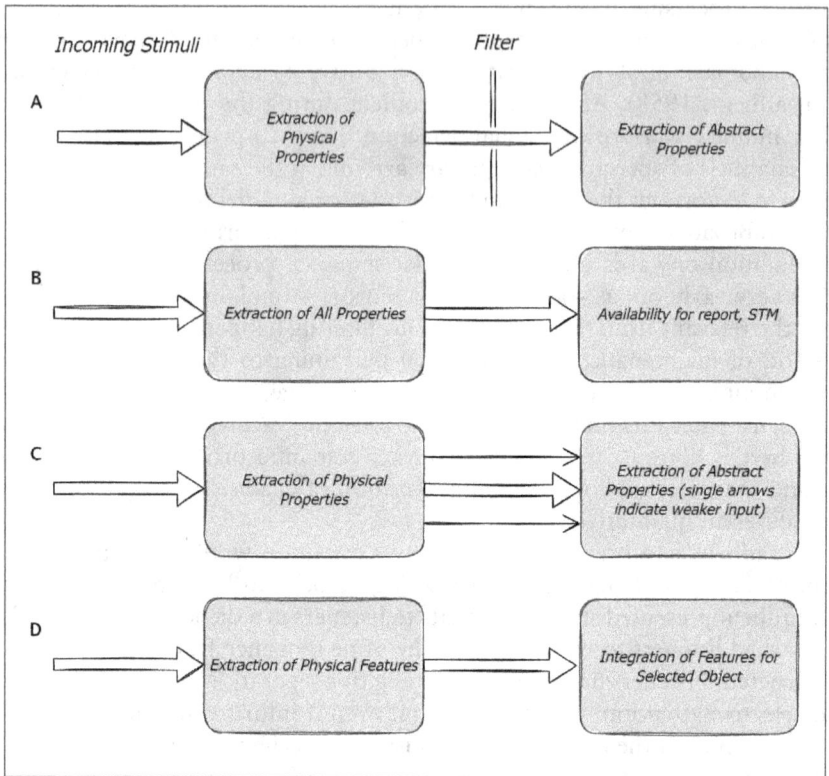

Figure 3.2 Schematic depiction of four influential accounts of selective attention. A) Broadbent's early-selection filter theory; B) a late-selection account; C) Treisman's (1969) "attenuation" model of Broadbent's theory; D) Treisman and Gelade's (1980) feature integration theory.

Source: Adapted from Driver (2001)

stimulus in the unattended channel is stronger than the attended stimulus, then it captures attention. Thus, Broadbent's ideas required modification. What is attended to, of course, enriches objective cognition, while what is not attended to or ignored still influences cognition.

In 1963, Deutsch and Deutsch (1963) published a short theoretical paper that had a new proposal on the issue of filtering. They proposed that instead of the filter rejecting irrelevant stimuli at the beginning of the information processing chain, all stimuli are considered until very late in the processing stream. This means all the stimuli beyond their physical examination also receive semantic consideration. This late selection model of selective attention allowed processing of all incoming stimuli until very late. The late selection model could explain the transient interference of goal-irrelevant stimuli during processing. Deutsch and Deutsch referred to the shifting frame of reference with regard to stimuli selection. An organism's current goals determine attentional selection keeping in mind the dynamic changes in the environment; i.e., one can't be fully sure what one wants to attend in the very beginning but this emerges over time. The late theory emphasises the goal-directed nature of semantic processing of the stimuli. O'Craven et al. (1999) examined the prediction of the late theory in a neuroimaging experiment. They presented two different stimuli superimposed on one another and induced motion in one of them. For example, they showed participants stimuli in which a face was superimposed on a house. When participants selectively attended to the face, then activity in the medial temporal areas was higher even if the house kept moving. In this case, attention selected particular features during processing which then led to semantic processing. The perceptual object which is cognised is an outcome of such attention processing which is always selective to certain features or objects. Thus, attention selects what is important for the agent at a certain time and context. However, what is not selected still influences cognition. This research tells us much about the usefulness of attention as a selective mechanism as well as about the general nature of the mind. However, having only a vague goal will not necessarily engage selective attention. The goals must be clear and taxing enough. If they are not, then distracting stimuli can sneak in and consume attentional resources. To what extent the mind is goal-oriented and focused is still a matter of debate.

Maintaining uninterrupted focus is cognitively demanding. Thus, selective attention is deployed when it is most essential. Nilli Lavie proposed that selective attention only operates under sufficient cognitive or perceptual load. Under high perceptual load, selective attention facilitates target processing (Lavie et al., 2004). Imagine a search task in which one has to find a target among some distractors. If the distractors are very different from the target, then this task can be easy. The participants need not exhaust all selective attention. However, if the distractors start resembling the targets, then this creates a situation of high perceptual load. Under this circumstance, the individual has to exercise cognitive control to reduce interference from the distractors. Similarly, one can also imagine dual-task scenarios or tasks with memory load. When task demands are higher, cognitive control mechanisms facilitate selective attention. Lavie has argued that even if the distractors are sufficiently different from the targets based on features, it may not be sufficient for inducing load. In most search tasks, load can be induced through increasing set size, which is the number of objects that are present in the search set. It is to be noted that a high perceptual load can reduce distraction, but a high cognitive load can increase distraction (Lavie, 2005). These studies show that selective attention operates at its peak when the maximal effort is necessary. Specific brain networks are used in the engagement of selective attention (Sarter et al., 2006).

Although the load theory of selective attention is very intuitive and has explained many experimental results, there is some criticism. For example, there are questions regarrding the true definitions of concepts like a perpetual or cognitive load. And what exactly is high load? Many others have also shown that even under so-called high perceptual load, distractor processing does not diminish (Benoni & Tsal, 2010). Further, different individuals can sustain load differently. As discussed before, those who play action video games can do very well under high load (Murphy et al., 2016). Also, perceptual load in visual and auditory domains is not the same (Murphy et al., 2017). But taken together, the load theory at least advances our fundamental understanding of the mechanism of selective attention. Selection of important stimuli implies inhibition of the irrelevant (Gazzaley & Nobre, 2012). What is currently selected occupies working memory (Engle & Kane, 2004). Therefore, attentional selection is a higher-order cognitive mechanism that involves executive control and its components than just goals and motivation.

What does attention operate on? Attention selects both objects that are external in the environment and also thoughts that are internal. In the visual domain, selective attention brings external objects into focus (Scholl, 2001; Shinn-Cunningham, 2008). There has been a continuing debate over whether selective attention operates on features of objects or on whole objects. There is evidence to suggest that selective attention operates on features. The perceptual object emerges as a function of rapid binding of features. Synchronised gamma activity in the range of 30–80 Hz has been linked to selective attention and its operation related to feature binding. Feature-based attention maintains a constant object when it moves through space (Melcher, 2009). Prefrontal areas send a top-down signal to parietal areas on the features to be selected and the ones to be suppressed. Additional visual sensory areas collaborate in this filtering process. The dorsolateral prefrontal and parietal regions maintain feature-based information and constantly suppress other features during the task (Lanssens et al., 2020). When the participants have to maintain attention between stimuli with overlapping features, then these areas exert top-down suppression. The early visual areas respond to more fine-grained features of objects while the higher areas maintain more abstract properties. Even the amygdala which has long been known to be responsive to emotional stimuli contributes to feature-based attention. Many studies have shown its activation to facial features and other such emotional objects (Gamer et al., 2013).

Thus, one of the major functions of attention, particularly selective attention, is to select items for higher-order goal-driven cognitive processing. Without selective attention, there would be nothing for the mind to work on in a focused manner. Various behavioural and neuroimaging studies have revealed its mechanisms and functions in a wide range of participants. The contents of the mind at any point in time may then be what attention has selected at that point. Often, if not always, it's the result of the agent's own goal and current task at hand.

2. Spatial attention

Cognitive psychology has focused on vision more than any other domain for clear reasons. Many theories of attention have evolved out of experiments conducted involving vision. For example, visuospatial attention helps us find objects of interest in the environment. We can orient our attention towards such objects in space without moving our eyes. This improves cognitive processing of such objects. Michael Posner used the spatial cueing task to measure such movement of attention in space and their cognitive consequences (Figure 3.3). When a location is briefly cued and then a visual target appears immediately at that location, participants are faster in identifying or discriminating the target. This could only be possible if attention were oriented towards that location led by the cue. When the cue is presented centrally it is called voluntarily controlled endogenous shift. When the target appears after a certain delay then there is a noticeable inhibition of the responses to the target at the cued location (Klein, 2000). Attention is reluctant in returning so quickly to a location where it was recently. The Posner cueing task

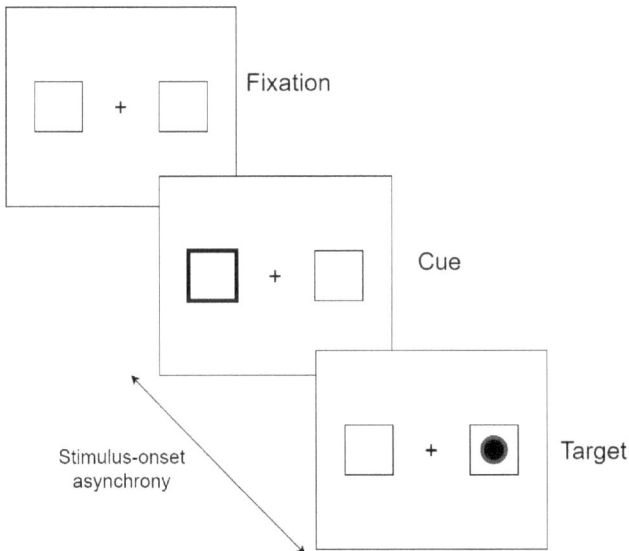

Figure 3.3 Illustration of Posner cueing paradigm used to study spatial attention. In a typical experiment, a peripheral cue is presented left or right of the fixation followed by a target that appears at the cued location or not. Responses are facilitated when the cue and target location match as opposed to when they don't.

revealed both facilitation and inhibition in target processing as a function of temporal delay between the appearance of cue and target.

The evolutionary function of spatial attention is to wander around and find goal-relevant objects (Klein, 2000). Current goals direct spatial attention towards relevant objects while suppressing the irrelevant objects. Sometimes, salient objects capture attention in a bottom-up manner. The executive control system is quickly engaged to disengage attention from such a trap. This engage-disengage and re-engage mechanism is key to the attention system. This fundamental mechanism determines the individual differences in cognitive capability (Posner, 2011). The frontal areas modulate activities of the subcortical areas in controlling the magnitude and extent of spatial attention that any object or location should receive (Fiebelkorn & Kastner, 2020). Visuospatial attention to selected areas enhances perception and awareness (Carrasco et al., 2004). Spatial attention, if mobilised towards any object or location, triggers activity in the posterior visual areas. Studies with primates have shown that spatial attention operates on priority maps. Salient items even if they are not part of the goal compete for attention (Desimone & Duncan, 1995).

Orienting attention in space is coordinated by frontal and parietal areas including some subcortical structures like the superior colliculus, thalamus, lateral geniculate nucleus, and others (Fiebelkorn & Kastner, 2020). In humans, the alpha band oscillations in the range of 8–12 Hz have been linked to the locus of spatial attention. Spatial attention influences the visual evoked potential measures through EEG in the timescale of 90–140 ms (Baumgartner et al., 2018). Spatial attention may enhance the signal of the behaviourally appropriate stimuli but they may not necessarily achieve this through suppression (Foster & Awh, 2019).

Visuospatial attention is linked to our cognitive states. For example, studies have found that positive or negative mood alters the span of spatial attention. Positive mood expands it while negative mood contracts it (Vanlessen et al., 2016). Even music can broaden the scope of spatial attention. In one study participants were asked to listen to happy, sad, or neutral instrumental music. The idea was to see if these experiences would alter the scope of spatial attention. Music broadened the scope of spatial attention and influenced the distractor's influence (Putkinen et al., 2017). Spatial attention is a flexible mechanism sensitive to different types of life experiences. For example, in the ageing population, inhibitory mechanisms with regard to spatial attention span are weaker (Lawrence et al., 2018). Ageing slows down cognitive control thus delaying wilful movement of spatial attention (Golob & Mock, 2019).

Does culture influence the span of spatial attention? East Asians have more of a holistic style of processing while the Westerners have more of an analytic style of processing. Easterners can spread their attention to a wider field of view while the Westerners can focus attention on the targets more locally. In one experiment, participants from different cultures saw targets at different fields of eccentricity. The Chinese participants committed more errors while the Westerners could find the targets easily (Boduroglu & Shah, 2017). This may suggest that although the Chinese were equally careful in finding the targets, they were more vulnerable towards the entire space. Experience with particular scripts and reading has been shown to modulate spatial attention (Haun et al., 2006). The line bisection task and symbol cancellation tasks, for instance, are used to measure spatial attention and focus. Arabs do this task very differently compared to Westerners (Muayqil et al., 2021) since they write the Arabic script from right to left. More experience with such literacy influences spatial attention in general.

One can train spatial attention by playing action video games (Dye & Bavelier, 2004). Such games because of their demanding nature broaden the useful field of view. Thus, expert players can deploy spatial attention over a broader area and find targets at any visual eccentricity compared to non-gamers (Green & Bavelier, 2006). Action video games improve spatial span and thus aid in reading in dyslexic children (Franceschini et al., 2013). There are of course some criticisms of such effects at methodological grounds (Dale et al., 2020). It is also possible that, not action video games per se, but other factors influence attention (Murphy & Spencer, 2009).

3. Attention and affective processing

In recent years, there has been an upsurge in research on affective processing. Although we gather objective knowledge through cognition, we also have experiential states. So far, we have seen attention's role in cognition as a vigilant gatekeeper. While it is obvious that what we attend to decides our objective knowledge, it also influences our affective states. What we experience emotionally of an object is an outcome of the amount of attention we have paid to it. If attention is disengaged or regulated, then emotional states would change too. Current research indicates that attention regulation modulates amygdala functions thus affecting the emotions and their magnitude we experience (Doll et al., 2016). Emotional states could also influence attentional mechanisms. For example, children with autism spectrum disorder show low attentional deployment to specific stimuli such as faces. They also show deficits in face processing and emotion recognition (Schultz, 2005). Patients with schizophrenia show an attention-emotion incongruity (Baudouin et al., 2002).

Humans have evolved a very selective sensitivity to stimuli that are high on affective valence. Such stimuli attract attention without our intention. The ERP component P300 is known to reflect attentional processing. This component is modulated when viewers see erotic or disturbing images. Such stimuli engage attention instantly (Schupp et al., 2007). Stimuli with negative valence engage attention at an earlier time scale than positive pictures (Olofsson et al., 2008). While the P300 may indicate the beginning of selective attentional processing, the late positive potentials have been linked to more evaluative processing (Hajcak et al., 2010). The effects of such stimuli and the manner in which they hold attention stays for a longer time (Hajcak & Olvet, 2008). This is particularly strong for the unpleasant stimuli. This has been dubbed the negativity bias. Negative emotions and perceptions continue to influence our cognitive states long after we have encountered them. Not just for pictures, these brain potentials have also been observed for negative or positive words (Kissler et al., 2009). Thus, emotional stimuli, because of their valence or arousal levels, hold and engage attention.

Emotional stimuli such as sad faces seem to engage a more local level of processing (Srinivasan & Hanif, 2010). That is, viewers look at them with greater focus to grasp details. Disengagement from such stimuli happens through executive control. Among the different components of executive functions, inhibitory control and cognitive flexibility are critical for such actions. Very young children who score higher on inhibitory control scale later show better emotion regulation (Carlson & Wang, 2007). On the other hand, children with ADHD have been found to be less capable of emotion regulation (Walcott & Landau, 2004). The role of attention and executive control in emotion regulation is well established (Zelazo & Cunningham, 2007). These studies are in harmony with neuroscience-based models that propose a dynamic interaction between the affective and the cognitive centres of the brain (Pessoa, 2008). For example, the frontal and the orbit frontal areas evaluate bottom-up signals sent by the amygdala. This top-down executive management makes sure that the power of the emotional stimuli is manageable. Research from meditation shows that in expert meditators, the frontal areas modulate effects of emotional stimuli (Manna et al., 2010).

These studies thus lead to applied issues in which attention and executive control training could help manage emotional distress in certain individuals (Ochsner & Gross, 2007). In sum, we study attention to understand how the mind selects stimuli for processing and how objective knowledge is acquired. Cognitive psychology has been indifferent to affect for a long time, since it was long believed emotions are impossible to be captured through the usual experiments. They are too subjective and vague, and verbal reports of participants are not to be trusted. However, affect, emotions, and their phenomenology don't arise in any cognitive vacuum. The usual cognitive systems and their computations give rise to these states. That's why attention and working memory including the higher executive control systems are involved in management of emotions. These studies also show that the traditional separation between cognition and emotion need not be a hurdle to experimental work using different methods. Once we understand how emotions arise and the power of the stimuli, it is possible to control them by training the mind. Continuing this line of thinking, next we will examine how well attention explains awareness and consciousness.

4. Attention, awareness, and consciousness

The human mind is conscious. It's also attentive in the usual sense. How then is attentiveness related to being conscious? One arguable attribute of consciousness is that it has content. That is, if I claim that I am conscious, then I have to say that I am conscious of *something*. Attention plays an important role in giving this *something* to the mind. What one attends to usually becomes the content of consciousness. Awareness on the other hand is often defined as some sort of subjective experience without critical knowledge. However, attention modulates awareness (Cohen et al., 2012). Awareness could be the gateway to later conscious perception (Posner, 1994). Ned Block proposed that there are two types of awareness (Block, 1995). One he termed "access" and another "phenomenal." Attention transforms phenomenal to access type when the mind's content becomes more detailed. For example, feeble visual stimuli become vivid when attended. Brain imaging studies show that when participants deploy spatial attention onto any object, the frontal areas show higher activity, and target discrimination improves (Van Gaal & Fahrenfort, 2008). Spatial attention makes invisible stimuli visible (Wyart & Tallon-Baudry, 2008). Thus, what we think we know about the world in objective terms is an outcome of attentional processing. Attention modulates the threshold at which stimuli become conscious. Thus, what begins as phenomenal awareness turns into access awareness. One can report, discriminate, and have objective knowledge. Awareness and attention could be separable mechanisms though they may show some connections (Lamme, 2003). Research has explored when engagement of spatial attention from awareness could be differentiated. In Lamme's model, there is a fast feed-forward sweep of information that floods the areas of the primary visual cortex in the first 80 ms of stimuli onset. At this stage, participants may not be aware of the stimuli. Later information spreads to attentional areas and then conscious processing may begin. Therefore, there is both a temporal and spatial nature of awareness and its eventual progression into conscious perception. It has to be clarified that different types of attention can induce awareness differently. Endogenous voluntary attention leads to a higher awareness of stimuli, whereas exogenous attention is captured by stimuli without awareness (McCormick, 1997). One study that used MEG (magnetoencephalography), reported variable gamma-band oscillations depending on the deployment of spatial attention (Magazzini & Singh, 2018). Therefore, both neural and behavioural signatures of states of awareness and attention can be observed. The important question has been under what circumstances attention becomes engaged under which the mind attends an objective knowledgeable state.

Helmholtz too believed that most of our visual processing is unconscious (Turner, 1977). There are states of the mind when people are never aware of events. They don't report details even when the event has just happened around them. There are two arguments on this phenomenon. When one has focused attention on some object then other objects slip into non-awareness. Inattentional blindness has been coined as a term to refer to this (Mack & Rock, 1998). In a classic demonstration, Daniel Simmons showed that a group of players who were focused on passing a ball to one another did not notice when a man passed by wearing a bear mask. This lack of notice was linked to their attention being focused on the ball. Thus, awareness of objects or events was defined as an outcome of attentional deployment. What we notice or don't notice depends on our current goals and the degree to which we have committed attention (Most et al., 2005). Task-specific cognition suffers when task-irrelevant items enter into our perception. It has been shown that even high perceptual load on the main task induces inattentional blindness towards task-irrelevant items (Cartwright-Finch & Lavie, 2007). If the task at hand is sufficiently demanding, then one can't notice what's around. In one experiment participants even failed to notice a pure tone that accompanied a visual task with high perceptual load (Macdonald & Lavie, 2011). In real-world settings basketball players who are not that experienced have been shown to experience high inattentional blindness compared to experts (Furley et al., 2010) since expert players have learnt how to focus attention in a sustained manner on the ball at all times. Most (2010) argued that sometimes both perceptual and cognitive types of inattentional blindness can be seen during experiments. When spatial attention is misdirected, it can induce a form of spatial inattentional blindness. At other times when the core task is of a very high demand then working memory may be tasked. This could lead to a more cognitive kind of inattentional blindness. This perceptual vs cognitive dichotomy of inattentional blindness as related to awareness can be seen in some tasks.

The spatial spread of attention is dependent on individual differences. For example, individuals with hearing impairment have been shown to have a larger spatial spread which means they can have awareness or notice events at the periphery (Bavelier et al., 2006). Attention orienting tasks also have shown that if cues are presented at a very extreme distance from the centre, lesser attention capture is seen in such individuals. Thus, both cognitive load and distance matter for awareness. It would be simplistic to assume that no processing occurs during inattentional blindness because there is evidence to suggest the contrary (Hutchinson, 2019). The alpha band oscillations indicate high levels of attentional processing leading to consciousness. In one study researchers used the transcranial alternating current stimulation over the occipital cortex. When such current was within the alpha band, participants could not notice any unexpected stimuli. This suggests that the frontal attentional areas control inattentional blindness by suppression of sensory input that does not reach consciousness (Hutchinson et al., 2020).

5. Attending to the unconscious

So far, from our discussion it appears that attention plays a key role in making the mind conscious in the sense that the mind has objective content to report and discriminate. However, we perceive a wide range of stimuli all the time that we don't notice and they remain unconscious. What happens to such stimuli? Early observations of Cherry and Treisman suggested that stimuli that have been rejected or filtered out by attention still influence behaviour. More recent research in cognitive psychology and cognitive neuroscience has explored how attention may play a role in unconscious perception. Johann Herbart (1776–1841) had first used the word subliminal to refer to stimuli that we can't be aware of. The Greek philosopher Heraclitus believed that our consciousness is basically philosophical awareness, the contents of which we can reflect on. Everything else remains unknown to us (Rankin, 1995). Galen believed that our inferences come from the unconscious. The Roman philosopher Plotinus was probably the first who suggested that our attention brings things into awareness from the unconscious (Tryon, 2014). William James believed in unconscious processing (Weinberger, 2000). James deliberated at length on the distinctions between the conscious and the unconscious in his chapter titled "The Mind-Stuff Theory" in *Principles of Psychology* (James, 2007, 1890). Probably, James identified both the unconscious and the conscious as two states of the mind. The Freudian take on the unconscious and its enormous influence on twentieth-century studies of psychopathology is well known.

In Ulric Neisser's first textbook, *Cognitive Psychology*, there was not much on the issue of unconscious processing (Neisser, 2014). The information processing model of the mind was to explain what the participant could report and respond to and not what he could not. Even cognitive psychology's foray into the studies of consciousness was a much later development. More recently, cognitive psychologists have looked at unconscious processing through the induction of sub-liminality. That is, there are such stimuli whose intensity is too weak to penetrate our consciousness. Bargh and colleagues write,

> Thus, it is unfair to measure the capability of the unconscious in terms of how well it processes subliminal stimuli because unconscious (like conscious) processes evolved to deal and respond to naturally occurring (regular strength) stimuli; assessing the unconscious in terms of processing subliminal stimuli is analogous to evaluating the intelligence of a fish based on its behaviour out of water. And as one might expect, the operational definition of the unconscious in terms of subliminal information processing has led to the confusions in the field.
>
> (Bargh & Morsella, 2008, p. 2)

It is, though, strange that unattended stimuli are selected for processing. It is possible that there is a type of attention which selects such stimuli that are below thresholds of awareness. More recently it has been dubbed "unconscious attention." In Baars's global workspace model of consciousness, the unconscious plays an important role (Baars, 2005). Dehaene and colleagues offer a useful historical review of the evolution of research and thinking in this area (Kouider & Dehaene, 2007). Masking is used to make stimuli almost invisible. This paradigm became very popular in psycholinguistics (Forster & Davis, 1984). In this paradigm, often a masked word related to a target is presented first. Results show that such invisible primes influence target processing. The usual explanation is that participants process the unconscious stimuli even though they don't see them (Björkman et al., 1993).

In spite of many demonstrations of subliminal effects in different tasks, the explanation of its mechanism remains obscure, primarily because it is not clear what role attention may play in such a case when the agent does not know about the stimuli. Dehaene and colleagues suggested that both top-down and bottom-up factors play roles during unconscious processing. There are three distinct stages of stimuli processing in this proposal (Dehaene et al., 2006, Figure 3.4). Brief stimuli generate some activity in the visual occipital areas depending on their strength. If stimulus strength is robust then it leads to large-scale whole-brain activity and reaches consciousness. Techniques such as masking and continuous flash suppression are employed to degrade the intensity of the stimuli so that it does not induce large scale brain activity. Barr proposed three distinct stages of processing of stimuli: pre-conscious, conscious, and subliminal. In the preconscious stage, the stimuli have very little strength to influence any higher brain activity and thus may only lead to some awareness. Subliminal processing refers to when a greater amount of processing occurs leading to unconscious perception. Full-blown consciousness requires both bottom-up strengths of the stimuli and top-down attention. More recently, Lamme has proposed a four-stage model of processing (Lamme, 2020):

Stage 1: Fully invisible
Stage 2: Subjectively invisible
Stage 3: Unattended (otherwise subjectively visible)
Stage 4: Subjectively visible and attended

It's important to understand the difference between stages two and three. In some experiments, participants do not experience any of the stimuli. In some other cases, they have not paid any attention but have subjective experience. How does one measure such a subjective experience? Lamme proposed to use a subjective evaluation scale during experiments. On this scale, participants can give a number depending on their experience of the

(a)

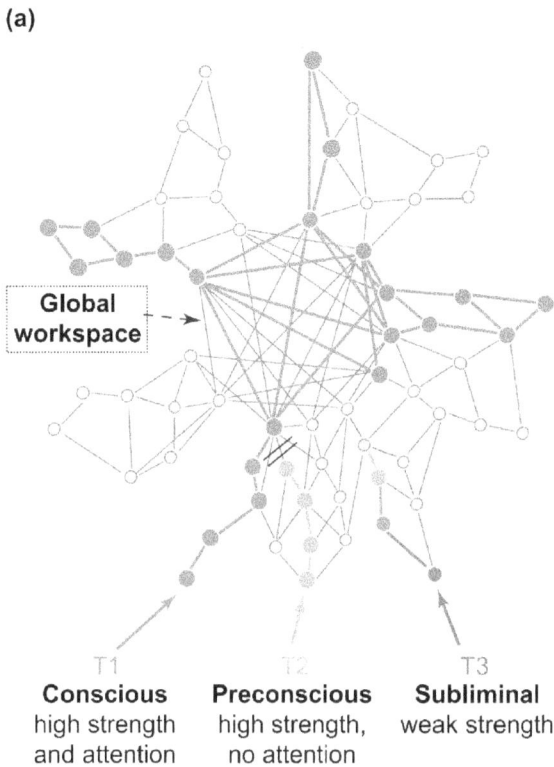

Figure 3.4 Global workspace model. A stimulus becomes conscious when there is a cascading activation of a set of central workspace neurons (T1, green). A stimulus of high perceptual strength can be unconscious because of no attention (T2, orange). A stimulus is called subliminal due to insufficient bottom-up strength (T3, red).

Source: Reprinted from *Trends in Cognitive Sciences*, Vol. 10, Stanislas Dehaene, Jean-Pierre Changeux, Lionel Naccache, Jérôme Sackur, Claire Sergent, "Conscious, preconscious, and subliminal processing: a testable taxonomy," 204–211, 2006, with permission from Elsevier

stimuli. In addition to experimental data, such qualitative instruments provide more information on subjective awareness.

It is likely that attention modulates awareness and consciousness. Attention brings feeble stimuli into full-blown consciousness. However, the issue of "visibility" remains controversial since we have not yet settled the very early stages at which the stimuli can induce subjective awareness. If awareness and attention are delinked as we have seen in the earlier discussion, then the role of attention on unconscious perception is clear. We also can't bypass the phenomenological aspects of unconscious or subliminal processing. Current experimental strategies do not measure phenomenality. Enormous emphasis on visual stimuli in such theories also offers only one side of the view. Unconscious processing can occur in many other modalities. A large number of studies have explored if unconscious stimuli capture attention while some have explored what attention does to otherwise invisible stimuli. They are not same things. For example, more recently many have shown that almost invisible and very brief cues can influence saccades (Huang et al., 2014; Prasad & Mishra, 2020). Thus, attention can act as a modulator to any stimuli and make them both visible and conscious. Finally, the exact role of attention on subjective and objective aspects of processing remains debated.

6. Attention and its training

It is possible to induce neuroplasticity by repeated training. Attention has been a key mental system that can be trained. According to many traditions, the key to a healthy mind and life is to learn to attend well. Cognitive psychologists' view of attention is limited in some sense and does not fully reflect the traditional conceptions found in different ancient cultures and traditions. A case in point is the manner in which the mind and attention are theorised in Zen Buddhism, which has remained very popular. Many scientific investigations have been carried out to examine how the practitioners enrich their minds through specific practices. Meditative practices in the three major Abrahamic monotheistic religions involve innocent forms of recitation, chanting, and visualisation of religious symbols. These religions do not prescribe technical practices in the control of attention or awareness as such, since such religions believed that technicality may interfere in the realisation of God which is the ultimate aim.

In Zen, the whole aim of the practice is to empty the mind of abstract conceptualisations, which is in sharp contrast to what attention does in our current theories (Suzuki, 2019). While one can attend to things to enhance present awareness, there is no need to be analytical and objective. In this sense, traditional practices have viewed the relationship between attention and consciousness differently. The defocusing of attention from things and its internal circulation around present ongoing sensations is a typical scenario in Zen. Suzuki compared the Zen state of mind to the mindset of Samurai warriors and also the evolution of Haiku poetry (Suzuki, 2019). At a deeper level, attention manifests in all these activities. For example, Haiku poets focus on the present sensations without worrying too much about ornamentation and forms. Its aesthetics lie in seeing and feeling things as they are and in themselves. In comparison to video games, Zen meditation strengthens attention in a qualitatively different way.

Mindfulness meditation emphasises paying attention to the present. Thoughts that are about the past or future are irrelevant. The Vietnamese Zen master Thich Nhat Hanh says that one can find joy and bring the mind to the body through one attentive breath. Technically speaking, attending to breathing systematically and intensely inhibits other distracting thoughts. These distracting thoughts are often about past regrets or future uncertainties. When the negative thoughts and images are suppressed, one feels lighter and happier. The cross-cultural popularity of mindfulness meditation speaks of its perceived effectiveness. At a behavioural level, practice of mindfulness leads to lesser impact of arousing emotional stimuli. Mindfulness teaches how to control attention to specific stimuli in a non-judgmental way. It is important to note that this conceptualisation of attention is different from what we have learnt so far, when attending greatly enhanced our ability to discriminate. Jon Kabat-Zinn, a well-known name in mindfulness training, writes that to be mindful is to attend in a specific way., to be non-judgmental towards the stimuli but to maintain awareness (Kabat-Zinn, 2015). Amidst this circular reasoning, it is unclear if we need to define selective attention with regard to mindfulness or examine mindfulness from contemporary theories of attention.

Brain imaging studies show that frontal areas of the brain establish better functional connections with the amygdala in mindfulness practitioners (Marchand, 2014). This connection, in essence, helps attention control towards emotional arousal. Mindfulness then helps the mind to suppress or not take cognisance of harmful thoughts that can negatively engage the emotions. This is so far the clearest link between attention regulation and control of rumination. Reoccurring thought patterns are controlled by moving attention to things that are present now. Some researchers have examined if such meditation practices also enhance attention as measured in typical cognitive psychological tasks. One study found that meditators perform better on the Stroop task than non-meditators since they can maintain superior sustained attention (Kozasa et al., 2012). Researchers have studied two different types of meditation practices as far as attention is concerned. For example, in focused attention meditation, practitioners focus on an object for a longer time uninterrupted. In the open monitoring meditation, participants observe contents of experience as they change from one moment to another. It is likely that both of these types of practices enrich different aspects of attention (Lutz et al., 2008). However, so far it has not been very clear how different practices influence different subsystems of attention (Tang & Posner, 2009).

A recent review (Britton, 2019) suggests that too much mindfulness training could have a negative impact. Excessive attention to current awareness could lead to a lack of sensitivity to both negative as well as positive emotions. Practising 45 minutes a day could be beneficial but anything more than that could inhibit some core psychological functions. What could be the reason for this? Since attention's main evolutionary purpose is to seek out novel information in the environment, its regulation and suppression can lead to a state of non-seeking. While this non-seeking, in general, is good for rumination for negative emotions, it's bad for cognition at large.

This point is debatable since it has to be linked to the individual's lifestyle and general ambitions. We probably can't survive, function, and succeed in today's world with non-sensitivity to stimuli all the time. Being mindful means to be aware in a non-judgmental manner. However, intentional actions include judgments. How can one act without clear discriminatory goals? Therefore, given the current status of research on the meditation-attention link, one has to be sceptical. Without a deeper understanding of the traditions, we will only evaluate meditation's influence on attention using traditional tasks. For example, we don't have any task as of now that can measure non-judgmental attention. All the tasks are designed to measure discrimination through attention. Nevertheless, these approaches certainly have enlarged our understanding of the mind in general and have brought ancient practices and modern scientific approaches close.

7. Summary

An entire book can easily be written on attention. The science of attention has grown so much and extends to so many disciplines today that it is difficult to keep track of all developments. Attention has become the holy grail of cognitive psychology and of the cognitive science enterprise. I have just covered a few important aspects that I think reveal the essential attributes of attention. It is still the case, as James proclaimed, that we still don't know how to define attention. I think it is better to ask the question of what attention does to one's cognition than of what it is. That way we remain focused on its valuable effects on our minds and everyday life. I have explored some key properties of attention that include selection, and also its links to higher mental processes such as consciousness. At the moment there are controversies in the field with regard to its neural and psychological dimensions but that's inevitable. In the end, attention is everything that we call "the mind" more metaphorically. The very content of the mind at each moment is a product of attention. Experimental research in the last several decades has clearly shown this. The future of attention research lies in replications in the cross-cultural dimension and also in the artificial systems. This chapter should help the reader understand other concepts related to cognition discussed in later chapters.

References

Baars, B. J. (2005). Global workspace theory of consciousness: Toward a cognitive neuroscience of human experience. *Progress in Brain Research*, *150*, 45–53.

Bargh, J. A., & Morsella, E. (2008). The unconscious mind. *Perspectives on Psychological Science*, *3*(1), 73–79.

Baudouin, J. Y., Martin, F., Tiberghien, G., Verlut, I., & Franck, N. (2002). Selective attention to facial emotion and identity in schizophrenia. *Neuropsychologia*, *40*(5), 503–511.

Baumgartner, H. M., Graulty, C. J., Hillyard, S. A., & Pitts, M. A. (2018). Does spatial attention modulate the earliest component of the visual evoked potential? *Cognitive Neuroscience*, 9(1–2), 4–19.

Bavelier, D., Dye, M. W., & Hauser, P. C. (2006). Do deaf individuals see better? *Trends in Cognitive Sciences*, 10(11), 512–518.

Benoni, H., & Tsal, Y. (2010). Where have we gone wrong? Perceptual load does not affect selective attention. *Vision Research*, 50(13), 1292–1298.

Björkman, M., Juslin, P., & Winman, A. (1993). Realism of confidence in sensory discrimination: The underconfidence phenomenon. *Perception & Psychophysics*, 54(1), 75–81.

Block, N. (1995). On a confusion about a function of consciousness. *Behavioral and Brain Sciences*, 18(2), 227–247.

Boduroglu, A., & Shah, P. (2017). Cultural differences in attentional breadth and resolution. *Culture and Brain*, 5(2), 169–181.

Britton, W. B. (2019). Can mindfulness be too much of a good thing? The value of a middle way. *Current Opinion in Psychology*, 28, 159–165.

Broadbent, D. E. (1958). *Perception and communication*. London: Pergamon Press.

Broadbent, D. E., & Gregory, M. (1963). Division of attention and the decision theory of signal detection. *Proceedings of the Royal Society of London. Series B. Biological Sciences*, 158(971), 222–231.

Carlson, S. M., & Wang, T. S. (2007). Inhibitory control and emotion regulation in preschool children. *Cognitive Development*, 22(4), 489–510.

Cartwright-Finch, U., & Lavie, N. (2007). The role of perceptual load in inattentional blindness. *Cognition*, 102(3), 321–340.

Carrasco, M., Ling, S., & Read, S. (2004). Attention alters appearance. *Nature Neuroscience*, 7(3), 308–313.

Cohen, M. A., Cavanagh, P., Chun, M. M., & Nakayama, K. (2012). The attentional requirements of consciousness. *Trends in Cognitive Sciences*, 16(8), 411–417.

Dale, G., Joessel, A., Bavelier, D., & Green, C. S. (2020). A new look at the cognitive neuroscience of video game play. *Annals of the New York Academy of Sciences*, 1464(1), 192–203.

Dehaene, S., Changeux, J. P., Naccache, L., Sackur, J., & Sergent, C. (2006). Conscious, preconscious, and subliminal processing: A testable taxonomy. *Trends in Cognitive Sciences*, 10(5), 204–211.

Deutsch, J. A., & Deutsch, D. (1963). Attention: Some theoretical considerations. *Psychological Review*, 70(1), 80.

Doll, A., Hölzel, B. K., Bratec, S. M., Boucard, C. C., Xie, X., Wohlschläger, A. M., & Sorg, C. (2016). Mindful attention to breath regulates emotions via increased amygdala – prefrontal cortex connectivity. *Neuroimage*, 134, 305–313.

Driver, J. (2001). A selective review of selective attention research from the past century. *British Journal of Psychology*, 92(1), 53–78.

Dye, M. W., & Bavelier, D. (2004). Playing video games enhances visual attention in children. *Journal of Vision*, 4(11), 40–40.

Engle, R. W., & Kane, M. J. (2004). Executive attention, working memory capacity, and a two-factor theory of cognitive control. *Psychology of Learning and Motivation*, 44, 145–200.

Fiebelkorn, I. C., & Kastner, S. (2020). Functional specialization in the attention network. *Annual Review of Psychology*, 71, 221–249.

Forster, K. I., & Davis, C. (1984). Repetition priming and frequency attenuation in lexical access. *Journal of Experimental Psychology: Learning, Memory, and Cognition, 10*(4), 680.

Foster, J. J., & Awh, E. (2019). The role of alpha oscillations in spatial attention: Limited evidence for a suppression account. *Current Opinion in Psychology, 29,* 34–40.

Franceschini, S., Gori, S., Ruffino, M., Viola, S., Molteni, M., & Facoetti, A. (2013). Action video games make dyslexic children read better. *Current Biology, 23*(6), 462–466.

Furley, P., Memmert, D., & Heller, C. (2010). The dark side of visual awareness in sport: Inattentional blindness in a real-world basketball task. *Attention, Perception, & Psychophysics, 72*(5), 1327–1337.

Gamer, M., Schmitz, A. K., Tittgemeyer, M., & Schilbach, L. (2013). The human amygdala drives reflexive orienting towards facial features. *Current Biology, 23*(20), R917–R918.

Gazzaley, A., & Nobre, A. C. (2012). Top-down modulation: Bridging selective attention and working memory. *Trends in Cognitive Sciences, 16*(2), 129–135.

Golob, E. J., & Mock, J. R. (2019). Auditory spatial attention capture, disengagement, and response selection in normal aging. *Attention, Perception, & Psychophysics, 81*(1), 270–280.

Green, C. S., & Bavelier, D. (2006). Effect of action video games on the spatial distribution of visuospatial attention. *Journal of Experimental Psychology: Human Perception and Performance, 32*(6), 1465.

Hajcak, G., MacNamara, A., & Olvet, D. M. (2010). Event-related potentials, emotion, and emotion regulation: An integrative review. *Developmental Neuropsychology, 35*(2), 129–155.

Hajcak, G., & Olvet, D. M. (2008). The persistence of attention to emotion: Brain potentials during and after picture presentation. *Emotion, 8*(2), 250.

Hatfield, G. (1998). Attention in early scientific psychology. *Visual Attention, 1,* 3–25.

Haun, D. B., Rapold, C. J., Call, J., Janzen, G., & Levinson, S. C. (2006). Cognitive cladistics and cultural override in Hominid spatial cognition. *Proceedings of the National Academy of Sciences, 103*(46), 17568–17573.

Huang, Y. F., Tan, E. G. F., Soon, C. S., & Hsieh, P. J. (2014). Unconscious cues bias first saccades in a free-saccade task. *Consciousness and Cognition, 29,* 48–55.

Hutchinson, B. T. (2019). Toward a theory of consciousness: A review of the neural correlates of inattentional blindness. *Neuroscience & Biobehavioral Reviews, 104,* 87–99.

Hutchinson, B. T., Pammer, K., & Bandara, K. (2020). tACS stimulation at alpha frequency selectively induces inattentional blindness. *Brain Topography,* 1–10.

James, W. (2007). *The principles of psychology* (Vol. 1). Cosimo, Inc.

James, W., Burkhardt, F., Bowers, F., & Skrupskelis, I. K. (1890). *The principles of psychology* (Vol. 1, No. 2). Macmillan.

Kabat-Zinn, J. (2015). Mindfulness. *Mindfulness, 6*(6), 1481–1483.

Kissler, J., Herbert, C., Winkler, I., & Junghofer, M. (2009). Emotion and attention in visual word processing – an ERP study. *Biological Psychology, 80*(1), 75–83.

Klein, R. M. (2000). Inhibition of return. *Trends in Cognitive Sciences, 4*(4), 138–147.

Kouider, S., & Dehaene, S. (2007). Levels of processing during non-conscious perception: A critical review of visual masking. *Philosophical Transactions of the Royal Society B: Biological Sciences, 362*(1481), 857–875.

Kozasa, E. H., Sato, J. R., Lacerda, S. S., Barreiros, M. A., Radvany, J., Russell, T. A., Sanches, L. G., Mello, L. E., & Amaro Jr., E. (2012). Meditation training increases brain efficiency in an attention task. *Neuroimage, 59*(1), 745–749.

Lamme, V. A. (2003). Why visual attention and awareness are different. *Trends in Cognitive Sciences, 7*(1), 12–18.

Lamme, V. A. (2020). Visual functions generating conscious seeing. *Frontiers in Psychology, 11.*

Lanssens, A., Pizzamiglio, G., Mantini, D., & Gillebert, C. R. (2020). Role of the dorsal attention network in distracter suppression based on features. *Cognitive Neuroscience, 11*(1–2), 37–46.

Lavie, N. (2005). Distracted and confused?: Selective attention under load. *Trends in Cognitive Sciences, 9*(2), 75–82.

Lavie, N., Hirst, A., De Fockert, J. W., & Viding, E. (2004). Load theory of selective attention and cognitive control. *Journal of Experimental Psychology: General, 133*(3), 339.

Lawrence, R. K., Edwards, M., & Goodhew, S. C. (2018). Changes in the spatial spread of attention with ageing. *Acta Psychologica, 188*, 188–199.

Lutz, A., Slagter, H. A., Dunne, J. D., & Davidson, R. J. (2008). Attention regulation and monitoring in meditation. *Trends in Cognitive Sciences, 12*(4), 163–169.

Macdonald, J. S., & Lavie, N. (2011). Visual perceptual load induces inattentional deafness. *Attention, Perception, & Psychophysics, 73*(6), 1780–1789.

Mack, A., & Rock, I. (1998). *Inattentional blindness.* MIT Press.

Magazzini, L., & Singh, K. D. (2018). Spatial attention modulates visual gamma oscillations across the human ventral stream. *Neuroimage, 166*, 219–229.

Manna, A., Raffone, A., Perrucci, M. G., Nardo, D., Ferretti, A., Tartaro, A., Londei, A., Del Gratta, C., Belardinelli, M. O., & Romani, G. L. (2010). Neural correlates of focused attention and cognitive monitoring in meditation. *Brain Research Bulletin, 82*(1–2), 46–56.

Marchand, W. R. (2014). Neural mechanisms of mindfulness and meditation: Evidence from neuroimaging studies. *World Journal of Radiology, 6*(7), 471.

McCormick, P. A. (1997). Orienting attention without awareness. *Journal of Experimental Psychology: Human Perception and Performance, 23*(1), 168.

Melcher, D. (2009). Selective attention and the active remapping of object features in trans-saccadic perception. *Vision Research, 49*(10), 1249–1255.

Moray, N. (1959). Attention in dichotic listening: Affective cues and the influence of instructions. *Quarterly Journal of Experimental Psychology, 11*(1), 56–60.

Most, S. B. (2010). What's "inattentional" about inattentional blindness? *Consciousness and Cognition, 19*(4), 1102–1104.

Most, S. B., Scholl, B. J., Clifford, E. R., & Simons, D. J. (2005). What you see is what you set: Sustained inattentional blindness and the capture of awareness. *Psychological Review, 112*(1), 217.

Muayqil, T. A., Al-Yousef, L. M., Al-Herbish, M. J., Al-Nafisah, M., Halawani, L. M., Al-Bader, S. S., . . . & Alanazy, M. H. (2021). Culturally influenced performance on tasks of line bisection and symbol cancellation in Arabs. *Applied Neuropsychology: Adult, 28*(3), 257–268.

Murphy, G., Groeger, J. A., & Greene, C. M. (2016). Twenty years of load theory – where are we now, and where should we go next? *Psychonomic Bulletin & Review*, 23(5), 1316–1340.

Murphy, K., & Spencer, A. (2009). Playing video games does not make for better visual attention skills. *Journal of Articles in Support of the Null Hypothesis*, 6(1).

Murphy, S., Spence, C., & Dalton, P. (2017). Auditory perceptual load: A review. *Hearing Research*, 352, 40–48.

Neisser, U. (2014). *Cognitive psychology* (Classic ed.). Psychology Press.

Ochsner, K. N., & Gross, J. J. (2007). The neural architecture of emotion regulation. *Handbook of Emotion Regulation*, 1(1), 87–109.

O'Craven, K. M., Downing, P. E., & Kanwisher, N. (1999). fMRI evidence for objects as the units of attentional selection. *Nature*, 401(6753), 584–587.

Olofsson, J. K., Nordin, S., Sequeira, H., & Polich, J. (2008). Affective picture processing: An integrative review of ERP findings. *Biological Psychology*, 77(3), 247–265.

Pessoa, L. (2008). On the relationship between emotion and cognition. *Nature Reviews Neuroscience*, 9(2), 148–158.

Peter, U. T. (2005). Voluntary attention modulates the brightness of overlapping transparent surfaces. *Vision Research*, 45(9), 1095–1098.

Posner, M. I. (1994). Attention: The mechanisms of consciousness. *Proceedings of the National Academy of Sciences*, 91(16), 7398–7403.

Posner, M. I. (2011). *Attention in a social world*. Oxford University Press.

Prasad, S., & Mishra, R. (2020). To look or not to look: Subliminal abrupton-set cues influence constrained free-choice saccades. *Journal of Eye Movement Research*, 13(4).

Putkinen, V., Makkonen, T., & Eerola, T. (2017). Music-induced positive mood broadens the scope of auditory attention. *Social Cognitive and Affective Neuroscience*, 12(7), 1159–1168.

Rankin, H. D. (1995). Heraclitus on conscious and unconscious states. *Quaderni Urbinati di Cultura Classica*, 73–86.

Sarter, M., Gehring, W. J., & Kozak, R. (2006). More attention must be paid: The neurobiology of attentional effort. *Brain Research Reviews*, 51(2), 145–160.

Scholl, B. J. (2001). Objects and attention: The state of the art. *Cognition*, 80(1–2), 1–46.

Schultz, R. T. (2005). Developmental deficits in social perception in autism: The role of the amygdala and fusiform face area. *International Journal of Developmental Neuroscience*, 23(2–3), 125–141.

Schupp, H. T., Stockburger, J., Codispoti, M., Junghöfer, M., Weike, A. I., & Hamm, A. O. (2007). Selective visual attention to emotion. *Journal of Neuroscience*, 27(5), 1082–1089.

Shinn-Cunningham, B. G. (2008). Object-based auditory and visual attention. *Trends in Cognitive Sciences*, 12(5), 182–186.

Srinivasan, N., & Hanif, A. (2010). Global-happy and local-sad: Perceptual processing affects emotion identification. *Cognition and Emotion*, 24(6), 1062–1069.

Suzuki, D. T. (2019). VII. Zen and Haiku. In *Zen and Japanese culture* (pp. 215–268). Princeton University Press.

Tang, Y. Y., & Posner, M. I. (2009). Attention training and attention state training. *Trends in Cognitive Sciences*, 13(5), 222–227.

Treisman, A. M. (1969). Strategies and models of selective attention. *Psychological Review*, 76(3), 282.

Treisman, A. M., & Gelade, G. (1980). A feature-integration theory of attention. *Cognitive Psychology*, 12(1), 97–136.

Tryon, W. (2014). *Cognitive neuroscience and psychotherapy: Network principles for a unified theory*. Academic Press.

Turner, R. S. (1977). Hermann von Helmholtz and the empiricist vision. *Journal of the History of the Behavioral Sciences*, 13(1), 48–58.

Van Gaal, S., & Fahrenfort, J. J. (2008). The relationship between visual awareness, attention, and report. *Journal of Neuroscience*, 28(21), 5401–5402.

Vanlessen, N., De Raedt, R., Koster, E. H., & Pourtois, G. (2016). Happy heart, smiling eyes: A systematic review of positive mood effects on broadening of visuospatial attention. *Neuroscience & Biobehavioral Reviews*, 68, 816–837.

Von Wolff, C. F. (1740). Psychologia rationalis. prostat in Officina libraria Rengeriana.

Walcott, C. M., & Landau, S. (2004). The relation between disinhibition and emotion regulation in boys with attention deficit hyperactivity disorder. *Journal of Clinical Child and Adolescent Psychology*, 33(4), 772–782.

Weinberger, J. (2000). William James and the unconscious: Redressing a century-old misunderstanding. *Psychological Science*, 11(6), 439–445.

Wyart, V., & Tallon-Baudry, C. (2008). Neural dissociation between visual awareness and spatial attention. *Journal of Neuroscience*, 28(10), 2667–2679.

Zelazo, P. D., & Cunningham, W. (2007). Executive function: Mechanisms underlying emotion regulation. In *Handbook of emotion regulation* (pp. 135–158). Guilford.

4 Current Research on Consciousness

1. The conscious mind: A historical sketch

It is difficult to write about consciousness with clarity encompassing all points of views in any single chapter. I aim to get straight into the heart of the issue among many that should bother cognitive scientists particularly. That is how one does come to defend the mind and even propose models of its workings within a visibly material universe. This was also the title that Jaewong Kim had chosen for his important monograph (Kim, 1998). Consciousness has been approached either as a metaphysical problem or more recently as a scientific one to be cracked with the tools of the modern brain and psychological sciences. However, reductionist approaches have been fiercely resisted as we will see later. Consciousness as a metaphysical problem has remained so for at least four thousand years. The question of consciousness was central to the writers of the Upanishads, probably the oldest writings by humans on philosophical issues (Scharfstein, 1998). The Buddha addressed it in his many discourses (Sharp, 2011). The Chinese too wrote on it since it was linked to human virtue (Oda & Bucci, 2020). Thus, consciousness as a phenomenon has always been very intriguing to scholars and thinkers. Today within the functionalist cognitive psychology and cognitive neurosciences, its study has become more sophisticated. Multiple theories exist within the philosophy of the mind of its nature and attributes (Parrington, 2021). Even then, there is no certainty of its mechanisms within our current systems of knowledge. It has proven to be very elusive for a materialistic framework which is the current scientific approach in many fields. Before we go to consciousness, we have to take a brief historical tour of the concept called the mind since consciousness is an attribute of the mind.

In Western civilisation speculations about the mind and its attributes have continued since the pre-Socratic Greeks, the Roman Stoics, and then the philosophers of the Renaissance. For example, the Greek atomists such as Democritus believed that everything that's there in the universe is made of material (Taylor, 2010). This materialism did not allow any substance that was not matter. Various Greek schools of philosophy that practised

DOI: 10.4324/9781003316053-4

Sophism and Stoicism were not particularly interested in the nature of the mind, although their philosophy was more geared towards solving everyday practical problems of life and attainment of virtue and serenity through right conduct (Hadot, 2002). The Roman Stoics such as Seneca and Cicero carried forward this Neoplatonist philosophical programme that again provided practical insights into living (Armstrong, 1981). The early and mediaeval Christian philosophy was Neoplatonist in its approach (Hadot, 2002). Writers such as St. Augustine wrote metaphysical treatises on issues that dealt with the mind and consciousness relating it to devotion to Christ. However, St. Augustine did not focus much on the relationship between the mind and the world outside in the traditions of the ancient Greeks. St. Augustine speculated that the origin of the human cognition, thinking, reasoning, and perceiving can be found in the human soul itself (O'Daly, 1987). Therefore, until the fourteenth century, there was no serious effort to understand the mind as a concept within philosophy. Aristotelian and scholastic philosophy that was popular in universities was slowly challenged. Thus, since Hellenistic philosophy until the late Middle Ages, there was no systematic independent philosophy of mind such as we have now. Later in the sixteenth century, both the scientific revolutions and the Renaissance led to more rational proposals in multiple domains (Shapin, 2018). Mystical beliefs on the supernatural were replaced by objective theories. Studies in anatomy and physiology provided the backbone for materialistic theories about the body and the mind. By this time the Aristotelian hold on philosophy had weakened (Des Chene, 2000). Knowledge of the natural world and its classifications was not enough to satisfy the many curiosities of man. Thus, the study of the mind in early modern philosophy adopted the naturalism of Aristotle but infused it with rationalism (Blackwell & Kusukawa, 2017). It began to be recognised that it was the human mind alone which produced all meaning and interpretations about itself and the world.

It was Descartes who first approached the problem of the mind and consciousness methodologically. Descartes proposed that humans are thinking beings who know who they are (Descartes, 2013). In his *Meditations*, Descartes attempted a philosophical method to explain all systems of knowledge as clearly as possible using objective rationalistic schemes, moving away from the mediaeval Aristotelian dichotomy of "matter" and "form" (Gaukroger, 2008). Descartes proposed that the human "soul" was capable of thinking, perceiving, sensing, and acquiring knowledge. This soul was equivalent to consciousness; it had intuitive knowledge of the world and about itself that could not be doubted. Later, he wanted to examine if the pineal gland produced consciousness, but this endeavour was not fruitful. Thus, Descartes brought a revolution to the metaphysics and epistemology in the study of mind and consciousness which was similar to the popular Copernican revolution (Ben-Yami, 2015). Descartes established that the mind is a separate entity in the material world with its own properties. This conjecture arises from the incorrigible belief of the human mind in itself, and does not depend on sense data, i.e., what is out there in the world. This led to a rational method to explain scepticism in multiple domains. David Hume rejected Descartes's rationalism and proposed that our knowledge is based on sense data that we acquire through experience (Hume et al., 1993). Thus began the competing philosophical traditions of rationalism and empiricism.

Kant, the most famous philosopher of his time, was a rationalist and proposed that cognition is to represent something with consciousness (Willaschek & Watkins, 2017). For Kant, the mind cognises objects through representations using intuitions and concepts. Conscious cognition was possible for even non-existent objects. Therefore, cognition on the part of the mind did not depend on sense data, i.e., what is out there in the world. Kant thus gave the mind the power to represent thoughts and ideas. This view has been the most dominant in contemporary cognitive science. However, Kant did not offer any definitions of "consciousness" as such but used this word in connection to the mind and its ability to represent ideas through cognition. The rationalism in cognitive science, therefore, can be safely attributed to these influences of Descartes and Kant among others. This influence allows us today to consider the mind and mentality irrefutable entities that have their own properties and that are not material.

A definite turn in philosophy came with the rise of the Vienna circle and its logical positivism. The logical positivists wanted to develop a scientific philosophy based on mathematics and logic and did not want to promote metaphysical speculations (Ayer, 1959). They used sentences to explore truth conditions using logic. Naturally for them there was no such thing called a rational mind in a Cartesian theatre that took sensible decisions. Logical positivism in general influenced the growth of analytical philosophy in the UK and later in the USA. Analytical philosophers were empiricists and studied language using logic (Dummett, 2014). Analytical philosophy examined sentences in order to understand the truth values of thoughts. The idea was to examine facts contained in sentences or truth conditions as a proxy for external reality. There was no need to summon the mind in such a case since sentences themselves stated facts about the world. It was thus empiricist and behaviourist in its approach. One should read Gilbert Ryle's famous book *Concept of the Mind* to get a flavour of this line of thinking which dominated philosophy for decades. Gilbert Ryle did not believe in the existence of any mind and called it a mere ghost in the machine. For Ryle there was no such thing as consciousness, emotion, and reasoning except observable behaviour. Thus, long before behaviourism in psychology began as a scientific movement it was already popular in analytical philosophy. Logical positivism thus influenced behaviourism both in philosophy and psychology in later decades. There was no philosophy of mind and there was no such thing called a mind, which is non-material in these traditions (Braddon-Mitchell, 2019). It is only with the rise of cognitivism in the 1950s that rationalism and mentalism returned to fuel the cognitive revolution.

A multidisciplinary exercise began to study the mind and its attributes which also included consciousness among other things (Greenwood, 1999). The cognitive revolution therefore was a reappraisal of the rationalist past in philosophy while acceptance of the empirical rigour of sciences. In sum, the proper investigations of psychological functions and their philosophical implications towards a general theory of the mind began only in the 1950s.

This very brief history, albeit sketchy, suggests that speculations on the nature of the mind and its place in the universe is not new and has a very long-running ancient tradition. I could not give many dominant ideas from Eastern traditions that have also contributed valuable ideas on this point. That humans have minds which are conscious has never been doubted since ancient times. The rise of logical positivism and subsequent behaviourist psychology briefly had put a pause in this long historical chain. From this point I will get into the question of consciousness properly, as an attribute of the mind, and explore its philosophical, psychological, and neurobiological basis. These constitute recent ideas from the post-cognitive revolution era.

2. Hard and easy problems

From the foregoing discussion, it seems that ancients thought that the human soul is conscious. It can make decisions; it has reason; and it feels pain and understands. It has its own "will" as German philosopher Arthur Schopenhauer would have thought (Schopenhauer, 2012). This conscious self/soul or will creates the illusion of reality. This was also a view that Plato had accepted. Today, we don't use words such as soul but mind. It is the conceptual entity that apparently is conscious and has a biological basis. The modern quest has been to understand its origin and attributes, and if animals and other agents also have them. In this section, I will examine "consciousness" as a phenomenon or a process that mind/brain scientists are trying to understand.

Conscious beings experience things far beyond gathering objective information about them. Philosophers have coined the term "qualia" to explain this phenomenal state linked to perception and cognition. For example, there is something we experience about a red rose beyond the objective reportable facts related to its colour and texture. David Chalmers suggested that the biggest problem in understanding consciousness is to explain how such experiential and phenomenal states arise in the first place, most likely in the brains. This he coined as the hard problem of consciousness (Chalmers, 1995, Figure 4.1). According to Chalmers, there are some tractable and some intractable aspects of consciousness. In his words:

> there is not just one problem of consciousness, "Consciousness" is an ambiguous term, referring to many different phenomena". Each of these phenomena needs to be explained, but some are easier to explain than

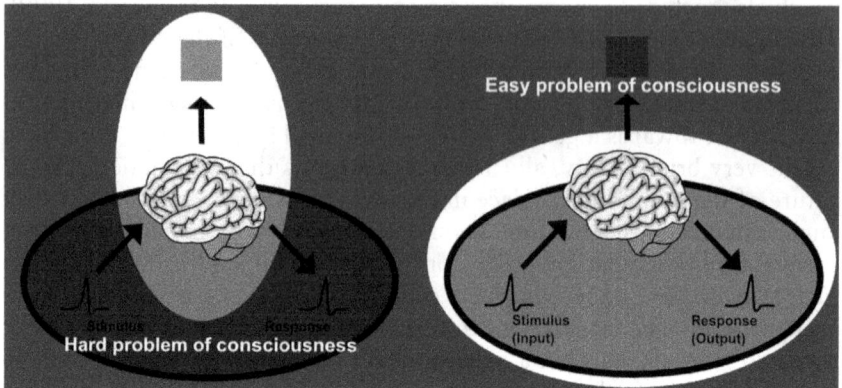

Figure 4.1 Hard and easy problems of consciousness. The easy problems are related
    to the contents of consciousness which are reportable. The hard prob-
    lems refer to the phenomenal, subjective experiences.

Source: Wikipedia Commons

others. At the start, it is useful to divide the associated problems of
consciousness into "hard" and "easy" problems. The easy problems of
consciousness are those that seem directly susceptible to the standard
methods of cognitive science, whereby a phenomenon is explained in
terms of computational or neural mechanisms. The hard problems are
those that seem to resist those methods.

(Chalmers, 1995, pp. 1–2)

Both cognitive psychology and cognitive neuroscience have distanced themselves from the hard problem and instead have tried to investigate the easy
problems; sometimes even reducing the problems to manageable units. One
such manageable strategy is to correlate visual perception with activity in
certain areas in the visual cortex. Koch's *Neural correlates of consciousness*
approach (Crick & Koch, 1998) led to the idea that there are clearly defined
and traceable neurobiological underpinnings of visual awareness. However,
such structure-function correlations say nothing about the phenomenological experience of the participants. Although the experiments reveal whether
one can report the identity of a stimulus, they do not throw light on the
hard problems as defined by Chalmers. There have been many well-argued
critiques of such strategies to explain consciousness using brain imaging and
computational methods (Koch et al., 2016; Metzinger, 2000).

Bernard Baars's "global workspace model" attempted to explain how
consciousness arises from dynamic interactions among different brain areas
simultaneously (Baars & Franklin, 2007). The model proposed that perceptual awareness and consciousness is the outcome of the neural networks

spread all over the brain. In this model, consciousness is imagined to arise from large-scale activity of the brain controlled by a central executive; when such activity does not occur, there is no consciousness. Without getting into the details of the model, for our purposes here it will be sufficient to say that the model still does not answer the hard problem. That is, how does phenomenal first-person experience arise from neural computation? That said, it is worth noting that the model is a fine culmination of decades of work in cognitive psychology, and advances in neuroimaging and computational theory. For example, the model uses theories of attention to explain emergence of conscious access from sensory perception (Newman & Baars, 1993). To Chalmers, these attempts are nothing but efforts to reduce the hard problems to simpler terms and exercise a functionalist approach using modern methods. Undeniably, the point that Chalmers is raising is intuitive and true. But if the problem escapes scientific methods, then how can one go about it? To Chalmers, "Explanation of functions does not suffice for the explanation of experience." In sum, although great advances have been made in functionalist cognitive psychology and cognitive neurosciences, we still have no idea about the nature of consciousness. As is expected, adherents of materialistic theories have tried to either reduce the problem of consciousness to explainable units or have completely denied it suggesting it is nothing but mere folk psychological assertions by humans.

How can then the hard problems be explained given what we know so far that mental phenomena are different from the physical, which precludes them from being studied using the usual tricks. Chalmers proposed a theory called naturalistic dualism. That is, both psychophysical and neurobiological knowledge will be used in understanding experience. Chalmers writes, "Where we have new fundamental properties, we also have new fundamental laws. Here the fundamental laws will be psychophysical laws, specifying how phenomenal (or protophenomenal) properties depend on physical properties. . . . [T]hey will be supervenience laws, telling us how experience arises from physical processes" (Chalmers, 1996, p. 127). This suggestion creates a scientifically acceptable form of dualism. We can still have the mental while explaining it through the physical.

Did evolution prefer us to have phenomenal consciousness? Everyday survival could very well go on with the access type of consciousness. There are suggestions that phenomenal consciousness came much later when the brain achieved a high degree of integrating capacity. Although evolutionary researchers have tracked down certain dates for specific functions such as working memory (Coolidge & Wynn, 2005) and language (Berwick & Chomsky, 2016), no one has proposed when phenomenal consciousness emerged. At the beginning, when the brain developed capacity for basic sensory processes, selection could be happening without the agent's phenomenality being attached to it. This stage was without what is now called conscious attention or attention. Now, what are they? Conceptuality deals with meaning. When agents are paying attention, they are extracting meaning and they are looking at the experience from a conceptual point of view. They're not just processing objects and their locations, but they have attached phenomenality to that experience. Attention's involvement with consciousness was probably delayed in our evolutionary history. At the beginning, it helped us just focus and find objects without entertaining with its qualia. There was just blue and no blueness of blue. Therefore, we have to explain in functional terms why phenomenal consciousness was necessary in the first place and what it does to our everyday cognitive life (Nichols & Grantham, 2000).

One can deny consciousness by claiming that it is not a scientific problem. The descriptions of its phenomenal attributes cannot be scientifically investigated or demonstrated. Therefore, if something cannot be demonstrated and objectively studied using the scientific methods, then we'd better not talk about them. Patricia and Paul Churchland are well known for this brand of philosophy (Churchland, 1989). The central thesis of this school of thought is that mental activity is brain activity. Any further talk on the mind in different ways is merely folk psychological and not scientific in nature. The Churchlands suggested that contemporary neuroscience research will have all the answers about the mind and its contents by examining the brain. Neurophilosophy assumes that all that we can do currently is to study the brain thoroughly and nothing else. Whatever we get from such studies must be sufficient for explaining all of behaviour and cognition. There is no point in creating a distinct category called the mental that cannot be tracked down to the material. Of course, such a proposal is bound to attract widespread criticism from those who still believe that consciousness is a distinct phenomenon and is just as real as the brain. The brain produces both logical reasoning and phenomenality. Current scientific progress in fields like neuroscience and cognitive psychology, however, has accepted the mind and the mental although the brain is studied for any clues.

Philosophers who took materialism and behaviourism seriously did not care for vague words such as mind or consciousness. Prominent among them is Daniel Dennett, who suggested that consciousness is an illusion and we have just believed in it for ages (Dennett, 1988). In his *From Bacteria to Bach and Back*, Dennett refers to our fascination with consciousness as a "user illusion" (Dennett, 2017). We have the language to talk about it, and there is nothing more to it. To Dennett, the idea that there is something unique to being a fly (in reference to Nagel's example of a bat in his famous paper (Nagel, 1974) or a polar bear is also equally false. It's similar to being like an escalator if that means anything to anyone. Writing a review of his book *From Bacteria to Bach and Back* in the pages of the *Times Literary Supplement*, David Papineau wrote the following:

> It is no accident that Daniel Dennett has gained such a wide readership. He is always fun to read. He has few equals at explaining complex topics, and his positive theories are never boring. But his public would do

well to take those theories with a pinch of salt. They are by no means the latest scientific insights that he cracks them up to be. The real source of his views is rather a set of peculiar philosophical assumptions that he acquired more than half a century ago.

("Competence without comprehension," TLS, 2017, June)

Dennett's denial of sentience and consciousness is grounded in the idea that we cannot find the mind. Any scientific approach can only explore the brain. Dennett is of the view that there has to be an attempt to solve the problem of consciousness in an objective way, since that is the way of science.

However, not every philosopher of the mind in the last few decades has been a fan of materialism. Influential papers like Nagel's *What Is It Like to Be a Bat?* (Nagel, 1974) and Frank Jackson's "What Mary Didn't Know" (Jackson, 1986) argued for the existence of subjectivity. There are limitations to understanding how subjective phenomenality arises during such objective analysis. That's why fields such as neuroscience (except cognitive neuroscience) and other computational sciences that are physicalist in their approach have not studied phenomenality but only the access mechanism. Thus, Chalmers's hard problems have not been answered but sometimes they have been simplified to make them easy. Consciousness, particularly its phenomenal quality, is well accepted today as a product of the brain, and several disorders are associated with it (Zhang et al., 2021). Therefore, it is not just folk psychological talk but it is real in that very sense in which the brain is real. The problem for the field is to explain it using our current neurobiological and computational knowledge of the brain. Consciousness may be a brain-based mechanism because the mental system arises in the physical system (Tümkaya, 2019). However, there is still widespread opposition to the idea that neurobiology will explain the mind in the future (Gold & Stoljar, 1999).

3. Theories of consciousness

Physicalist theories have to explain how the neurons through their activity give rise to subjective states that agents experience. Sophisticated data from brain imaging and computational modelling along with neurobiological explorations with other animal brains have made it possible to characterise, at a neuronal level, how consciousness might have emerged. Tononi and Edelman's dynamic core hypothesis (1998) linked the emergence of consciousness to brain activity in different areas. The theory proposed that consciousness is integrated and is also highly differentiated (Tononi & Edelman, 1998). They operationalise these concepts in terms of "functional clustering" which gives rise to the integration of experience and a measure of "neuronal complexity" that is behind differentiation. According to the authors, conscious experiences are always integrated and they are experienced from the first-person point of view holistically. In contrast to split-brain patients, healthy individuals can't entertain two different conscious experiences if two different stimuli are presented in two different eyes. They create one complex stimulus, binding the two, resulting in one experience. Conscious experiences are also extremely differentiated since no two experiences are the same. They may rapidly change with time and thus we can differentiate among experiences. One major idea of the dynamic core hypothesis is the availability of hundreds of conscious experiences out of which only one is selected at a time for our experience and report. The theory proposes that the thalamocortical posterior network works in a parallel and distributed manner from which consciousness emerges. The frontal attention and planning areas also work in a distributed manner and collaborate with the thalamocortical areas. The key is the dynamic integration of information in widely distributed neuronal populations over time that create holistic and unique phenomenal experiences. The theory does not propose that some specific groups of anatomically selective neurons give rise to conscious precepts. Rather, different groups of neurons may dynamically create a core functional binding that leads to the experience of a certain conscious percept. This is a radical proposal in the sense that it does not regard particular neurons or brain areas relevant to consciousness. The theory distinguishes between conscious and unconscious states. Brain areas whose activity is not part of a dynamic core don't contribute to conscious states. Therefore, the emphasis is on the dynamic dissociation between neural states and functional states that gives rise to conscious experience.

Even if we want to explain consciousness in the brain and create a scientific model, the biggest problem is also accounting for what the 80 billion neurons do and how they decide on their connections. Merely saying that neuronal networks and their connections create mental states is not enough. It is a very difficult job since no available technology today in neuroimaging allows us to track the dynamic interactions of all these neurons. However, neuroimaging provides us with some snapshots of the state of the brain and some neuronal networks and their activity in real-time and space (Owen, 2013). From neural data, computational models can be created that are useful in explaining mental states and behaviour. More recently, AI-powered algorithms have been trained with such data to bring in more synergy between AI and neuroscience relevant for consciousness research (Chella & Manzotti, 2007). However, one important problem remaining is to understand and accept whether physical systems that have their parts (e.g., neurons) can be conscious at all. Without resorting to dualism, we have to work towards a theory that indeed explains this. The integrated information theory of consciousness (IIT) developed by Tononi and colleagues is one such comprehensive and multidimensional theory that attempts to ground and measure consciousness in any physical system (Tononi et al., 2016). It is beyond the scope of this present book to fully explain and cover the many aspects of this comprehensive theory. However, it is important to explain some key features of it since it is now a major theory of consciousness.

IIT relies heavily on the notion of "information" that physical systems have. It explains "conscious" states in such physical systems as a measure of their "phi" (Tononi & Koch, 2015). Phi is a measure of the integrated information of any system. According to IIT, parts of the system may have their phi but the total phi of the system is not a summation of these parts. This total may be more or less than the individual phi of the parts. Phi represents the various feedback and exchange of information among the parts of the system. IIT also proposes a "conceptual" structure that systems have for a given phi. This is the embodied state of the system at any given moment in time. If a system is conscious, then its conceptual structure specifies the max phi value for it. Those systems that have a max phi = 0 can't be said to be conscious, since their causes and effects are explained completely by the individual causes and effects of the parts. This means there is nothing extra the system as a whole generates beyond what the parts generate. The theory correctly proposes that our conscious experiences are holistic and unified, and they are about one thing at a time. Readers can track the resemblance of this idea to Edelman's dynamic core hypothesis. It is no coincidence that Tononi was trained under Edelman, and I think the base proposal of IIT is built on the dynamic core theory except that it is mathematically more elaborate and neurally implementable. Therefore, the holistic experience or consciousness of a system is certainly not the summations of the activities of its parts. Some systems generate more consciousness given their intrinsic nature than other systems and our brains are a good example. Even if we measure the phi of each neuron that we have at any given moment and compute their contribution of information, the overall phi of the brain is going to be more than the sum. This means that it is not completely reducible to its parts. It is one of the major assumptions of the theory that some physical systems are more conscious than others given their phi.

IIT proposes that in the human brain, for example, the cerebellum does not have any intrinsic consciousness of its own since patients who have structural deficits in this area do not show any noticeable deficits in their consciousness. We may not have exact biometrical data on this proposal but IIT does distinguish different brain areas and units based on their phi. For example, neurons in the visual cortex and basal ganglia have non-zero phi and thus have intrinsic consciousness. At the moment, these are proposals that allow scientific testing and eventual falsification. Christoph Koch, who originally developed the neural correlates of consciousness framework (Crick & Koch, 1990) is a major supporter of the IIT. In his book *Consciousness* he suggested that the proposals of IIT may lead us to panpsychism (Koch, 2012). Panpsychism is the idea that all physical things in the universe including the universe itself have consciousness to different degrees. Thus one can go on measuring "phi" of all material bodies. There have been several criticisms of the IIT since it has many loose threads. For example, although it tries to measure integrated information in units of the brain, it does not clarify what "information" is. We can't yet measure the phi of individual units of the brain with any certainty. It does not explain how a system that has integrated information also has first-person experiential states, a prime feature of consciousness. IIT's main idea that a certain quantum of information in any complex system is "conscious" is a conjecture.

At the very heart of IIT lies the strong assumption that only systems that produce heavily integrated information from their constituents have higher consciousness. That state is a global state yet differentiated as far as experience is concerned. IIT also postulates that the structural density of connections of brain regions makes them more or less conscious. For example, neurons in the cerebral cortex have more dense connections predicting more integrated information than those in the cerebellum. At the moment, it does not explain why subjectivity should arise in physical systems even if they have integrated information and have dense connectivity. The theory is a good middle ground between dualism and total reductionism or even theories that are in complete denial of consciousness such as eliminative materialism. Christoph Kock rightly says that IIT is a scientific version of panpsychism (Koch, 2021). We may not accept that information, however rich, is "conscious" and also that all matter has some amount of "consciousness," but a scientific approach to this ancient problem probably has to assume these to progress, which is what IIT does with best intentions.

I briefly referred to the global workspace model of Baars (2005) earlier which deserves to be elaborated on here. It has been hailed as the most popular theory of consciousness of the last two decades. I will point out here how this model differs from IIT and other such ideas and why it is so popular (Signa et al., 2021). The global workspace model has been proposed as a cognitive model of consciousness. Baars abandoned metaphysical speculations on consciousness, the kind of question that begins with "What does it feel like?" and instead grounded it to its functional role in the human brain. The theory makes a clear distinction between conscious and unconscious information or states of the brain. He asserted that some information is reportable and agents are conscious at certain times, and other information stays unconscious. However, this unconscious information that agents cannot report still influences brain activity and behaviour. Baars's model of global workspace, as the name suggests, is built around classical notions of information processing, memory representations, dynamic integration, selective attention and filtering of information, and computation as studied in cognitive psychology. Aptly, Baars refers to his model as a cognitive architecture with a well-defined role for consciousness. The brain is a global workspace where different types of sensory information acquired and processed through different modalities compete to be conscious. Information processing in the brain is viewed as massively parallel; handled by specialised neural processors, an idea that goes back to early theorists of cognitive architecture like Alan Newell (Newell, 1994). In the global workspace, only one type of information reaches the reportable conscious level of access to the agent and this mechanism operates serially. For example, right now as

I write, I am fully conscious of the words and sentences I am writing, and nothing else. The moment I shift my goals – for example, if I wish to attend to the whizzing sound of the fan or the dim light of the table lamp – the conscious state related to writing will be correspondingly replaced.

Baars writes, "GW theory may be thought of as a theatre of mental functioning. Consciousness in this metaphor resembles a bright spot on the stage of immediate memory, directed there by a spotlight of attention under executive guidance. Only the bright spot is conscious, while the rest of the theatre is dark and unconscious" (Baars, 2005). This statement signifies the critical role of attention in making things conscious, the spotlight model popular in cognitive psychology, since the time of James. According to Baars, both internal and external states can become conscious, if attention selects them for the agent. Once something is conscious, it is redistributed throughout the brain, to specialised processors for further processing. The notion of redistribution is central in global workspace theory because it predicts specific neural mechanisms. For example, the frontoparietal networks of the brain, that exercise executive control and selective attention, influence or modulate the activity of subcortical areas such as the amygdala or insula during a conscious experience (Baars, 2003).

The global workspace theory "operationalises" consciousness by giving it the job of broadcasting representations throughout the brain. Based on neuropsychological data, where consciousness is compromised, it argues that without this responsibility of consciousness, representations will remain unconscious (Bartolomei et al., 2014). However, operationalising any idea does not mean defining it in its epistemological or ontological sense. The theory does not tell us why consciousness does what it does or what it is. It also does not explicitly state that it is an emergent property of brain activity. It offers consciousness a central management role that's about distributing information throughout the brain which agents experience. More recently, there have been several proposals to modify and fine-tune the theory so that it also answers other important questions. For example, more recently it has been suggested that the global workspace theory should have a metacognition component attached to it (Shea & Frith, 2019). Metacognition is the extra awareness and confidence that agents have about the contents of their consciousness as certain definite experiential states. That's how they can use these representations and report them in social situations or perform actions. If the representations are just conscious but lack metacognition, then they are of no use in the real world. We have to remember that we have conscious representations of things or ideas since that helps us perform targeted actions and make decisions in the real world. They also help us find out the intentions of other people in the environment and predict future scenarios. Further, the global workspace theory does not explain how phenomenal consciousness and subjective states arise in the brain even if there is global broadcasting of information. Nevertheless, it remains a highly cited theory that drives current research on consciousness.

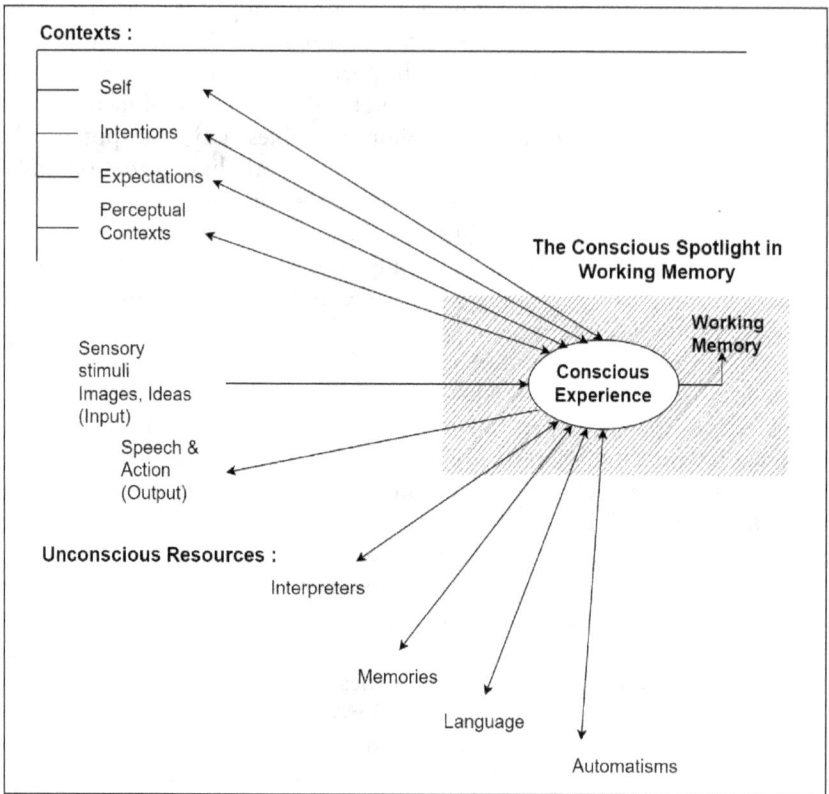

Figure 4.2 Schematic diagram of the global workspace model.

Source: Reprinted from *Progress in Brain Research*, Bernard J. Baars, Global workspace theory of consciousness: toward a cognitive neuroscience of human experience, 45–53, 2005, with permission from Elsevier

Both GW and IIT base their notion of "consciousness" on information and its transmission in the brain. They both adopt a "functionalist" approach to the mind and consciousness. While being technically sound, they both either stay neutral or say little on the "phenomenal" states that agents experience. Therefore, it's natural that there has to be a means to bring "phenomenality" into such models and then see where to find that in the brain. Higher-order theories of consciousness (Gennaro, 2004; Lau & Rosenthal, 2011) claim that theories like GWT are first-order theories and hence do not explain how phenomenal inner awareness arises during conscious processing. The higher-order theories further propose that agents have inner awareness of their mental contents or what they are processing apart from objective knowledge. It's like experiencing the "redness" of red apart from identifying that it is red and not green. The weakness in the GW theory is that although it postulates global broadcasting, it assumes that local processing is unconscious. Implicitly it does not assume any inner superior phenomenal experiential states associated with consciousness. Higher-order theories assume that apart from first-order processing – that is being able to know what a stimulus is – higher-order representations arise in frontal areas that produce inner experience. For example, in Figure 4.3, the higher-order theory bestows phenomenal consciousness to frontal areas and first-order stimuli processing to more posterior visual areas. Higher-order theorists think that theories such as GW are first-order theories since they only explain conscious stimuli processing using a cognitive architecture. Is higher-order theory merely metaphysical? Many will likely think the higher-order theories are too philosophical and are adding extra noise to what is consciousness and do not offer any empirical predictions. That may be true, but scholars who work within this theory have also neural evidence to show in support. For example, studies with patients with blindsight show that they can't experience phenomenal consciousness but at the same time, they can report the details of the stimuli above the chance level (Brown et al., 2019). This means that there is a dissociation between higher-order representations and first-order representations at the neural level. The higher-order theories also assume that the frontal areas evolved long before to support phenomenal consciousness and later only took up the additional responsibility to deal with a more objective access type of consciousness. There may not be solid empirical testimony to this claim but the theory remains popular among more philosophically minded scholars.

The higher-order theories postulate that an additional representation is necessary for the representations created by first-order theories to be

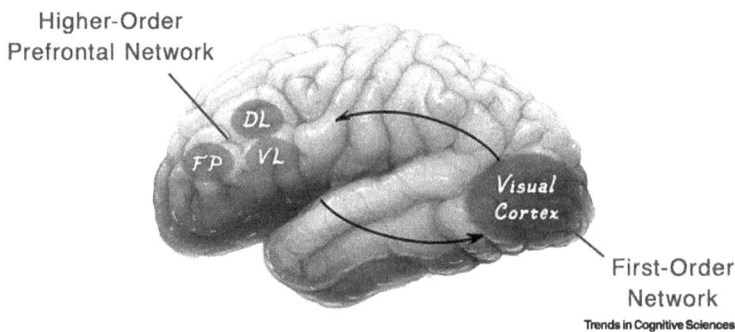

Figure 4.3 The brain areas implicated in first-order and higher-order processing according to higher-order theories of consciousness.

Source: Reprinted from *Trends in Cognitive Sciences*, Vol. 23, Richard Brown, Hakwan Lau, Joseph E. LeDoux, Understanding the Higher-Order Approach to Consciousness, 754–768, 2019, with permission from Elsevier

phenomenally conscious. Everyday experience may suggest that while we may report and identify several stimuli in the environment because of sensory processing we don't experience rich phenomenal states associated with all stimuli. Thus, the difference could be because of the role frontal areas play in modulating how information transmitted by primary sensory areas in the brain is to be experienced and to what extent. It is difficult to take a position on the issue of phenomenal consciousness being the most important condition of consciousness given the current state of affairs. Therefore, the empirical success of theories such as the GWT has to be evaluated on the phenomenal side of things.

It appears that from the early neural correlates of consciousness proposals (Koch et al., 2016) to the global workspace theory, we have progressed in our empirical understanding of conscious states of the brain in psychological and neural dimensions. These theories have made the study of consciousness a "scientific" enterprise as opposed to traditional metaphysical speculation or simple thought experiments. At the same time, there is strong criticism of these approaches that argue against reductionism (Goff, 2017a). Theories such as IIT and GWT have missed the true essence of what it feels like to be an agent experiencing phenomenality. These theories also fail to show any designated neural network that produces such phenomenality. It is one thing to find out that the brain processes information but it is another to explain how it achieves self-awareness through this mechanism. Therefore, it has not been possible to ground subjectivity in the brain or create a potential mathematical model. Hence, higher-order theories protect phenomenality while respecting empirical reduction.

The idea that what we attend to becomes the "object" of our current consciousness is a popular narrative. It was William James who linked selective attention or focus to consciousness (James, 1892). To some extent this is also correct since the brain's capacity is limited; we can only fully attend to one thing at a time. For example, if we attend to a visually presented object, like fruit, we can describe its features. However, attending to any object and extracting objective knowledge of its features are not synonymous with subjectively experiencing that object. Subjective phenomenal states can be different from objective knowledge states (Overgaard, 2018). The role of attention becomes important in this scenario as a cognitive system. The *attention-schema* theory exactly proposes to explain this connection (Graziano & Webb, 2015). It attempts to explain how subjective awareness emerges from the act of attending to objects. Graziano and colleagues bring concepts such as the self and attention together in the attention-schema theory. They propose that while attending to something, the brain also becomes aware of its own "self" (Wilterson et al., 2020). The brain creates an attention schema that tells it that it is experiencing some phenomenal state as a self.

According to the attention-schema theory, when an agent perceives any visual object, they also construct a relationship between the visual representation and the self as a mental agent. *That* relationship is attention. Thus, attention is conceptualised not as something that illuminates an object but as something which glues the self with the external object, creating a subjective state in the agent. Viewed in this way, the emergence of subjective states related to stimuli perception in an agent's mind is an interaction between the "self" and the object. The attention-schema theory is a materialistic theory of consciousness (Graziano, 2017). The theory says that there is no such thing as a phenomenal subjective experience beyond the physical measurable events. However, the theory does not say so explicitly, unlike the illusion theory of Dennet (2016), but more in an implicit manner, taking the example of machines. The theory predicts that machines may also have a feeling of inner awareness of their workings which they can only express in loose terms, just as humans do. The brain creates a gross schema of attention and feels that it has some subjective experience associated with it. Therefore, claims of phenomenal consciousness for the machine or the brain are nothing but self-talk in inexact language. Because brains do not have detailed knowledge of the physical basis of attention, it creates a schema of it. Therefore, when asked to express our subjective awareness, we say things like, "It feels like," "I am experiencing something like," and so on. These vague phrases do not refer to the actual physical mechanism. Therefore, according to the attention-schema theory, subjectivity is nothing but the brain's vague sense of it attending to something. The creator of the theory, Graziano, drew his ideas from the *body-schema* theory (Graziano, 2020). The parallelism is that the body also constructs a schema of its movement and the way it attends to things. The theory thus claims that both machines and brains have incorrigible tendencies to claim subjectivity where there is none since they are trapped in their construction of a schema of their physical workings which they take as real. In more recent times, the theory has also been applied to social cognition, whereby people ascribe subjectivity to others (Graziano, 2018). While it is not clear why the brain even goes all that far to create a schema of its state, which has no real use, and believes in it, the theory has attracted followers who are materialists. Also, it is not clear why "attention" assumes such an important role in the model.

If the brain merely creates some imprecise hallucinatory schema and is obliged to believe in it, then the theory must explain why evolution preferred it that way. It has no real purpose since it does not precisely explain its mechanism. The attention-schema theory empowers the possibility of machine consciousness indirectly and is a direct descendant of eliminative materialism. There is not much scope here to offer a comprehensive critique of this theory but a few things can be said. For example, the theory relies excessively on the mechanisms and notion of attention, drawing from the biased competition account (Desimone & Duncan, 1995) and other theories of cognitive psychology. However, there is no certainty yet on what exactly attention is at a mechanistic level and there are massive disagreements among researchers (Anderson, 2011). Secondly, the proposal that the brain is merely creating a schema of attention and which it thinks of as a separate substantive phenomenal experience is just a conjecture. There is yet no empirical verification of this claim. The theory compares the subjective states of both machines and humans and it is known that they are not the same (Harnad, 1989). The theory implies that we are in no position to deny machine consciousness, just as we can't deny ours. The attention-schema theory considers the brain's illusion about others' attentional states as its own experience of their subjective states (Doerig et al., 2021). Therefore, it reduces social cognition or our mapping of others' mental states to some illusion about their ways of attending or even our inability to exactly express their attention modelling. But the theory itself does not offer any computational or neural model of attention nor it does say how attention modelling explains subjective states. However, it is the most sophisticated illusionist theory of consciousness we have currently.

Dissatisfaction with materialistic theories, despite their neural or computational sophistication, is natural since we can't give up our subjectivity. Any attempt to reduce it to neural or computational or psychological states seems problematic. How about a theory that not only accepts phenomenality but makes the radical claim that everything in the universe has consciousness? Panpsychism is the theory which takes this radical position (Bruntrup & Jaskolla, 2016) which has seen a recent resurgence (Goff, 2017b). We saw earlier that even mechanistic theories such as IIT implicitly accept panpsychism (Mørch, 2019a). Even philosophers in ancient Greece such as Thales held the view that minds are a fundamental property of the universe (Skrbina, 2017). Panpsychism states that consciousness is a fundamental property of nature. Many influential psychologists such as William James and philosophers such as Arthur Schopenhauer believed that the universe is conscious. However, in our times, there is an attempt to explain the "emergence" of consciousness from non-conscious matter. Thomas Nagel is a prolific defender of panpsychism, apart from David Chalmers, who thinks that our only way to avoid the trap of emergentism is to accept panpsychism (Bruntrup & Jaskolla, 2016). That is, we have to accept that the micro-units, let's say neurons in our case, have some amount of consciousness themselves or they are self-aware. If that view is taken, then we don't have to explain how consciousness emerges from the material base. There are many versions of this theory and many defenders but all of them believe that consciousness is a basic feature of things that the universe has. They all hold that phenomenality is not an emergent property of physical matter but it is intrinsic to it. Bertrand Russel, in his "neutral monism" on which he elaborated in his book *The Analysis of Mind*, had said that scientific investigation of matter tells us about its external features but not what matter is in itself (Russell, 2005). Thus, we can't decipher those aspects of the matter that are already a part of it, for example, its consciousness.

It is of course difficult for us to imagine what objects are in themselves and from their point of view. For this to be the case, as Nagel had said, we have to be bats to know what bats feel about themselves. Panpsychism assumes that since we don't know what objects are in themselves, we can't deny that they don't have any consciousness. How do we know that fundamental building blocks of nature are conscious themselves? The strength of panpsychism lies in its power of explanation and not its rejection of emergentism (Ney, 2021). Panpsychism also makes sense since current neuroscience can't accept that basic units such as neurons are conscious. If so, then how can they be part of any mechanism that becomes conscious? This is the summation problem which has no explanation as of yet (Seager, 1995). The defenders of panpsychism hold the view that, as of now, the theory is philosophical and it may be decades or centuries before we have empirical data that support its claims. But the theory certainly is a serious challenge to the neuroscience-based theories that attempt to explain consciousness as an emergent feature of matter. Either we accept that matter is conscious, to begin with, or we explain how consciousness can emerge from things that are not conscious. Recent scholars have tried to defend panpsychism using the arguments of "causation" (Mørch, 2019b). We experience things directly as they are. Therefore, things have causal power in them to bring change since they have consciousness. Otherwise, no causation is possible in the usual sense. Physicalist theories don't ascribe agency to material bodies when they cause events. They ascribe it to them having certain properties which bring causal effects. Nevertheless, panpsychism and its revival have also led to its applications in other areas such as religion and theology (Leidenhag, 2019). No doubt, panpsychism is counterintuitive to our scientific worldview and therefore accepting it requires bringing a radical modification to our understanding.

There are more theories of consciousness than what can be covered here. A recent meta-analysis of theories classifies them into several categories and examines their empirical success (Seth & Bayne, 2022). Signorelli et al. (2021) classify and compare 14 different models of consciousness. Their approach is very comprehensive and they classify the theories on a few important criteria. According to them, all theories of consciousness can be classified as either "mechanistic" or "unificationist." Mechanistic theories aim at causal explanations of consciousness in neural or psychological terms. For example, the global workspace theory is mechanistic since it explains how any system becomes conscious. On the other hand, theories like IIT are unificationist since they propose to integrate and offer a holistic explanation of several phenomena that are part of consciousness. Unificationist theories may also have neural or psychological predictions that can be demonstrated empirically. Theories of consciousness can also be broadly divided based on their main "motive." According to Signorelli et al., all theories of consciousness currently available either attempt to explain "access" or "phenomenal" aspects of consciousness, a distinction popularised by Ned Block (1995). The access theories are functionalist since they explain if someone is conscious then that must be manifested in behaviour. Theories that stress the "phenomenal" aspect tend to be more on the "what it feels like" side of the story. Finally, theories explain either what is "consciousness" in mechanical terms or they attempt to explain what it means to be conscious, which are different things. At the moment there is no good or bad theory of consciousness. Even though there are 14 theories, we still don't know how to properly define consciousness. What we see now certainly is a collective attempt to make this a scientific problem and study it as such following well-known paradigms of science, mostly to offer falsifiable predictions, while at the same time keeping some of the most baffling aspects of consciousness of agents within these approaches.

4. Attention, phenomenality, and the unconscious

If you take a cognitive psychological view, then you have to think more in terms of functionality. What are the functions of consciousness, just as we have functions of memory, and functions of emotion? If you take a philosophical view, it will be discussed in terms of its metaphysical quality. What is it? Functionalism is the view that everything that's there serves a function. If evolution has selected consciousness and phenomenality, then they have functions that we can describe and measure by experiments. This approach saves us from unnecessary metaphysical speculations. Cognitive psychology adopted this approach long ago (Churchland, 2005). It is strange that there are no coherent arguments about why phenomenality and subjectivity should exist beyond one's ability to gather objective facts about things and what their true functions are. This has allowed materialists as we saw earlier to say that they are nothing but illusions. The matter is not simple since we know that our subjectivity means much to our mental lives and we cannot easily give them up. In the following, I examine the role of attention if at all in inducing subjectivity within a functionalist psychology to see if that reveals any answers.

Cognitive psychologists view attention as a brain mechanism that allows us to acquire detailed information about the world. Thus, its evolutionary significance in our survival is clear (Patel et al., 2015). It is probably the most studied cognitive process in the mind-brain sciences. An obvious question is if attention plays any role in phenomenality. Baars (1997) explained consciousness in terms of attention. Attention plays a causal role in bringing objects to full-blown consciousness from awareness (Cohen et al., 2012). Chalmers defines awareness as follows: "Awareness in this sense is simply the process, describable in neuroscientific terms, of making the sensory qualities conscious for the subject" (Chalmers, 1996). Since Chalmers indicated that our main effort should be to explain experiential phenomenology, awareness is a good candidate for that. When we are aware of something, we do have experiential states without objective knowledge. Psychologically speaking we have not yet directed our focal attention to gather complete usable knowledge. But that state is undeniably true and has some vividness to it.

Full blown attentive states of the brain provide objective conscious knowledge. Awareness on the other hand creates phenomenal experience. Many debates have occurred on the relationship between conscious awareness and attention (e.g., Koch & Tsuchiya, 2007). When attention is paid in a focused manner, what is in awareness becomes more vivid and detailed. Thus, attention is the mechanism that leads from awareness to conscious states. Ned Block suggested looking for consciousness at the interactions of phenomenology of consciousness and awareness (Block, 1995). Block dissociated consciousness into two types and these two types do not interact and cannot be reduced to one. The access part of consciousness is all about basic cognitive processing that utilises attention, working memory, and perceptual processes. The phenomenological part is about subjective experience or qualia.

Attention amplifies sensory stimuli that reach consciousness. Our consciousness increases depending on the strength of amplification. If attention has not been able to amplify much, then perceptual stimuli does not reach full-blown consciousness and can't be reported. Lamme (2003) first proposed a causal link between attention and consciousness through a decision model (Figure 4.4). This model does not explain phenomenality but can predict a good amount of behavioural and neural data in experiments. Many have shown that when attention is paid more strongly, peoples' subjective awareness increases. However, the way subjective awareness is measured in such studies should not be confused with qualia. There is hardly a method that can measure subjectivity yet. Nevertheless, many brain imaging studies have also shown that the frontal attentional areas are active and correlate with conscious states (Dehaene & Changeux, 2011). Thus, bringing conscious states to decision states is a well-grounded attempt to develop a mechanistic model. Does this mean that subjective conscious states can't exist without attention? Does phenomenality depend on attention?

Block specifically asks how we can separate the neural mechanism of subjectivity from cognitive access. According to modular theories of cognition, cognitive access is an encapsulated mechanism (Fodor, 1983). Do representations related to cognitive access that provide objective information have phenomenality? This will pave the way for integrating both phenomenality and access types to the same representation. On the other hand, if representations related to access consciousness do not have phenomenality, then we have to search for them elsewhere within the brain (Block, 2007). Block proposes a radical solution to this theoretical problem. He suggests that whenever we can confidently find neural mechanisms for phenomenal consciousness, we can afford to assume that these mechanisms do not have access type properties. Thus, in a strict sense, the Fodorian module that has access representations is not phenomenally conscious. In simple terms, this debate leads to the tentative conclusion that we still can't be sure if the so-called neural correlates of consciousness include phenomenality. Christoph Koch and colleagues attempted to answer this issue by reviewing

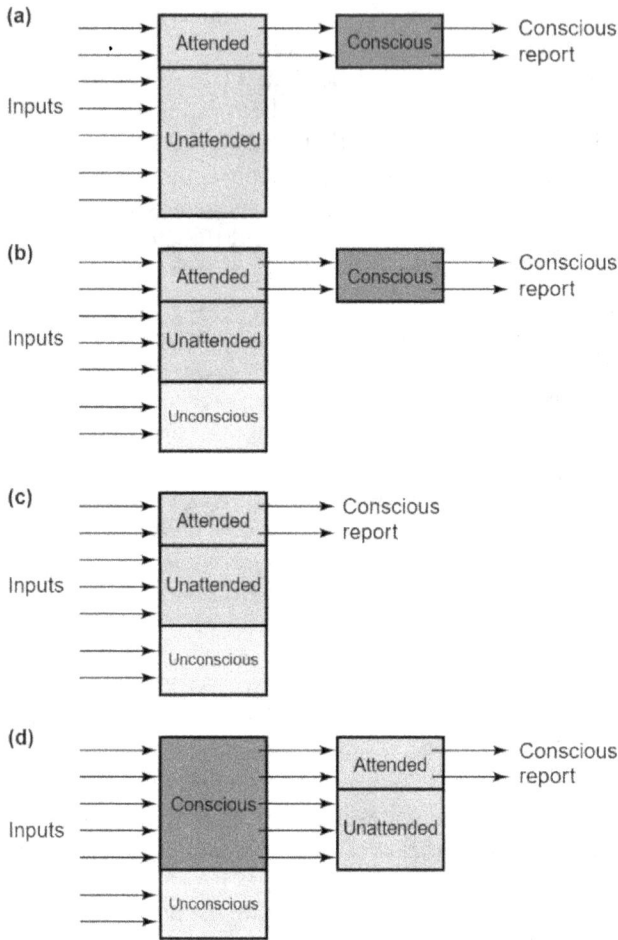

Figure 4.4 Four possible models of the relationship between attention and awareness. The models all show different filters which decide when visual input
reaches the level of conscious report.

Source: Reprinted from *Trends in Cognitive Sciences*, Vol. 7, Victor A.F. Lamme, Why visual
attention and awareness are different, 12–18, 2003, with permission from Elsevier.

many instances of consciousness and its absence in different circumstances
(Koch & Tsuchiya, 2007). Let us consider the case of people that go into
long-term comas or vegetative states and sleep. They argued that consciousness is not a single monolithic mechanism and is differently manifested in
different scenarios. Further, different types of brain mechanisms in terms
of their temporal and spatial parameters can inform about these types.

Therefore, it's possible that while some brain states may have phenomenality along with the access type of consciousness, others may have just the access type (Tononi & Koch, 2008). From the ongoing transient activity of the brain and the feed-forward as the feedback states, it's possible to uncover neural correlates for both types of consciousness. Koch's popular book (2012) on this subject sums up his reductionist views on consciousness.

Catherine Tallon-Baudry writes,

> Probing the nature of the links between the cognitive function, attention and consciousness, therefore taps right into the debate on the definition of consciousness: if consciousness is intrinsically related to attention, then its functional role and evolutionary advantage should pertain to executive functions. Alternatively, if attention and consciousness are distinct, then consciousness should no longer be considered as an executive function, but be defined by its experiential properties.
>
> (Tallon-Baudry, 2012, p. 1)

This assertion means, if at all, we have to scientifically explain consciousness, then we have to link it to executive control. As noted earlier, conscious attention is part of executive control. According to some, it evolved much later and is linked to intentionality, agenthood, and sense of self, among others. Catherine Tallon-Baudry's balanced and well-informed critique of the neuroimaging data is related to the attention consciousness research enterprise. Many have proposed that the activation of the frontoparietal areas reflect conscious states. However, studies with EEG show that an early attentional component like the N2pc can show up indicating attention capture but the participants may not be conscious of the stimuli. Neural signatures for attention and consciousness can also show double dissociation. Therefore, even within the functionalist information processing view, there is disagreement if attention and consciousness should be linked or if they should be treated differently. Attention as the gatekeeper of consciousness seems intuitive. How about the alternative view that our consciousness determines our attention? How can I attend if I have no consciousness? This view, if taken seriously, will entail executive control as an additional supra-mechanism that controls attention. However, current models of executive control do not have consciousness as a component. Nevertheless, the attention-consciousness separation seems more futuristic than attention and consciousness relatedness. This at least saves the subjectivity component of consciousness which is probably all that matters to many.

Given our limited ability to focus and gather information from the environment, we are nevertheless endowed with the capacity to generate a holistic and rich phenomenology. For example, consider a situation in which you are presented with several alphabets at one time and are asked to report them. At any time, you can likely attend to a few and report them objectively. However, you may have an awareness of many others even without any objective knowledge. The famous experiment of Sperling is often used to demonstrate this (Sperling, 1960). In this experiment, participants, when cued, reported awareness of items compared to what they directly attended to. How does one explain this vivid experience which was possible without attention? Dennett suggests that we have to refer to different types of attention to understand this and crack the mystery of so-called phenomenology. We receive objective knowledge by attending finally to that which we can report objectively. However, at the same time, other items that we don't attend to completely do receive some attention which is distributed. So, attention has two modes. Once we accept this, we can explain that even if attention is not directed at something, we get some items into our awareness by distributed attention. Several neuropsychological cases show that in the absence of focal attention, participants show subjective awareness. Therefore, we can explain consciousness through functionalist approaches without claiming that it's mysterious and unexplainable. If we break down the concept of consciousness into its basic properties, we can see that we are in a position to explain some of them using our current knowledge of brain activity. Dennett challenges those who claim dissociation between cognitive and experiential states. According to him, stronger faith in science should help us to explain consciousness without the speculations.

The word "unconscious" was not so popular within cognitive psychology a few decades ago, but it is not the case now. It is not only the Freudians, but also experimental psychologists who refer to it. That's because there is growing evidence that objects and events that we are not aware of somehow enter into consciousness and influence behaviour. It seems obvious that we can "attend" to things that we can see. Objects that we cannot see would therefore not be attended to. The role of attention in this unconscious cognition is not yet clear but it's a growing field of inquiry (Koch & Tsuchiya, 2007; Kiefer, 2007). Our visual system and the sensory apparatus are not designed to perceive very brief stimuli, such as stimuli that are presented for as little as 10 ms. Such subliminal stimuli have been shown to influence cognition and behaviour nonetheless (e.g., Dehaene et al., 2006). If that is so then it's also likely that such stimuli operating below thresholds of our awareness can also produce phenomenality. It is kind of intuitive since many of our ongoing transient thoughts and subjective states do not seem to have an immediate explicit trigger. Since myriad stimuli of various intensities are constantly bombarding our system, it's possible that many feeble ones still somehow rise to the surface and influence us. The idea of unconscious processing is controversial for apparent reasons since it defies known theories of attention. It is possible that if we go by Block's distinction between phenomenal and access consciousness, such invisible stimuli may cause phenomenality while access is the result of focal attention that we wilfully pay.

Many have studied the effect of stimuli on behaviour that operates outside our conscious perception or awareness. Subliminal stimuli are generally brief and masked; they are presented before participants discriminate a target often in a visual task. Masking has a very long history in priming studies of various types (Breitmeyer & Öğmen, 2006). Researchers manipulate the relationship of these subliminal primes to targets and also in some cases top-down goals of participants to see the influence on behaviour. Such designs can effectively demonstrate any relationships between unconscious and conscious states. Strangely, attention has been shown to play a role in unconscious processing. For instance, Koivisto and Neuvonen (2020) examined how masking could influence the effect of subliminally presented stimuli on later discrimination. It is well known that patients with blindsight can discriminate stimuli that are presented to their blindsight. They have no awareness of the stimuli but they can act on it. It appears that some of these patients do have some awareness of the stimuli at a certain level of feature, like colour, while others do not. The researchers examined if manipulation of features such as colour and orientation influences discrimination differently in people who don't have blindsight. We know from models of attention that in the very early stages of object perception features are bound by attention (Treisman & Gelade, 1980). Of course, this is debatable, since we always perceive the whole object, i.e., a red apple and not its features. Our qualia or experiential states are holistic about the objects and not their parts. The data show that when such features are manipulated differently on Gabor patches, they influence decision making. To conclude, subliminally presented stimuli can act on our decision making without our knowledge. It is likely that attention plays a role in this and this can be referred to as "unconscious attention" (see Prasad & Mishra, 2019 for a recent review).

Studies show that top-down control can be exercised on subliminal stimuli (Ansorge et al., 2014). Current goals and motivational states influence to what extent subliminal stimuli may be processed. For example, subliminal primes that are linked to rewards or our current goals have greater influence than those that are not linked (Prasad & Mishra, 2020). Another technique has been to induce implicit biases about such primes in advance and then examine their influence on cognition and decision making (Lambert et al., 1999). Essentially it means we can acquire some knowledge of the primes and how they are related to our current goals implicitly. The whole mechanism remains unconscious to us but influences behaviour. Thus, what we refer as unconscious could be a storehouse of schemas of our intended actions. Additionally, higher control systems can regulate them so that we benefit in our actions. Even though these experiments show the influence of subliminal entities on decision states, they don't speak on subjective awareness. However, more recently there have been some developments in which subjectivity is measured through self-reports (e.g., Perceptual Awareness Scale, Ramsøy & Overgaard, 2004). Sometimes on such scales, participants report that they do have some idea or awareness of the prime but not to the extent that they have objective knowledge. Researchers take this as evidence that the stimuli are truly operating below awareness. Taken together the research on unconscious processing has illuminated another dimension of attention. It raises fundamental questions about the fluidity of cognition. From unconscious to conscious – the time and distance may seem very short. But attention still plays a role in it. These results have influenced philosophical investigations on the nature of consciousness and the role of attention (Block, 2014).

Cognitive psychology so far has not been able to integrate these two views, the phenomenality, and selective attentional processing. The strict functionalism of contemporary cognitive psychology has gone in the direction of reductionism. It wants to approach the subjective question with that same approach, reducing it to basic operations. This has been met with criticism. The widely popular bottom-up stimulus-driven capture of attention, for instance, has no phenomenality to it. Consider the Posner cueing paradigm (Posner, 1980) when attention is captured by a brief cue. When a cue attracts attention, our objective knowledge becomes vivid. That's access consciousness. How about phenomenality in such a task? Interestingly we never ask participants about that, and this remains unreported. This is just a random example from many in which we regularly collect data on objective knowledge but not on phenomenal experience. Of course, when intentional agents perform any task, they get subjective experience. The errors we detect in such experiments could reflect lapses in phenomenality but not in objective knowledge. These issues remain to be explored.

Chalmers more recently (Chalmers, 2018) has emphasised that all phenomenal mental states are conscious or else they are not worth anything. It is not clear if attention is necessary for experiencing subjectivity. Some theorists have proposed "mitigating" or "decompositional" ideas to unite the conscious and the unconscious to some psychological mechanism (Polák & Marvan, 2019). There are mental states which are phenomenal but we don't experience them. For example, someone can be in pain for a very long time but may consciously experience it at some time because of causal interference of attention. Evidence from patients with neglect shows that some part of their visual experience of the same stimuli is conscious but some other parts remain unconscious but with phenomenal character. The model proposed by Lamme (2003) involved a feed-forward sweep which led to visual processing at an early level. Only later "recurrent" processing activates consciousness that we experience. Even the global workspace model allows some bifurcation of mental states that are unconscious and that are conscious. What needs to be explained is how some phenomenal non-conscious states become conscious. Chalmers's "hard problem" views the problem of consciousness as unitary. But the unitary view fails to accommodate how we perceive non-conscious stimuli and how visual neglect patients react to stimuli of which they have no consciousness, such as in cases in which patients have non-conscious pain (Bain et al., 2019). It is still not clear if phenomenal consciousness depends on the functioning of higher-order cognitive systems or if they are independent of it (Rosenthal, 1986). In any case, there are certain benefits in studying the cognitive systems such as attention that influence subjective perception in different ways.

5. Animal consciousness

Descartes denied mentality to animals whatsoever (Descartes, 2013). He took them as mere machines devoid of any self-consciousness. But over time, this view has changed. Animals are considered to have subjective states as well but probably not of the type we have. Nagel famously declared that only a bat could understand how another bat feels (Nagel, 1974). Currently, there are some developments in the domain of animal consciousness research. Animals have experiences, emotions, and awareness. The idea is to discover what type of consciousness animals may have and what we can learn from them about the evolution of our consciousness. These comparative biological approaches have much value albeit they may be restrictive. For example, just like humans, many animals seek out altered states of consciousness by consuming psychotropic substances (Samorini, 2002). They drug themselves in order to experience hallucination and some sort of altered state. Thus, animals "know" as agents what they are up to in a general way. Animals lack language and therefore we can't know their subjective states even if they experience subjectivity. Can this be a barrier to our scientific understanding of animal consciousness (Griffin, 1985)?

Some scholars think that we have to focus on animals' social signalling, which also carries hints about their subjective states. The social signalling hypothesis has an evolutionary origin. We have to also understand that hominins' evolution took millions of years and language is of a very recent origin. But they produced symbolic behaviour depicting subjective states much earlier than this. Therefore, symbolic behaviour such as signalling in animals can offer some empirical basis to our understanding of their consciousness. Peter Carruthers has suggested that animals may have some subjective states but they may not have higher-order phenomenal states (Carruthers, 2005). They may not have a theory of mind like us that is required to know others' mental states (Baron-Cohen, 1997). One can also say that in animals such states are less well developed than in us (Carruthers, 2000). Sophisticated consciousness of the sort we display requires sophisticated brains and animals do not have them. However, these assumptions may just be anthropomorphic biases unless science proves otherwise.

A more parsimonious position would be that animals have subjectivity to the extent which natural selection has preferred for them and no more. Many studies have shown that animals have memory, spatial cognition, emotions, decision making, and selective attention (Gabay et al., 2013). They may not be as sophisticated as we are but these skills do help them go about their lives (Heyes, 2008). Animals may also have sentience (Brown, 2015). Sentience is linked to the concept of experiencing pain or pleasure. We know that animals do suffer from pain. But again, their expression of it remains unclear to us since they do not have the linguistic ability. Humans can not only experience pain and pleasure, but also can express the phenomenality of it using language. If we accept animal sentience, then we can approach the question of animal consciousness (Duncan, 2006). Some neuroscientists argue that if we consider consciousness as simply a brain process then the brain areas that are linked to consciousness can also be found in animals. For example, data from neurophysiological studies show changes in chemical levels in specific brain regions as animals experience pain (Boyle, 2009).

Insects are considered some of the lowest forms of animals. Could they have consciousness? Entomologists have long studied their social behaviour. Insects may have a very rudimentary form of consciousness depending on their nervous systems. Klein and Barron wrote a target article on the question of insect consciousness and invited criticism (Klein & Barron, 2016). Their main points defending insect consciousness dealt with both neurobiology and behaviour. Klein and Barron (2016) proposed that the evolution of basic subjective awareness in insects can be traced to the Cambrian explosion (see also Feinberg & Mallat, 2019, Figure 4.5). This is when many diverse types of animal species emerged and they had to learn to adapt to novel challenges for survival. Key adaptations included spatial navigation and emotion. They learned to fear other predators who were not present in that environment earlier. The evolution of the amygdala can be traced to this stage.

Higher consciousness requires a very big cerebral cortex with billions of neurons. Most insects lack a cerebral cortex but have some subcortical structures like the midbrain. One proposal is that the insect midbrain is capable of subjective awareness. Michel Tye, a prominent philosopher of the mind, seems to think that we have created too much hype around the notion of consciousness (Tye, 1999) and that stops us from looking around in other species. Subjective awareness is a very basic form of awareness and insects should have it. This basic awareness can be supported by structures like the midbrain. However, they may not have a self-reflective ability or metacognition. From the insects' point of view, this basic awareness could mean awareness of their environment, how they navigate and go about their lives. It does not involve the Thomas Nagel-type self-awareness and self-reflection or the Block-type rich phenomenality. Insects may not know who they are.

Everyone knows that ants display a high degree of collective group-level activity. Their social hierarchy, just like bees, allows them to scout food and maintain territories in an organised way. Friedman and Søvik (2019) have proposed thought experiments based on ants to examine if they display any attributes of consciousness that humans have set. Although the authors display the usual cynicism and pessimism on the current state of theories of consciousness we have for us, they propose a dichotomous theoretical model to explore consciousness – the forward and reverse framework to study consciousness. The main claim is that social insects display some of the traits of subjective awareness that we display. Further, evolutionarily, some of

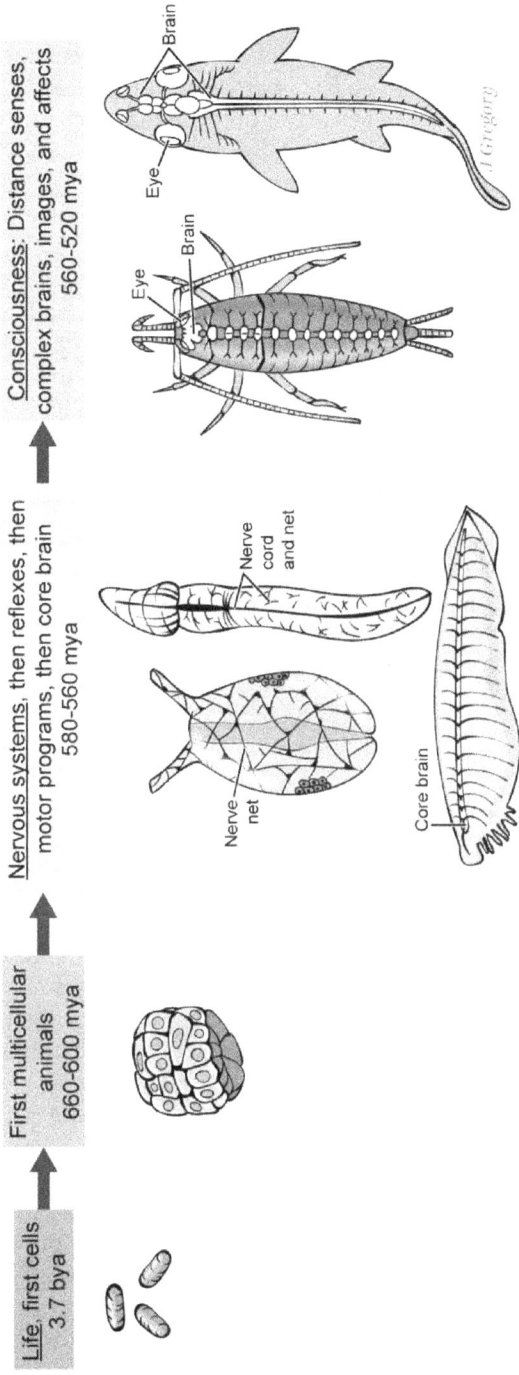

Figure 4.5 Stages of evolution in animal consciousness. Stages of evolution from single-celled organisms to complicated organisms with more complicated nervous systems.

Source: From Feinberg & Mallat (2019)

the attributes of consciousness have developed in all species. Researchers who have proposed theories of human consciousness have neglected the long-running evolutionary, ecological, and behavioural data that others have gathered. Thus, it is time to go backwards and reverse our framework to include some of these models. They even propose that such an enterprise can be easily accommodated within the global workforce model. The problem with this idea is that animal behavioural studies have been very limited in accommodating conceptual developments in cognitive science and often they look like sophisticated extensions of behaviourism.

These evidences may seem reasonable for us to grant animals some form of consciousness. However, we still don't have any unified notion of consciousness. What we have are many theories and proposals on different attributes of consciousness. This may itself make it difficult for us to recognise consciousness in species other than us (Tye, 2016). Animals certainly have experience and they are conscious in the way we are conscious (Tye, 2016). However, if the debate is on phenomenal consciousness that is more about abstract content, then we cannot yet be sure if animals have them. Certain frameworks such as the integrated information theory (Mallatt, 2021) propose that consciousness is an emergent property of biologically complex systems. Following this, animals may have some form of consciousness depending on the complexity of their nervous systems. The debate continues until we have more empirical data and theoretical integration across disciplines.

6. Summary

We saw that the current approaches to the question of consciousness stands between our scientific commitment to materialism and our incorrigible attitudes to our mind's phenomenal awareness. Fields like cognitive psychology and cognitive neuroscience have made much progress. However, given their functionalism, they have not been able to capture certain key attributes of consciousness. We also saw that giving up consciousness and calling it an unscientific folk psychological issue or reducing it to manageable units has its own problems. Therefore, it's a problem that can be called one of the last frontiers in our scientific quest to understand ourselves. There are many disorders that are linked to consciousness and thus a study of it will help such people. As explained, the evolutionary theories of the emergence of consciousness remain in dark or denial. We simply don't understand how and for what purpose consciousness has evolved. But the fact that we experience phenomenality in addition to our cognition is real. We also examined the nature of attention and if it could be a window to our understanding of consciousness. What is missing in the field is not data or technological progress but a theory that can unify the diverse nature of findings.

Bernard Hommel has most recently raised some serious doubts on the methodologies of both cognitive science and cognitive neurosciences. Hommel makes historical references to doing science or explaining phenomena either from the Aristotelian or the Galilean approaches (Hommel, 2019). The Aristotelian approach is about the systematic categorisation of the new phenomena into already understood units. Once a phenomenon shows identifiable attributes then it is classified, just as biologists classify newly found species. This approach does not go for explaining the functions of the structure in terms of its components. How do the components and their specific interactions give rise to the overall function of the organism or structure and why so?

We don't have a mechanistic explanation of the functions of consciousness. All that we have are accidental correlations. The brain imaging data and its correlation with mental states are of this sort. Hommel diminishes them saying no neural data can ever explain psychological data. That's not a new assertion of course. What about the Galilean approach? Hommel thinks that this approach does not force strict categorical dichotomies, but seeks to understand a problem using all possible means. For example, we should try to explain the evolutionary, the psychological, the neural, and the computational aspects together as interrelated components. Currently, within cognitive science, this is not the case. The dissociation between the behavioural and the neural data won't help in building mechanistic models. It is easy to see the very different manner in which cognitive psychologists, neuroscientists, and computational researchers develop their theories of attention or consciousness. The question is not why we have attention or consciousness, but if we have it then what can be a mechanistic model that explains the whole of it? Hommel's call is encouraging but it again may have issues. If I stretch it to the question of consciousness then the hard problem of experience comes. Can we have a mechanistic model of the Galilean type for experience? This is exactly where the philosophers will move the goal post. However, we have to be hopeful about the enterprises of cognitive (neuro) sciences. As Hommel rightly invokes Marr, the levels of analysis idea is still useful. That is what has allowed scientific work so far in this area. The current and future requirement will be the integration of frameworks and finding more mechanistic explanations.

References

Anderson, B. (2011). There is no such thing as attention. *Frontiers in Psychology*, 2, 246.

Ansorge, U., Kunde, W., & Kiefer, M. (2014). Unconscious vision and executive control: How unconscious processing and conscious action control interact. *Consciousness and Cognition*, 27, 268–287.

Armstrong, A. H. (1981). *An introduction to ancient philosophy* (No. 418). Rowman & Littlefield.

Ayer, A. J. (Ed.). (1959). *Logical positivism* (Vol. 2). Simon and Schuster.

Baars, B. J. (1997). In the theatre of consciousness: Global workspace theory, a rigorous scientific theory of consciousness. *Journal of Consciousness Studies, 4*(4), 292–309.

Baars, B. J. (2003). The global brainweb: An update on global workspace theory. *Science and Consciousness Review, 2.*

Baars, B. J. (2005). Global workspace theory of consciousness: Toward a cognitive neuroscience of human experience. *Progress in Brain Research, 150,* 45–53.

Baars, B. J., & Franklin, S. (2007). An architectural model of conscious and unconscious brain functions: Global workspace theory and IDA. *Neural Networks, 20*(9), 955–961.

Bain, D., Brady, M., & Corns, J. (Eds.). (2019). *Philosophy of suffering: Metaphysics, value, and normativity.* Routledge.

Baron-Cohen, S. (1997). *Mindblindness: An essay on autism and theory of mind.* MIT Press.

Bartolomei, F., McGonigal, A., & Naccache, L. (2014). Alteration of consciousness in focal epilepsy: The global workspace alteration theory. *Epilepsy & Behavior, 30,* 17–23.

Ben-Yami, H. (2015). *Descartes' philosophical revolution: A reassessment.* Springer.

Berwick, R. C., & Chomsky, N. (2016). *Why only us: Language and evolution.* MIT Press.

Blackwell, C., & Kusukawa, S. (2017). *Philosophy in the sixteenth and seventeenth centuries: Conversations with Aristotle.* Routledge.

Block, N. (1995). On a confusion about a function of consciousness. *Behavioral and Brain Sciences, 18*(2), 227–247.

Block, N. (2007). Consciousness, accessibility, and the mesh between psychology and neuroscience. *Behavioral and Brain Sciences, 30*(5–6), 481–499.

Block, N. (2014). Rich conscious perception outside focal attention. *Trends in Cognitive Sciences, 18*(9), 445–447.

Boyle, E. (2009). Neuroscience and animal sentience. *Neuroscience, 112.*

Braddon-Mitchell, D. (2019). Behaviorism. In *The Routledge companion to philosophy of psychology* (pp. 90–98). Routledge.

Breitmeyer, B., & Öğmen, H. (2006). *Visual masking: Time slices through conscious and unconscious vision.* Oxford University Press.

Brown, C. (2015). Fish intelligence, sentience and ethics. *Animal Cognition, 18*(1), 1–17.

Brown, R., Lau, H., & LeDoux, J. E. (2019). Understanding the higher-order approach to consciousness. *Trends in Cognitive Sciences, 23*(9), 754–768.

Bruntrup, G., & Jaskolla, L. (Eds.). (2016). *Panpsychism: Contemporary perspectives.* Oxford University Press.

Carruthers, P. (2000). The evolution of consciousness. In *Evolution and the human mind: Modularity, language and meta-cognition* (pp. 254–275). Cambridge University Press.

Carruthers, P. (2005). Why the question of animal consciousness might not matter very much. *Philosophical Psychology, 18*(1), 83–102.

Chalmers, D. (2018). The meta-problem of consciousness. *Journal of Consciousness Studies, 25*(9–10), 6–61.

Chalmers, D. J. (1995). Facing up to the problem of consciousness. *Journal of Consciousness Studies, 2*(3), 200–219.

Chalmers, D. J. (1996). Facing up to the problem of consciousness. In *Toward a science of consciousness: The first Tucson discussions and debates* (pp. 5–28). MIT Press.

Chella, A., & Manzotti, R. (2007). *Artificial intelligence and consciousness* (pp. 1–8). Association for the advancement of Artificial Intelligence Fall Symposium.

Churchland, P. M. (2005). Functionalism at forty: A critical retrospective. *The Journal of Philosophy*, 102(1), 33–50.

Churchland, P. S. (1989). *Neurophilosophy: Toward a unified science of the mind-brain*. MIT Press.

Cohen, M. A., Cavanagh, P., Chun, M. M., & Nakayama, K. (2012). The attentional requirements of consciousness. *Trends in Cognitive Sciences*, 16(8), 411–417.

Coolidge, F. L., & Wynn, T. (2005). Working memory, its executive functions, and the emergence of modern thinking. *Cambridge Archaeological Journal*, 15(1), 5–26.

Crick, F., & Koch, C. (1990). Towards a neurobiological theory of consciousness. In *Seminars in the neurosciences* (Vol. 2, pp. 263–275). Saunders Scientific Publications.

Crick, F., & Koch, C. (1998). Consciousness and neuroscience. *Cerebral Cortex*, 8(2), 97–107.

Dehaene, S., & Changeux, J. P. (2011). Experimental and theoretical approaches to conscious processing. *Neuron*, 70(2), 200–227.

Dehaene, S., Changeux, J. P., Naccache, L., Sackur, J., & Sergent, C. (2006). Conscious, preconscious, and subliminal processing: A testable taxonomy. *Trends in Cognitive Sciences*, 10(5), 204–211.

Dennett, D. C. (1988). Quining qualia. In *Consciousness in modern science*. Oxford University Press.

Dennett, D. C. (2016). Illusionism as the obvious default theory of consciousness. *Journal of Consciousness Studies*, 23(11–12), 65–72.

Dennett, D. C. (2017). *From bacteria to Bach and back: The evolution of minds*. W. W. Norton & Company.

Descartes, R. (2013). *Meditations on first philosophy*. Broadview Press.

Des Chene, D. (2000). *Physiologia: Natural philosophy in late Aristotelian and Cartesian thought*. Cornell University Press.

Desimone, R., & Duncan, J. (1995). Neural mechanisms of selective visual attention. *Annual Review of Neuroscience*, 18(1), 193–222.

Doerig, A., Schurger, A., & Herzog, M. H. (2021). Hard criteria for empirical theories of consciousness. *Cognitive Neuroscience*, 12(2), 41–62.

Dummett, M. (2014). *Origins of analytical philosophy*. A&C Black.

Duncan, I. J. (2006). The changing concept of animal sentience. *Applied Animal Behaviour Science*, 100(1–2), 11–19.

Feinberg, T. E., & Mallatt, J. M. (2019). Subjectivity "demystified": Neurobiology, evolution, and the explanatory gap. *Frontiers in Psychology*, 10, 1686.

Fodor, J. A. (1983). *The modularity of mind*. MIT Press.

Friedman, D. A., & Søvik, E. (2019). The ant colony as a test for scientific theories of consciousness. *Synthese*, 1–24.

Gabay, S., Leibovich, T., Ben-Simon, A., Henik, A., & Segev, R. (2013). Inhibition of return in the archer fish. *Nature Communications*, 4(1), 1–5.

Gaukroger, S. (Ed.). (2008). *The Blackwell guide to Descartes' meditations*. John Wiley & Sons.

Gennaro, R. J. (Ed.). (2004). *Higher-order theories of consciousness: An anthology* (Vol. 56). John Benjamins Publishing.

Goff, P. (2017a). *Consciousness and fundamental reality*. Oxford University Press.

Goff, P. (2017b). The case for panpsychism. *Philosophy Now, 121*, 6–8.

Gold, I., & Stoljar, D. (1999). Interpreting neuroscience and explaining the mind. *Behavioral and Brain Sciences, 22*(5), 856–866.

Graziano, M. S. (2017). The attention schema theory: A foundation for engineering artificial consciousness. *Frontiers in Robotics and AI, 4*, 60.

Graziano, M. S. (2018). The attention schema theory of consciousness. In *The Routledge handbook of consciousness* (pp. 174–187). Routledge.

Graziano, M. S. (2020). Consciousness and the attention schema: Why it has to be right. *Cognitive Neuropsychology, 37*(3–4), 224–233.

Graziano, M. S., & Webb, T. W. (2015). The attention schema theory: A mechanistic account of subjective awareness. *Frontiers in Psychology, 6*, 500.

Greenwood, J. D. (1999). Understanding the "cognitive revolution" in psychology. *Journal of the History of the Behavioral Sciences, 35*(1), 1–22.

Griffin, D. R. (1985). Animal consciousness. *Neuroscience & Biobehavioral Reviews, 9*(4), 615–622.

Hadot, P. (2002). *What is ancient philosophy?* Harvard University Press.

Harnad, S. (1989). Minds, machines and Searle. *Journal of Experimental & Theoretical Artificial Intelligence, 1*(1), 5–25.

Heyes, C. (2008). Beast machines? Questions of animal consciousness. *Frontiers of Consciousness, 259–274*.

Hommel, B. (2020). Pseudo-mechanistic explanations in psychology and cognitive neuroscience. *Topics in Cognitive Science, 12*(4), 1294–1305.

Hume, D., Biro, J., Fogelin, R. J., & Haakonssen, K. (1993). *The Cambridge companion to Hume*. Cambridge University Press.

Jackson, F. (1986). What Mary didn't know. *The Journal of Philosophy, 83*(5), 291–295.

James, W. (1892). The stream of consciousness. *Psychology, 179–202*.

Kiefer, M. (2007). Top-down modulation of unconscious' automatic'processes: A gating framework. *Advances in Cognitive Psychology, 3*(1–2), 289.

Kim, J. (1998). *Mind in a physical world: An essay on the mind-body problem and mental causation*. MIT Press.

Klein, C., & Barron, A. B. (2016). Insects have the capacity for subjective experience. *Animal Sentience, 1*(9), 1.

Koch, C. (2012). *Consciousness: Confessions of a romantic reductionist*. MIT Press.

Koch, C. (2021). Reflections of a natural scientist on panpsychism. *Journal of Consciousness Studies, 28*(9–10), 65–75.

Koch, C., Massimini, M., Boly, M., & Tononi, G. (2016). Neural correlates of consciousness: Progress and problems. *Nature Reviews Neuroscience, 17*(5), 307–321.

Koch, C., & Tsuchiya, N. (2007). Attention and consciousness: Two distinct brain processes. *Trends in Cognitive Sciences, 11*(1), 16–22.

Koivisto, M., & Neuvonen, S. (2020). Masked blindsight in normal observers: Measuring subjective and objective responses to two features of each stimulus. *Consciousness and Cognition, 81*, 102929.

Lambert, A., Naikar, N., McLachlan, K., & Aitken, V. (1999). A new component of visual orienting: Implicit effects of peripheral information and subthreshold cues on covert attention. *Journal of Experimental Psychology: Human Perception and Performance*, 25(2), 321.

Lamme, V. A. (2003). Why visual attention and awareness are different. *Trends in Cognitive Sciences*, 7(1), 12–18.

Lau, H., & Rosenthal, D. (2011). Empirical support for higher-order theories of conscious awareness. *Trends in Cognitive Sciences*, 15(8), 365–373.

Leidenhag, J. (2019). The revival of panpsychism and its relevance for the science-religion dialogue. *Theology and Science*, 17(1), 90–106.

Mallatt, J. (2021). A traditional scientific perspective on the integrated information theory of consciousness. *Entropy*, 23(6), 650.

Metzinger, T. (Ed.). (2000). *Neural correlates of consciousness: Empirical and conceptual questions*. MIT Press.

Mørch, H. H. (2019a). Is the integrated information theory of consciousness compatible with Russellian panpsychism?. *Erkenntnis*, 84(5), 1065–1085.

Mørch, H. H. (2019b). The argument for panpsychism from experience of causation. In *The Routledge handbook of panpsychism* (pp. 269–284). Routledge.

Nagel, T. (1974). What is it like to be a bat?. *The Philosophical Review*, 83(4), 435–450.

Newell, A. (1994). *Unified theories of cognition*. Harvard University Press.

Newman, J., & Baars, B. J. (1993). A neural attentional model for access to consciousness: A global workspace perspective. *Concepts in Neuroscience*, 4(2), 255–290.

Ney, A. (2021). Panpsychism and the limits of physical science. *Journal of Consciousness Studies*, 28(9–10), 181–193.

Nichols, S., & Grantham, T. (2000). Adaptive complexity and phenomenal consciousness. *Philosophy of Science*, 67(4), 648–670.

Oda, T., & Bucci, A. (2020). Izutsu's Zen metaphysics of I-consciousness vis-à-vis Cartesian cogito. *Comparative Philosophy*, 11(2), 7.

O'Daly, G. J. (1987). *Augustine's philosophy of mind*. University of California Press.

Overgaard, M. (2018). Phenomenal consciousness and cognitive access. *Philosophical Transactions of the Royal Society B: Biological Sciences*, 373(1755), 20170353.

Owen, A. M. (2013). Detecting consciousness: A unique role for neuroimaging. *Annual Review of Psychology*, 64, 109–133.

Parrington, J. (2021). *Mind shift: How the human brain acquired consciousness*. Oxford University Press.

Patel, G. H., Yang, D., Jamerson, E. C., Snyder, L. H., Corbetta, M., & Ferrera, V. P. (2015). Functional evolution of new and expanded attention networks in humans. *Proceedings of the National Academy of Sciences*, 112(30), 9454–9459.

Polák, M., & Marvan, T. (2019). How to mitigate the hard problem by adopting the dual theory of phenomenal consciousness. *Frontiers in Psychology*, 10, 2837.

Posner, M. I. (1980). Orienting of attention. *Quarterly Journal of Experimental Psychology*, 32(1), 3–25.

Prasad, S., & Mishra, R. K. (2019). The nature of unconscious attention to subliminal cues. *Vision*, 3(3), 38.

Prasad, S., & Mishra, R. K. (2020). Reward influences masked free-choice priming. *Frontiers in Psychology*, 11, 576430.

Ramsøy, T. Z., & Overgaard, M. (2004). Introspection and subliminal perception. *Phenomenology and the Cognitive Sciences*, 3(1), 1–23.

Rosenthal, D. M. (1986). Two concepts of consciousness. *Philosophical Studies, 49*, 329–359. https://doi.org/10.1007/BF00355521

Russell, B. (2005). *Analysis of mind*. Routledge.

Samorini, G. (2002). *Animals and psychedelics: The natural world and the instinct to alter consciousness*. Simon and Schuster.

Scharfstein, B. A. (1998). *A comparative history of world philosophy: From the Upanishads to Kant*. SUNY Press.

Schopenhauer, A. (2012). *The world as will and representation* (Vol. 1). Courier Corporation.

Seager, W. (1995). Consciousness, information and panpsychism. *Journal of Consciousness Studies, 2*(3), 272–288.

Seth, A. K., & Bayne, T. (2022). Theories of consciousness. *Nature Reviews Neuroscience*, 1–14.

Shapin, S. (2018). *The scientific revolution*. University of Chicago Press.

Sharp, P. (2011). Buddhist enlightenment and the destruction of attractor networks: A neuroscientific speculation on the Buddhist path from everyday consciousness to Buddha-awakening. *Journal of Consciousness Studies, 18*(3–4), 137–169.

Shea, N., & Frith, C. D. (2019). The global workspace needs metacognition. *Trends in Cognitive Sciences, 23*(7), 560–571.

Signa, A., Chella, A., & Gentile, M. (2021). Cognitive robots and the conscious mind: A review of the global workspace theory. *Current Robotics Reports, 2*(2), 125–131.

Signorelli, C. M., Szczotka, J., & Prentner, R. (2021). Explanatory profiles of models of consciousness-towards a systematic classification. *Neuroscience of Consciousness, 2*, niab021.

Skrbina, D. (2017). *Panpsychism in the West*. MIT Press.

Sperling, G. (1960). The information available in brief visual presentations. *Psychological Monographs: General and Applied, 74*(11), 1.

Tallon-Baudry, C. (2012). On the neural mechanisms subserving consciousness and attention. *Frontiers in Psychology, 2*, 397.

Taylor, C. C. W. (2010). *The atomists, Leucippus and Democritus: Fragments: A text and translation with a commentary* (Vol. 5). University of Toronto Press.

Treisman, A. M., & Gelade, G. (1980). A feature-integration theory of attention. *Cognitive Psychology, 12*(1), 97–136.

Tononi, G., Boly, M., Massimini, M., & Koch, C. (2016). Integrated information theory: From consciousness to its physical substrate. *Nature Reviews Neuroscience, 17*(7), 450–461.

Tononi, G., & Edelman, G. M. (1998). Consciousness and complexity. *Science, 282*(5395), 1846–1851.

Tononi, G., & Koch, C. (2008). The neural correlates of consciousness: An update. *Annals of the New York Academy of Sciences, 1124*(1), 239–261.

Tononi, G., & Koch, C. (2015). Consciousness: Here, there and everywhere?. *Philosophical Transactions of the Royal Society B: Biological Sciences, 370*(1668), 20140167.

Tümkaya, S. (2019). On the proper treatment of the Churchlands. *Erkenntnis*, 1–14.

Tye, M. (1999). Phenomenal consciousness: The explanatory gap as a cognitive illusion. *Mind, 108*(432), 705–725.

Tye, M. (2016). *Tense bees and shell-shocked crabs: Are animals conscious?* Oxford University Press.

Willaschek, M., & Watkins, E. (2017). Kant on cognition and knowledge. *Synthese*, 1–19.

Wilterson, A. I., Kemper, C. M., Kim, N., Webb, T. W., Reblando, A. M., & Graziano, M. S. (2020). Attention control and the attention schema theory of consciousness. *Progress in Neurobiology*, *195*, 101844.

Zhang, B., Huang, K., Karri, J., O'Brien, K., DiTommaso, C., & Li, S. (2021). Many faces of the hidden souls: Medical and neurological complications and comorbidities in disorders of consciousness. *Brain Sciences*, *11*(5), 608.

5 Neuroplasticity

1. Plasticity of the brain: A brief history

No contemporary discussion on cognition or the mind is possible without referring to the brain. Even though many philosophical viewpoints exist on the relationship between the mind and the brain, scientific advancement on the study of the brain and its contribution to mental states has reached a level of sophistication that is hard to ignore. In the mind/brain sciences today, reference to brain activity for all types of cognitive functions is very common. Cognitive scientists accept the structure-function relationship, and the mental and psychological states depending on the brain functions. Minds are what brains produce. Any change in the brain and its structure or connectivity results in a change in mental attributes. Brains also modify themselves over a period of time; the amount of time the modification takes depends upon experience. Both nature and nurture play roles in such changes. This experience-dependent change in the brain is termed neuroplasticity. It is the brain's ability to constantly reorganise itself both structurally and functionally (Cramer et al., 2011). Neuroplasticity thus refers to changes in the mental functions including behaviour due to adaptive changes in the brain. Cramer and colleagues write,

> Neuroplasticity can be broadly defined as the ability of the nervous system to respond to intrinsic and extrinsic stimuli by reorganising its structure, function and connections; can be described at many levels, from molecular to cellular to systems to behaviour; and can occur during development, in response to the environment, in support of learning, in response to disease, or in relation to therapy.
>
> (Cramer et al., 2011, p. 1592)

This means that neuroplasticity could have many underlying reasons and could also produce good or bad results for the organism. Much recent research has focused on the nature of neuroplasticity in the cognitive domain. That is, how does the continuous practice of specific cognitive tasks change

DOI: 10.4324/9781003316053-5

the brain for the benefit of the individual? The chapter aims at exploring some of the main ideas in this domain.

The idea that experience alters and modifies the brain is old. William James wrote in 1890,

> Plasticity, then, in the wide sense of the word means the possession of a structure weak enough to yield to an influence, but strong enough not to yield all at once. . . . Organic matter, especially nervous tissue, seems endowed with a very ordinary degree of plasticity of this sort: so that we may without hesitation lay down as our proposition the following, that the phenomena of habit in living beings are due to the plasticity of the organic materials of which their bodies are composed.
>
> (James et al., 1890, vol. I, p. 105; cited in
> Berlucchi & Buchtel, 2009)

James had speculated that activations between the neurons that are connected may strengthen over time. He had also speculated on the nature of experience- or habit-dependent plasticity. However, at that time, there was no clear description of neural information flow or synapse. Importantly, being a psychologist, he traced the matter of plasticity to changes in the inner structure of the brain. James's description was not entirely hypothetical and was based on nascent knowledge of the nervous system available then. Charles Sherrington had coined the word *synapse* but did not have much to say on the issue of plasticity. However, scholars such as Eugenio Tanzi and his student Ernesto Lugaro in Italy first proposed the hypothesis on the direct influence of the environment on neuronal plasticity (Berlucchi, 2002). This was the time when Cajal had already discovered the intricate nature of the organisation of the neurons in Spain, and in Italy, Golgi had developed his methods to visualise these connections. Lugaro discovered that the ability of the neurons to remain plastic slows down with ageing. This indicated that experience-dependent neuroplasticity is constrained by age and many other factors.

While the idea that our daily habits and experiences are enough to induce neuronal plasticity is common today, it was not so during the early stages of neuroscience's evolution. For instance, the Romanian neuroscientist Marianesco had observed that the nerve cells show morphological reactions to toxic pathological effects (Shaywitz, 1999). This kind of modification did not result from learning or experience. Cajal, who later speculated on the mental properties resulting from the pyramidal cells, believed that their structures and connections determine how different individuals attain their psychological powers. Although William James had approached the issue of neuroplasticity without much empirical data in hand, by the time we reach Cajal, the idea reappears with more knowledge of the neurons and their connections. Cajal proposed that new skills can only be learnt with the modifications of the existing neuronal connections (Azmitia, 2007). He observed that existing connections resist any new sudden modifications. If one persists with great force, the connections give up their resistance and the skill is acquired. Cajal's psychological association to neurons and their evolving structures is fascinating and also interesting given that historical climate. Cajal postulated that neurons could change their connections as a function of the force of will. The question is whether plasticity is just the natural unfolding of the growth patterns of the neuronal systems as designed, or is a result of consciously felt experience and will of the organism. Donald Hebb popularised the idea that the neurons and their connections change as a function of repetitive nature of stimuli and experience becomes acceptable (Hebb, 2005). The Hebbian association was taken to be an important example of neural plasticity. Behavioural modification through repeated practice could lead to structural cases of modifications in brain cells and networks.

Cajal was influenced by both Darwin and James. His neuron doctrine, therefore, was a result of thinking both in evolutionary and psychological terms. Cajal held the notion that the connections that one sees among different neurons in the cerebral cortex are an outcome of evolutionary processes. Additionally, Darwinian evolution primarily focuses on the adaptability of the organism to natural selection for survival. Thus, brains and their connections evolved to facilitate natural selection and were under selection pressure to change. Reticular theory of the organisation of the nervous system proposed by Joseph von Gerlach assumed a fixed set of connections frozen in time (Stahnisch, 2015). Cajal, however, imagined that these connections cannot remain static under constant stimulation and "mental gymnastics." Mental gymnastics refers to the will of the organism to combat environmental pressure (Monte Ferreira et al., 2014). Cajal had discovered that there exists a definite structural hierarchy in the way different types of neurons are organised. This influences the manner in which they transmit information to one another. The important question is why this hierarchical mechanism exists and who controls it. Cajal's "psychomotor" neurons and the "association" neurons had a direct interface between the neuronal substrate and the environment (Stahnisch, 2015). Therefore, the environment modified the connections as required for the organism. In this way, he was seeking an evolutionary angle to the neuron theory.

From this brief historical sketch, it appears that some of the founding fathers of neuroscience were guided by the general principles of psychology and evolution. They attempted to explain structure in terms of the organism's goals and evolutionary urges. Both James and Cajal understood and wrote on plasticity from converging points of views. Given the tensions between psychology and neuroscience in the later part of the twentieth century and its continuation at the moment, the question becomes to what extent structural modifications of the central nervous system are governed by the will of the organism. Can the organism modify its neural structures to fulfil its psychological will? This is of utmost importance now given that several training programs exist to enhance brain plasticity, more on which will be discussed later.

2. Cognitive neuroplasticity

The mind can change the brain and its functioning. How can subjective states influence the material body and induce changes? The mind still remains a folk psychological construct to the many inheritors of logical positivism and analytical philosophy and other neuro/computational behaviourists. Therefore, the talk on neuroplasticity has become brain-centric in general. Changes in particular structures of the brain are seen because of cognitive training. How is this possible and how can we accept and explain these within our commitment to materialism? How can psychological states – even if they are real – modify the brain? I will give some examples from contemporary fields to show that this phenomenon is very much real and accepted within fields like cognitive science and cognitive neuroscience.

Neuroplasticity can be seen in many different domains including cognition. Continuous and extreme training of the mind or its specific components brings notable changes in the functions. For example, professional musicians, who are trained for a long time, show structural patterns in their brains that are qualitatively different from others (Tervaniemi, 2009). For instance, experienced musicians show increased representations in their auditory processing areas (Pantev et al., 1998). Cortical representation of digits in long-term string players differs between the left and the right hands (Elbert et al., 1995). Of course, it is not the case that all musicians will display such changes. It depends upon their richness of practice, genetics, and a range of other factors. Such changes or modifications to the brain and in turn to the cognitive skills are seen in many other domains as a result of sustained long-term effort.

Cognitive ageing refers to the maintenance of optimal mental functions in the face of eventual biological slowdown (Salthouse, 2004). Concepts like "cognitive scaffolding" and "cognitive reserve" have become popular to refer to this. The neuropsychological view of plasticity deals with the brain's ability to self-repair or transfer functions to other domains. Ageing adults report that they are increasingly facing challenges of cognitive nature. This could be related to decision making, memory retrieval and language use, or even emotion processing (Park & Schwarz, 2012). These functions deteriorate at a certain rate over the entire lifespan. The key question is how the brain slows down the rate of decay of important cognitive functions. The scaffolding theory of ageing suggests that the brain prepares itself by recruiting additional resources to take care of any requirements that may arise (Park & Reuter-Lorenz, 2009, Figure 5.1). It refers to the brain's self-organising behaviour in the face of challenges with fewer resources. For

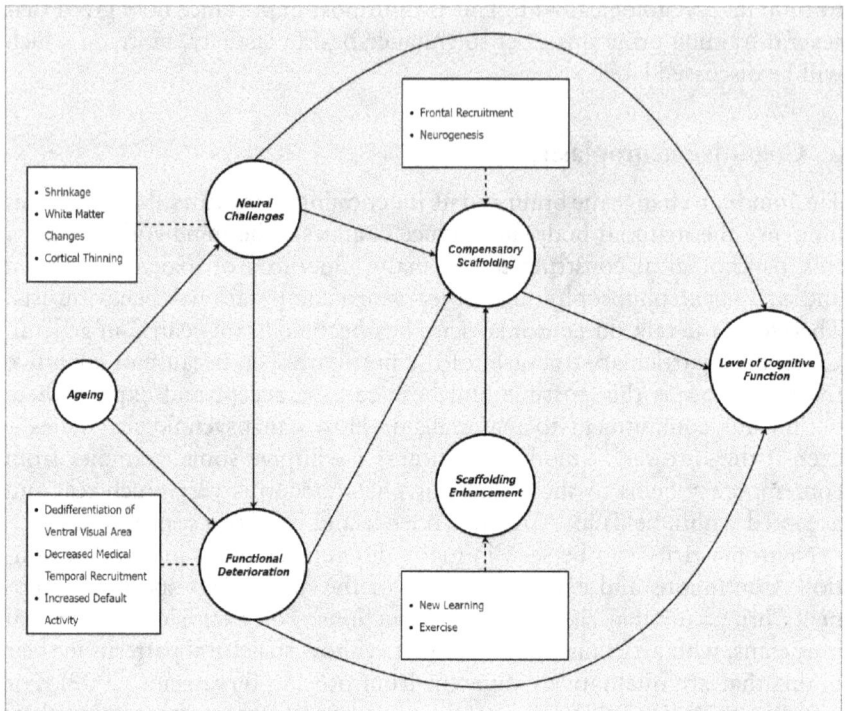

Figure 5.1 Scaffolding theory of ageing and cognition. Adverse structural and functional changes in the brain such as cortical thinning, shrinkage, and decreased functional connectivity caused due to ageing contribute to compensatory scaffolding. These interact with explicit interventions such as new learning or exercise to help the dynamic adaptation of the ageing brain.

Source: Adapted from Park & Reuter-Lorenz (2009)

instance, the prefrontal cortex typically shrinks due to atrophy in older adults. To compensate, increased prefrontal activation during many cognitive functions is seen in the aged brain. Scaffolding has also been seen in the alteration of the anterior-posterior functional connectivity in ageing adults (Zhang et al., 2017) which modifies functional connectivity as seen during cognitive tasks.

Recent research effort has been to boost the scaffolding mechanism with external stimulation (Goh & Park, 2009). Circumstances of life and the demands on cognition change as one ages. The prefrontal cortex manages these responsibilities through a wide range of cortical areas. With age and experience, the brain learns to execute cognitive functions with more economy. Research also shows that, as part of scaffolding, not just the prefrontal cortex but the also cerebellum establishes newer connections in old age (Filip et al., 2019). It's not clear why some cortical areas develop newer connections at this age. It should also depend on an individual's life history and cognitive demands. Most brain imaging studies, however, indicate that such re-organisation does occur and it indicates natural neuroplasticity.

The other important concept that has been very popular is cognitive reserve. It is a kind of bank balance of cognitive resources that can be used in old age when cognitive functions are on decline. Cognitive reserve is an outcome of lifelong experiences. The more varied, sustained, and richer the experience is, the greater the cognitive reserve (Whalley et al., 2004). Activities such as literacy, bilingualism, sport, or other mentally demanding life-long activities can lead to cognitive reserve. Depending upon the extent of cognitive reserve, the onset of many neurodegenerative diseases are delayed (Stern, 2009). Cognitive training and demanding tasks can boost cognitive reserve. Most researchers seem to agree on the notion that one must invest while being young to gain benefit later in old age. This means that young people that engage in a higher level of mental engagement and challenge will harvest a higher cognitive reserve. The concept of "reserve" has both psychological/cognitive and neural attributes (Barulli & Stern, 2013). Neural reserve is about brain volume, cellular density, the strength of connections, and so on (Stern, 2009). Cognitive reserve refers to the manifestation of neural reserve in actual cognitive tasks (Lövdén et al., 2010). Variables such as literacy rate, socio-economic status, IQ, and onset of diseases such as Alzheimer's disease (AD) or Parkinson's disease (PD) modulate neural reserve.

As is evident from the schematic diagram in Figure 5.2, most brain imaging studies so far on the issue of cognitive or neural reserve have followed different protocols. The difference in brain activity between the young and the old observed for particular tasks is important. The young are investing while they can in building those neural resources. Therefore, the issue of cognitive reserve is a longitudinal problem and cannot be investigated with cross-sectional studies at any single time point. The point related to efficiency and capacity of certain brain networks is also critical. It is possible that at a certain age in an individual, the capacities of the networks are constrained for various reasons and do not show the appropriate efficiency. With cognitive adaptation and acquisition of new skills, these may become efficient. The same goes for older adults who acquire a new skill during ageing and make the networks more competitive. Each individual at any point during the lifespan may acquire any one of these abilities. This poses a serious methodological question on the way brain imaging measurements of cerebral blood flow are interpreted concerning cognitive or neural reserve.

Stern (2009) proposed that the benefits of cognitive reserve are wide-ranging and related to a lot of variables. The issue of individual differences is critical in understanding cognitive reserve. Different individuals have different compensatory mechanisms and can resist the onset of the neurodegenerative conditions in different ways. However, this can only be true if

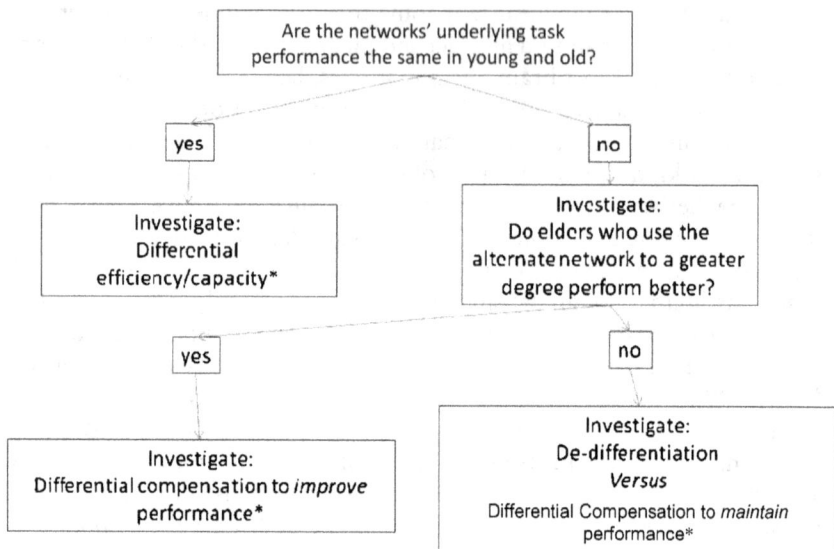

*In each instance, investigate: How do individual differences relate to proxy measures of cognitive reserve?

Figure 5.2 Approaches used for studying cognitive reserve. The figure gives an overview of the hierarchy of questions that must be addressed in studies of cognitive reserve. The first and the most important step is in determining whether the young and the old population use the same brain networks for a given task. Further investigations should be determined based on this.

Source: Reprinted from *Neuropsychologia*, Vol. 47, Yaakov Stern, Cognitive reserve, 2015–2028, 2009, with permission from Elsevier.

they have maintained a high degree of engagement with demanding mental skills and training throughout their lifespan. Further, it is currently being explored if cognitive reserve shows up when there is a pathology of the brain. In one recent study, it was found that cognitive reserve predicted the maintenance of executive functions in individuals only if they had AD and not otherwise (McKenzie et al., 2020). The presence or absence of a neurodegenerative condition thus explains if cognitive performance will remain intact via cognitive reserve or if it will slow down. If cognitive reserve predicts resistance or coping only in the event of the onset of a neurodegenerative condition, then the question arises on its general implications. Studies have shown that in some people, cognitive reserve is spent quickly as the severity of diseases increases and then there is a very stiff decline in cognitive functions (Bettcher et al., 2019). Literacy also modulates cognitive reserve throughout life (Mungas et al., 2018).

A general theory of neuroplasticity must have both descriptive and explanatory powers like any theory. It should also explain a wide range of both predicted and novel phenomena related to brain functions and behaviour. One of the most important shortcomings is that the concept of neuroplasticity has been mostly based on neuropsychological data. Therefore, it speaks very little about the natural maturation and eventual weakening of brain resources in healthy adults over the lifetime. Further, the distinction between neural and cognitive reserve questions the sole emphasis on brain networks and their activations to cognitive tasks as a measure of plasticity. It is not all about the brain since psychological experiences also induce changes in the brain. At this point, there are a few psychologically motivated theories of cognitive reserve or cognitive neuroplasticity. Researchers should also be careful about the uses of the words cognitive and neural reserve.

3. Enhancing neuroplasticity

The concept of neuroplasticity has caught the popular imagination since it has great practical utility. As cultures become knowledge economies, increasing one's mental abilities has become a necessity. The discussion so far in this chapter dealt with some theoretical concepts related to cognitive neuroplasticity. There are many ways to improve cognition which have been studied scientifically. They extend from playing demanding computer games to art therapy. In this section I have picked a few domains where current research has shown positive results. The list is by no means exhaustive but indicative. These activities have been shown to positively influence cognitive capacity throughout lifespan. Of course, they are in no way culture-neutral, but are being adopted everywhere. There is also individual variability with regard to the effectiveness of these methods.

3.1. Food

The idea that what you eat affects your brain and the eventual longevity of the mind is interesting. Enhancing our cognitive life through food has cultural and civilisational history. For example, in Eastern traditions, people live a very well-endowed long life with complete cognitive competence but they do not focus much on eating. In the Indian traditions, the meditators and monks up in the mountains live long and eat little. The tribals in India who live in far-flung areas eat what they get. Therefore, our culture has given us what we mainly eat, and this takes care of our brain's health. In Western traditions, a variety of protein-rich food is consumed. The definite relation of certain types of food on cognition is well accepted. What is still not known is which food directly influences particular types of cognitive mechanisms such as attention, memory, decision making, etc. The studies with rats and mice in laboratories do indicate that food rich in bad fat slows down the brain and produces anxiety. The same is also seen in humans.

With both Westernisation and urbanisation, such food is getting consumed at a higher rate now than in the past. There has not been a magic formula of food that can certainly speed up neuroplasticity or offer lifelong protection against cognitive erosion.

Omega-3 fatty acids and polyphenols influence metabolic events and strengthen synaptic health. An intake of these has been shown to modulate epigenetic events in the long run (Gomez-Pinilla & Tyagi, 2013). Metabolism and other basic biological functions are one thing but what about subjective states of the mind? Does Omega-3 influence psychological states? More recent studies have directly linked food intake of certain types and psychological states such as mood. Food enriched with probiotics and prebiotics can enhance mood, and reduce anxiety and depression (Taylor & Holscher, 2020). Intake of polyphenols and simultaneous speed training modulates cognitive neuroplasticity. In an intervention study with older adults with a low level of literacy, a combination of food and cognitive training supposedly led to structural neuroplasticity (Clark et al., 2019). The Mediterranean diet, which induces neuroplasticity providing prevention against such diseases, has been very popular around the globe. The occurrence of dementia in older populations is found to be lower in Greece where the Mediterranean diet is popular (Kosmidis et al., 2018); however, there are not many clinical trials that justify this correlation (Petersson & Philippou, 2016). Although educational attainment has often been found to be a strong predictor of cognitive reserve. Therefore, at the moment, there is no clear evidence that a particular type of diet leads to cognitive reserve only if we leave other variables. Furthermore, food intake is a highly cultural and lifestyle-related issue. The diagnosis of dementia and depression and a range of such cognitive disorders are also not done universally in the same way. Given that very little cross-cultural validation exists, it is not easy to recommend a particular type of food-based intervention. Although food certainly plays a key role in bodily functions, its exact role in different types of complex cognitive processes is not known.

3.2. Exercise/sport

Humans have been engaged in sport and exercises ever since the dawn of civilisation. One finds people indulging in sports in every culture since the Greeks, who emphasised physical endurance and started the Olympics. Can exercise and sport create neuroplasticity? Even a single spell of moderate aerobic exercise could modulate the brain deprived of neurotrophic factors and thus can boost neuroplasticity. Adults who engage in this kind of high intensity exercise have been shown to build cognitive reserve against diseases (McDonnell et al., 2013). Exercises that are of high intensity increase oxygen intake to the brain and stimulate the frontal and motor cortices. Physical activity protects against dementia and boosts cognitive reserve. It appears that those who engage in physical activity already have a high level of cognition, are more health-conscious, and can afford leisure time. Socio-economic factors also influence one's ability to indulge in exercises and have good health. In most studies of this nature, people are asked to give data in a subjective questionnaire on the degree of their physical activity (Hötting & Roder, 2013). Figure 5.3 shows the many variables that can come into play when we try to correlate exercise with neuroplasticity and cognition. Factors such as gender, culture, and education influence such complex interactions. In addition to physical activity, cultural and intellectual activities could also provide similar neural boost (Richards et al., 2003). Continuous exercising over the years is necessary to maintain any structural neuroplasticity that may be achieved. People who have been exercising all their lives show very little memory impairments when they are over 60 (Rovio et al., 2010). Interestingly those who have been doing exercises until they were middle-aged and then stopped showed rapid decline later. Neural and cognitive benefits due to exercise are linked to everyday continuous practice.

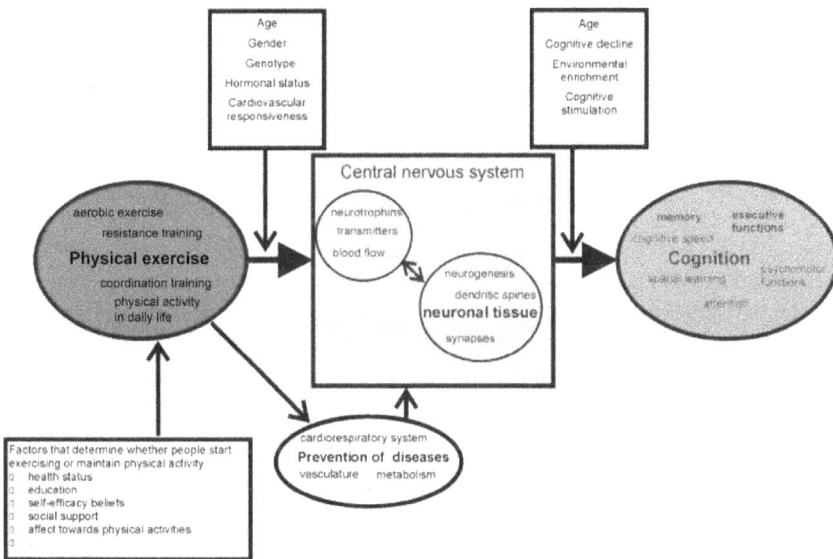

Figure 5.3 Relationship between exercise, neuroplasticity, and cognition. Schematic representation of the many variables that play a role in determining whether one exercises (health status, education, etc.) and the variables that mediate the effects of exercise on brain plasticity (gender and genotype, among others). The subsequent effects of the brain-related changes on cognition also depends on factors like age, existing cognitive deficiencies, and environmental factors.

Source: Reprinted from *Neuroscience & Biobehavioral Reviews*, Vol. 37, Kirsten Hötting, Brigitte Röder, Beneficial effects of physical exercise on neuroplasticity and cognition, 2243–2257, 2013, with permission from Elsevier.

Thus, what is important is regular and sustained stimulation of the brain for any long-term and lasting benefits.

Most studies have looked into how cardiovascular exercises influence performance on different cognitive tasks that require attention, memory, or decision making. However, it is not clear if such exercises can boost cognition more generally or only a few components are affected (Kramer et al., 2001). Aerobic exercises have been shown to facilitate executive functions including inhibitory control. Even resistance training is linked to superior cognition. One year of resistance training can significantly boost performance on a Stroop task, a task that measures inhibitory control (Liu-Ambrose et al., 2010). Thirty minutes of vigorous high-intensity aerobic exercise can immediately modulate the reactive type of inhibitory control mechanisms more than the proactive type (Chacko et al., 2020). Reactive and proactive types of control refer to suppression of undesirable action plans vs more top-down avoidance of unintended actions (Braver, 2012). EEG measurements have revealed neural activity pre- and post-exercise. In this particular study, a group of individuals did high-intensity cycling and another group of individuals browsed the internet for that time. Participants performed a visuomotor discrimination task. This task calls for sustained selective attention throughout the experiment. The ERP measurements showed that the exercise group showed modulation of the early components such as the pN1. This exercise did not have any modulatory effect on the components arising in the frontal and premotor areas that could have indicated more proactive control (Chacko et al., 2020).

It appears that the lasting benefits of exercises on cognitive reserve or cognition, in general, have to do with the intensity and duration of the practice. While high-intensity exercises do show some positive results, low and moderate exercises do not. For example, intensity of exercise modulates the plasticity of the motor cortex (Andrews et al., 2020). High-intensity exercises such as boxing may not show quick facilitation on tasks that require learning and memory (Lorås et al., 2020).

3.3. Bilingualism

The previously discussed methods to induce neuro- or cognitive plasticity are not cognitive, at least at the input level. One can exercise, eat well, and achieve some benefits in the long run eventually. However, there are training methods whose input is cognitive. For example, the practice of bilingualism leads to changes in the brain and cognitive reserve (Mishra, 2018). Most people in the world today are bilinguals because of many geopolitical, social, cultural, and economic reasons. Many adults who never grew up in a location learning two languages have to learn a new language during their adulthood for economic or social reasons. This additional mental exercise influences the structures and functions of the brain. Speaking a language involves most critical areas of the brain and this was known to the early neuropsychologists of the nineteenth century. Bilingualism induces such important changes in the brain networks over a period of time. The bilingual brain is essentially different from the monolingual brain (Fabbro, 2001). Studies show structural changes in key areas in bilinguals' brains compared to monolinguals'. For instance, structural changes have been observed in the grey matter in the left inferior parietal cortex (Mechelli et al., 2004) in the bilingual brain. Such changes in the brain are correlated with the degree of proficiency attained in the second language and the age at which it was acquired. With increasing practice of bilingualism, the brain's language and control areas show increased functional connectivity (Sulpizio et al., 2020). The white matter connectivity of the bilinguals' brains is also related to their amount of immersion in the bilingual environment (Stein et al., 2014). Immersion refers to the situation in which a bilingual individual lives in a context which is bilingual, and is exposed to a second language in a controlled environment such as the classroom. Bilinguals control their languages depending on the interlocutors and the environmental contexts (Green & Abutalebi, 2013). Language control and selection is the mechanism which leads to such experience-driven neuroplasticity in the long run.

The practice of bilingualism is different from other forms of behaviour. Bilingualism has been compared to juggling. The bilingual mind constantly activates two languages. Therefore, during speaking, the bilingual person has to select one by inhibiting another. This idea was captured by David Green (Green, 1998), who linked language control in the bilinguals to a generalised executive control system of the brain. The brain recruits the same executive control areas for language control as it does for other such stimuli. If so, then the practice of bilingualism should modulate the activity of these areas. The neuroscience of bilingualism has emerged as an intense area of research over the years. For example, fMRI studies have shown changes to the bilingual brains with regard to grey matter volume, white matter integrity, and cortical thickness (Li et al., 2014, Figure 5.4).

The critical variables that correlate with neural changes are the age of acquisition and proficiency in the second language (Abutalebi & Green, 2016). Proficiency has been broadly defined as one's ability to shift, switch, and use language in a context-sensitive manner with increased demands. Cognitive demands on bilinguals could differ widely between cultures, and differed as a function of the many language-use variables. In spite of the differences in studies, there is consensus that bilingualism is a key method to induce brain neuroplasticity in the long run (Perani & Abutalebi, 2015). It is important to note the difference between bilingualism, sports, and food as external variables of neuroplasticity. While sports and food are things one can do in isolation, bilingualism requires a speech community. Language is the currency of cognitive interactions among individuals in a society. Therefore, the degree of actual use over time in a real bilingual community influences the degree of neuroplasticity. Bilingualism brings in some structural or

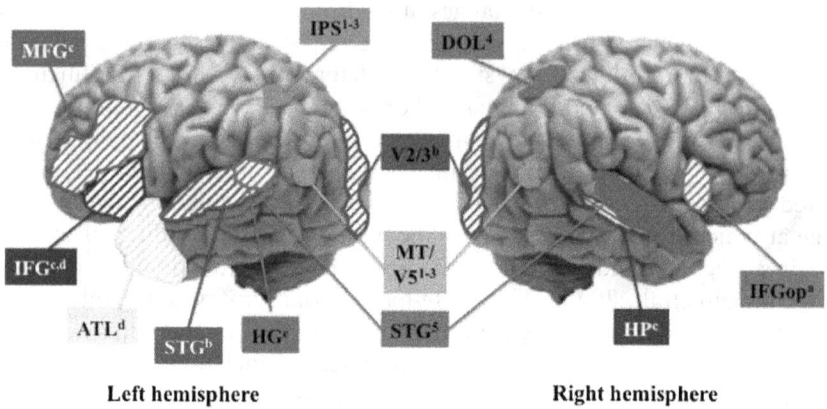

Left hemisphere   **Right hemisphere**

Figure 5.4 Increase in grey matter volume as a function of linguistic (shaded) or non-linguistic (solid) training.

Source: Reprinted from *Cortex*, Vol. 37, Ping Li, Jennifer Legault, Kaitlyn A. Litcofsky, Neuroplasticity as a function of second language learning: Anatomical changes in the human brain, 301–324, 2014, with permission from Elsevier.

functional connectivity through long-term changes and influences cognitive ageing/cognitive reserve in a positive way.

We have seen earlier that the cognitive scaffolding theory predicts reorganisation of the structural and functional aspects of key brain areas during ageing. This was more evident in the older population close to the onset of a neurodegenerative disease. Interestingly, lifelong practice of bilingualism has been shown to modulate cognitive reserve (Bak & Alladi, 2014). The practice of bilingualism is considered to delay the onset of neurodegenerative diseases. A study published from India attracted worldwide attention when it reported that in a large sample of patients with AD, those who were bilinguals reported a later onset of symptoms (Alladi et al., 2013). This advantage in terms of a delay in the onset of symptoms was linked to bilingualism.

My group conducted an experimental study with normal healthy older adults (Mishra et al., 2018) in Hyderabad. The idea was to see if the performance of such bilingual older adults on executive control tasks correlates with their second language proficiency. The study did not find that second language proficiency predicts such advantage in task performance. However, in many previous studies with younger adults in India (e.g., Singh & Mishra, 2012, 2013, 2015), it has been observed that those who are excellent with their second language perform better on cognitive control tasks. A recent meta-analysis on the issue of bilingualism and cognitive ageing (Zhang et al., 2020) concluded that while there are studies linking bilingualism to neuropathology via the age of onset, there are a few studies that do not show any link between bilingualism and cognitive decline during normal ageing. Secondly, the degree to which anyone has been bilingual over a significant amount of time is highly variable around many pockets in the word. Further, key psycholinguistic variables such as language shifting, switching, and contextual engagements also change over a lifetime. Therefore, it is not a homogeneous population that we are talking about, although neuroimaging studies comparing bilinguals and monolingual routinely find differences. Interestingly, many studies also have reported that bilinguals and monolinguals may differ with regard to brain imaging data but not on behavioural tasks. This psychology vs neuroscience difference with regard to actual experimental data and their interpretation on the question of cognitive reserve (Mishra, 2018) remains debated. Neural data do not predict behavioural outcomes and vice versa. Finally, what we know from neuropsychology cannot be used to theorise on normal population.

Even if we go with the general idea that bilingualism delays the onset of certain severe cognitive diseases such as AD, we have a few important questions to answer. The symptoms of AD are not homogeneous and they appear differently in different patients. It is not, therefore, clear which symptoms are delayed by so-called accumulated cognitive reserve through bilingualism. This has to be also linked to what exactly bilinguals practise so that they end up restructuring specific brain networks that are useful for certain cognitive functions. These could be in the domain of cognitive flexibility, attention, memory, set-shifting, creativity, decision making, or even emotion judgment. It is likely that by just controlling two languages we do not exercise all these brain areas that control this variety of functions. There is some evidence that bilingualism delays the clinical symptoms of AD (Mendez et al., 2020). It is understood that clinical symptoms do include many important cognitive functions. But we can't be sure which particular cognitive abilities will get restored or get disturbed in AD if the patient has been bilingual. In spite of these limitations, many studies do affirm the idea that bilingualism is a critical tool to enhance neuroplasticity of the brain, particularly domains related to higher cognition.

3.4. Literacy

Literacy is a strong modulator of cognition and cognitive reserve. Literacy involves formally acquiring reading and writing abilities through training. Humans have been using the auditory-verbal language for at least eighty thousand years. However, literacy is only four thousand years old. First evolved in the ancient civilisations of Egypt and China, it quickly took over as the most sophisticated means of communication and has remained so. Literacy training led to educational practices. As time went by, literates and illiterates created different cultures. In the past several decades, the scientific study of reading and writing within cognitive psychology has attracted great attention. Multiple theories and frameworks exist on how the brain processes visual letters and creates meaning. More recently researchers have been keen to know if literacy leads to cognitive plasticity. It is possible that many illiterate people are not bilingual speakers or do not exercise or play any sport. If they can get the benefit of being readers and writers then it could lead to a lot of advantages. It is very difficult to keep track of changes that literacy training brings, if it is acquired during childhood, since this may get confounded with many other input systems that can modify the brain during the growing years. There are still many pockets in the world where we find adult illiterates. Because of different cultural and socio-economic reasons these individuals could not afford formal training in literacy. They are today called either low literates or functional illiterates (Huettig & Mishra, 2014). These individuals show low ability in reading and writing. It would be interesting if it could be shown that literacy training in functionally illiterate individuals changes the structural patterns in the brain. This hypothesis has been tested in very few longitudinal studies on adult illiterates.

Huettig and colleagues (Skeide et al., 2017) trained a large number of functionally illiterate individuals in the Indian city of Lucknow, for about a year. These individuals had never gone to school before and had very low levels of literacy. The training included activities related to learning to read. A control group of similar functionally illiterate individuals were recruited who did not undergo any literacy training. As the training progressed, these individuals underwent brain imaging on simple tasks. The idea was to see to what extent this literacy training would change important cortical networks related to language, vision, and attention. The longitudinal changes in the brain of the training group revealed important changes in those regions and enhanced functional connectivity. A more recent re-examination of the same data further revealed higher cortico-cortical connections resulting from literacy training (Hervais-Adelman et al., 2019). Literacy training could create functional connectivity in distant subcortical areas linking the occipital lobe and the thalamus. These were probably the world's first longitudinal brain imaging studies to explore literacy-induced neuroplasticity. Many others have also observed a fundamental difference between literates and illiterates with regard to brain organisation (Dehaene et al., 2015). However, before these Indian studies, it was not known that even a short period of literacy training would lead to noticeable neuroplasticity in important cognitive networks. These results are very startling, but what is its effect on cognitive reserve? The researchers have not followed up to examine if the participants maintained their practice of reading and writing. Therefore, without this data, it is not possible to predict if this intervention will lead to any cognitive reserve in such individuals.

Constant practice over a long time seems to be the key to eventual cognitive reserve or any sustained neuroplasticity. It would be interesting to re-examine these individuals after a few years and see if their structural and functional connectivity has remained intact without such practice. The visual word form area which specifically evolved to take care of letter processing changes after long years of training (Dehaene-Lambertz et al., 2018). It is not clear if one year of training in adult illiterates can lead to the emergence of a visual word form area which will remain functional later. Currently, there is no data on neural changes in people who stopped or reduced reading later in life. In today's world of digital addiction, people are no longer reading traditionally. Further, it is not known how reading a book vs reading on digital platforms may change the brain differently.

3.5. Relationships

In countries like Japan and Sweden, solo living is on the rise (Druta & Ronald, 2020). The traditional formats of sustained relationships such as marriages are no longer taken seriously. Many popular news reports indicate that single people are more vulnerable to suicide and die younger than their married peers (Wyder et al., 2009). For that matter, any sustained relationship has also been shown to bring in additional neural health. It is therefore of interest to examine how relationships contribute to overall cognitive health. Cohabitation may be evolutionarily preferred since it enhances social binding and responsibilities. Besides, child care and care for the elderly within a family increases self-control. Interestingly, those who became widowed or divorced face higher risks of dementia similar to those who were never married (Håkansson et al., 2009). Relationships are continuous experiments with trust, empathy, and care that may, but not necessarily always do, include romantic love. Relationships induce a causal association between emotional states and attention/working memory. Love and marriage have been around for a long time. In spite of increased divorce rates around the world, cohabiting with a romantic partner remains a preferred choice. Studies show that there is higher activation of the brain's reward circuitry in individuals who experience romantic love than those who do not (Savulescu & Sandberg, 2008). Love and attachments modulate many important neurotransmitters in the brain. It is also a public perception that those who are in any long-term sustained relationship commit fewer crimes and show greater social adaptation. In one study, researchers administered the emotional Stroop task to a group of people who were in romantic love and compared them to those who were single. The emotional Stroop task requires one to stop responding to faces depicting positive or negative emotions. People in romantic love were better at suppressing their responses in the face of negative emotions than those who were single (Song et al., 2016). Interestingly, early-stage lovers showed greater inhibitory control on the emotional Stroop task than people who had been in long-term relationships. It may be because during the early courtship period, partners do their best to present their best selves forward and suppress any negative thoughts that can impair the evolving relationship. In another study, it was found that women who were in love performed lexical decision task more quickly if their partner's names were subliminally presented (Bianchi-Demicheli et al., 2006). This indicates that relationship status has a far-reaching effect on key components of cognition that may include early perception, decision making, and emotion regulation.

If we accept the logic that the reward circuitry is active and facilitates bonding between individuals in the beginning of any romantic relationship, then as the relationship grows, the stimuli may not exert the same power and the reward circuitry may not get activated to the same extent. With passing time, in long-term romantic relationships, wellbeing, life satisfaction, and self-esteem replace early obsession (Acevedo & Aron, 2009). The initial variables of quick gratification are replaced with a more sustained focus on mutual wellbeing. Apart from the usual effects of wellbeing and emotional stability, relationship status also has been linked to cognitive reserve. Those who are married seem to develop higher cognitive reserve compared to those who have had marital failure or are single (Håkansson et al., 2009). Marriage particularly boosts neural reserve that may delay the onset of dementia (Sommerlad et al., 2018), but it is not clear how exactly marriage improves one's cognitive health. It is likely that married people live in more socially networked situations and therefore can get much support in challenging conditions.

3.6. Video games

Humans have always played games for entertainment and building social cohesion. Children begin their early cognition through games. Apart from the benefits at the level of the body, games can also influence cognition. Technological progress, particularly the digital revolution, brought internet-based video games. These games not only provided recreation but also intellectual challenges. In the last few years, a growing number of researchers have found that playing cognitively demanding video games could enhance cognition and thus may bring cognitive neuroplasticity. Closed-loop video games are both immersive and interactive. They dynamically update the level of challenge the player experiences depending on their current performances. This can seriously excite the reward control systems of the brain and requires a high degree of selective attention. Video games mimic cognitive psychology tasks and expect the player to use similar brain networks for playing well (Mishra et al., 2016). These games use the latest technology such as virtual reality, motion tracking, and augmented reality including the best of display and physiological measures. Individuals can also be fitted with neurofeedback to know how they are dynamically adapting to the challenges of the game. Video games can be both action and non-action type. The action video games are more dynamic and immersive and have been shown to activate all major brain networks related to attention and motor control.

In one study, a group of older adults played a commercially available mind-training package for 20 hours. At the end of the training, data showed that players had enhanced performance on attention and visual memory tasks and scored higher on a scale that measured wellbeing compared to a control group, (Ballesteros et al., 2014). The results did not indicate any improvements in executive control, specifically in inhibitory control. However, in another study with a similar design, older people who were trained on non-action video games showed improvements in executive control (Basak et al., 2008). The discrepancies could be because of the method of training or conceptualisation of the different components of cognition. Attention and working memory are part of the schema of executive functions (Miyake et al., 2000). If one trains them there is a likelihood that overall executive control also gets boosted. When older adults are trained with such games, the cognitive benefits are immediate but disappear after three months if there has not been any periodic boosting (Ballesteros et al., 2015).

An important question is why video games that look and feel so different should strengthen performance on laboratory-based tasks. Figure 5.5 from Bavelier et al. (2012) exemplifies the scenario well. The different tasks that measure different cognitive functions that are used in playing video games look very different. These tasks have no immersive quality nor are they dynamic. Likely, they don't challenge the reward system or the control systems as a video game. Then why should there be any transfer effect at all, on playing these games? It is unlikely that playing a particular video game teaches only a particular skill. Bavelier et al. (2012) suggest that video game playing makes the individual more sensitive and capable towards environmental stimuli. They can then bring in the resources that they internalised in the game to any novel situation. Good players develop a high degree

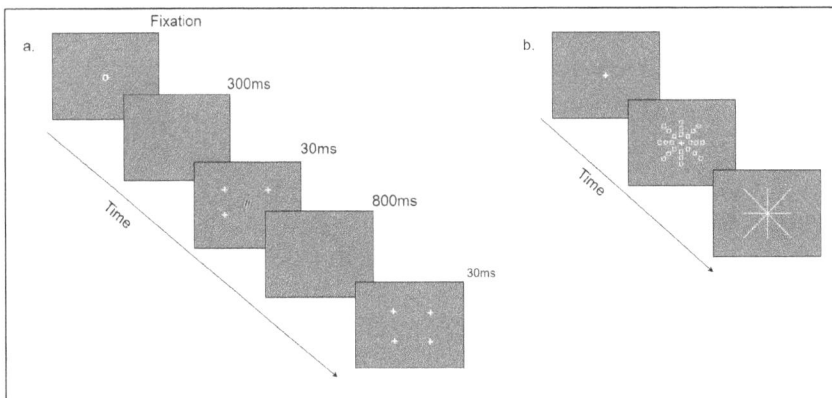

Figure 5.5 Example of the laboratory tasks. These tasks measure (a) contrast sensitivity and (b) visual search capacity.

Source: Adapted from Bavelier et al. (2012)

of sustained attention and decision-making ability for any novel situation. Attention training and measurements can be done in a variety of tasks. This view can generalise the effects of game-induced plasticity to novel domains.

There is another side to this story in that increased video game playing has been linked to the manifestation of pathological behaviour and changes in the brain. After all, compulsive video game playing is an addiction like others. In one study, it was found that those who play violent video games at least four hours every day show a decrease in grey matter volume. Behaviourally, they show less empathy (Mohammadi et al., 2020). Many experiments in the field of addiction psychology have shown that individuals addicted to long hours of playing such games show impulsive behaviour and abnormal grey matter volume or atrophy (Lee et al., 2016). We can't be entirely certain that measurements of grey matter changes have a direct and causal relationship to psychometric assessments. Addictive practices involving hours of self-absorption may likely lead to behaviour patterns that are not indicative of social and emotional wellbeing, just like one finds in gamblers or some groups of narcissistic criminals. It is important to note that the laboratory-based tasks that are done to measure attention or memory or cognitive control do not lead to long-term addiction. The action video games that utilise the same brain networks, however, can be addictive. The key difference is their immersion. Current reports from the world of virtual reality also suggest that it is very addictive and bad for overall mental health (Johnson et al., 2013). Internet addiction has already been declared to be a global health problem. Such addiction in the long term does not train attention in any healthy manner but rather impairs it. At the moment, we are not in a position to recommend the quantity of video gaming that will be beneficial beyond which there can be negative consequences. But one take-home message is that sustained playing of these games does induce changes in the brain/behaviour, and can be considered to contribute to neuroplasticity. It is also not clear if life-long playing of such games leads to any cognitive reserve or neural reserve against diseases.

4. Brain simulation

The physiological complexity of the human brain is unique in the natural world. It has 80 billion neurons and their intricate connections. These connections are the structural basis of computation. All learning and memory from stimuli and our knowledge are an outcome of changes in these structures and connections. So it makes perfect sense to attempt to make artificial brains with neurons and make them learn and see what structural or functional changes are observed as a function of that learning, or even create a faulty brain with faulty connections and see how any repair brings back learning and activates older knowledge systems. These are the basic assumptions of brain simulation and computation. Systems neuroscience attempts to model such connections using mathematical logic to understand the mechanistic principles of the brain. By simulation one can learn how the brain organises itself and learns from the outside world. Two major projects such as the American Brain Coalition's BRAIN Project and the European Human Brain Project have unearthed a vast amount of data from the brain. Modelling this data could reveal the nature of several diseases as well as pathologies. Brain simulation is a potentially useful method to learn about the brain artificially. The central problem is in artificially mimicking the biological complexity. Although there is no dearth of models that mimic computation carried out by neurons in specific brain areas, it has not been easy to model the cortical columns and large networks (dynamics of sparsely connected networks of excitatory and inhibitory spiking neurons). With an increase in computational power, it has become possible to model large networks that have hundreds of neurons. However, such adventure only aims for a mechanistic explanation of firing rates and tries to correlate it with behaviour (Devor et al., 2013).

Why does one need to simulate the brain? Most neuroscientists believe that computation can explain behaviour although they don't often use words such as mental states or phenomenology with regard to animals from whom such electrophysiological data is collected. The most dominant philosophy behind such an approach is to understand the brain by creating a model of it. This model may not be biological like the real brain but are complicated mathematical equations that are simulated on a computer platform. Brain simulation is a tool that can be used to understand the intricate nature of pathology and behavioural changes thereof in selected cases (Einevoll et al., 2019). Researchers use different "levels of analysis" during the modelling of biophysical data in the case of the brain. For instance, the organism *C. elegans* has 302 neurons and 500 synapses that have been modelled. One can imagine the complexity that is involved in such an enterprise or the human brain.

The focus of this chapter is neuroplasticity. It is about the fact that the brain learns and adapts to new stimuli and that has been important for our survival. Technically speaking, learning here in a strict neuroscience sense refers to noticeable structural changes in the brain. These changes could be in specific modules, those assumed specialised neural hubs that process specific types of information, or more general areas. I have also discussed the functional neuroplasticity induced by cognitive training and various habits that we engage with. Neuroplasticity is now being shown to be induced in just a few weeks of training and that shows improvements in various mental tasks (Zerilli, 2020). Various pre- and post-fMRI studies have shown that changes happen at the structural level of the brain with intense training. However, how does one simulate neuroplasticity in an artificial computational network? The assumption here is derived from the fact that neural networks learn with repeated exposure to stimuli that change some dimensions of the network itself. Of course, in the artificial world, there won't be any structural changes, but learning will induce functional connections among networks that are widely distributed. For example, when children with a learning disability are trained over weeks, then functional connections emerge within different networks in frontal, parietal, and other attentional areas (Iuculano et al., 2015). In particular, brain networks that did not communicate before start communicating to serve specific tasks as a function of training. In a simulated neural architecture, this would mean having artificial neurons whose connections change indicating learning and neuroplasticity. For example, in one study, researchers created a virtual organism that had only nine neurons (Wang & Orchard, 2017). As a function of learning, they observed the evolution of neuroplasticity in this network over some time. This may seem absurd if we compare it to the complexity at the human scale, but artificial simulation at the moment is just that.

Neuroplasticity for the human brain does not merely mean acquiring concrete knowledge of things but also the many other experiential and subjective aspects of using them, and being with them. This is not possible to simulate in an artificial network of few neurons. In other chapters of this book, I have addressed the clear weakness of deep learning algorithmics and the general problem with AI. They are relevant here on the question of testing neuroplasticity with artificial networks that are not brains. Biological brains learn and modify themselves in mysterious ways which we then see in behaviour. Therefore, even if we make an artificial brain and allow it to learn and change itself, we may not see it developing phenomenological knowledge of that learning. Of course, if we have very accurate neurological knowledge of brain diseases, we can simulate a similar network and create the disease and then see where the fault lies. However, our current knowledge of such diseases is also at best minimal and therefore, this also plagues our attempt to simulate such complicated human diseases in animal models or computer networks. Fundamentally then, we have to question and understand what " 'learning" and "adoption" mean in the artificial and how significantly they are different from the biological brains on all those important parameters that we care about.

5. Future of neuroplasticity

The concept of neuroplasticity is an elusive one. It is mysterious that everyday things that we do intensely can change our brain. Since the times of James and Cajal, our interest in the brain and its working has only increased. The increase in brain-based diseases worldwide across different population groups has created more awareness in the public regarding brain health. Increasing technological advancements and lifestyle changes and their impact on the health of the brain are yet to be understood fully. Neuroplasticity is understood as the brain's ability to change itself as a function of both internal and external changes. In this section I will raise a few final points that will be of value in understanding this concept in a holistic manner.

It has to be clear from the outset that we are talking about both brain states and mental states when we refer to concepts like neuroplasticity. Concepts like cognitive neuroplasticity and cognitive reserve point towards a brain-mind interaction. Historically, this concept has mostly been projected from a neural point of view. The dissociation between mental states and their corresponding brain states remains debated within cognitive science. However, neuro-psycho causality is the main theoretical question in the study of neuroplasticity. Given this, a somewhat strict differentiation between neural and cognitive reserve as concepts is necessary. One pertains to changes in the psychological attributes manifested as behaviour, and the other to structural changes in the brain with or without any clear psychological feature. For example, in the domain of bilingualism advantage, there is no correlation between changes in the brain and performance on psychological tasks. It is possible that someone may have a very good neural reserve, but not appropriate cognition. Most studies do not consider lifelong experiences of participants but report sketchy details at one point in time. This can seriously hinder our understanding of neuroplasticity as a dynamic mechanism which keeps changing with regard to challenges of life's circumstances.

The other most challenging issue is that of cultural and individual differences in neuroplasticity. Human experience is embodied in specific cultures and is diverse. The experiential angle of neuroplasticity is culture bound. The growing field of cultural neuroscience (Chiao, 2009) shows that neural functions are different in different populations who come from different cultures. Such differences come down all the way to specific cognitive mechanisms like attention, working memory, and visual perception. If one's cognition is relative to one's culture, then no universal theory is possible. Therefore, the type of neuroplasticity that may be induced, say staying a lifetime in New York City, is not the same as staying in Papua New Guinea. That is because cognitive demands are very different in each location and therefore, we can't use the same instrument of measurements. Of course, the fundamental operations of the brains of all humans are similar despite their other differences but within this, there may be similarities. This is also valid for different cognitive functions such as attention, memory, and decision making. It is possible that in some cultures people do not need a lot of selective attention while in other cultures its demand is very high (Kitayama & Murata, 2013). Therefore, neuroplastic changes in attention will be different in different cultural groups. Future studies on neural or cognitive reserve will have to focus on cultural and individual variation.

Another limitation is the exceptional emphasis on neuropsychology in the conception and theory of neuroplasticity. The concept of cognitive reserve is usually linked to the ability of the brain to withstand the appearance of any neurodegenerative diseases. However, we must first find out how the brain changes and creates neuroplasticity during normal living and everyday wear and tear. It is essential to first develop theories of a normal healthy brain's maturation and plasticity. Very few studies have focused on the link between a healthy brain and longevity. There are many cases in which people attain great longevity without any extra cognitive training whatsoever. Therefore, it is not clear from the neuropsychological models what is the role of cognitive reserve if the person remains healthy. There are also insufficient models of normal maturation of different cognitive systems. Most cognitive systems such as attention, executive control, and memory start to decline around 30 years of age (Reisberg, 1984). In sum, the brain-based theories of neuroplasticity have their limitations since we know little of the brain functioning anyway. A proper convergence of theories of cognitive psychology and neuroscience models of the human brain is the need of the hour.

Theodor Dobzhansky had said that everything can only be understood in the light of evolution. Evolution and its mechanism of natural selection are the forces that predict changes in material systems. The human cerebral cortex has evolved in the last 3 million years or so to reach its current state and of course, the forces of evolution are still at work. Language, attention, memory, and a range of higher-order cognitive systems have evolved recently. If the higher-order cognitive systems are so recent then our cognitive evolution is in its infancy. The Upper Palaeolithic cultural revolution which is often linked to cognitive evolution happened about 50,000 years ago (Sophie et al., 2009). Seen in the light of evolution we might understand neuroplasticity differently. Technological progress has always led to evolutionary shifts. Immersion of modern humans in digital technologies is being viewed with perplexity at the moment. Ultimately evolution will prefer that the brain architecture and cognitive functions are beneficial to the species. For instance, after COVID-19, most people on earth have adapted quickly to a digital world since it is the requirement of the time. If this continues, I can speculate that brains will permanently adapt to these changes. Online internet and virtual life will be the preferred norm of experience. However, it is not easy to predict which attribute natural selection will select. The gradual changes in the frontal and the parietal lobes are taken as evidence of the cognition-ready brain. Therefore, increasing demands on cognition will bring in further changes to such important structures (Anderson & Finlay, 2014). Further, most cognitive and neuroscientists take a modular approach to the systems they deal with. If cognition is modular and is made of different interactive modules, then we cannot be sure of the rate of change of individual modules as a function of evolution. Many studies also show dynamic interactions among apparently different modules (Burkart et al., 2017). Michel Anderson in his *After Phrenology: Neural Reuse and the Interactive Brain* suggests that the current description of the term neural reissue is not very clear (Anderson, 2014). Changes in the brain's structures to adapt to a new demand is based on already existing older structures. Therefore, it is unlikely that any new structures will emerge from new activities.

However, the kind of activities that humans adapt to and which ensure the continuation of the species will be preferred by natural selection. For example, when humans started to develop culture and arts around 40,000 years ago, they had no idea that these activities would remain a part of human affairs. Similarly, when agriculture began some 11,000 years ago it was not known if humans would still depend on this community-based food production in the distant future. Today those who produce symbolic art are highly valued in any society. Interestingly art, music, dance, and even doing science have been linked to better mental health and wellbeing. Will the same happen for playing video games or internet browsing? Cultural adaptation to certain behaviours influences neural changes in the long term (Colagè & d'Errico, 2020). Apart from neuroplasticity at the individual level, there can also be collective neuroplasticity. Large scale changes in an entire population in any location can show different adaptive skills. For example, Yamada et al. (2016) measured cognitive changes and dementia in a large population of atomic bomb survivors in Hiroshima, Japan. Interestingly, radiation level did not influence dementia percentage or cognitive decline. However, more natural causes like old age and other habits did predict slowing down of cognition. The study is interesting, being one of the few large-scale longitudinal studies on a very specific population that has seen one of the worst man-made horrors in the modern world. It is possible that having seen such horror and lived through it, many developed resilience that prevented the kind of decline expected to result from such a catastrophe. Similarly, children from war-ravaged countries may develop extreme resilience that is necessary for their survival. Therefore, large-scale effects such as wars, famines, or even what we are seeing in the form of coronavirus and its impact can change collective human behaviour and have the potential to induce neuroplasticity. After all, an individual only functions within the large canopy of cultures and in the network of other humans. The role of culture and evolution in human cognition is undeniably strong. Therefore, we should shift our focus from neurodegenerative diseases slightly and look at the larger picture of human adaptation in the real world as evidence of collective neuroplasticity.

6. Summary

Neuroplasticity and its many variations are currently the most debated topic in a variety of brain and mind sciences. The simple reason is that it shows the potential for application. Once we know how to change our brains and in turn our minds knowledgeably, we can ensure our survival and longevity. However, there is no agreement that mental states are direct results of changes in the neural strata. Therefore, I like to view neuroplasticity and cognitive plasticity differently. They may interact at times but their relationship is not causal. However, given the state of current research advancements, it is likely that many new recommendations will come for enhancing neuroplasticity in future. Novel discoveries in brain sciences will influence thinking in the mind sciences. What if after these considerations, we still do not know why we need sophisticated cognition? It cannot be a matter of human greed that we have displayed elsewhere. We need to know clearly why boosting our brain power is so essential for our individual and community-based survival. There are also questions of ethics involved in this issue that I have not dealt with in this chapter. To what extent are externally induced brain changes ethical? This also has the potential to induce a bias in society. For example, a group of children who can afford brain-training programs and are motivated to practise and develop will have a different baseline from others who cannot. At the moment, there are no regulatory bodies that are looking into these questions. Given the massive expected use of AI and VR, the future of neuroplasticity research will be different from what it looks like now.

References

Abutalebi, J., & Green, D. W. (2016). Neuroimaging of language control in bilinguals: Neural adaptation and reserve. *Bilingualism: Language and Cognition, 19*(4), 689–698.

Acevedo, B. P., & Aron, A. (2009). Does a long-term relationship kill romantic love? *Review of General Psychology, 13*(1), 59–65.

Alladi, S., Bak, T. H., Duggirala, V., Surampudi, B., Shailaja, M., Shukla, A. K., Chaudhuri, J. R., & Kaul, S. (2013). Bilingualism delays age at onset of dementia, independent of education and immigration status. *Neurology, 81*(22), 1938–1944.

Anderson, M. L. (2014). *After phrenology: Neural reuse and the interactive brain.* MIT Press.

Anderson, M. L., & Finlay, B. L. (2014). Allocating structure to function: The strong links between neuroplasticity and natural selection. *Frontiers in Human Neuroscience, 7,* 918.

Andrews, S. C., Curtin, D., Hawi, Z., Wongtrakun, J., Stout, J. C., & Coxon, J. P. (2020). Intensity matters: High-intensity interval exercise enhances motor cortex plasticity more than moderate exercise. *Cerebral Cortex, 30*(1), 101–112.

Azmitia, E. C. (2007). Cajal and brain plasticity: Insights relevant to emerging concepts of mind. *Brain Research Reviews, 55*(2), 395–405.

Bak, T. H., & Alladi, S. (2014). Can being bilingual affect the onset of dementia? *Future Neurology, 9*(2), 101–103.

Ballesteros, S., Mayas, J., Prieto, A., Toril, P., Pita, C., Laura, P. D. L., Reales, J. M., & Waterworth, J. A. (2015). A randomized controlled trial of brain training with non-action video games in older adults: Results of the 3-month follow-up. *Frontiers in Aging Neuroscience, 7,* 45.

Ballesteros, S., Prieto, A., Mayas, J., Toril, P., Pita, C., Ponce de León, L., Reales, J. M., & Waterworth, J. (2014). Brain training with non-action video games enhances aspects of cognition in older adults: A randomized controlled trial. *Frontiers in Aging Neuroscience, 6,* 277.

Barulli, D., & Stern, Y. (2013). Efficiency, capacity, compensation, maintenance, plasticity: Emerging concepts in cognitive reserve. *Trends in Cognitive Sciences, 17*(10), 502–509.

Basak, C., Boot, W. R., Voss, M. W., & Kramer, A. F. (2008). Can training in a real-time strategy video game attenuate cognitive decline in older adults? *Psychology and Aging, 23*(4), 765.

Bavelier, D., Green, C. S., Pouget, A., & Schrater, P. (2012). Brain plasticity through the life span: Learning to learn and action video games. *Annual Review of Neuroscience*, *35*, 391–416.

Berlucchi, G. (2002). The origin of the term plasticity in the neurosciences: Ernesto Lugaro and chemical synaptic transmission. *Journal of the History of the Neurosciences*, *11*(3), 305–309.

Bettcher, B. M., Gross, A. L., Gavett, B. E., Widaman, K. F., Fletcher, E., Dowling, N. M., Buckley, R. F., Arenaza-Urquijo, E. M., Zahodne, L. B., Hohman, T. J., & Vonk, J. M. (2019). Dynamic change of cognitive reserve: Associations with changes in brain, cognition, and diagnosis. *Neurobiology of Aging*, *83*, 95–104.

Berlucchi, G., & Buchtel, H. A. (2009). Neuronal plasticity: Historical roots and evolution of meaning. *Experimental Brain Research*, *192*(3), 307–319.

Bianchi-Demicheli, F., Grafton, S. T., & Ortigue, S. (2006). The power of love on the human brain. *Social Neuroscience*, *1*(2), 90–103.

Braver, T. S. (2012). The variable nature of cognitive control: A dual mechanisms framework. *Trends in Cognitive Sciences*, *16*(2), 106–113.

Burkart, J. M., Schubiger, M. N., & van Schaik, C. P. (2017). The evolution of general intelligence. *Behavioral and Brain Sciences*, *40*.

Chacko, S. C., Quinzi, F., De Fano, A., Bianco, V., Mussini, E., Berchicci, M., Perri, R. L., & Di Russo, F. (2020). A single bout of vigorous-intensity aerobic exercise affects reactive, but not proactive cognitive brain functions. *International Journal of Psychophysiology*, *147*, 233–243.

Chiao, J. Y. (2009). Cultural neuroscience: A once and future discipline. *Progress in Brain Research*, *178*, 287–304.

Clark, D. O., Xu, H., Moser, L., Adeoye, P., Lin, A. W., Tangney, C. C., Risacher, S. L., Saykin, A. J., Considine, R. V., & Unverzagt, F. W. (2019). MIND food and speed of processing training in older adults with low education, the MIND-Speed Alzheimer's disease prevention pilot trial. *Contemporary Clinical Trials*, *84*, 105814.

Colagè, I., & d'Errico, F. (2020). Culture: The driving force of human cognition. *Topics in Cognitive Science*, *12*(2), 654–672.

Cramer, S. C., Sur, M., Dobkin, B. H., O'Brien, C., Sanger, T. D., Trojanowski, J. Q., Rumsey, J. M., Hicks, R., Cameron, J., Chen, D., & Chen, W. G. (2011). Harnessing neuroplasticity for clinical applications. *Brain*, *134*(6), 1591–1609.

Dehaene, S., Cohen, L., Morais, J., & Kolinsky, R. (2015). Illiterate to literate: Behavioural and cerebral changes induced by reading acquisition. *Nature Reviews Neuroscience*, *16*(4), 234–244.

Dehaene-Lambertz, G., Monzalvo, K., & Dehaene, S. (2018). The emergence of the visual word form: Longitudinal evolution of category-specific ventral visual areas during reading acquisition. *PLoS Biology*, *16*(3), e2004103.

Devor, A., Bandettini, P. A., Boas, D. A., Bower, J. M., Buxton, R. B., Cohen, L. B., Dale, A. M., Einevoll, G. T., Fox, P. T., Franceschini, M. A., & Yodh, A. G. (2013). The challenge of connecting the dots in the brain. *Neuron*, *80*(2), 270–274.

Druta, O., & Ronald, R. (2020). Living alone together in Tokyo share houses. *Social & Cultural Geography*, 1–18.

Einevoll, G. T., Destexhe, A., Diesmann, M., Grün, S., Jirsa, V., de Kamps, M., Migliore, M., Ness, T. V., Plesser, H. E., & Schürmann, F. (2019). The scientific case for brain simulations. *Neuron*, *102*(4), 735–744.

Elbert, T., Pantev, C., Wienbruch, C., Rockstroh, B., & Taub, E. (1995). Increased cortical representation of the fingers of the left hand in string players. *Science*, 270(5234), 305–307.

Fabbro, F. (2001). The bilingual brain: Cerebral representation of languages. *Brain and Language*, 79(2), 211–222.

Filip, P., Gallea, C., Lehéricy, S., Lungu, O., & Bareš, M. (2019). Neural scaffolding as the foundation for stable performance of aging cerebellum. *The Cerebellum*, 18(3), 500–510.

Goh, J. O., & Park, D. C. (2009). Neuroplasticity and cognitive aging: The scaffolding theory of aging and cognition. *Restorative Neurology and Neuroscience*, 27(5), 391–403.

Gomez-Pinilla, F., & Tyagi, E. (2013). Diet and cognition: Interplay between cell metabolism and neuronal plasticity. *Current Opinion in Clinical Nutrition and Metabolic Care*, 16(6), 726.

Green, D. W. (1998). Mental control of the bilingual lexico-semantic system. *Bilingualism: Language and Cognition*, 1(2), 67–81.

Green, D. W., & Abutalebi, J. (2013). Language control in bilinguals: The adaptive control hypothesis. *Journal of Cognitive Psychology*, 25(5), 515–530.

Håkansson, K., Rovio, S., Helkala, E. L., Vilska, A. R., Winblad, B., Soininen, H., Nissinen, A., Mohammed, A. H., & Kivipelto, M. (2009). Association between mid-life marital status and cognitive function in later life: Population-based cohort study. *The BMJ*, 339, b2462.

Hebb, D. O. (2005). *The organization of behavior: A neuropsychological theory*. Psychology Press.

Hervais-Adelman, A., Kumar, U., Mishra, R. K., Tripathi, V. N., Guleria, A., Singh, J. P., Eisner, F., & Huettig, F. (2019). Learning to read recycles visual cortical networks without destruction. *Science Advances*, 5(9), eaax0262.

Hötting, K., & Röder, B. (2013). Beneficial effects of physical exercise on neuroplasticity and cognition. *Neuroscience & Biobehavioral Reviews*, 37(9), 2243–2257.

Huettig, F., & Mishra, R. K. (2014). How literacy acquisition affects the illiterate mind–A critical examination of theories and evidence. *Language and Linguistics Compass*, 8(10), 401–427.

Iuculano, T., Rosenberg-Lee, M., Richardson, J., Tenison, C., Fuchs, L., Supekar, K., & Menon, V. (2015). Cognitive tutoring induces widespread neuroplasticity and remediates brain function in children with mathematical learning disabilities. *Nature Communications*, 6(1), 1–10.

James, W., Burkhardt, F., Bowers, F., & Skrupskelis, I. K. (1890). *The principles of psychology* (Vol. 1, No. 2). Macmillan.

Johnson, D., Jones, C., Scholes, L., & Carras, M. (2013). *Videogames and wellbeing: A comprehensive review*. Young and Well Cooperative Research Centre.

Kitayama, S., & Murata, A. (2013). Culture modulates perceptual attention: An event-related potential study. *Social Cognition*, 31(6), 758–769.

Kosmidis, M. H., Vlachos, G. S., Anastasiou, C. A., Yannakoulia, M., Dardiotis, E., Hadjigeorgiou, G., Sakka, P., Ntanasi, E., & Scarmeas, N. (2018). Dementia prevalence in greece. *Alzheimer Disease & Associated Disorders*, 32(3), 232–239.

Kramer, A. F., Hahn, S., McAuley, E., Cohen, N. J., Banich, M. T., Harrison, C., Chason, J., Boileau, R. A., Bardell, L., Colcombe, A., & Vakil, E. (2001). Exercise, aging and cognition: Healthy body, healthy mind. *Human Factors Interventions for the Health Care of Older Adults*, 91–120.

Lee, D., Lee, J., Yoon, K. J., Kee, N., & Jung, Y. C. (2016). Impaired anterior insular activation during risky decision making in young adults with internet gaming disorder. *NeuroReport*, *27*(8), 605–609.

Li, P., Legault, J., & Litcofsky, K. A. (2014). Neuroplasticity as a function of second language learning: Anatomical changes in the human brain. *Cortex*, *58*, 301–324.

Liu-Ambrose, T., Nagamatsu, L. S., Graf, P., Beattie, B. L., Ashe, M. C., & Handy, T. C. (2010). Resistance training and executive functions: A 12-month randomized controlled trial. *Archives of Internal Medicine*, *170*(2), 170–178.

Lorås, H., Haga, M., & Sigmundsson, H. (2020). Effect of different exercise modes at high intensity on immediate learning and arousal. *International Journal of Sport and Exercise Psychology*, *18*(1), 33–45.

Lövdén, M., Bäckman, L., Lindenberger, U., Schaefer, S., & Schmiedek, F. (2010). A theoretical framework for the study of adult cognitive plasticity. *Psychological Bulletin*, *136*(4), 659.

Mechelli, A., Crinion, J. T., Noppeney, U., O'Doherty, J., Ashburner, J., Frackowiak, R. S., & Price, C. J. (2004). Structural plasticity in the bilingual brain. *Nature*, *431*(7010), 757–757.

McDonnell, M. N., Buckley, J. D., Opie, G. M., Ridding, M. C., & Semmler, J. G. (2013). A single bout of aerobic exercise promotes motor cortical neuroplasticity. *Journal of Applied Physiology*, *114*(9), 1174–1182.

McKenzie, C., Bucks, R. S., Weinborn, M., Bourgeat, P., Salvado, O., Gavett, B. E., & Alzheimer's Disease Neuroimaging Initiative. (2020). Cognitive reserve predicts future executive function decline in older adults with Alzheimer's disease pathology but not age-associated pathology. *Neurobiology of Aging*, *88*, 119–127.

Mendez, M. F., Chavez, D., & Akhlaghipour, G. (2020). Bilingualism delays expression of Alzheimer's clinical syndrome. *Dementia and Geriatric Cognitive Disorders*, 1–9.

Mishra, J., Anguera, J. A., & Gazzaley, A. (2016). Video games for neuro-cognitive optimization. *Neuron*, *90*(2), 214–218.

Mishra, R. K. (2018). *Bilingualism and cognitive control* (Vol. 6). Springer.

Miyake, A., Friedman, N. P., Emerson, M. J., Witzki, A. H., Howerter, A., & Wager, T. D. (2000). The unity and diversity of executive functions and their contributions to complex "frontal lobe" tasks: A latent variable analysis. *Cognitive Psychology*, *41*(1), 49–100.

Mohammadi, B., Szycik, G. R., te Wildt, B., Heldmann, M., Samii, A., & Münte, T. F. (2020). Structural brain changes in young males addicted to video-gaming. *Brain and Cognition*, *139*, 105518.

Monte Ferreira, F. R., Nogueira, M. I., & DeFelipe, J. (2014). The influence of James and Darwin on Cajal and his research into the neuron theory and evolution of the nervous system. *Frontiers in Neuroanatomy*, *8*, 1.

Mungas, D., Gavett, B., Fletcher, E., Farias, S. T., DeCarli, C., & Reed, B. (2018). Education amplifies brain atrophy effect on cognitive decline: Implications for cognitive reserve. *Neurobiology of Aging*, *68*, 142–150.

Pantev, C., Oostenveld, R., Engelien, A., Ross, B., Roberts, L. E., & Hoke, M. (1998). Increased auditory cortical representation in musicians. *Nature*, *392*(6678), 811–814.

Park, D. C., & Reuter-Lorenz, P. (2009). The adaptive brain: Aging and neurocognitive scaffolding. *Annual Review of Psychology*, *60*, 173–196.

Park, D. C., & Schwarz, N. (Eds.). (2012). *Cognitive aging: A primer*. Psychology Press.

Perani, D., & Abutalebi, J. (2015). Bilingualism, dementia, cognitive and neural reserve. *Current Opinion in Neurology, 28*(6), 618–625.

Petersson, S. D., & Philippou, E. (2016). Mediterranean diet, cognitive function, and dementia: A systematic review of the evidence. *Advances in Nutrition, 7*(5), 889–904.

Reisberg, B. (1984). Stages of cognitive decline. *The American Journal of Nursing, 84*(2), 225–228.

Richards, M., Hardy, R., & Wadsworth, M. E. (2003). Does active leisure protect cognition? Evidence from a national birth cohort. *Social Science & Medicine, 56*(4), 785–792.

Rovio, S., Spulber, G., Nieminen, L. J., Niskanen, E., Winblad, B., Tuomilehto, J., . . . & Kivipelto, M. (2010). The effect of midlife physical activity on structural brain changes in the elderly. *Neurobiology of Aging, 31*(11), 1927–1936.

Salthouse, T. A. (2004). What and when of cognitive aging. *Current Directions in Psychological Science, 13*(4), 140–144.

Savulescu, J., & Sandberg, A. (2008). Neuroenhancement of love and marriage: The chemicals between us. *Neuroethics, 1*(1), 31–44.

Shaywitz, B. A. (1999). Development, learning, and neuroplasticity: Where we are now. *The Changing Nervous System: Neurobehavioral Consequences of Early Brain Disorders, 389*.

Singh, N., & Mishra, R. K. (2012). Does language proficiency modulate oculomotor control? Evidence from Hindi – English bilinguals. *Bilingualism: Language and Cognition, 15*(4), 771–781.

Singh, N., & Mishra, R. K. (2013). Second language proficiency modulates conflict-monitoring in an oculomotor Stroop task: Evidence from Hindi-English bilinguals. *Frontiers in Psychology, 4*, 322.

Singh, N., & Mishra, R. K. (2015). The modulatory role of second language proficiency on performance monitoring: Evidence from a saccadic countermanding task in high and low proficient bilinguals. *Frontiers in Psychology, 5*, 1481.

Skeide, M. A., Kumar, U., Mishra, R. K., Tripathi, V. N., Guleria, A., Singh, J. P., Eisner, F., & Huettig, F. (2017). Learning to read alters cortico-subcortical crosstalk in the visual system of illiterates. *Science Advances, 3*(5), e1602612.

Sommerlad, A., Ruegger, J., Singh-Manoux, A., Lewis, G., & Livingston, G. (2018). Marriage and risk of dementia: Systematic review and meta-analysis of observational studies. *Journal of Neurology, Neurosurgery, and Psychiatry, 89*(3), 231–238.

Song, S., Zou, Z., Song, H., Wang, Y., d'Oleire Uquillas, F., Wang, H., & Chen, H. (2016). Romantic love is associated with enhanced inhibitory control in an emotional stop-signal task. *Frontiers in Psychology, 7*, 1574.

Sophie, A., Coolidge, F. L., & Wynn, T. (Eds.). (2009). *Cognitive archaeology and human evolution*. Cambridge University Press.

Stahnisch, F. W. (2015). Joseph von Gerlach (1820–1896). *Journal of Neurology, 262*(5), 1397–1399.

Stein, M., Winkler, C., Kaiser, A., & Dierks, T. (2014). Structural brain changes related to bilingualism: Does immersion make a difference?. *Frontiers in Psychology, 5*, 1116.

Stern, Y. (2009). Cognitive reserve. *Neuropsychologia, 47*(10), 2015–2028.

Sulpizio, S., Del Maschio, N., Del Mauro, G., Fedeli, D., & Abutalebi, J. (2020). Bilingualism as a gradient measure modulates functional connectivity of language and control networks. *NeuroImage, 205*, 116306.

Taylor, A. M., & Holscher, H. D. (2020). A review of dietary and microbial connections to depression, anxiety, and stress. *Nutritional Neuroscience, 23*(3), 237–250.

Tervaniemi, M. (2009). Musicians-same or different?. *Annals of the New York Academy of Sciences, 1169*(1), 151–156.

Wang, L., & Orchard, J. (2017). Investigating the evolution of a neuroplasticity network for learning. *IEEE Transactions on Systems, Man, and Cybernetics: Systems, 49*(10), 2131–2143.

Whalley, L. J., Deary, I. J., Appleton, C. L., & Starr, J. M. (2004). Cognitive reserve and the neurobiology of cognitive aging. *Ageing Research Reviews, 3*(4), 369–382.

Wyder, M., Ward, P., & De Leo, D. (2009). Separation as a suicide risk factor. *Journal of Affective Disorders, 116*(3), 208–213.

Yamada, M., Landes, R. D., Mimori, Y., Nagano, Y., & Sasaki, H. (2016). Radiation effects on cognitive function among atomic bomb survivors exposed at or after adolescence. *The American Journal of Medicine, 129*(6), 586–591.

Zerilli, J. (2020). *The adaptable mind: What neuroplasticity and neural reuse tells us about language and cognition*. Oxford University Press.

Zhang, H., Lee, A., & Qiu, A. (2017). A posterior-to-anterior shift of brain functional dynamics in aging. *Brain Structure and Function, 222*(8), 3665–3676.

Zhang, H., Wu, Y. J., & Thierry, G. (2020). Bilingualism and aging: A focused neuroscientific review. *Journal of Neurolinguistics, 54*, 100890.

6   Artificial Intelligence and Agency

1. Artificial Intelligence (AI) and philosophical issues

When we talk of artificial intelligence systems (henceforth referred to as "the AI") within the ambit of mind-brain sciences, the immediate question one can ask is this: Can they ever be like us? That is, will they have minds like us and do things unsupervised? It is widely believed that the AI is not natural intelligence and does not arise automatically in nature (Henderson, 2007). It is artificial since humans have created it and they control it. However, there has been much debate in recent years on the AI having a kind of consciousness that can be termed "machine consciousness." While some have used the AI and computational modelling to study human consciousness, others have tried to explore if consciousness is possible in the artificial (Clowes et al., 2007). While the former is widely used today by cognitive scientists as a tool, the latter is thought to be nearly impossible. Although the AI do not have consciousness and agency defined in the conventional sense – they have vast computing powers. This power gives them the ability to quantify, find patterns, generalise, and finally make predictions. Big data mining coupled with such predictive ability makes them solve multidisciplinary problems better than humans. More recent progress has seen massive use of the AI in domains such as weather forecasting, telemedicine, and space science. Expert opinions suggest that in a few decades the AI will have its uses in most domains of our lives and will be super intelligent (Müller & Bostrom, 2016). They will have high embodied intelligence and will solve mega-problems such as global warming and poverty. However, the major questions on the AI today are not as much about their utility given their computational powers but more about their having those attributes of the mind that we humans have.

Since the cognitive revolution, Artificial Intelligence has consistently made progress in spite of both philosophical and empirical scepticism. Alan Turing's paper "Can Machines Think?" led to the emergence of the field of AI (see Figure 6.1 for a representation of the test of intelligence developed by Turing). Since then, there has been a massive growth in AI's computational powers. At the same time, many philosophical concerns

DOI: 10.4324/9781003316053-6

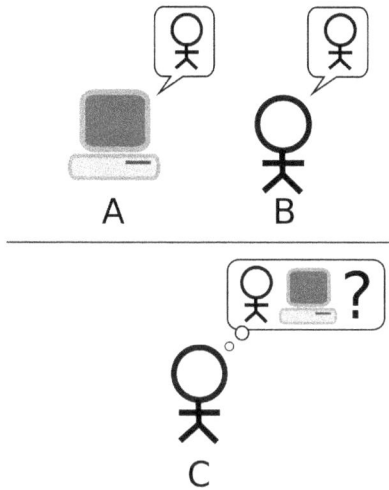

Figure 6.1 Schematic representation of Turing test (Saygin et al., 2000). The computer A passes the Turing test if a person C interacting with a computer A and a human B can't differentiate between the two. This would suggest that the computer A was able to successfully mimic the responses of a human being.

Source: Image: Wikipedia Commons

have posed challenges, mainly if AI has a mind and consciousness of the type we humans have. Therefore, the approach to AI has been rather pessimistic inside mainstream cognitive science. Since cognitive scientists care about the mind and higher-order cognitive functions which the AI simply do not have. Very early on, Hubert Dreyfus had suggested that machines just can't think and be like us (Dreyfus, 1979). John Searle's Chinese room argument had maintained that machines can't generate biological consciousness (Searle, 1980) and that they don't have minds. The argument was that machines may use syntax but they have no inherent semantics. Concepts like intentionality, self-consciousness, and voluntary goals are not to be found in the artificial, even if they may demonstrate superior computational powers, i.e., calculators and computers. Therefore, in principle there has to be a distinction between what biological machines like our brains can do and what artificial machines cannot do. Highly sophisticated machines do not naturally project meaning like brains do. They don't have a personalised model of the world as we do which gives us self-awareness. Therefore, machines may follow instructions but they are not agents that experience anything. Humans have not been able to accord the AI the status of moral agents that have their own selves. Personhood is intrinsically linked to agency, intentionality, and such higher properties that are only unique to biological agents that have consciousness (Behdadi & Munthe, 2020).

Let us agree that the machines have no consciousness, intentionality, and subjectivity of the type we have. If this is true, then they are not true agents in the natural world and have no phenomenal experience. This assertion flows from the position that our claims to subjectivity, consciousness, and experiential selves are unquestionable. They are ontological facts of nature. However, this point of view has also been criticised by others who pose a materialistic theory of the mind and consciousness. For example, according to the prominent philosopher Daniel Dennett, the problem that the AI poses is philosophical and we can easily sort it (Dennett, 1978). Dennett says that we are just computational machines and are very similar to robots. Our brains are made of millions of components although they are of natural origin (Dennett, 1988) that give rise to so-called consciousness and our various claims about mentality. An extreme version of such a proposal even denies any mention of mentality and consciousness (Churchland, 1981). Although such proposals do not attract much attention these days, they do pose questions about consciousness. This legacy goes all the way to Fodor's "Computational Theory of Mind" and computational behaviourism that has been the mainstream in neurosciences (Fetzer, 2004).

Both humans and AI use symbols for computation. Cognitive scientists believe that the human mind creates representations of objects and ideas using symbols. Since we cannot directly perceive external reality and have no access to what's out there, we have to represent them. However, Gibson challenged this view in the 1960s, proposing his theory of direct perception (Gibson, 2002). The Gestalt psychologists have similarly attempted to explain perception through direct sensory experience and phenomenology of objects given their organisation. These views became secondary in mainstream cognitive science that adopted the information processing approach and mind was considered to be a computational device that uses symbols. Even if both the AI and humans use "symbolic logic," the symbols have perceptual grounding for the biological brains. While the human brain could very well be a computing device, this does not explain how it generates "phenomenal experience." Therefore, currently there is no motivation for humans to suspend their claims to consciousness following such proposals but to understand it and then extend it to the AI, if that's possible, while we remain intuitively convinced that the AI does not have those powers that we have in the domains of "thinking," "perceiving," and "feeling."

There are yet other proposals that extend consciousness to everything. For example, in a subfield of philosophy of the mind called panpsychism, it is assumed that even non-biological agents may have consciousness. Consciousness is everywhere and not unique to the living (Strawson, 2016). This theory views everything that's there in the universe as having some sort of consciousness. Since it has not been possible to demonstrate how mental properties arise from the physical, we have to accept the proposal that the physical might also have mental aspects to it. Otherwise, the mental just can't emerge from a vacuum (Strawson, 2006). Following this reasoning, we can thus say that the AI, being physical systems, may also have mental properties. But the connection between panpsychism and the AI has not been fully fleshed out yet.

It is possible that very sophisticated AI machines do have some attributes of consciousness that we humans have. For example, one important feature of our consciousness is to provide us objective information about things in the world. Attention plays a key role in this mechanism. Image processing algorithms can "find" objects using attention – whatever that may mean in the context of the AI. However, they may have no "experience" of what they find. According to Ned Block, we have both phenomenal and access consciousness (Block, 2011). Phenomenal consciousness gives us the qualia about our feelings when we say things like "redness of roses," etc. Qualia refers to the deep subjective feelings that we have about things beyond objective knowledge of them. Access consciousness, however, refers to the objective knowledge that we have about things. According to Block, phenomenal consciousness belongs to natural brains. Access consciousness can be explored through psychology and computational techniques. It is possible that artificial agents may end up having the access types of consciousness given their vastly improved ability to crunch data and generalise from sensors but might never have phenomenal consciousness. They can gather information from the environment and act on it but will not have any phenomenal experience associated with it. Even if the AI has robotic vision and attention, it will not be "conscious" of things in the world.

Martin Heidegger had proposed the term *Dasein* to explain the everyday phenomenology of our existence in the world (Heidegger, 1927). *Dasein* implies being present in the world and being conscious of it. Artificial agents certainly do not have this. They do not know their existence in the world which comes naturally to us. Heidegger had further elaborated Husserl's philosophy of phenomenology. Heidegger wrote an essay on the future of technological progress and its effect on mankind (Heidegger, 1954). There he said that our fully embodied selves are much more than an outcome of our intelligence. As long as we view the robots as intelligent tools that are helping us live better lives, we need not fear them. They will never be more than intelligent. Hubert Dreyfus, who critiqued AI for many years, held this view as well (Dreyfus, 1979). Thus, the issue of agency and morality for the AI cannot be explained using the same theories of mind that we apply to humans. The AI do not have any idea about their "presence" in the world.

Human consciousness, intentionality, morality, and other higher-order functions evolved out of both biological and cultural evolution. The AI do not have any evolutionary history and thus the concept of biological or cultural evolution is not applicable to them. Unless there is social and cultural evolution in such agents, there may not be much consciousness and self-reflective power (Singer, 2021). Our model of the world is based on both current and evolutionary contingencies and our history of actions. Our sense of the world and consciousness is not just here and now, which is the case mostly with the AI. Their internal world is not contextualised and therefore they don't display the embodied selves that we have. Some scholars think that it is very premature to discuss consciousness and morality in the AI since there is a very fundamental difference in how such things have evolved in us vs them (Singer, 2021).

With this very brief and incomplete overview of some important philosophical perspectives, we can conclude that the AI do not have consciousness. They are not intentional agents who act freely in the world. Their symbolic reasoning is decontextualised and is not an outcome of any evolutionary processes. Mainstream materialistic theories within philosophy of the mind may deny consciousness and experience in humans, but that will not explain why the AI do not have these things. While we are yet to understand how our minds work, we have to keep track of the computational sophistication of the AI. Searle (1992) had said that minds may be computational but they have content. It is this content that is missing in the AI. The question of human acceptability of AI as agents rests on clarifications to such philosophical issues. It is mysterious how in spite of being limited in our computational capability we experience rich phenomenology but the AI do not.

2. Machine learning and generalised intelligence

According to Boden (2016), AI has two main aspects to it. One is technological in that it is used to solve real-world problems. The second is scientific in that psychologists can use it to create powerful models of mind-brain interaction. For example, algorithms trained on neural data can track billions of neurons that interact in real time creating mathematical models of representations and cognition. However, Boden questions if they are to be called intelligent the way we define intelligence for natural minds. The usual answer to this is that they don't have general intelligence like us since they don't have a "theory of mind" (Chollet, 2017). Theory of mind is defined as the ability to grasp others' mental states including any emotions (Frith & Frith, 2005). For example, we intuitively get to know someone's mental state, at least to some extent, by merely looking at them. This ability has been taken as a core attribute of our minds. Theory of mind is one aspect of generalised intelligence that allows us quick access to others' minds which is absent in the AI. In this section, I will discuss the real-world applications of AI, most importantly the machine learning algorithms. Since any empirical validation of theory of mind has to consider what well-trained machines can do, even if they are limited and are not quite like us.

Machines may not yet have a theory of mind that we can accept, but they can have artificial intelligence and be very good at solving many real-world problems. Machines can be trained to analyse a vast amount of data, which humans cannot do. Dubbed "machine learning," these applications are based on mathematical modelling, statistical data mining, and extracting useful "intelligence" to solve novel problems. We don't know if machines have consciousness and entertain subjective states like us or if they can make decisions, but they can certainly be trained to do very complicated things that we simply can't. That is because we are limited in our computational power and memory and cannot handle massive data and generate statistical information. Humans have always been fascinated with the idea of creating a machine that would be just like them in terms of their thinking and logical reasoning abilities. Ever since Alan Turing proposed the foundations of computation, its influence has been pervasive in many fields. It gave rise to the creation of computer algorithms that could run on some hardware and perform tasks. Although this chapter is on AI, we have to discuss the concept of machine learning because it is an important application of AI.

When you type the word "dog" into Google Images, you get hundreds of pictures of various types of dogs. Interestingly, with this string of letters as input, the algorithm used by Google does not present images of cats but only of dogs. This means that the algorithm is trained to "know" what dogs as entities are as far as images are concerned. Now, if you type "German shepherd" it similarly gives us images of only this breed and no other breed of dogs. It has acquired, therefore, categorical knowledge about things and their classes. Google Images runs on an algorithm that is trained on billions of images and has extracted features (Fergus et al., 2004). These features are used for learning the algorithm that it uses. The same general logic goes for other search engines that we use to find things on the internet; for example, searching for objects or books on Amazon. At the heart of this technology lies machine learning. Machine learning simply means that machines could be trained to perform simple and even complex applications with real-world data. Algorithms are sets of instructions that are written in different computational languages for the machines. In machine learning, the idea is to train the machine to extract statistical information from a vast set of data to learn to predict and to apply that knowledge. Thus, machine learning is an important part of an AI enterprise in which machines are trained to learn from data and extract information and then apply it to new incoming information. That could involve classifying new patients' data to diagnose cancer, finding a face in the crowd, or even predicting the weather.

What is important here is to train the machine on a vast scale of real-world data so that the algorithm extracts statistical information and uses mathematical models to mimic some aspects of human decision making and prediction (Lei et al., 2020). Of course, we humans believe that no machine could deduce logical structures as we can and think as we can. However, it is to be noted that, just as Searle had said, machines do have enormous computational power compared to humans and they can do certain things much faster than we can. Machine learning today is used in a vast range of real-world scenarios in which humans would fail. Andrew Ng, a prominent

AI researcher at Stanford University, aptly says that machine learning and AI are the new electricity of our age (Ng, 2018). Just as electricity transformed our lives in the nineteenth century, today applications of machine learning through vastly improved computational power has its presence in most aspects of our everyday lives. Let's now discuss the types of machine learning algorithms that are in use currently and how they are considered a part of the AI program more generally.

How does a computer program learn anything? It learns things the way children learn and many philosophical controversies have surrounded this issue (Marcus, 2003). However, computer programs can be trained to learn from a vast amount of data and then they can use that knowledge to perform new tasks. In this specific case, learning involves extracting features from stimuli and then using that knowledge to either identify or discriminate new input. For example, an algorithm can be trained on various pictures of cars to train it to correctly identify new pictures of cars. The program learns the prototypical features that must be present in any image of the car presented in any manner. However, cars may come in many other formats and shapes and at times such algorithms can't identify them.

There are mainly three classes of learning scenarios or algorithms that are used in machine learning: supervised learning, unsupervised learning, and reinforced learning (Ayodele, 2010). As the name suggests, in supervised learning, the algorithm is trained with labelled data for it to learn (Figure 6.2). For example, images of cars and other vehicles are labelled as such and the model learns to correctly classify an input with an output later. It is supervised since the model is already given the correct output to some inputs. Then it's tested in a subset of the images later to check if its performance is error-free. Supervised learning is the most basic type of machine learning algorithm that has vast applications in areas such as image classification and pattern recognition. In this case, the model is trained on huge quantities of data for it to learn and therefore it requires a lot of memory in the system. An unsupervised algorithm is very similar to the human cognitive processing style, at least conceptually (Barlow, 1989). Humans don't process already labelled data as input and output in the real world. They have to encounter objects of diverse nature and then they find similarities and patterns which they discover using their cognition to make sense and make decisions. Similarly, the unsupervised algorithm is not given any labelled data set to begin with; therefore it has no idea about the data. It has to extract features from the data itself and that is its learning. For example, if images of cars and cycles are given to the algorithm without labels, it has to extract similar features and cluster the objects based on those features. It must learn what is a car or a cycle from this exercise. Therefore, the unsupervised algorithm uses feature clustering with feature association as its main strategy of learning. In association, it can predict if one image occurs with a certain feature, then another will occur with some other feature. This has great relevance for predicting buying behaviour of customers in

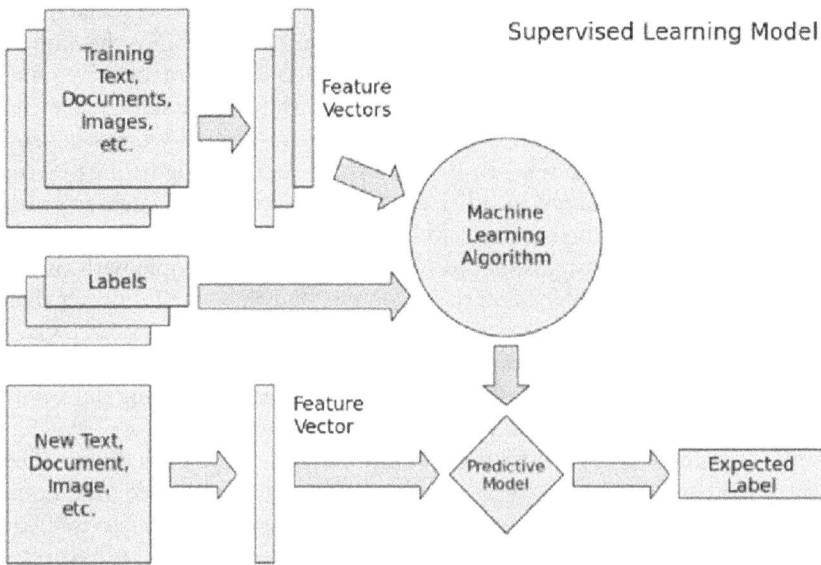

Figure 6.2 An overview of the supervised learning model.

Source: Nasteski (2017). Image source: https://radimrehurek.com/data_science_python/

supermarkets. When the images of what they buy are analysed, the unsupervised algorithm can predict the types of products the customers buy together generally. It's obvious that unsupervised learning is more difficult and time-consuming than supervised learning but it reflects the features of AI since it generates its intelligent analysis from any amount of input and works on that knowledge to clarify further novel input.

One of the most popular video-sharing platforms is YouTube. Billions of people watch billions of videos of different types on it every moment. Viewers also upload hours of videos constantly to the site each moment. How do YouTube suggestions work for each viewer that often appear to be very close to expectations? YouTube programmers have trained machine learning algorithms that track the viewing history as well as time spent on each video of millions of users (Arthurs et al., 2018). The algorithm is trained on this constantly updated dataset to predict correct suggestions. These algorithms also have been trained to flag any video that's judged as unsafe for the public. Interestingly when only humans were used to classify the videos as unsafe, the rate was only 8%. After the machine learning algorithms have been trained to do the job the accuracy has now gone up to almost 80% (Kurdi et al., 2020). Naturally, the algorithm can also wrongly classify some videos as unsafe and remove them from the site; therefore YouTube employs a vast number of human observers to keep track of the algorithm's activity.

Similar algorithms are used by other social media sites such as Instagram and Facebook. There have been many ethical questions about these social media sites' operations and their addictive influence on humans. Since the amount of time viewers engage with these sites and watch their content drives their advertising revenue, it's natural that these algorithms are designed in such a way that they keep the viewer hooked to them for hours by throwing suggestions that they are bound to like. Machine learning algorithms of this type are also used heavily in other e-commerce operations such as online ticketing or finding hotels on the website. Most recently, these algorithms have also been used successfully to influence groups of people with similar political orientations by feeding them content that they like to attract them towards a certain voting pattern (Golam Mostafa, & Junayed, 2021). Overall, machine learning algorithms have transformed the way we live in the world today since they can influence our world view by tracking our online behaviour and constantly feeding us content that we like.

The final class of algorithms that are more complex and are a direct reflection of the use of AI are the deep learning networks (Shrestha & Mahmood, 2019). These are very different from the supervised and unsupervised categories of algorithms. The true computational power of the AI is harnessed through what is called "deep learning" (Figure 6.3). According to Gary Marcus, an American scientist and entrepreneur, deep learning is a statistical technique to classify, quantify, and seek patterns in the vast amount of data using multiple layers of neural networks (Marcus, 2018). Loosely based on how neurons are connected and communicate in the brain, artificial neurons in the neural net also transfer information and learn. This learning involves mapping between different properties of the input; for example, speech sounds and some words or labels. Once they have been trained on a wide range of such data, they develop the ability to generalise to new inputs.

These algorithms try to mimic the neural networks of the human brain and how neurons communicate to learn. Figure 6.3 represents a basic form of neural network that's a deep algorithm. As you will see there are artificial neuronal networks of different classes. The input neurons receive the inputs from the dataset. The middle invisible hidden layers process the information and generate knowledge. The output layers produce the desired outputs and predictions. Deep learning algorithms learn unsupervised. In this type of machine learning, the algorithm is only given some initial input sensory data. But there are no explicit instructions about domain knowledge. The idea is to let the algorithm learn from its experience and create categories. However, in contrast to this, adaptive intelligence in biological systems lies in learning from input data. An infant generalises from infrequent given input and then projects this knowledge to solve a problem in novel encounters. Biological agents are endowed to do unsupervised learning throughout their lives. We humans also learn unsupervised from the start. Chomsky's poverty of stimuli argument (Chomsky, 1975) exemplified this in the domain of language learning. This was a core argument against the behaviourism of

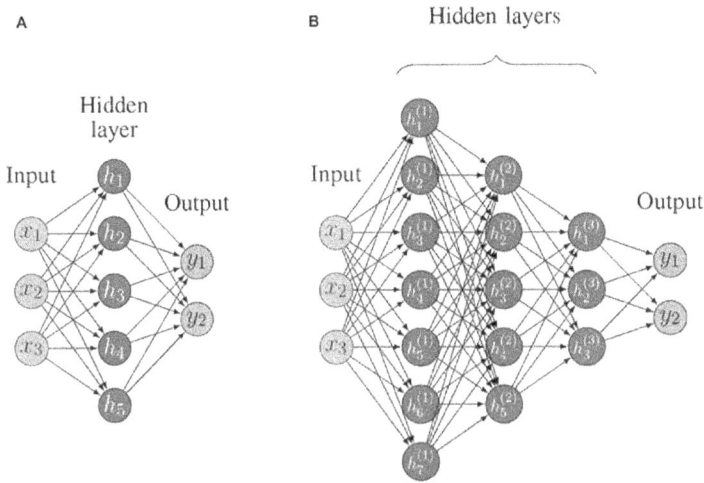

Figure 6.3 Examples of shallow (left) and deep (right) neural networks.
Source: From Emmert-Streib et al. (2020)

Skinner (Chomsky, 1959). Google's Deep Mind is an AI that is left unsupervised to play the demanding video game Breakout. In this game, it has to hit the ball against a wall, but it has to anticipate and learn gradually that the best way to hit the ball is to dig a hole in the wall. But it learns this only after about two hours of practice. This has been taken as a good demonstration of unsupervised learning in which the agent extracts conceptual knowledge to solve a problem dynamically. The unsupervised image classification algorithm Alexnet was created by Alex Krizhevsky (Krizhevsky et al., 2017). The algorithm was trained on a massive scale of natural scenes. The idea was to make it learn the classification of such scenes without any outcome reference. Its learning over time showed that it could develop generalisations. For example, it could find a horse or a mountain in a complex natural scene despite some differences.

In his book on deep learning, Terrence Sejnowski (Sejnowski, 2018) writes that deep learning neural nets transform the experience of the outside world into internal patterns of activity, much like neurons in the brain. At a more fundamental level, if we have to trust theories of neuroscience, then learning and action or even memory representations are carried out by billions of interconnected neurons that can be modelled mathematically. Deep learning algorithms use AI to crunch massive amounts of data that are simply beyond human capability and generate predictive models that have real-world applications in many fields. For example, deep learning algorithms powered by AI are used in medical diagnosis (Serag et al., 2019) and also in education (Perrotta & Selwyn, 2020). Every other day these algorithms are becoming even more powerful by mimicking human decision making. However, humans generate real-world semantics and experience the meaning of their learning that machines are not capable of. So far, the artificial neural network remains a very simplified and gross approximation of what neurons do in the biological brain. To overcome this conceptual barrier, currently, great effort is being made to integrate AI with neuroscience and cognitive science research. Deep learning neural networks are being trained on neural data to understand how brains effortlessly do what they do. Although deep learning networks use mathematical weights as the equivalent of synapses in the brain, which is not what it is, they are based on similar logic. Current brain imaging techniques such as fMRI allow researchers to analyse hundreds of images of the brain from actual human performance on cognitive tasks. Then the network is trained to create a predictive model of the actual mechanism (Savage, 2019).

To some extent, these efforts have been successful but they have posed other problems. Many times, with slightly different input than the one the system was trained on, the algorithm commits errors. Being unsupervised, they fail to generate new hypotheses about new situations. Neural networks thus trained can both generalise on the relationships of input on which they have been trained or extrapolate to new input (Marcus, 2018). While such deep learning mostly works, the serious objections relate to their use of a massive range of input data for training. Humans don't need that kind of data to generate abstract representations and project conceptual knowledge. This remains a very fundamental difference between how we "think" and what is "thinking" for such systems. Marcus (2018) goes on to provide several other objections or limitations of deep learning systems on both practical and epistemological grounds. For example, deep learning systems do not integrate prior knowledge, an ability which is unique to us. He says that these are systems that are self-insulated and are hermeneutic. Therefore, their generalisations are not related to guidance from previous experiences that are more conceptual. Further, these systems do not distinguish causation from correlation in their learning. Such distinctions between the artificial and the natural remain contested among various scholars.

From the foregoing discussion it appears that AI does not yet display generalised intelligence despite its immense capacity for deep learning. Deep learning may be flawed but it shows promise in the domain of artificial intelligence. Many experts have predicted its wide success in many tasks that humans will never be able to complete in real time which would transform our world (Sejnowski, 2018). These systems display what is now called artificial general intelligence which has similarities to human intelligence but is not equal. Intelligence can be defined as an agent's ability to accomplish self-defined goals in a wide range of situations (Legg & Hutter, 2007). Artificial agents thus now display this behaviour in a range of tasks that include general reasoning and cognitive flexibility. However, researchers think that in the near future such intelligence won't come any closer to natural intelligence (Shevlin et al., 2019). The proponents of generalised artificial intelligence think that there is an infinite possibility of minds, and what we think of minds is limited. This means there is no limit to which intelligence in the artificial can grow and therefore since our cognitive capacities are biologically limited there is no point in such comparisons. At first, it appears that the human tendency to dismiss artificial intelligence is unnecessarily anthropomorphic and biased. It also involves unreasonable comparisons between two very different categories of systems (Yampolskiy & Fox, 2012). If the intelligence of the artificial is going to be qualitatively of a very different type, then there is potentially no issue with it. However, if their collective intelligence is to overcome human intelligence then there are issues to be addressed.

3. Ethics and morality

Rapid technological progress always leads to ethical issues that we don't understand immediately – for example, the moral and ethical issues with gene editing or people's right to abortion. At this point in time, innovations in AI have increasingly posed ethical dilemmas of this sort. There are two main aspects to these ethical concerns. One is related to the AI's increasing powers and the potential to override humans in the domain of intelligence. Many philosophical and social points relate to how far we can allow the involvement of AI in our lives. One of the main issues related to privacy and the interference of AI in our everyday affairs is the issue of driverless cars. The other problem relates to humans' ethical treatment of the AI, particularly the humanoid robots. Human beings have evolved to treat others with dignity. But whether they can extend this to the AI is not yet clear. In this section I address these issues with certain examples.

Many subfields have developed at the intersections of moral psychology, AI and moral philosophy have addressed the questions related to moral agency in artificial agents (Torrance, 2008). These fields examine how humans view the actions of the AI in their lives and their ever-increasing encroachment, and how humans extend ethical treatments to the AI. These issues are intertwined and theories from both moral psychology and moral philosophy are implicated in their understanding. In spite of much work it remains debated if human moral decision making is rational or emotional (Greene & Haidt, 2002). Brain imaging studies on humans have revealed the neurobiological basis of human moral decision making in simple tasks (Greene, 2009). Older philosophical theories of human moral actions provide the basis for analysis of such empirical facts.

Cognitive psychologists have used the "trolley problem" to examine moral decision making. Take for example the human performance on the trolley task. The problem demonstrates that humans make moral decisions depending on what would be maximally good for the maximum number of people. I have explained other aspects of experimental investigations on morality in Chapter 7. The point here is that when it comes to the AI, such theories have their limitations since the key questions are related to their being conscious agents and having sentience. Torrance (2008) proposed that in spite of superior computational power the AI will not have sentience and thus will not have emphatic rationality which is required for a moral agent. Mere computational success does not automatically entail agency.

Others think that with increasing computational and technical sophistication these agents can perform certain actions that are morally acceptable without any phenomenal experience (Franklin, 2003). Sentience is accorded to biological agents who have minds and agency and act morally. The AI can perform acts that humans regulate and instruct but cannot decide for itself what is good. This is the central tenet of human actions since they are judged to be utilitarian and good beyond selfish interests. Thus, artificial moral agents are not like us in this phenomenal and subjective sense. They don't have intrinsic rationality that empowers them to make moral decisions the way we expect them to. In sum, these debates have raised fundamental questions about theories of "mind," "consciousness," "agency," and "morality," and to whom we can accord them. Establishing these criteria has not been easy in the last several decades.

Considering the rapid growth in this area, there are multiple issues related to the AI in which humans feel concerned that their freedom is being compromised (Figure 6.4). An important privacy concern relates to the mass surveillance by large corporations who do not seek requisite consent before employing the AI. There is a growing fear that such surveillance may permanently modify human behaviour considering every human movement is being analysed for which individuals can be prosecuted. Surveillance and civil liberties do not go together. A coalition comprising many human rights groups including the American Civil Liberties Union (ACLU) has sent letters to large corporations such as Google, Amazon, and IBM raising serious ethical questions about video analytics used by them ("Nationwide coalition of over 85 groups urges companies commit not to provide face surveillance to the government," ACLU Blog, 2019). The union in a policy document demands government approval for any AI-related activity by private companies that deal with a massive amount of human data. The fears are genuine since these corporations can use this information for their financial ends, and also sell them to illegitimate agencies who will further exploit them. The recent governmental investigations into Facebook's data abuse and sale to third parties are in line with these concerns. In the last decade, Chinese companies such as Baidu, Huwai, and iFlytek have been developing AI on a massive scale. Given the track record of China on human rights and the recent reports of surveillance on the Uyghur Muslims, the Western democracies are worried that China will abuse AI even more. Any speech or visual data collected from anyone can be used for profiling at various levels, which is already happening with the Uyghur Muslims and their oppression. The

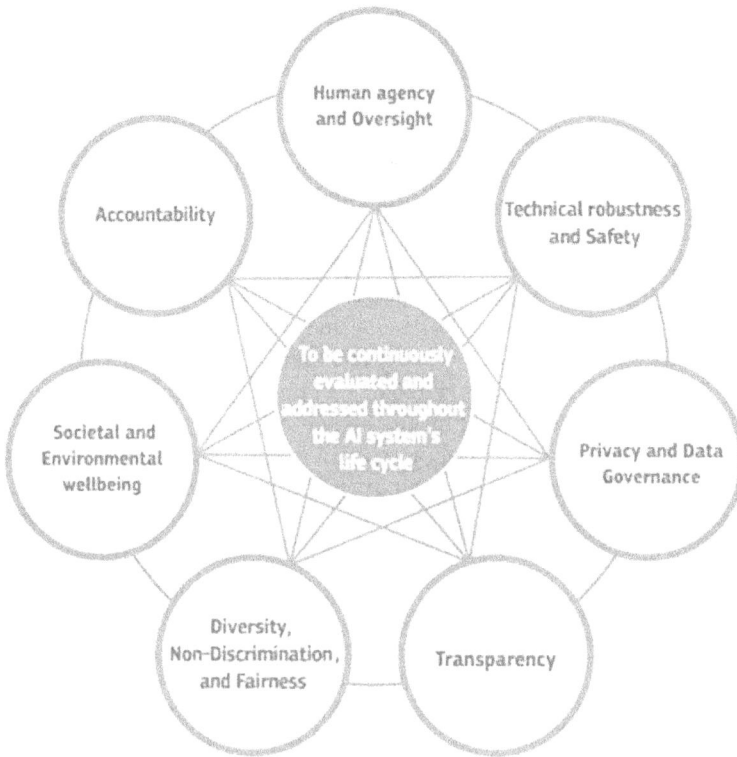

Figure 6.4 The guidelines list of key requirements that AI systems should meet to be trustworthy and ethically responsible.

Source: Digital Strategy website, European Commission

war on AI is alongside our age-old concerns for ethics. These concerns do not suggest that the AI algorithms are doing these out of their own will. These are being manipulated by humans for their own economic or military interests. Therefore, these fears do not pertain to the AI but how humans are using the AI. Therefore, the onus of ethics falls on humans here instead of the AI, which is not conscious and is not a moral agent.

Algorithms that use AI to sort out and extract general patterns from scale data are different than hominoid robots that run on the technology of AI as well. This distinction has to be clear because humans are more sensitive to such humanoid robots than to computer programs that they can't see or interact with. The question of agency appears to be more striking for such robots that humans interact with. In this case the concerns that arise are different from the ones I mentioned earlier. For example, artificial embodied robots are recruited to provide psychotherapy to patients in many clinics.

Armed with data, they often make their own decisions without human control (Fitzpatrick et al., 2017). Imagine a virtual personal psychotherapist who listens to your problems, and you even trust its judgments. The virtual assistant then has a conversation with you on sensitive topics, and you confide. This intimacy develops through questions and answers. The virtual therapist using AI can suggest things to you that might work. And if it seems agreeable to you, you develop confidence in the virtual therapist knowing fully well that it is not a human being. Such trust with virtual agents is possible, and is already happening. Take for example the artificial therapist Woebot. It has been developed by scientists at Stanford who have been therapists for a long time. Their vast accumulated experience of dealing with different types of patients now is being fed into an AI system. In a study, young adults with depression were given therapy through Woebot for two weeks roughly for 20 sessions (Fitzpatrick et al., 2017). Another group was given the National Institute of Health's pack for depression. The group that received the therapy from Woebot showed improvement later. Many claim that therapy by Woebot is not much different from therapy by humans. The important question is how it is that humans assign agency to an artificial agent in such scenarios. The artificial therapist assumes the role of an experiential being who is "understanding" the perspectives of the human patient. But we know from Searle (1982) that this cannot be termed "understanding" in that sense since the virtual agent does not have a mind, sentience, or consciousness. The fascinating fact is that humans are still able to extend trust and confidence to such agents. While patients trust the AI therapist, they also know that since they are not real people, there is no stigma. The therapists are not judging them if they disclose sensitive matters. This shows that patients don't assign agency to these therapists in the same sense as they do to human therapists and thus feel secure. While they are close to feeling like they are talking to someone real who is understanding them, they don't feel burdened by such communication. The virtual therapist thus becomes an interactive agent without natural agency.

Particular problems arise when such therapists are used for treatment of children who may have autism spectrum disorder (ASD). Such children are known to have developmental problems in communication, emotion, and social interaction including language use (Baron-Cohen, 2004 but see Nuske et al., 2013). These children need special therapy in multiple domains that are aimed at enhancing their social communicative experience. Robots can come handy in such cases providing therapy aiming at specific simulations of experience.

For example, a humanoid robot called KASPAR (Kinesics and Synchronisation in Personal Assistant Robotics, Figure 6.5), developed by scientists at the University of Hertfordshire in the United Kingdom, helps such children develop their social and linguistic skills. This robot responds to children's distress and also encourages them to modify their behaviour. The robot shows sensitivity to touch, an important aspect of cognition. Such

Figure 6.5 KASPAR robot developed by researchers at University of Hertfordshire to teach language and social skills to children.

Source: From Wainer et al. (2014)

tactile feedback coupled with real-time body movements reinforces learning in such children. Multiple research articles claim that such interactions are very fruitful in a therapeutic context (Dautenhahn & Werry, 2004; Rudovic et al., 2017). Interestingly, it has been observed that such children are keen to communicate with the robots but not with the human therapists. This may be problematic since the whole enterprise of giving therapy is to make the children competent to talk and deal with other human beings, not just with artificial agents. If they develop an affinity towards artificial agents and do not like real humans, then they may not be able to be part of the wider society. The developers think that once the children have learnt key skills through the robots, then they will be able to transfer them to human communication. However, it is not yet clear how any "theory of mind" abilities acquired through human-machine interaction are to be transferred to a human-human scenario. Robots of course do not reflect the subtle complexity of human interactions that include language, body, emotions, and social cognition.

From the examples discussed in the previous paragraphs it is evident that there is no clarity on the issues related to morality and the mind in human-machine interaction. On one hand, humans have existential fear of their worlds being crushed and changed by the AI manipulated by corporations; on the other, they find robots running on AI technology useful in a variety of situations. Therefore, it is clear that humans have specific sets of fears and appreciations for the AI. They both feel concerned and show indifference to the AI agents given the fact that they don't accord them agency and consciousness. The patient feels comfortable since the therapist is not a human agent with phenomenology. The same lack of agency and a moral self becomes a problem for other surveillance algorithms since they can do things without realising their consequences. Only agents with natural minds and moral selves with their own rationality can do good. Next, I address why there are fundamental reasons for humans not to trust and accept the AI as agents. These reasons are embedded in our psychology and biology which make it impossible to accept the virtual as real. So far, we have addressed issues pertaining to the AI not having consciousness and mentality. This we access instantly even if we deal with them in practical matters such as therapy. As AI agents assume more real-life appearances, humans will find the separation between the real and the virtual diminishing. However, as I show in the following, there are very deeply rooted reasons why the virtual still looks fake.

4. Human-machine interaction

Ian McEwan is an acclaimed British fiction writer. His new novel *Machines Like Me* deals with the morality of androids and their social interactions with humans. The novel, set in the 1980s, has a protagonist who purchases a humanoid robot to live with him. McEwan imagines a Britain where Alan Turing, the creator of AI, has become famous, and people are buying AI products. But in reality, Turing was hunted and faced social exclusion for being homosexual and committed suicide (Hofstadter, 2013). In the novel, the robot is an integral part of the narrative, along with other human characters. It is intelligent but has no sense of morality or consciousness. The algorithms that run it do not generate moral dispositions or a mind.

Although humans have their suspicions about virtual agents being incapable of many things, they are nevertheless vulnerable to their influences. We take them seriously and develop emotional attachments towards them as in many video games. Now companies are using virtual avatars as influencers to advertise their products. Since flesh and blood models have their limitations and can only work in a constrained manner, virtual models are a suitable replacement. For example, the clothing brand Calvin Klein recently used a virtual model alongside a real human model in one of their publicity ads. Lil Miquela, the virtual model who looks like a 19-year-old, has 1.6 million Instagram followers. It was created in a studio in Los Angeles.

The widespread human acceptance of such virtual models indicates that we can transcend the subjectivity between the real and the virtual ("These Influencers Aren't Flesh and Blood, Yet Millions Follow Them," NYT, 2019). The Chinese media company Xinhua has introduced a virtual news anchor who can work all the time, unlike human anchors. Human creators behind these virtual models can manipulate them in any way they want, sometimes even unrealistically.

One of the most bizarre things you can come across is a man marrying a robot or a virtual hologram as a companion. Many are now seeking sustained companionships with these agents in countries like Japan and China. Those who are lonely but do not want human companions are finding happiness with these agents. Such happiness with an artificial companion can't be derived if the human agents think of them as lowly machines devoid of minds. The YouTube advertisement of the Gatebox virtual robot ("Gatebox – Promotion Movie," YouTube, 2016) shows it all. A lonely office worker in Japan finds happiness having this robot at home. The robot texts with him as he would expect from a loving girlfriend and also makes sure that he carries an umbrella. The man falls for these gestures and feels fulfilled. Before he enters his apartment, the robot makes sure that the lights are on. A Chinese man named Zheng Jiajia who was an employee of Huawei married the robot which he had created in 2017 ("Chinese man 'marries' robot he built himself," *Guardian*, 2017). Sociologists think men are getting into these since the male-to-female ratio is uneven in some countries like China. But what if human-robot emotional relationships become too widespread and normal? These few examples may seem to be acts of eccentricity or publicity stunts by few. But given the adaptive nature of humans, deep attachment may likely develop between humans and robots. It is speculated that by 2050, such marriages will have legal status ("A.I. expert David Levy says a human will marry a robot by 2050," CBC, 2017). Companies that are making robotic brides earn in millions in a few countries. While conceptually we may still assign no agenthood to the artificial, we will show some empathy towards them. This thin line between acceptance and non-acceptance is purely qualitative and not linked to their computational powers.

Being like us means to appear and behave like us. The life-size robotic dolls are a good example of this approximation. They don't look bizarre with wires, they look like us in many ways. Humans have this ability to tag emotion to any virtual or real face. Neuroscience of face perception research suggests that we have a specific cortical site that engages in facial identification and evaluation (Kanwisher et al., 1997). If we can map emotion onto such faces, then unwillingly we also consider them as agents who have their own identity and maybe even consciousness. This may look superficial, but it works in many cases. For example, humans do not seem to make a big distinction between virtual and real faces on emotion identification tasks. When humans look for emotion on virtual faces, the same brain areas are active more or less, such as the fusiform face area (FFA, de Borst & de

Gelder, 2015). However, this distinction disappears with old age, since older people do not engage with social media a lot and therefore do not encounter such expressive avatars (Dyck et al., 2008). Acceptance of the AI is a kind of social learning that is happening rapidly. Today's generation of young children who are growing up spending substantial time on the internet are bound to encounter virtual agents a lot more than real ones. When they grow old their ability to recognise emotions on real faces compared to virtual faces may decrease.

The key question is to what extent humans are able to accept such a façade of realism in the virtual. Interestingly when the facial features and emotions of the virtual agent become very close to real humans, then human agents find it odd. They feel a kind of unease, which has been dubbed the "uncanny valley" effect. When the resemblance is close to 100%, humans feel a strong eeriness with such avatars. The roboticist Masahiro Mori had predicted this in the 1970s (Mori et al., 2012, Figure 6.6). Humans are fine with virtual agents that resemble them in facial structures and emotions. But when they start resembling them totally, the eeriness begins; as if something stops them from accepting the artificial agent completely. Humans

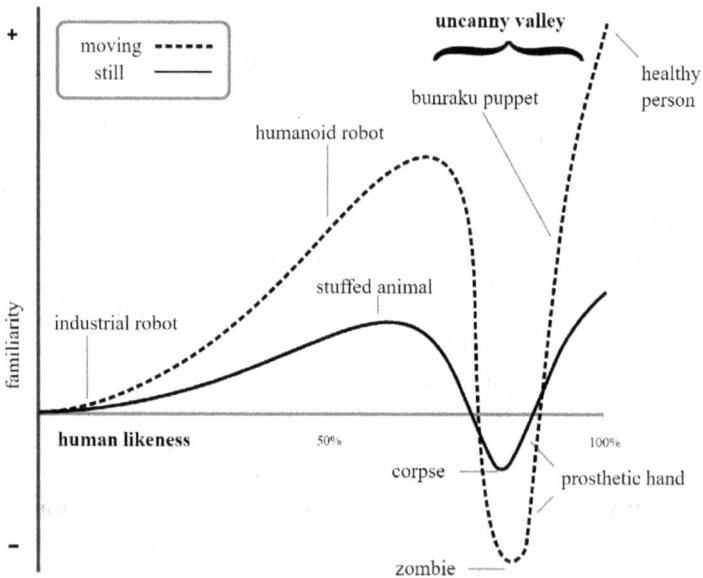

Figure 6.6 Uncanny valley effect. The perception of artificial objects by human observers is plotted hypothetically as a function of the similarity of the artificial objects to human agents. Mori proposed that there would be a dip ("valley") at a certain point in the perception of realness as the similarity of the artificial agents with human agents increased.

Source: Image: Wikipedia commons, by Smurrayinchester

get the same feeling with corpses and lifelike prosthetic body parts. Mori also predicted that these strange feelings grow if these agents start moving. The source of this conflict may lie with their identities as humans. The artificial agents challenge our intuitive understanding of what it means to be a human. We know they are not real agents, but they start resembling the "real" so much that we are perplexed.

Typically developing children show this strangeness towards virtual characters, which resemble actual humans a lot. Designers are capable of creating avatars that are flawlessly humanlike visually and that are capable of mimicking emotions such as the case of Lil Miquela. But human observers do not consider these agents to be experiencing beings that are capable of generating their own emotions and making decisions. This cognitive assessment is a projection of our own theory of mind onto others. Humans can probably confer agenthood status to these avatars that can do something but not the status of experiencing mental beings (Stein & Ohler, 2017). If the uncanny valley hypothesis is correct, then we have to accept our biological limitations. We won't ever be able to accept artificial agents fully and completely irrespective of their resemblance to us. They are only good until the point we treat them as artificial, lifeless, and controlled by us. However, the rise of avatars indicates that this may not be true completely. They do have a certain hold on us, and we are willing to bury the real-artificial difference. At least we don't bring that difference to consciousness when we interact with them. The uncanny valley hypothesis still has its hold on researchers in AI and cognitive science to date. It is still not known what leads to the strange feelings.

The uncanny valley effect does not however constrain human interactions with the robots at several intimate levels. Humans are social animals that can act while entertaining contradictory emotions and mental states; for example, eating animal meat while being an animal rights' activist. That is, they can have cognitive dissonance in their thoughts and actions. In the domain of the commercial adult sex market, AI has now come in in a big way. Today there are almost life-like sex dolls that can mimic behaviour (Fosch-Villaronga & Poulsen, 2020). This industry is now changing the way sex is sold and consumed in the market. In Germany, there are brothels that have only sex dolls ("Inside Bordoll, a German sex-doll brothel in Dortmund," DW, April 2018). With excellent-quality material that resembles human flesh and the power of AI, these dolls can provide a sensorimotor experience that is almost real. It is interesting to put the uncanny valley argument to this situation. If the customers think that these dolls are lifeless and are not experiencing beings, then how can they enjoy them sexually? It is possible, since humans can apply cognitive dissonance while interacting with such companions that are artificial. It is not that those humans are suspending their belief about their being artificial but they can still get along with their acts. At this point in time there is not much research to indicate how the human brain is able to accommodate such a dichotomy and if this has evolved to adapt to such changes. The eeriness of the uncanny valley remains a problem to be solved.

In Japan, a man named Shin Tagaki has founded a company Trottla ("This Guy Makes Life-Size Child Dolls Wearing Lingerie," *Vice*, 2013) that sells child sex robots catering to unique demands of the consumers. Customers can ask him to manufacture a child robot with unique facial expressions. Since one can have desires fulfilled in a non-consensual way with sex robots, when they are designed to offer some resistance then the customers attack them, just as they would do to real humans, resulting in rape. Data suggest that many who buy such robots also attack and mutilate them if they feel that there is resistance or non-cooperation. This non-resistance is not natural that is flowing out of some agent but has been programmed by the manufacturer. This scenario suggests that humans expect the robots to act like humans in specific situations. It is unclear whether only some are capable of maintaining this dissociation between the artificial and real or whether it is a basic attribute of human nature. Many governments are finding it difficult to classify such acts as criminal since they are not conducted with real persons. Further, if this is controlled, then it may also be infringement on personal freedom (Maras & Shapiro, 2017).

Another dimension of man-machine interaction relates to how they can shape our behaviour in a more general way. Nicholas A. Christakis has studied how interaction with robots may change how we interact among ourselves. Everything that we have technologically developed has modified our behaviour towards other humans. It has been observed that humans either show more sensitivity or more unreasonableness towards one another, depending on the presence of robots. In one study, Christakis examined how robots influence group-level cohesion among humans at work (Shirado & Christakis, 2017). Humans started to feel free and worked collaboratively when the robot was among them and acted like one of them. The robot committed a mistake and accepted it just as humans do. When the robot acted stubbornly, the humans also reflected it. This means when humans see a robot more like them with the frailties and uncertainties, they feel more assured. They include it in their social groups ("How AI Will Rewire Us," *the Atlantic*, 2019). Frequency of interactions in specific contexts such as this modulates acceptance of robots by humans (Whelan et al., 2018). It looks as if humans assign at least some agency to robots when they interact with them closely and more frequently. Further, when robots have identities and names like us, our behaviour towards them changes. For example, children kicked and abused a robot less when it had a name than when it did not have one. However, there is no definite theory as of yet that predicts when humans assign agency to robots and when they do not.

The foregoing examples still do not suggest that humans accord moral agency to robots even though they derive pleasure interacting with them. That is why they can inflict pain on them without feeling guilty. Since antiquity, through the Greeks and then the Roman Stoics, we have developed standard protocols for exercising morality. But do they apply to machines? Do machines deserve moral treatment from us (Risse, 2019)? This is where we don't understand how to stop paedophiles that extract perverse pleasure by humiliating child sex robots. Extensions of our laws of morality to include the artificial will require important revisions in our understanding of a few things. The most important question is who deserves moral treatment. If this is only restricted to experiencing beings that have autonomous consciousness to feel and think, then robots as of now don't qualify.

Thomas Tylor in his 1972 book *A Vindication of the Rights of Brutes* argued for ethical treatments of animals and brutes. The problem is that humans do not consider animals as moral agents capable of reasoning. Philosophers who wrote on ethics did not include animals in their analysis. For example, Kant did not consider that animals have any ability to reason (Kant, 1798). G. E. Moore, the analytic philosopher famous for his book *Principia Ethica* (1903), did not bother about animals at all. Of course, the strain comes from Descartes who was categorical that animals have no minds and no reasoning. Descartes did not consider animals as conscious beings – but mere machines that function mechanically. Interestingly, he was searching for the site of consciousness in brains of cadavers in the butcheries of Amsterdam – which he did not find. J. M. Coetzee, the Nobel prize-winning novelist, delivered his Tanner lectures on human values at Princeton University titled *The Lives of Animals* (delivered on Oct 15–16, 1997). What does a literary novelist know about the minds of animals? The protagonist in *Elizabeth Costello* delivered a lecture to an academic audience in an American college in which she compares killings of animals for meat to the slaughters of the Third Reich. Every day we kill millions of animals for food without bothering about their pain. Are we biologically incapable of feeling such pain or have we rationalised and chosen to ignore it? Philosophers such as Frege (1948) held that experiences are meaningless without subjects that are capable of experiencing them. It is then our assessment of subjecthood that decides who gets the status of a moral being. Interestingly, merely having consciousness and the ability to feel pain do not seem sufficient for such an identity. As for the robots, we have to first accept them as agents capable of experiencing something in a unique way which is not the case now (Colin McGinn, 1995). Agents are identified as unique persons but without a sense of "self."

5. Singularity and evolution

In the domain of technological progress, singularity means a point of no return – when large-scale technological changes become irreversible and change human civilisation significantly. Our fear of the AI takeover is related to singularity. Do we see this happening with the AI? That kind of change will alter how humans have lived and viewed themselves and when our sense of agency is taken away forever. It is not merely the control of humans by AI systems but complete submission to them. Developers of self-driven cars such as Elon Musk predict that while AI singularity is a real possibility, it may take a lot of time until we get there. Robotic experts and futurists who see AI as a future tool for collective human welfare do not yet want to predict on this. The singularity fear is not shared by all yet. Ray Kurzweil thinks that humanity is going to change (for the better) in just a few decades. Philosophers and psychologists who fundamentally believe that robots simply do not have the agency to control us think this prediction is nonsense. But what is our confidence that we will be able to maintain and assert our unique selves and agency to the artificial who have become very intelligent and are gazing deep into our motives?

I. J. Good was a British mathematician who worked with Alan Turing as a cryptologist. Good (1966) first wrote about technological singularity and its consequences on humans. He wrote,

> Let an ultra-intelligent machine be defined as a machine that can far surpass all the intellectual activities of any man however clever. Since the design of machines is one of these intellectual activities, an ultra-intelligent machine could design even better machines; there would then unquestionably be an "intelligence explosion," and the intelligence of man would be left far behind. Thus, the first ultra-intelligent machine is the last invention that man need ever make.
>
> (Good, 1966, p. 33)

We have to reject this idea on some solid conceptual ground. The proponents of strong AI and singularity are technocrats. Their ideas have led to the creation of companies that earn billions. Therefore, they are entitled to beat their drums even more loudly. Who gains from an eventual technological singularity whereby humans have lost their humanity? This way of looking at it is not trivial since it is quite possible that a bunch of technologists and fans of futurism are already inclined to lower their judgment of what is intelligence and thus can accept a scenario in which machines and human intelligence have no difference, just as only some of us, but not everyone, can accept artificial AI dolls as emotional partners.

While philosophical disputes on the nature of the mind and agency continue, there is an exponential increase in the computational power of the AI. This increase has the potential to completely change the way we manage our affairs now. AI is to be first understood as a product of human intelligence. In itself, it has no ontological status quo. Therefore, evolutionary forces may shape the human brain in order to comfortably deal with the challenges posed by the AI in different dimensions. Once humans put checks and balances in place on ethical issues related to the AI, the AI's influence will not be uncontrolled. It is a mistake to accept that humans' acceptance of the utility of the AI indicates their judgments about them. They still remain entities without consciousness, agency, and minds. This projection itself is an outcome of our own rationality which has evolved through millions of years. This evolution not only gave the human brain its computational power but consciousness and capacity of phenomenal experience. It's only between 10,000 and 35,000 years before that the complete evolution of the *Homo sapiens* brain size took place (Neubauer et al., 2018). This timeline corresponds to the beginning of culture and technology and behavioural modernity.

Stephen Jay Gould believed that since the last 40,000 to 50,000 years, there have not been any significant changes in the human brain biologically (Gould & Gold, 1996). However, human cognitive evolution may be happening much more quickly than before given our ability to adapt to more difficult challenges and tame nature (Templeton, 2010). Our increasing resistance against diseases along with global travel and migration, adaptation to technology, as well as cultural and social progress are all signs that human evolution is still on (Solomon, 2016). Thus, while we may fear the doomsday linked to AI, we have to also consider the adaptive forces of our own evolution that are at work in parallel. As of now, there is no definite prediction on the competitive timeline of human vs AI evolution. There is a possibility that the future will see hybrid agents who are capable of interacting with humans as autonomous agents mimicking human cognition (Maldonato & Valerio, 2018). Since humans have created AI, human brains are also evolving to adapt to the ever-increasing demands. Even in such a scenario, humans will know how to control and dismiss the AI on conceptual grounds. For example, in critical sectors such as healthcare, AI is used but under human supervision. The surgeons are not obliged to consider the decisions of the AI even if it comes from massive amounts of data mining and predictive models.

6. Summary

The chapter was an excursion into the world of the artificial in the context of cognition and philosophy of the mind. Its nihilistic flavour reflects what is currently the state of theory. Our claim to our unique mentality is not merely an anthropomorphic vanity, it is an ontological fact of the universe. It is not to be found in any other artificial system. Our resistance to the AI thus has a deep biological basis that's related to our own minds. The future of AI seems robust from a business and technological point of view. But if we apply fundamental notions of agency, consciousness, and phenomenal experience then they seem just like toys. They may have sophisticated computational power but no agency. Therefore, we will always enslave them; albeit this may lead to some unethical behaviour on our part. But humans have evolved self-correcting devices and soon will establish laws for their proper regulation. Thus, viewed as a philosophical question, artificial intelligence makes little sense unless we want a drastic revision of what we mean by intelligence. The human fear of our lives being taken over by the artificial is just immature at best. However, the study of the artificial and their learning should be of interest to cognitive scientists since we still can learn so much about how our minds work from this. How do brains work and why can't we replicate them with the artificial? Future research in multiple fields will only reveal how unique and rare our phenomenology is in this material universe. I have no problem with humans adapting to the artificial in their everyday lives that includes emotional and social interactions. But the fine line that separates them will be "agency" and, by implication, morality.

References

Arthurs, J., Drakopoulou, S., & Gandini, A. (2018). Researching youtube. *Convergence, 24*(1), 3–15.

Ayodele, T. O. (2010). Types of machine learning algorithms. *New Advances in Machine Learning, 3,* 19–48.

Barlow, H. B. (1989). Unsupervised learning. *Neural Computation, 1*(3), 295–311.

Baron-Cohen, S. (2004). The cognitive neuroscience of autism. *Journal of Neurology, Neurosurgery & Psychiatry, 75*(7), 945–948.

Behdadi, D., & Munthe, C. (2020). A normative approach to artificial moral agency. *Minds and Machines, 30,* 195–218.

Block, N. (2011). Perceptual consciousness overflows cognitive access. *Trends in Cognitive Sciences, 15*(12), 567–575.

Boden, M. A. (2016). *AI: Its nature and future.* Oxford University Press.

Chollet, F. (2017, July 17). The limitations of deep learning. *The Limitations of Deep Learning.* https://blog.keras.io/the-limitations-of-deep-learning.html

Chomsky, N. (1959). Review of "verbal behaviour" (Skinner, 1957). *Language, 35,* 26–58.

Chomsky, N. (1975). *Reflections on language.* Pantheon Books.

Churchland, P. M. (1981). Eliminative materialism and propositional attitudes. *The Journal of Philosophy, 78*(2), 67–90.

Clowes, R., Torrance, S., & Chrisley, R. (2007). Machine consciousness. *Journal of Consciousness Studies, 14*(7), 7–14.

Dautenhahn, K., & Werry, I. (2004). Towards interactive robots in autism therapy: Background, motivation and challenges. *Pragmatics & Cognition, 12*(1), 1–35.

de Borst, A. W., & de Gelder, B. (2015). Is it the real deal? Perception of virtual characters versus humans: An affective cognitive neuroscience perspective. *Frontiers in Psychology, 6,* 576.

Dennett, D. (1988). Conditions of personhood. In *What is a person?* (pp. 145–167). Humana Press.

Dennett, D. C. (1978). Artificial intelligence as philosophy and as psychology. *Brainstorms: Philosophical Essays on Mind and Psychology,* 109–126.

Dreyfus, H. L. (1979). *What computers can't do: The limits of artificial intelligence* (Vol. 1972). Harper & Row.

Dyck, M., Winbeck, M., Leiberg, S., Chen, Y., Gur, R. C., & Mathiak, K. (2008). Recognition profile of emotions in natural and virtual faces. *PloS One, 3*(11), e3628.

Emmert-Streib, F., Yang, Z., Feng, H., Tripathi, S., & Dehmer, M. (2020). An introductory review of deep learning for prediction models with big data. *Frontiers in Artificial Intelligence, 3,* 4.

Fergus, R., Perona, P., & Zisserman, A. (2004, May). A visual category filter for google images. In *European conference on computer vision* (pp. 242–256). Springer.

Fetzer, J. H. (2004). The philosophy of AI and its critique. *The Philosophy of Computing and Information*, 119.

Fitzpatrick, K. K., Darcy, A., & Vierhile, M. (2017). Delivering cognitive behavior therapy to young adults with symptoms of depression and anxiety using a fully automated conversational agent (Woebot): A randomized controlled trial. *JMIR Mental Health*, 4(2), e19.

Fosch-Villaronga, E., & Poulsen, A. (2020). Sex care robots: Exploring the potential use of sexual robot technologies for disabled and elder care. *Paladyn, Journal of Behavioral Robotics*, 11(1), 1–18.

Franklin, S. (2003). A conscious artifact?. *Journal of Consciousness Studies*, 10 (4–5), 47–66.

Frege, G. (1948). Sense and reference. *The Philosophical Review*, 57(3), 209–230.

Frith, C., & Frith, U. (2005). Theory of mind. *Current Biology*, 15(17), R644–R645.

Gibson, J. J. (2002). A theory of direct visual perception. *Vision and Mind: Selected Readings in the Philosophy of Perception*, 77–90.

Golam Mostafa, I. A., & Junayed, M. S. (2021). Investigation of different machine learning algorithms to determine human sentiment using Twitter data. *International Journal of Information Technology and Computer Science (IJITCS)*, 13(2), 38–48.

Good, I. J. (1966). Speculations concerning the first ultraintelligent machine. In *Advances in computers* (Vol. 6, pp. 31–88). Elsevier.

Gould, S. J., & Gold, S. J. (1996). *The mismeasure of man*. W. W. Norton & company.

Greene, J. D. (2009). The cognitive neuroscience of moral judgment. In M. S. Gazzaniga, E. Bizzi, L. M. Chalupa, S. T. Grafton, T. F. Heatherton, C. Koch, J. E. LeDoux, S. J. Luck, G. R. Mangan, J. A. Movshon, H. Neville, E. A. Phelps, P. Rakic, D. L. Schacter, M. Sur, & B. A. Wandell (Eds.), *The cognitive neurosciences* (pp. 987–999). Massachusetts Institute of Technology.

Greene, J. D., & Haidt, J. (2002). How (and where) does moral judgment work?. *Trends in Cognitive Sciences*, 6(12), 517–523.

Heidegger, M. (1927/2010). *Being and time*. SUNY Press.

Heidegger, M. (1954). The question concerning technology. *Technology and Values: Essential Readings*, 99, 113.

Henderson, H. (2007). *Artificial intelligence: Mirrors for the mind*. Infobase Publishing.

Hofstadter, D. (2013). *Alan Turing: Life and legacy of a great thinker*. Springer Science & Business Media.

Kant, I. (1798/2010). Anthropology from a pragmatic point of view. In R. Louden & G. Zoller (Eds. & Trans.), *Anthropology, history, and education* (pp. 227–429). Cambridge Edition of the Works of Immanuel Kant. Cambridge University Press.

Kanwisher, N., McDermott, J., & Chun, M. M. (1997). The fusiform face area: A module in human extrastriate cortex specialized for face perception. *Journal of Neuroscience*, 17(11), 4302–4311.

Krizhevsky, A., Sutskever, I., & Hinton, G. E. (2017). Imagenet classification with deep convolutional neural networks. *Communications of the ACM*, 60(6), 84–90.

Kurdi, M., Albadi, N., & Mishra, S. (2020, December). "Video unavailable": Analysis and prediction of deleted and moderated YouTube videos. In *2020 IEEE/ACM international conference on advances in social networks analysis and mining (ASONAM)* (pp. 166–173). IEEE.

Legg, S., & Hutter, M. (2007). Universal intelligence: A definition of machine intelligence. *Minds and Machines, 17*(4), 391–444.

Lei, Y., Yang, B., Jiang, X., Jia, F., Li, N., & Nandi, A. K. (2020). Applications of machine learning to machine fault diagnosis: A review and roadmap. *Mechanical Systems and Signal Processing, 138*, 106587.

Maldonato, M., & Valerio, P. (2018). Artificial entities or moral agents? How AI is changing human evolution. In *Multidisciplinary approaches to neural computing* (pp. 379–388). Springer.

Maras, M. H., & Shapiro, L. R. (2017). Child sex dolls and robots: More than just an uncanny valley. *Journal of Internet Law, 21*, 3–17.

Marcus, G. F. (2003). *The algebraic mind: Integrating connectionism and cognitive science*. MIT Press.

Marcus, G. F. (2018). Deep learning: A critical appraisal. *arXiv Preprint*, arXiv 1801.00631.

McGinn, C. (1995). Animal minds, animal morality. *Social Research*, 731–747.

Moore, G. E. (1959). *Principia ethica: 1903* (Vol. 2). Cambridge University Press.

Mori, M., MacDorman, K. F., & Kageki, N. (2012). The uncanny valley [from the field]. *IEEE Robotics & Automation Magazine, 19*(2), 98–100.

Müller, V. C., & Bostrom, N. (2016). Future progress in artificial intelligence: A survey of expert opinion. In *Fundamental issues of artificial intelligence* (pp. 555–572). Springer.

Nasteski, V. (2017). An overview of the supervised machine learning methods. *Horizons. B, 4*, 51–62.

Neubauer, S., Hublin, J. J., & Gunz, P. (2018). The evolution of modern human brain shape. *Science Advances, 4*(1), eaao5961.

Ng, A. (2018). *AI is the new electricity*. O'Reilly Media.

Nuske, H. J., Vivanti, G., & Dissanayake, C. (2013). Are emotion impairments unique to, universal, or specific in autism spectrum disorder? A comprehensive review. *Cognition & Emotion, 27*(6), 1042–1061.

Perrotta, C., & Selwyn, N. (2020). Deep learning goes to school: Toward a relational understanding of AI in education. *Learning, Media and Technology, 45*(3), 251–269.

Pinar Saygin, A., Cicekli, I., & Akman, V. (2000). Turing test: 50 years later. *Minds and Machines, 10*(4), 463–518.

Risse, M. (2019). *Human rights, artificial intelligence and Heideggerian technoskepticism: The long (worrisome?) view*. Carr Centre.

Rudovic, O., Lee, J., Mascarell-Maricic, L., Schuller, B. W., & Picard, R. W. (2017). Measuring engagement in robot-assisted autism therapy: A cross-cultural study. *Frontiers in Robotics and AI, 4*, 36.

Savage, N. (2019). How AI and neuroscience drive each other forwards. *Nature, 571*(7766), S15.

Searle, J. R. (1980). Minds, brains, and programs. *The Behavioral and Brain Sciences, 3*, 417–424.

Searle, J. R. (1982). The Chinese room revisited. *Behavioral and Brain Sciences, 5*(2), 345–348.

Searle, J. R. (1992). *The rediscovery of the mind*. MIT Press.

Sejnowski, T. J. (2018). *The deep learning revolution*. MIT Press.

Serag, A., Ion-Margineanu, A., Qureshi, H., McMillan, R., Saint Martin, M. J., Diamond, J., O'Reilly, P., & Hamilton, P. (2019). Translational AI and deep learning in diagnostic pathology. *Frontiers in Medicine*, 6, 185.

Shevlin, H., Vold, K., Crosby, M., & Halina, M. (2019). The limits of machine intelligence: Despite progress in machine intelligence, artificial general intelligence is still a major challenge. *EMBO Reports*, 20(10), e49177.

Shrestha, A., & Mahmood, A. (2019). Review of deep learning algorithms and architectures. *IEEE Access*, 7, 53040–53065.

Shirado, H., & Christakis, N. A. (2017). Locally noisy autonomous agents improve global human coordination in network experiments. *Nature*, 545(7654), 370.

Singer, W. (2021). Differences between natural and artificial cognitive systems. In *Robotics, AI, and humanity* (pp. 17–27). Springer, Cham.

Solomon, S. (2016). *Future humans: Inside the science of our continuing evolution*. Yale University Press.

Stein, J. P., & Ohler, P. (2017). Venturing into the uncanny valley of mind – the influence of mind attribution on the acceptance of human-like characters in a virtual reality setting. *Cognition*, 160, 43–50.

Strawson, G. (2006). Realistic monism: Why physicalism entails panpsychism. *Journal of Consciousness Studies*, 13(10–11), 3–31.

Strawson, G. (2016). Mind and being: The primacy of panpsychism. In Godehard Brüntrup & Ludwig Jaskolla (Eds.), *Panpsychism: Contemporary perspectives* (pp. 75–112). Oxford University Press.

Templeton, A. R. (2010). Coherent and incoherent inference in phylogeography and human evolution. *Proceedings of the National Academy of Sciences*, 107(14), 6376–6381.

Torrance, S. (2008). Ethics and consciousness in artificial agents. *AI & Society*, 22(4), 495–521.

Wainer, J., Dautenhahn, K., Robins, B., & Amirabdollahian, F. (2014). A pilot study with a novel setup for collaborative play of the humanoid robot KASPAR with children with autism. *International Journal of Social Robotics*, 6(1), 45–65.

Whelan, S., Murphy, K., Barrett, E., Krusche, C., Santorelli, A., & Casey, D. (2018). Factors affecting the acceptability of social robots by older adults including people with dementia or cognitive impairment: A literature review. *International Journal of Social Robotics*, 10(5), 643–668.

Yampolskiy, R. V., & Fox, J. (2012). Artificial general intelligence and the human mental model. In *Singularity hypotheses* (pp. 129–145). Springer.

7   Mind, Cognition, and Religion

1. Evolution of religion

Soon after they appeared, religions had their effect on the collective consciousness of humankind that shaped their history. Marx had rightly called religion "the opium of the masses." This referred to the manner in which religion takes possession of rational selves and makes the believer accept the unknown and the mysterious. The hold of religion on the human psyche is all-pervasive and distinct. While the believer accepts the mysterious, the atheist deals with rationality. This rationality does not allow any category of God that cannot be demonstrated through objective means. Thus, being religious is to have one type of mental attributes, rather than being not religious. This oversimplification will be dealt with later in the chapter since many cognitive scientists have started to look into religion's effects on the mind. Religions brought culture and civilisation to the polytheistic pagans. Throughout history, different religions influenced different aspects of cognition. For example, while Buddhism aimed at enlightening the soul through self-examination and renunciation of worldly passions, Hinduism emphasised humanity beyond the individual and afterlife. Christianity instilled the hearts of its followers with piety and forgiveness and Islam again brought back the absolute faith in the all-powerful creator. The rituals, scriptures, buildings for gods, art, prayers, everything came along to make the religious experience worth living for. Religions, apart from their fanfare and relics, modified core aspects of human cognition forever. Under the pretext of providing guidelines for a virtuous and regulated life, they moulded cognition to make life more meaningful. The religious mind accepted the unknown and the mysterious for eternal peace and tranquillity. This chapter explores the cognitive science of religion, a well-established domain of scientific inquiry now with many theories and applications. Particularly, the chapter looks into how religions influence the minds of those who practise them. It also examines how the modern mind engages with religion when we have accepted a rational and objective world view following the scientific revolutions of Copernicus and Galileo.

DOI: 10.4324/9781003316053-7

Religion could be the by-product of the mind's evolution itself. There is little consensus on the exact timing of the origin of religion as an organised social phenomenon. Development of group-level collective social cognition was likely conducive for its evolution (Bulbulia, 2007). Religious belief recommends entertaining transcendence in an otherwise material world. Religion rises above the Cartesian distinction between mind and matter. At a very fundamental level of analysis, religion begins when people ascribe agenthood and animacy to natural phenomena. The myriad artefacts, objects of rituals, relics, and iconography used in everyday religious practices suggest this. Probably, along with the ability to focus, for objective knowledge, the human mind evolved this ability to achieve transcendence. It is difficult to say if this was a by-product of cognitive evolution, like language, or it was something more specific. Early ancestors wanted to project animacy to objects in the environment and also to the invisible (Guthrie & Guthrie, 1995). The phenomenology of the transcendence, mixed with a feeling of the mystery of existence, led to the religious mood. This required suspending information gathered through the rational mind and the objective facts of nature. Barrett (2000) has proposed that the human mind developed a "hyperactive agency detecting device" which was used as a radar to find potential agents in the environment. Alertness towards agents was helpful for survival and planning. This tendency led to ascribing agenthood to objects that were not even there. This became the foundation of belief structures attached to the unseen and elicited reverence.

The mind's ability to entertain the supernatural is behind religion's success. Since the dawn of the scientific age, enormous emphasis has been given to rationality and objectivity. One would assume that given the rise of science, religion would disappear at least from the advanced countries that have tilted more towards objectivity. Rational intelligence and objective knowledge are the complete opposite of supernatural beliefs (McPhetres & Nguyen, 2018). Interestingly, however, all forms of organised and non-organised religions, cults, and assemblies are on the constant rise throughout the world even though there has been great progress in science. The United States may be the world's most advanced country with regard to investments in science. Yet, overall scientific literacy in the USA remains low (Miller, 2010). Interestingly, data suggest that religion has played an active role in many states in the USA, for example, on matters related to school curriculum, laws on abortion, and vaccination. Lately, religion has also been popular in China, which is a Communist country (Sun, 2017). Interestingly, the USA and China are industrialised countries with tremendous scientific advancement. Therefore, we cannot say that the rise in science diminished the influence of religions across the world. In more technologically advanced countries, both rational objectivity and religious beliefs have evolved in parallel and stabilised. Therefore, there is no *a priori* theory which predicts a decrease in religious sentiments and a rise in atheism in a world that is largely ruled by modern scientific temper. For cognitive scientists the question then is to explain how the mind incorporates this conflict between the rational and the irrational.

Richard Dawkins's *The God Delusion* is a cult classic on the new atheism (Dawkins, 2006). Dawkins supports the idea that religion might have evolved as a by-product of the more general evolution. Therefore, there cannot be any scientific objective ground to entertain a supernatural god and mysticism. The rise of atheism in earlier centuries has been attributed to both Darwinism and social theories of Marx and others (LeDrew, 2012). The atheist's rejection of God is taken to be a sign of superior intelligence (Kanazawa, 2010). Social change and modernity led to the search for greater objectivity. Does atheism reflect the rise of the new scientific mind? H. Allen Orr had criticised Dawkins's book in the pages of *New York Review of Books* calling it amateurish and non-serious propaganda (Allen Orr, 2007, January, *New York Review of Books*). The claim was that the article did not do much to prove the non-existence of God to the believers in any serious manner. In response, Daniel Dennett attacked Orr claiming that Dawkins's book was a popular one and not intended to be a treatise on religion (Dennett, 2007, May, *New York Review of Books*). He further said that Orr and the likes of him were trying to protect a religious world that is quickly disappearing. Dennett's collusion with Dawkins fits well with his materialistic behaviouristic theory of the mind and cognition. God cannot emerge in a mechanistically explained world or brain. If beliefs, mysticism, and the supernatural have to be accepted as products of the mind then consciousness and the many other folk psychological attributes also have to be accepted.

Dawkins accepted that the emergence of religion could be explained as simply as the emergence of natural consciousness is. Therefore, there is no need to invoke the supernatural or mystical. Naturalising religion would allow it to be explored in the brain. Religion could be a tool to study cognition (Bulkeley, 2005). Religion can be seen as an evolutionary adaptive brain function that relies on important brain networks subserving emotion, mental imagery, and belief as seen through brain activity (Kapogiannis et al., 2009). However, with this approach the evolution of organised religions cannot be understood without going back in time and explaining the evolution of pro-sociality and group solidarity. Religions manifest a very high-level evolutionary adaptation towards large-scale collective cognition (Atran & Henrich, 2010). Religion was beneficial from a material and economic point of view since it involved collaboration. Therefore, religion could be viewed as a co-product of cultural evolution that had a wide range of advantages to its practitioners. The natural attributes of the mind were conducive to religions (Bellah, 2011). Attributes such as socialising, inferring, repetitive behaviour, mental imagery, and others are seen in many other habits that we have. Therefore, the human mind has all the psychological tendencies that make faith and belief possible. Therefore, a careful study of the human mind and its attributes should reveal the foundations of religion. Evolutionary psychology, cognitive archaeology, and neuroscience today have techniques that can throw light on this (Boyer, 2008).

A widely popular view considers that religion evolved as cultural adaptation. Religion therefore was not a specific product of the brain's evolution but uses the systems that have other functions (Sosis, 2009). It worked well as an adaptation since it extended the scope of human cooperation. Other scholars have viewed religion's emergence in terms of historical shifts from early humans being egalitarian to trans-egalitarian hunter-gatherers. Our ancestors developed systematic rituals and organised structures related to ancestor worship around the Palaeolithic period (Rossano, 2006). Evidence of such shifts in rituals and practices are seen in cave paintings and other artefacts. Thus, the religious mind evolved out of changes in everyday life itself. Some have also suggested that religions evolved out of changes in mating strategies (Van Slyke & Szocik, 2020). Religion helped in successful and stable mating strategies within a community by putting a structure in place. Also, importantly, although higher primates show qualities such as empathy and theory of mind, they don't have anything like religion. It is an exclusively human evolution that is deeply rooted in culture and collective consciousness. The evolution of human morality has also to do with evolution of religion (Campbell, 1975) since most religions recommend a moral life and impose guidelines of good behaviour.

Therefore, multiple viewpoints exist on the issue of religion's evolution. It is difficult to pinpoint exactly what material or psychological circumstances led to religion's emergence. Whether it evolved as the brain's natural evolution or later as an adaptation for social reasons, its links with cognition are clear. Religious practices reflect cognitive operations at a fundamental level. In the following, we explore which cognitive systems are functionally related to the religious mind. Many scholars have also examined if believers and non-believers differ on their cognitive abilities. Experimental cognitive psychology offers possibilities to know how the religious mind differs from the non-religious.

2. Religion and cognitive systems

Cognitive psychologists study cognitive systems using both behavioural and neuroimaging methods. This has been put to use in studying the effect of religion on the mind, or more specifically on selected systems such as attention and executive control. Collective attention lies at the very foundation of organised religions. Understanding the cognitive science of religion would require models of collective attention. Both peaceful and violent outcomes of religion are group effects. Organised religions are like musicians playing a great symphony under a master conductor. They play individual instruments yet they have a common goal that keeps evolving throughout the symphony. Religions show how well the human mind has evolved to synchronise with other minds. It is one of the finest manifestations of the evolution of our social mind (Johnson, 1979). Group-based contemplative practices, common in many regions, train collective attention. Importantly, religious groups behave as if they have a common goal and a common mind to pursue those goals. This is the phenomenon that needs to be studied within the ambit of cognitive psychology. More recently, many researchers in mind/brain sciences have broken down these concepts into manageable hypotheses and have conducted experiments. This has led to the possibility of studying religion through empirical means.

With the growth in organised cultures, population, objects, and other stimuli (including many animals), there is an attentional overload. In such a scenario, to reduce the cognitive load, attention adapted to be more selective. Brains' higher control systems evolved to allow some flexibility in the manipulation of attention (Coolidge & Wynn, 2018). Religions evolved much later, probably with the evolution of social cognition and the mind's ability to struggle with higher-order metaphysical thoughts. It also evolved to calm the mind amid the flux of stimuli that were more internal with some moral education for a good life. Religions pushed attention more inwards and encouraged its manifestation at a larger collective scale. For example, many people in spite of their cognitive diversity could attend to one relic or object of worship. It was not necessary that this object had to be a physical one but could be immaterial. Thus, it allowed collective attending with shared goals.

In today's internet age, millions of people are capable of paying attention collectively to the same information even when they are dislocated physically (Wu & Huberman, 2007). Televised religious sermons similar to soccer matches attract the attention of millions together. When people see performances together, their brain activity shows synchronisation over time (Pollick et al., 2018). Collective attention has been evolutionarily helpful in the formation of culture and has supported innovation (Muthukrishna & Henrich, 2016). Human cooperation and collaboration on a massive scale require collective attention. The key question is how the individual can maintain rational control of the mind within a large group's collective goal? Mass mobilisations must mean some kind of suspension of individual rationality. The extension of Western liberalism, individualism, and scientific awareness is precisely in a collision against religions since they have fundamental differences with regard to individual vs collective goals. Religions demand a kind of suspension of individual goals for a larger collective purpose linked to the supernatural, guided by someone who claims to know more about such things. Atheism gives the individual all the power to reject such things and make decisions. Thus, religious practices modulate attention differently that involves higher-order cognition. Religions fundamentally alter the cognitive identity of the individual (Mavor & Ysseldyk, 2020).

Cognitive science of religion examines the effect of religion on everyday cognition and behaviour. On the surface, believers and non-believers, of course, appear not very different. However, practitioners of specific religions look at the world uniquely. This unique way of perceiving reality could be because of deploying attention to objects and features differently. Let's examine two well-known religions and see if their followers show significant difference on some cognitive tasks. Calvinism began as a reaction to Catholicism by John Calvin in Switzerland (Kuyper, 2008). Its philosophy is different from mainstream Protestantism. It emphasises hard work for self-development and encourages material possession for happiness. Many even say that Calvinism is responsible for Switzerland being a rich nation and the banker to the world (Hart, 2013). Followers of Calvinism accept individual growth through hard work and do not think there is any kind of virtue in being poor.

The Netherlands has had a strong Calvinist tradition since the sixteenth century. William of Orange who waged the Eighty Years' War with the Spanish was a Calvinist (Hyma, 1938). In more modern times, the Dutch have continued to be followers of Calvinism although a majority of them are atheists. The Dutch way of life has a reverence for a few traits that are central to Calvinism. Given these traits of the Calvinist, it is likely that their cognitive orientation will also be different from others. In a study, Colzato and colleagues (Colzato et al., 2008) compared students at Leiden University who were either Calvinists or atheists as per their self-report. The authors examined if their different religious persuasion would lead to deployment of attention differently in an experimental task. Attention can be deployed either at a global or a local level (Figure 7.1). Navon had first demonstrated this with hierarchical figures (Navon, 1977). For example, in the case of the numeral six written with small sixes, one can either attend

```
E E E E E E E E E E      E E E           E E E
E E E E E E E E E E      E E E           E E E
E E E                    E E E           E E E
E E E E E E E E E E      E E E E E E E E E E E
E E E E E E E E E E      E E E E E E E E E E E
E E E                    E E E           E E E
E E E                    E E E           E E E
E E E E E E E E E E      E E E           E E E
E E E E E E E E E E      E E E           E E E
```

            Congruent   Incongruent
             Global E   Global H
             Local E   Local E

Figure 7.1 Example of stimuli used in Navon task. Participants are faster in responding when both the global and the local features match (congruent condition: E made of smaller E's) as opposed to when they don't match (incongruent condition: H made of smaller E's).

Source: Image from Watson (2013)

to the holistic number or the parts. It's the difference between looking at the forest vs the trees. It is probably the case that we tend to attend to the forest or the big picture before we go more objective and local with our perception. Colzato and colleagues proposed that the Calvinists deploy more local attention compared to the atheists if they are tested on a local-global attention task. It was indeed the case that the Calvinists deployed more local attention. The Calvinists showed decreased processing of global features (Figure 7.2).

In another study, the same group of authors wanted to know if religion affects attention control more directly in a comparative study. They compared Dutch Calvinists and Italian Catholics with seculars and atheists on a Simon task (Hommel et al., 2011). The Simon task measures one's ability to suppress a prepotent action. The Simon effect is linked to attention control in general and is widely popular in cognitive psychology and neuropsychology. Calvinists showed a lower Simon effect than the Catholics. This could mean that the Calvinists were capable of suppressing a prepotent action pattern more successfully than the Catholics. The authors suggested that Calvinism encourages greater independent decision making and responsibility

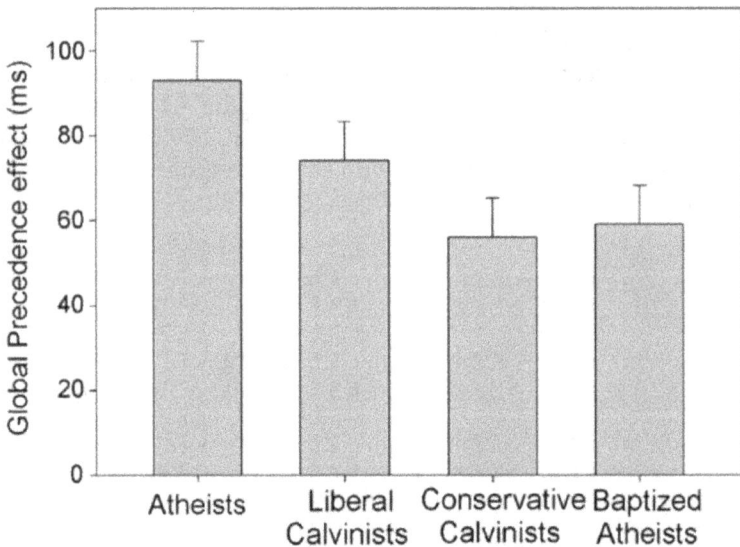

Figure 7.2 Global precedence effect (GPE) in practitioners of different religions. GPE on a Navon task indicates the extent of processing of global features. In this study, Dutch Calvinists showed reduced processing of global information compared to atheists which was reportedly attributed to the Dutch Calvinism's emphasis on individual responsibility.

Source: Reprinted from *Cognition*, Vol. 117, Lorenza S. Colzato, Ilja van Beest, Wery P.M. van den Wildenberg, Claudia Scorolli, Shirley Dorchin, Nachshon Meiran, Anna M. Borghi, Bernhard Hommel, God: Do I have your attention?, 87–94, 2010, with permission from Elsevier

whereas Catholicism encourages a more collective style of behaviour and belief system. Calvinists did not show much surprise when the Simon task presented incongruent stimuli since they were not very surprised when the stimulus-action rules were broken. It is as if they could anticipate all types of contingencies that were related to the task and were prepared for them. However, Catholics were surprised and this led to a bigger Simon score. The results reveal religion's effect on specific components of cognition, more specifically attention regulation and action control. Of course, capturing the effect of something as complex as religion on simplified tasks could be considered an exaggeration. However, these studies do open up the opportunity to evaluate empirically the religious mind's cognitive strategies.

Religious practices also affect the affective aspects of cognition. Devotional rituals induce emotional states in believers. The nature of attention in believers thus may have an affective side to it. When believers deploy attention on their object of reverence, they also experience happiness. Focused attention modulates the affective states of the brain, i.e., the amygdala (Pessoa et al., 2005). Deep and sustained religious practice must act like rewarding stimuli to engage the attentional network along with the emotion regulation mechanism. In laboratory tasks, stimuli that are associated with reward orient attention even when the participants are not aware of them (Custers & Aarts, 2010). This invisible association between reward and attention is an interesting link which can explain why some people are excessively religious more than others. In one study, researchers measured brain activity in devout Mormons (Ferguson et al., 2018). During the fMRI scanning, the participants were exposed to Mormon religious stimuli. The frontal attention areas, the temporal lobe, and other areas were found to be active during their religious experience. Attention thus plays a key role in religious experience through its functional association with the reward circuitry. In addition to the frontal areas, the parietal lobe also shows activation which is linked to "self-awareness" and spiritual experience in practitioners (Miller et al., 2019). These neuroimaging studies suggest a clear link between religious practices, attention, and affective states of the mind.

Atheism comes from Greek *a* (without) and *theos* (god). The appearance of the word in the English language probably coincides with the age of enlightenment and scientific progress as seen in the English translation of Plutarch's *Atheotes* (Bullivant, 2013). We can't understand the mind of the believer without considering that of the non-believer. The atheist believes in the non-existence of God or any supernatural. Applying rationality and known objective facts of the universe, such certainty is reached. The question then is, does one require cognitive effort in maintaining such non-belief systems? Rationalists assume that the religious believer's mind is weak cognitively. Proponents of scientific rationality would say that the human mind has evolved to understand, question, and conquer religion. The consideration of the supernatural is only a weakness seen in some. Liberals and atheists are considered more intelligent since they are considered to have a scientific outlook and open attitude (Kanazawa, 2010). However, a study of believers and their intelligence in 137 countries showed that this correlation may be weak (Lynn et al., 2009).

In contrast to atheists, some religious fundamentalists take belief to another level of extremity. While ordinary believers may be content with spiritualism and its experience, fundamentalists are more into the politicisation of the belief. A group of Polish scientists observed that religious fundamentalists differ from moderates on an important cognitive variable (Senderecka et al., 2019). The Error Related Negativity (ERN) response in EEG indicates the brain's awareness of errors that one might commit. The scientists asked the participants to do a stop-signal task. In this task, one has to stop responding on certain trials when indicated to do so. Most people perform this task well under normal circumstances in many experiments. However, the ERN response in religious fundamentalists has been found to be much higher. It could mean they were monitoring their errors more and were also distressed by it. Fundamentalists may lack cognitive flexibility. Studies show that devoutly religious people score low on psychological tasks that measure cognitive flexibility such as the Wisconsin Card Sorting Task (Zmigrod et al., 2019). Cognitive flexibility is considered a core component of fluid intelligence. Those who are cognitively flexible can adapt more quickly to the demands of a changing situation. Such findings make sense since fundamentalists generally don't adapt to growing social and technological changes in cultures.

Cognitive science of religion assumes that religion and its evolution in humans is only natural. What is unnatural is possibly atheism (Geertz & Markússon, 2010). This viewpoint took a stronghold probably because religion seems to have given mankind many good things. For example, it has strengthened pro-social behaviour (Norenzayan et al., 2016) and it has also helped in achieving cooperation and minimising conflict (Norenzayan, 2013). Therefore, it is only natural to see that so many adopt religious practices and become believers. Some scholars think that the many varieties of atheism have also evolved similarly like religions. For example, contemporary brain-based studies show that religious belief and disbelief share the same underlying pathways (Norenzayan & Gervais, 2013). In sum, cognitive science studies on religion are beginning to unearth the fundamental biases of the mind with regard to belief. There are of course many metaphysical issues that need to be sorted out before any coherent theory emerges that links the brain to religion.

3. Faith and violence

Strong religious sentiments have also led to violence and many unacceptable behaviours. The studies that were discussed earlier portray religion as a powerful force of positive cognitive transformation. However, a close look at the other side of the fence suggests that religion could also lead to loss of control and fuel hatred. It encourages tendencies that can at times establish harmonious living. Let us examine the case of Buddhism in the context of its cognitive benefits and other consequences. Just as the Roman Stoics such as Seneca and others thought that controlling our minds is necessary for the attainment of health and virtue, Buddhist practices offer guidelines for a clean and peaceful life. Buddha simplified and changed the meditation techniques taught to him by his Brahminical teachers like Alara Kalama and Uddaka Ramaputta (Wynne, 2007). The very motive to meditate has remained the same for 2,500 years, to silence the mind and make it free of delusional thoughts that affect our emotions. However, the prescriptions for contemplation and peace do not happen in some vacuum. It happens within our social political structures, and then comes violence. The structure of organised religions encourages territoriality, political battles, racism, and often violence.

While so far studies have looked at individual-level attention, it is not clear how attention works in a collective of people who have a similar intensity of belief and purpose. Researchers in one study examined the basis of support for suicide attacks among religious people. The participants were Indonesian Muslims, Mexican Catholics, British Protestants, Russian Orthodox, Israeli Jews, and Indian Hindus. Those who attended religious services regularly showed the propensity for support to suicide attacks. Those who just did the prayers, but were not that regular, did not show this propensity (Ginges et al., 2009). Attending religious services with other like-minded people, of course, enhances pro-social behaviour (Galen, 2012). This pro-sociality has not been actually studied comprehensively with regard to violence. Just as pro-sociality can lead to developmental work and progress, it can bind people with similar negative thoughts and can cause great harm.

Yuval Noah Harari in his book *Sapiens* (Harari, 2014) offers a clear analysis of the origin and motives of polytheist and monotheist religions. It is important to consider this basic difference in order to understand the nature of violent tendencies in religions. Polytheist religions like Hinduism accepted an all-powerful and supreme being that did not bother about human considerations. Later, monotheistic religions accepted humans as God. Each cult's God was projected as supreme. The historical violence between Christianity and Islam is the fight between two groups who think their God is supreme and is the creator of everything. Monotheistic religions evolved from competing sects within polytheistic religions. Buddhism and Jainism arose from Hinduism. They are known to preach non-violence and mental introspection. Buddhists are known to be more philosophically evolved and practise non-violence. They also have a long history of meditation and mindfulness practice. The case of Buddhism is different from other larger and older religions since its adherents preach non-violence more and are known to be more accepting and compassionate. However, recent reports from a Buddhist country like Sri Lanka indicate that even they commit crimes. Buddhist Sinhalas have been at war against the minority Christians and Muslims for a long time (Deegalle, 2006). Japan is a largely Buddhist country but the crime rate in its biggest cities are no less (Leonardsen, 2010). In Myanmar, Buddhist monks are at war against the minority Muslim Rohingyas (Walton, 2015). In Thailand, a country with Buddhism as its state religion, the majority Buddhists have been waging a war against the minority Muslims on grounds of ethnicity. Many commentators in international media have agreed that although Buddhism is based on compassion and non-violence, its practitioners are equally vulnerable to political terror. Therefore, any group of religious believers can be fundamentalists and can inflict terror on the minority in their territories. More recently there have been many instances and reports of rising Hindu fundamentalists in India and crimes against minorities too (Balakrishnan, 2018). In southern Thailand where the Muslim population is more than 80% and the Buddhists are a minority, the young monks have taken up arms for self-protection. The government interestingly provides the monks military training equipped with arms (Jerryson, 2012).

Here again, we see a different face of a monotheistic religion known for forgiveness and peace. Leaving their core doctrine of compassion and enduring suffering, the monks take up arms and turn into vigilantes. The monks do their regular dhamma but also fight with state sponsorship (Jerryson, 2011). There are many instances in literature in which violence has been preached by Buddhists (Hinnells & King, 2007). While Buddha understood that one could understand reality and probably be happy by mind control and correct interpretation, he also knew that his subjects are human beings after all. He knew that his rational teachings could only go thus far. Therefore, he did not object to violence for self-defence (Gray, 2007). Every young man in Thailand has to be a monk for some years and renounce everything mundane. But if renouncement of worldly concerns is central to Buddhism, then violence has no place. These scenarios from different cultures indicate that religious groups can fight wars and dominate with a collective mind. The individual does not have much will in this case even if they have moral objections. It is this side of religion's hold on the human psyche that is of interest to scholars of cognition.

One of the ancient practices of religion is to gather more followers. In the monotheistic religions, followers often have a missionary purpose. For example, the sects may lure an individual, offering him greater liberty or release from the repression by others. Either way, the tendency to propagate and become larger with enriched socio-political power is seen with these sects. For example, in India people belonging to lower castes often convert to Buddhism (e.g., Gokhale, 1986). Many social activists and politicians convince them that upper-caste Hindus are fundamentalists and their emancipation lies in leaving Hinduism altogether. While such conversions are okay from one individual's free will point of view, this is viewed as an attack by a minority group on Hinduism. Specifically, in 1956, there was a large-scale mass conversion of Hindu Dalits into Buddhism, on the day of

Buddha Jayanti (Deegalle, 2015). How would Buddha himself have viewed this? Buddha was aware of lay people's attraction towards himself and his teaching. When anyone met him and expressed a desire to follow him, he suggested that they also keep their former teachers and religion. That way he was secular and took a broader world view about faith (Coleman, 2002). The government in Sri Lanka has now passed bills to keep track of involuntary conversions in the country. Even during the time of Buddha, some of the followers committed violence against those who did not want to convert. The early spread of Islam happened through the conquest over the Persians in the seventh century. The conquerors used coins that had inscriptions in Arabic on both sides. On one side it had, "There is no God but God alone without a companion." The other side had, "He is God the one God, the everlasting refuge, who has not begotten and has not been begotten and equal to Him is not anyone" (Koran, chapter 112.).

Michael Cook, one of the world's most renowned scholars on early Islam and Muhammad, takes this as the first evidence of Islam's endeavour for monotheistic tribalism (Cook, 2000). Everyone else had to accept Islam since it was distinct. Those who did not accept had to face the consequences. This was happening soon after the death of Muhammad when the Koran was finally in the form of a book of verse in AD 650. Thus, religions have a clear agenda of socio-political conquest through their followers. This can only work when individual followers' judgments are suspended. Studies show that an extreme nature of goal-directed attention is behind such acts of terror (Kruglanski et al., 2019). Once goals are set and clear, the agents try to rationalise, not to suppress them. Complete involvement with a goal has been shown to shield any inhibition that can operate at the level of awareness. Most who join violent groups and carry out suicide missions have an ongoing schema of inhibition that they do not perceive. Kruglanski et al. (2019) cite a story about the recruiting methods of a suicide squad of Liberation Tigers of Tamil Eelam (LTTE) members that's worth considering. When new members come to join this group, first they are asked to walk through a foyer. Later they are asked what they saw or noticed during their walk and waiting. Those who report very minimal stuff are considered. This means that those who could not notice anything were fully engrossed with their cause and were judged as fit to join the mission. Thus, selective attention either to an all-important individual or group cause can inhibit all other rational considerations.

Ancient Japanese Samurai were also monks. They spent their days in meditation and esoteric practice but were also tireless fighters. They unified the essence of a calm fearless mind with the toughness that allowed them to accept death easily. The evolution of Zen has played a key role in Japanese culture, wars, nationalism, poetry, and tea ceremony (Suzuki, 2003). The Samurai warriors were practitioners of Zen. How could Zen be about violent aggression and wars? The Western understanding of Zen as a peaceful meditative practice in serene monasteries and gardens is what the public thinks of it. Brian Victoria's book *Zen at War* highlighted the military past of Zen (Victoria, 2006). Zen leaders of Kyoto's famous Myoshin-ji shrine of the Rinzai Zen Buddhism in 2001 issued a public apology for past crimes committed by Zen monks. This past includes military expansionism, brutality, and crimes against innocents. How could a Zen state of mind that aims for Sartori (calm meditative state) be violent? Knowing this past is important since millions of practitioners of Zen today use it as a mind training program. However, we cannot overlook the deep metaphysics within which Zen evolved in Japan in ancient times. Ancient Japanese warriors following Zen did not differentiate between life and death. Usual dichotomies did not matter and they were ready to accept death any moment. In more modern times, Japanese military generals and soldiers followed Zen as a mind training method to be mentally tough against the enemy. The Khmer Rouge leader Pol Pot was a Buddhist monk in his youth who killed millions of his own people. Buddhist tendencies allowed Pol Pot to be psychologically immune from massacres and practise indifference. This is quite similar to modern claims that extreme meditation can make one insensitive to emotional stimuli by deactivating amygdala functions (Cebolla et al., 2017). In Bangkok, pig slaughterhouses are hidden far away from public gaze, since they are banned and the butchers are Catholic immigrants from Vietnam (Osborne, 2012, Forbes). Killing animals is not sanctioned in Buddhism but meat is eaten by Buddhists around the world. Thus, if we look around, many contradictions are found between the professed ethical behaviour of a religion and its manifestation in reality.

The Amish are found in many states in rural America who come from a Swiss-German stock. They are known for their isolationist way of life and rigidity in religious behaviour. The Amish value traditional lifestyle and do not approve of modernity. They do not marry outsiders and make every attempt to stop any social interactions with the non-Amish population. This is an example of a religious community that stays amid one of the most advanced and liberal countries on earth and yet maintains isolation. The Amish still use horse-driven buggy carts for transportation and go to their own schools. Interestingly, data suggest that they enjoy a high standard of living despite such lifestyle and belief systems (Cross & McKusick, 1970). Multiple reports on Amish show that they have low levels of cognitive disorders such as autism and dementia. Maintenance of pure genetic stock, high level of lifestyle and nutrition, and lack of outside interference may be some of the reasons. However, crime among the Amish is on the rise. In 2013, there was an interesting case in which a group of Amish members were accused of cutting beards of members of the other group because of their rebellion (Green, 2004, *The Atlantic*). Torah Bontrager in her book *An Amish Girl in Manhattan* recounted how growing up in an Amish community, she was raped for many years by men of her own family (Bontrager, 2018). Low levels of education, a closed-door devout culture, and submissiveness make women vulnerable to crimes in such communities. Therefore, a devout religious attitude is no guarantee against crimes. One can find similar stories about the members of Mormon church (Mason, 2019).

While we study many dimensions of religion using experimental paradigms, we have not yet come to grasp its enormous societal implications at a collective level. The facts that I have mentioned are discomforting because we often build our theories around prevailing clichés. Take for example, "Buddhists are non-violent." Cognitive science of religion has to study both the good and the bad aspects of such practices using modern experimental methods. This also includes understanding negative aspects of excessive meditation. At the moment, all studies on such methods are about their positive influence which is only one side of the story. Importantly, the effect of religions and their effects on the human mind can't be understood in any de-contextualised manner. It has to be understood only in the collective societal sense.

4. Cognitive science of religion: Challenges

What's the future of cognitive science or religion? We have no idea about the stage where we are now in our cognitive evolution. We can look back on our histories through records of skull and cave art but there is no data on evolution of cognition. Cognitive archaeology is throwing light on the evolution of cognitive mechanisms such as attention and working memory (Wynn, 2002). Selective attention and working memory might have evolved just some 40,000 years ago. Thus, cognitive evolution is in its infancy considering the timeline of the evolution of *Homo sapiens*. In this context, it has not been easy to map in realistic terms when our minds became equipped to embrace religion. It is tremendously commendable that cognitive scientists and others who subscribe to empiricism are taking up a very abstract and sensitive topic like religion to explore. But the problem with the current experimental approaches is that they are traditional and the complexity of the issues involved are often oversimplified. Thomas Nagel, famous for his landmark paper on consciousness (Nagel, 1974), and a dualist, has called for a second scientific revolution. The cognitive science of religion has to work at the interface of traditional thinking governing our scientific attitudes since the sixteenth century and the new world that's shaping up with the internet age. We have to explain with the best of our scientific knowledge why a cult like Mormonism is on the rise in the most scientifically advanced and liberal democracy like the USA. The existence of religions or even their rise does not pose any contradictions to anything but only shows some fundamental and invariant aspects of the human mind.

A proper study of the cognitive science of religion has to be pursued both locally and globally (Barrett, 2011). Religions impact the minds of people embodied within a cultural context. This point is important since it matters for replications of scientific findings since followers of the same religion may practise it differently in different cultures. For example, Buddhism is practised differently in the USA as compared to in many Asian countries (Mitchell, 2016). There is currently a growing agreement that cultures shape even the neurobiological basis of the mind (Ames & Fiske, 2010). Religions, being part of the cultures broadly, thus influence both psychology and biology in unique ways in different populations. The Japanese rose as a strong capitalist country post-Second World War and also have preserved their cultural heritage such as Zen. It is not the same now with the younger generation who are becoming video game addicts and isolationists. Suicide rates among the young are very high in Japan (Reader, 1991). Technological progress, more than anything, has put unachievable demands on our cognition. It is therefore interesting to see how effectively cultures where the dominant religion has favoured more meditative serenity and tranquillity, such as Japan, deal with such emerging challenges (Nelson, 2013). Thus, overall societal changes and their influence on religion must be considered.

The cognitive science of religion began as a multidisciplinary effort to "science up" the study of religion. This was an enterprise aimed to bring about an empirical investigation of religious phenomena in individuals and groups from different perspectives. Its original questions, some twenty years ago, dealt with cognitive science-based explanations of various types of anthropological and cultural facts associated with religions. The scholars who engaged in it primarily wanted to investigate religion from an empirical standpoint. How is the human mind able to accommodate religion and its demands? Since religion consists of belief in the supernatural and a devotion towards esoteric practices that include visions of the afterlife, the scholars used both explanatory and interpretative approaches. This is important since otherwise, only explanatory approaches will not be sufficient to understand religion's interaction with the mind. Further, the field has also evolved to establish links with neuroscience and evolutionary psychology more recently. The discipline studies the mind and its limits with regard to the acceptance of religion using multiple theoretical and empirical approaches. From this point of view, the discipline examines the extent and limits of human rationality using objective methods.

Barrett (2011) reviewed the accomplishments and the future directions of cognitive science of religion. According to Barrett, cognitive science of religion thus has accomplished a true interdisciplinary methodology to study minds in relation to religion. However, there are only a few areas that seem promising considering the various degrees of interfaces of participating subjects. For example, cognitive science of religion should benefit from direct collaborations with cognitive psychology and evolutionary biology because many theorists use psychological concepts in explaining the mind's limitations and powers with regard to religion. Psychological phenomena such as theory of the mind, pro-social behaviour, and subliminal priming (Pichon et al., 2007) among others have revealed the basis of religious belief. Considering the tremendous growth in theories and paradigms in cognitive psychology, it is likely that we would know more about the religious mind as well as the mind of the non-believer. Similarly, it has not been resolved if religions began as a by-product of general evolution or as an adaptation to something else (Barrett, 2000). The idea that core cognitive and psychological mechanisms of the mind are behind religion's emergence does not have enough empirical grounding yet. Similarly, even if we assume that it emerged as an adaptation since it helped in forging pro-social behaviour or led to greater harmony and health, the data is not clear (Boyer, 1994). Therefore, more close understanding of both evolutionary concepts and psychological underpinnings taking into account cultural and social factors should help us crack the mind-religion nexus. However, Barrett (2011) is less optimistic about the "neuroethology" approach which some scholars have taken recently. That is, to look at brain activity as neural proxies for religious beliefs. The problem is that there is no framework to understand these mappings now since the disciplines are new and still evolving. This comment is more general to the cognitive neuroscience approaches prevalent in many other areas where no fixed brain area has been found for any cognitive functions. In sum, the future of the discipline lies in more innovative approaches in domains of cognitive psychology and evolutionary theories.

Cognitive science of religion began with the cognitive revolution of the 1950s. The human mind was brought back to focus and every kind of behaviour was explained in terms of mental representations. Cognitive science's influence on religious studies led to an assault on cultural theories (White, 2021) since cultural theorists and anthropologists were keen on cultural relativism and explained religions in terms of unique cultures. Dan Sperber (Sperber, 1996) proposed his theory of "epidemiology of representations" which critiqued both cultural relativism and determinism as explanations for the growth of religions in human societies. Drawing inspiration from cognitive science theories of the mind, Sperber suggested that without understanding the core properties of the human mind, one cannot explain how religious ideas are transmitted across cultures or how they evolve. The mind has the key to understanding how it accommodates religious belief in different cultures. Therefore, this mentalistic perspective was key to the emergence of more biological and psychological concepts in understanding religions. However, even current approaches do have some constraints even if a largely cognitive approach has become popular in the study of the mind and religion. Since cognitive scientists aim at discovering a general framework for the mind for all, they have specific challenges while studying religions. Since religions and their practitioners show much diversity worldwide. It has not been easy to explain using cognitive psychology how different people are rooted in different cultures and practise different belief systems and conduct different rituals. Therefore, future research should be aimed at accommodating this diversity while maintaining the empirical approaches in the discipline.

5. Summary

The study of religion and the mind is certainly very interesting. The discipline known as cognitive science of religion has been on the rise that forges interdisciplinary collaborations between anthropology, sociology, and mind/brain sciences. In this chapter, I dealt with some points related to the evolution of religions. But given the fact that religion always becomes a very sensitive topic, both creationists and evolutionists have radically different theories of its beginning. However, religion can be understood at a very fundamental level in terms of a few cognitive components. Essentially, it trains collective attention, which has both good and bad sides to it. Further studies on both believers and non-believers have revealed different cognitive processing strategies. In the absence of large-scale studies, we may not be in a position now to explain how religions have shaped cultures and societies. Future studies will take into account this methodological limitation. The studies showing religion's effect on specific types of attentional modulations are very encouraging. They can reveal how religion has moulded specific types of people and their everyday behaviour. It can explain why some cultures live in more conflict and wage more wars than others. Since the unholy nexus of religion and politics is very ancient, they can't be separately looked at. I also pointed out that the naïve news of some cognitive neuroscientists studying the effects of meditation in Buddhists on the mind and attention has probably provided a biased view of the whole issue. A cognitive science study of religion has to also show how some practitioners of such a religion indulge in violence and ethnic cleansing. Science just can't project one aspect of the phenomenon and not consider what is exactly happening at the larger societal level. I deliberated considerably on the very important question of the nexus of religions and violence. We have to explain the human mind's exceptional ability to both focus on calm beautiful things and also indulge in violence. That conflict has shaped our evolution and created civilisations. It is time cognitive scientists take the studies of religions very seriously at the broadest level possible.

References

Ames, D. L., & Fiske, S. T. (2010). Cultural neuroscience. *Asian Journal of Social Psychology, 13*(2), 72–82.

Atran, S., & Henrich, J. (2010). The evolution of religion: How cognitive by-products, adaptive learning heuristics, ritual displays, and group competition generate deep commitments to prosocial religions. *Biological Theory, 5*(1), 18–30.

Balakrishnan, R. (2018). India and the crime-terrorism Nexus. *Counter Terrorist Trends and Analyses, 10*(9), 11–17.

Barrett, J. L. (2000). Exploring the natural foundations of religion. *Trends in Cognitive Sciences, 4*(1), 29–34.

Barrett, J. L. (2011). *Cognitive science, religion, and theology: From human minds to divine minds.* Templeton Press.

Bellah, R. N. (2011). *Religion in human evolution*. Harvard University Press.

Bontrager, B. (2018). *The hidden Amish girl*. Amazon. https://www.amazon.com/Hidden-Amish-Girl-Betty-Bontrager-ebook/dp/B07GBWJHPG

Boyer, P. (1994). *The naturalness of religious ideas: A cognitive theory of religion*. University of California Press.

Bulbulia, J. (2007). The evolution of religion. In Louise Barrett, and Robin Dunbar (Eds.), *Oxford Handbook of Evolutionary Psychology* (pp. 621–636). Oxford Library of Psychology.

Bulkeley, K. (2005). *The wondering brain: Thinking about religion with and beyond cognitive neuroscience*. Routledge.

Bullivant, S. (2013). Defining atheism. In *The Oxford handbook of atheism* (pp. 11–21). Oxford University Press.

Boyer, P. (2008). Being human: Religion: Bound to believe?. *Nature*, *455*(7216), 1038.

Campbell, D. T. (1975). On the conflicts between biological and social evolution and between psychology and moral tradition. *American Psychologist*, *30*(12), 1103.

Cebolla, A., Demarzo, M., Martins, P., Soler, J., & Garcia-Campayo, J. (2017). Unwanted effects: Is there a negative side of meditation? A multicentre survey. *PLoS One*, *12*(9), e0183137.

Coleman, J. W. (2002). *The new Buddhism: The western transformation of an ancient tradition*. Oxford University Press.

Colzato, L. S., van Beest, I., van den Wildenberg, W. P., Scorolli, C., Dorchin, S., Meiran, N., Borghi, A. M., & Hommel, B. (2010). God: Do I have your attention?. *Cognition*, *117*(1), 87–94.

Colzato, L. S., van den Wildenberg, W. P., & Hommel, B. (2008). Losing the big picture: How religion may control visual attention. *PLoS One*, *3*(11), e3679.

Cook, M. (2000). *The Koran: A very short introduction*. Oxford University Press.

Coolidge, F. L., & Wynn, T. G. (2018). *The rise of Homo sapiens: The evolution of modern thinking*. Oxford University Press.

Cross, H. E., & McKusick, V. A. (1970). Amish demography. *Social Biology*, *17*(2), 83–101.

Custers, R., & Aarts, H. (2010). The unconscious will: How the pursuit of goals operates outside of conscious awareness. *Science*, *329*(5987), 47–50.

Dawkins, R. (2006). *The God delusion*. Houghton Mifflin Company.

Deegalle, M. (Ed.). (2006). *Buddhism, conflict and violence in modern Sri Lanka*. Routledge.

Deegalle, M. (2015). Buddhists on religious conversion. In *Religious conversion: Religion scholars thinking together* (p. 2497852). Wiley.

Ferguson, M. A., Nielsen, J. A., King, J. B., Dai, L., Giangrasso, D. M., Holman, R., Korenberg, J. R., & Anderson, J. S. (2018). Reward, salience, and attentional networks are activated by religious experience in devout mormons. *Social Neuroscience*, *13*(1), 104–116.

Galen, L. W. (2012). Does religious belief promote prosociality? A critical examination. *Psychological Bulletin*, *138*(5), 876.

Geertz, A. W., & Markússon, G. I. (2010). Religion is natural, atheism is not: On why everybody is both right and wrong. *Religion*, *40*(3), 152–165.

Ginges, J., Hansen, I., & Norenzayan, A. (2009). Religion and support for suicide attacks. *Psychological Science*, *20*(2), 224–230.

Gokhale, J. B. (1986). The sociopolitical effects of ideological change: The Buddhist conversion of Maharashtrian untouchables. *The Journal of Asian Studies*, 269–292.

Gray, D. B. (2007). Compassionate violence? On the ethical implications of tantric Buddhist ritual. *Journal of Buddhist Ethics*, 14, 239–271.

Green, F (2004, September). Violence among the Amish. *The Atlantic.*

Guthrie, S. E., & Guthrie, S. (1995). *Faces in the clouds: A new theory of religion.* Oxford University Press on Demand.

Harari, Y. N. (2014). *Sapiens: A brief history of humankind.* Random House.

Hart, D. (2013). *Calvinism: A history.* Yale University Press.

Hinnells, J., & King, R. (Eds.). (2007). *Religion and violence in South Asia: Theory and practice.* Routledge.

Hommel, B., Colzato, L. S., Scorolli, C., Borghi, A. M., & van den Wildenberg, W. P. (2011). Religion and action control: Faith-specific modulation of the Simon effect but not stop-signal performance. *Cognition*, 120(2), 177–185.

Hyma, A. (1938). Calvinism and capitalism in the Netherlands, 1555-1700. *The Journal of Modern History*, 10(3), 321–343.

Jerryson, M. K. (2011). In Buddha's company: Thai soldiers in the Vietnam war. In *Southeast Asia: Politics, meaning, and memory.* University of Hawaii Press.

Jerryson, M. K. (2012). *Buddhist fury: Religion and violence in Southern Thailand.* Oxford University Press.

Johnson, H. M. (1979). Religion in social change and social evolution. *Sociological Inquiry*, 49(2–3), 313–339.

Kanazawa, S. (2010). Why liberals and atheists are more intelligent. *Social Psychology Quarterly*, 73(1), 33–57.

Kapogiannis, D., Barbey, A. K., Su, M., Zamboni, G., Krueger, F., & Grafman, J. (2009). Cognitive and neural foundations of religious belief. *Proceedings of the National Academy of Sciences*, 106(12), 4876–4881.

Kruglanski, A. W., Bélanger, J. J., & Gunaratna, R. (2019). *The three pillars of radicalization: Needs, narratives, and networks.* Oxford University Press.

Kuyper, A. (2008). *Lectures on calvinism.* Hendrickson Publishers.

LeDrew, S. (2012). The evolution of atheism: Scientific and humanistic approaches. *History of the Human Sciences*, 25(3), 70–87.

Leonardsen, D. (2010). *Crime in Japan: Paradise lost?* Springer.

Lynn, R., Harvey, J., & Nyborg, H. (2009). Average intelligence predicts atheism rates across 137 nations. *Intelligence*, 37(1), 11–15.

Mason, P. Q. (2019). *Mormonism and violence: The battles of Zion.* Cambridge University Press.

Mavor, K. I., & Ysseldyk, R. (2020). A social identity approach to religion: Religiosity at the nexus of personal and collective self. In *The science of religion, spirituality, and existentialism* (pp. 187–205). Academic Press.

McPhetres, J., & Nguyen, T. V. T. (2018). Using findings from the cognitive science of religion to understand current conflicts between religious and scientific ideologies. *Religion, Brain & Behavior*, 8(4), 394–405.

Miller, J. D. (2010). The conceptualization and measurement of civic scientific literacy for the twenty-first century. *Science and the Educated American: A Core Component of Liberal Education*, 136, 241–255.

Miller, L., Balodis, I. M., McClintock, C. H., Xu, J., Lacadie, C. M., Sinha, R., & Potenza, M. N. (2019). Neural correlates of personalized spiritual experiences. *Cerebral Cortex*, 29(6), 2331–2338.

Mitchell, S. A. (2016). *Buddhism in America: Global religion, local contexts.* Bloomsbury Publishing.

Muthukrishna, M., & Henrich, J. (2016). Innovation in the collective brain. *Philosophical Transactions of the Royal Society B: Biological Sciences*, *371*(1690), 20150192.

Nagel, T. (1974). What is it like to be a bat?. *The Philosophical Review*, *83*(4), 435–450.

Navon, D. (1977). Forest before trees: The precedence of global features in visual perception. *Cognitive Psychology*, *9*, 353–383.

Nelson, J. K. (2013). *Experimental Buddhism: Innovation and activism in contemporary Japan.* University of Hawaii Press.

Norenzayan, A. (2013). *Big Gods: How religion transformed cooperation and conflict.* Princeton University Press.

Norenzayan, A., & Gervais, W. M. (2013). The origins of religious disbelief. *Trends in Cognitive Sciences*, *17*(1), 20–25.

Norenzayan, A., Shariff, A. F., Gervais, W. M., Willard, A. K., McNamara, R. A., Slingerland, E., & Henrich, J. (2016). The cultural evolution of prosocial religions. *Behavioral and Brain Sciences*, *39*.

Osborne, L. (2012, July 11). Are Buddhists violent? *Forbes.* Retrieved September 15, 2022, from https://www.forbes.com/2009/04/14/bangkok-violent-buddhists-opinions-contributors-thailand-cambodia-burma.html?sh=1f0742cd7d36

Pessoa, L., Padmala, S., & Morland, T. (2005). Fate of unattended fearful faces in the amygdala is determined by both attentional resources and cognitive modulation. *Neuroimage*, *28*(1), 249–255.

Pichon, I., Boccato, G., & Saroglou, V. (2007). Nonconscious influences of religion on prosociality: A priming study. *European Journal of Social Psychology*, *37*(5), 1032–1045.

Pollick, F. E., Vicary, S., Noble, K., Kim, N., Jang, S., & Stevens, C. J. (2018). Exploring collective experience in watching dance through intersubject correlation and functional connectivity of fMRI brain activity. *Progress in Brain Research*, *237*, 373–397.

Reader, I. (1991). *Religion in contemporary Japan.* University of Hawaii Press.

Rossano, M. J. (2006). The religious mind and the evolution of religion. *Review of General Psychology*, *10*(4), 346–364.

Senderecka, M., Kossowska, M., Sekerdej, M., & Szewczyk, J. (2019). Religious fundamentalism is associated with hyperactive performance monitoring: ERP evidence from correct and erroneous responses. *Biological Psychology*, *140*, 96–107.

Sosis, R. (2009). The adaptationist-byproduct debate on the evolution of religion: Five misunderstandings of the adaptationist program. *Journal of Cognition and Culture*, *9*(3–4), 315–332.

Sperber, D. (1996). *Explaining culture: A naturalistic approach.* Cambridge University Press.

Sun, Y. (2017). The rise of protestantism in post-Mao China: State and religion in historical perspective. *American Journal of Sociology*, *122*(6), 1664–1725.

Suzuki, S. (2003). *Not always so: Practicing the true spirit of Zen* (p. 176). HarperOne.

Van Slyke, J. A., & Szocik, K. (2020). Sexual selection and religion: Can the evolution of religion be explained in terms of mating strategies?. *Archive for the Psychology of Religion*, *42*(1), 123–141.

Victoria, B. D. (2006). *Zen at war*. Rowman & Littlefield Publishers.

Walton, M. J. (2015). Monks in politics, monks in the world: Buddhist activism in contemporary Myanmar. *Social Research*, 82(2), 507–530.

Watson, T. L. (2013). Implications of holistic face processing in autism and schizophrenia. *Frontiers in Psychology*, 4, 414.

White, C. (2021). *An introduction to the cognitive science of religion: Connecting evolution, brain, cognition, and culture*. Routledge.

Wu, F., & Huberman, B. A. (2007). Novelty and collective attention. *Proceedings of the National Academy of Sciences*, 104(45), 17599–17601.

Wynn, T. (2002). Archaeology and cognitive evolution. *Behavioral and Brain Sciences*, 25(3), 389.

Wynne, A. (2007). *The origin of Buddhist meditation*. Routledge.

Zmigrod, L., Rentfrow, P. J., Zmigrod, S., & Robbins, T. W. (2019). Cognitive flexibility and religious disbelief. *Psychological Research*, 83(8), 1749–1759.

8   Self, Morality, and Cognition

1. The evolution of morality

Evolution of morality is a significant question of scientific and philosophical importance. For centuries, from the Greek philosophers to more modern thinkers, speculation has been continuous on the origin of morality in our species. Charles Darwin, in his *Descent of Man* (Darwin, 1871), suggested that it is our moral self that distinguishes us from all other animals. It is unique in the biological world. Darwin advanced the thesis that the origin of human morality is biological. Basic categories of morality could also be universal. It is also the case that human morality is influenced by cultural forces and they manifest differently in different people and places. Darwin's position on moral behaviour pushed the idea that morality is of biological origin and therefore it should be studied scientifically. However, philosophers have long held the position that morality is cultural or religious, since it is widely different in people with regards to its practices (Avise & Ayala, 2010). Thus, the question of morality being of natural origin vs cultural origin has been debated for a long time without much resolution.

Departing significantly from philosophical speculation before him, Darwin, based on his observations, noted that human morality is an outcome of a highly developed faculty of intelligence – intelligence that endows the human animal rationality, capacity of thinking, and the ability to know the consequences of one's actions on others. Even though these abilities have a biological basis, they could vary depending on individual and cultural forces. Thus, Darwin brought higher cognition, that is intelligence, to theories on the nature of morality and ethical actions in humans. Darwin also held the view that other animals could be capable of morality of the type that humans have, only if they could be as intelligent as humans. Therefore, the lack of morality in animals is justified on the grounds that they do not possess the level of sophisticated intelligence that we humans have. Today this view may be contested, but the underlying idea is still in circulation. Darwin's views brought the debate on evolution of morality to more scientific turf.

DOI: 10.4324/9781003316053-8

Ayala has argued that the human moral self is exaptation and not an adaptation (Ayala, 2010). Exaptations are by-products of natural selection. Ayala has suggested that human morality could be understood in terms of a few clearly defined traits that are biological: firstly, the ability to anticipate the effects of actions on other individuals; secondly, the ability to ascribe values to choices made; and finally, the ability to select the best alternative, keeping moral virtue in mind. These traits have evolved as an outcome of the emergence of superior cognition in our species. Therefore, morality is not an adaptation that evolved to support some specific function in our social and cultural evolution. A close study of evolution of bipedalism, tool use, and extensive use of hands for creating symbolic products all have led to scenarios that are related to moral actions. For example, when tools that could kill someone were created, the human mind also started to evaluate the consequences of such actions on the victim (Ayala, 2014). However, cultural theorists think that human morality evolved as a function of cultures. They emerged as a response to rigid cultural norms that were agreed upon. These conventions led to choices of actions that were either virtuous or immoral for each community. The individual thus developed a system of evaluation of personal actions that were moral and just (Cosmides et al., 2010).

Steven Pinker has claimed that human morality is an instinct (Pinker, 2017). Humans are biologically endowed to express moral and ethical thinking to begin with. As a strong nativist position, this view makes our morality a core part of our biological makeup. Of course, later learning further makes it suitable for various people and cultures. A strong test of such a hypothesis would be if infants that have not been exposed to the ways of the world manifest moral behaviour. It appears that preverbal infants do make moral judgments about individuals as pro-social or antisocial (Van de Vondervoort & Hamlin, 2016). Infants also show an intuitive sense of fairness already (Sloane et al., 2012). Citing such studies, many theorists have claimed that human infants already come with a moral core which is unique to our species and not seen in others (Hamlin, 2013). It is of course possible that such early moral intuitions may be modified according to experience in specific cultures.

Not all theorists take the view that humans are moral by their very biology. For example, Frans de Waal has defended the view that human morality is a choice and not a biological trait (De Waal et al., 2006). Humans have learnt to display moral behaviour that is pro-social, as a result of long cultural evolution and learning. According to De Waal, one can also see patterns of moral behaviour, such as reciprocal pro-sociality, in many other animals. Animals also have moral lives that we don't understand since we have committed to a highly anthropomorphic view of our own morality as special (Bekoff & Pierce, 2009). De Waal's view makes sense if we consider the fact that humans are capable of brutality at all ages and cultures. These seem spontaneous and part of our core make-up, just the way Pinker thinks that our good nature is part of our core make-up. Even small children commit crimes, indicating there is no biological constraint that inhibits brutality (Streib, 1983). Therefore, given the current status of research, it is difficult to conclude if our moral nature is strictly biological or is an outcome of cultural evolution and is thus modifiable. Further, it is also not possible to conclude whether we learn morality from social interactions or it is an instinct. Developmental psychologists currently stand divided on this important point.

The evolution of social relations and kinship among our ancestors does not tell us anything directly about how morality evolved (Ruse, 1984) since morality refers to doing good because it is just and virtuous without any expectation of rewards. Evolutionary social history of mankind does not offer clear hints about the emergence of the mind's moral attributes. Either it is possible that morality evolved as cultural adaptation over a long period of time or it emerged accidentally at a certain point in time (Joyce, 2007). The sudden emergence could be linked to the appearance of extraordinary intelligence and social cognition supported by cognitive systems in our ancestors. This cognitive perspective with regard to emergence of necessary brain networks that support moral behaviour becomes important for mind/brain scientists, which is the perspective I will take in this chapter (Bekoff, 2001). Among the cognitive systems that evolved, only a few directly influence moral behaviour, and those are being studied currently within cognitive psychology (Strohminger & Nichols, 2014): the involvement of attention, memory, and consciousness in moral decision making. Therefore, although cultural, social, and philosophical accounts of the evolution of morality have revealed much on the subject, mind/brain scientists have now started to study the mechanisms of morality as a function of the brain. The important question is how and when the brain acts morally and what the constraints are.

2. The science of morality

Our moral self is natural, intuitive, and mostly incorrigible. But we all know what it means since we all have a moral self however good or bad it may be. Morality is the internal radar that decides what's good or bad for us (Schwartz, 1987). Morality helps guide us towards virtuous behaviour as set by the society we live in. In any situation we know instinctively what is right, what should be done. From individual lives to lives of nations, morality guides all actions. When actions are rational but are judged as immoral, they are not undertaken (Overing, 2013). In all religions, the high ideals of a good life as well as a smooth transition to the afterlife depends on our moral behaviour. Our moral nature governs our worldly decisions and the positions we take every day towards anything. Humans aspire towards morally virtuous actions as if they are evolutionarily designed to be so. Actions and thoughts that do not align with the prevailing morality of a society or culture are looked down upon. This may suggest that morality was evolutionarily selected to be part of our cognition since it does common good. This assumption, though it seems natural, needs empirical support. This chapter is about current research in mind-brain sciences that study the moral attributes of human nature. Most philosophical doctrines evolved to understand and preach the moral life that is achievable. The cognitive science approach to this question is to understand the theoretical assumptions of morality in connection to the brain and general theories of human psychology. With advancements in brain imaging methods and cognitive psychology, this has now been made possible.

The most important question is if morality is part of cognition in general. Cognition includes moral decisions that help execute social and ethical responsibilities. Concerns for morality introduce experiences linked to virtue, guilt, fear, and a range of other emotions. Morality is associated with self-consciousness and agency. Moral agents have intentionality and goal-directed behaviour. Understanding the cognition behind morality is also important to understand the diversity of human actions and their consequences in everyday life. What humans do and do not do depends on their moral radar. It has not been easy to explain to what extent humans can exercise morality or evaluate actions based on their moral consequences. Philosophers have devised many elegantly thought-out experiments to examine human actions from the perspective of moral decision making, such as the trolley problem. It is also fascinating to think what our world and social life would have been like in the absence of our moral concerns. Cognitive science is about developing models of the mind and its operations using psychological, neurobiological, computational, and philosophical approaches. This also includes linguistic and anthropological points of view.

At the outset, it may appear that the question of morality is much too subjective and philosophical to be part of cognitive explorations. However, on the contrary, since the eighties, a distinctive field has evolved within the cognitive sciences. Joshua Greene, in an interesting article, proclaimed that moral cognition has grown as a field more rapidly than other fields in recent decades (Greene, 2015). Although it has been classically studied in philosophy, psychological and neurobiological methods have now allowed us a glimpse of the very foundations of our moral nature. It's being widely recognised that our conceptions of our own moral nature are an extension of our psychological self. Cognitive systems that include attention, working memory, and executive control influence our moral behaviour. Greene noted that once we frame the key problems and questions of morality, we can see that the current models of cognitive science are well suited. The question of morality is not all about our altruistic nature or empathic self, but cognitive operations that influence them. Since morality is one of the functions of the brain and mind, a functional approach has allowed us to look at the distinctive psychological and neural mechanisms of morality (Sunar, 2009). The functional perspective of our moral nature considers mechanisms such as attention, perception, memory, emotion, and decision making including social cognition. Jonathan Haidt (2007) has expanded the domain of moral cognitive science that explains concepts such as purity, treason, and disrespect from a larger cultural point of view. Haidt has explained the cognitive science of morality beyond the considerations of guilt, harm, and fairness.

Albert Bandura studied the development of our moral nature over many years and made some important contributions (Bandura, 2014). The key question for him was to examine both the good and the bad moral actions at the interface of individual and social forces. How do we choose to act morally and when do we suspend it? History tells us that people disengage from their moral sanctions under many conditions, most particularly when they are manipulated by authority or when they are convinced that their actions and resultant guilt will be on someone else. At times they also make adjustments to this self-censoring by sanitising language. The most fundamental question is whether individuals are programmed to perform the most morally valid actions or social forces influence this. According to Bandura, people generally don't engage in abstract rational thinking on their moral actions. Individuals engage in a self-reacting style of thinking when they evaluate the consequences of their actions. That is, they evaluate if their own and others' actions are similar or different from the moral standards that they have set for themselves. Humans have uniquely different moral standards given particular developmental, social, and cultural influences. Although Bandura's perspective was not from experimental psychology, he did develop a theory on morality from the social cognitive point of view (Bandura, 1977; Figure 8.1). He theorised that individual moral actions can be amplified towards the proactively good by structuring the social forces accordingly.

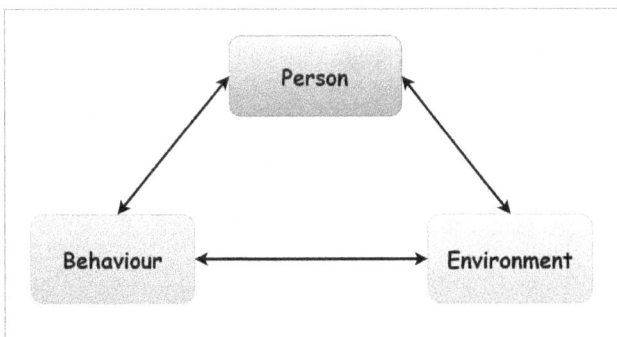

Figure 8.1 Bandura's social cognitive theory of development. Behaviour is learned from an environment by observing others' behaviour. In this way, he combined the behaviouristic principles with social factors in building a theory of human behaviour.

Source: Adapted from Bandura (1977)

In his example, the hierarchical nature of command flow in our political and bureaucratic structures makes good people commit crimes that they otherwise would not have committed. For example, in the command chain, the top decision-maker is away from the execution scene but the person who implements remains close to actions. Those who are in the middle do not feel much emotionally since they merely act like messengers. Take, for example, the religious leaders at the top issuing commands and the field soldiers carrying out the crimes on the ground. Thus, Bandura found that these various means of command flow can decide an individual's moral compass and nature of guilt. In sum, our moral compass has origins in both individual and contextual forces. While the individual may be responsible for any actions and their moral dimensions, larger societal and cultural forces, including the power of bureaucracy, cannot be neglected. Bandura makes the interesting observation that it's equally important to also understand under which circumstances we create proactive control settings for our good actions. Both disengaging from morally corrupt actions and engaging with good actions are part of this control setting. This dichotomy is important and has connections with the current theories of executive control and action planning theories in experimental psychology. For example, executive control can mean both proactive and reactive types of control settings (Braver, 2012). Most scientific attention has been given to moral failings as opposed to moral good, particularly the factors that lead to morally awkward actions in otherwise intelligent people. Milgram in a highly cited paper (Milgram & Gudehus, 1978) found that even decent people can perform morally reprehensible actions when they are freed from the ownership of their actions.

Moral actions are always about available options. The philosophical speculation on the morality question has been on what we choose to do and why, particularly when we face moral dilemmas that involve questions of life and death. A famous thought experiment in this domain is the trolley problem (Figure 8.2) which examines how individuals evaluate moral options and decide on suitable actions. The problem was developed by Phillipa Foot in 1967 to highlight the fact that our moral decisions during difficult situations are guided by our concerns for utilitarianism (Foot, 1967). We prefer to make rational decisions considering the maximum utility of our actions. This view gives prominence to our rationality more than emotional impulsivity. The trolley problem thus has become the starting point for many cognitively inclined scientists since it allows for non-metaphysical speculations. Imagine you are standing on a railway platform and you see a carriage approaching quickly. You also see that five men are sitting on the track unmindful of the approaching doom. There is a lever which – if pulled – will stop the trolley and the five lives can be saved. However, if the train is diverted into another track, it might hit one single person who is also sitting unmindful. Will you pull the lever to save five lives even if your action ultimately kills one person? Many philosophers

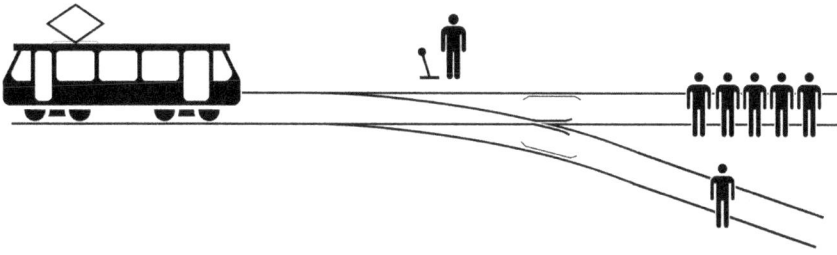

Figure 8.2 Schematic representation of the trolley problem commonly used in moral psychological experiments. Participants are asked to imagine a situation in which a runaway trolley is speeding down a track. Ahead, there are five people unable to move who will be killed if the trolley goes ahead. The participants then have to imagine that they are standing next to a lever. If they pull the lever, they can divert the trolley which would then kill only one person on that track. Would they pull the lever?

Source: Wikipedia commons

have argued that in such a scenario, most people will say that they won't hesitate to pull the lever since it saves a greater number of lives. In another variation of the problem, in place of the single man, there is a fat man on a bridge on top of the tracks. If you push him, the trolley will stop and the five people can be saved. Studies have shown that people are now hesitant to push the fat man although the end result is the same: one person dies and five people are saved. This problem forces different people to reach different speculations. It has been shown that two distinct types of psychological systems are at work on the two variations. In the first instance, we use the rational side of our decision making to judge that one life can be sacrificed in place of five. In the latter case, the emotional control system dominates the decisions. The trolley problem has been stretched to many real-world problems and decision making. A case in point is the decision to go into war and drop bombs even if it is known that there will be some civilian casualties.

Most people approach the decisions in the trolley problem aiming at larger public good without any bias. The problem activates both rational and empathetic thinking. Daniel Kahneman had observed that there are two kinds of decision-making systems in the brain, one fast automatic and the other slow, more deliberate (Kahneman, 2011). Therefore, different people approach the trolley problem differently. Some take a more rational position while others evaluate the situation more emotionally. Also, much research shows that decisions are often based on biases and heuristics (Gigerenzer & Gaissmaier, 2011). At times, such biases can be ideological (Redlawsk, 2002). For example, in the political domain, liberals and conservatives view the same things differently. While one group votes for going to war, the other opposes it. While one group thinks that immigrants are bad for culture and economy, the other thinks that free mobility and citizenship is for the greater good of humanity (Brandt et al., 2014).

The trolley problem has been devised by philosophers to prove the point that human rational actions are a result of a careful thinking process. The logical approach to such problems and the actions people take leave no scope for the emotions. The role of emotions in moral decision making has been long studied in psychology. William James had recognised that our mental states are also emotional states (James, 1890). The body first enacts the feelings long before the mind generates any propositional structures. The neurologist Antonio Damasio, in his *Looking for Spinoza: Joy, Sorrow, and the Feeling Brain*, explored the highly unusual effects of brain damage to selective regions on patients' emotional and pro-social behaviour. Patients with damage to the prefrontal cortex or the medial prefrontal cortex lost their ability to make rational decisions of the kind that we expect in the trolley task. They became emotional or suffered from depression. Any miscalculation during epileptic surgery led to similar situations with many patients. Damasio explained the highly interconnected relationship between our emotions and the thinking brain in terms of the brain regions. Therefore, the implicit role of emotions in moral decision making remains unexplored.

Daniel Kahneman thought that there is no such thing called rational decision making. We humans merely make emotionally limp/limply decisions following heuristics. For the trolley problem, individual decisions would be at this intersection of emotional triggers and some rational analytical thinking. Depending on how emotional one is, or how much one understands utilitarianism, decisions will be made. In an important paper, Moll et al. (2005) demonstrated that the brain networks that subserve the so-called moral brain comprise both the frontal executive control areas and the emotion-processing areas. It's also likely that in some conflicting situations, our rationality overrides the emotions when we make moral decisions and the opposite happens in other states. Depending on the problem – if it's personal or impersonal – such a dissociation can be seen. Experimental data demonstrate such double dissociation during moral decision making (Moll & de Oliveira-Souza, 2007). In sum, the logical philosophical approaches may be limited in explaining the complexity of human moral decision making fully. We have to include emotional states for such an analysis. This also perfectly suits our current repulsions towards fundamental views of classical cognitive science. The emotion angle sits well with views that are more embodied.

3. Language and morality

It may appear that morality is a mental cognitive state with a designated neural network supporting it. There are many contingencies that affect this state. An important point concerns the expression of moral positions.

Language expresses our very deep moral values using its structures. Moral positions are expressed as truth conditions. The functional connection of language with thoughts and consciousness influences moral decision making. Given the tremendous growth of research on language and its interaction with other cognitive systems such as vision, attention, and memory, including executive control, it's possible to seek functional and causal relationships among them (Mishra, 2015). Wallace Chafe long ago claimed that language and consciousness are functionally linked (Chafe, 1974). How one feels about a situation in connection to the self is reflected in language that is used. Fodor's algorithmic view of language did not include such phenomenological aspects. Language was viewed as the main driver of our mind's computational engine (Clark, 1999). Cognitive science has brought back experience and phenomenology into discussion and real-world applications. Moral states are experiential states that humans undergo. Therefore, scientific efforts should be to explore the underlying mechanism of these experiential states both in behavioural and neural terms. One strand of research in recent years has examined if language influences moral decision making in this embodied sense which is a valid question since language carries the strains of our emotional states (Pratt & Kelly, 2008). Many studies have shown that when we use language our emotional brain is also active. For example, during language use the sensorimotor areas of the brain are active (Mishra & Marmolejo-Ramos, 2010). These areas coordinate both stimuli perception and cognitive reactions to it. This may suggest a causal relationship between language and our affective self. Therefore, it is likely that the expression of morality or even its very origin in the mind has a linguistic character to it. How exactly language codes the moral position could be debatable since there are many linguistic theories. My focus here is not to get into linguistic theories but to treat language as an important mechanism that influences our moral thinking via a sense of self and consciousness. In that respect it becomes a question for cognitive science rather than linguistics. It enters into psychological and neurological dimensions.

More recently, a strand of research has examined how people differ in the expression of their morality depending on the language they are using. For example, most bilinguals show less moral concern when they use their non-native language compared to when they are using their native language (Costa et al., 2014). Albert Costa was one of the pioneers of the study of language-morality interaction in recent times. Working in Barcelona, he had witnessed first-hand the linguistic uprising of the separatist movements (Hargreaves, 2000). In Barcelona, people speak Catalan while they look down upon Spanish, a symbol of the imperialism of Madrid. Maybe that was his context of examining how such people expressed their moral decisions in Spanish, which is a language they considered foreign, or even English which few spoke as a foreign language. In one study, he and his colleagues administered the footbridge version of the trolley problem in both the native and second languages of the participants (Costa et al., 2014). The participants spoke a different second language while their native language was Spanish. The authors wanted to know if participants showed more utilitarian decision making while using the second language. Indeed, the results showed that people's behaviour was more utilitarian in their second language compared to the first language. The researchers theorised that people are more emotionally distant in their second language. Therefore, they could think more in an abstract manner of the consequence of their actions and not emotionally. They also speculated that since the second language decreases cognitive fluency, this might have led to more abstract decision making. Thus, socio-political ideologies influence how language and moral judgments interact.

There is yet another theory that governs the foreign language effect on moral decision making. Our mental processing can be either analytic and effortful or fast and effortless. Many theorists since Kahneman have denoted these two mechanisms as fast and slow cognitive operations. One requires focused attention and analysis and the other is more intuitive and faster. Researchers recently examined how linguistic context may influence moral decision making (Geipel et al., 2016). They particularly examined a given scenario in which participants are presented with hypothetical actors and their intentions and how they take moral positions on their outcomes. Actions can have rewards or punishments. The linguistic context was manipulated between first and second language. If the second language induced a slow deliberate mechanism, then this should induce more rational decision making. The results indicated that, in some instances, this was the case. For example, scenarios like this were presented: "Cristiano deliberately and intentionally gave a homeless man his only jacket, even though it was freezing outside. One hour later two guys saw the homeless person with Cristiano's jacket and beat him up because they thought that he had stolen the jacket." Participants were less emotional when these scenarios were presented in the second language. Why does the native language have such a powerful influence on our moral judgment? Some scholars think it's because the native language is often learnt in a highly emotionally charged environment with all its nuances. The early developmental pragmatics of the native language is very rich. The second language is learnt often in a decontextualised manner for a certain specific purpose.

More recently, scholars from Belgium have examined the foreign language effect in the judgment of criminal cases. Description of crimes and its narration in a particular language has important consequences for analysis and judgment. Woumans and colleagues hypothesised that criminal investigators will be less affected by the narration of a case if it's in the foreign language (Woumans et al., 2020). The authors presented crime scenarios either in native or a foreign language for judgment of severity. It was found that crimes described in a second language were judged as less severe compared to the native language. The authors argue that it's because emotional processing in a foreign language is less sensitive. It's to be noted that some other authors have argued that the foreign language effect could also be because of a more rational and analytical type of processing in the foreign language. However, it has not been demonstrated clearly how both emotional processing and rational thinking interact during such processing. In Belgium, the Flemish-speaking region of Ghent has been at language-war for decades. Social and political establishments operate both in Dutch and French. Therefore, this sort of research has important consequences for everyday life.

Li and Tomasello (2021) have recently argued that language and morality have to be viewed as social actions in the evolutionary sense. That is, people use language both to forge and preserve social cooperative moral relations. The theoretical positions we discussed before looked at language and morality as an "interactionist" cognitive mechanism. However, according to Li and Tomasello, language and morality are two important interacting mechanisms for everyday social behaviour. Our moral actions with fellow humans are expressed through specific patterns of language. Language facilitates social commitments in moral decision making. Therefore, evolution of morality could be understood as similar to the evolution of language, particularly when we look at morality as a wider social phenomenon. Kennedy et al. (2021) examined how individual moral concerns are expressed through language using data from Facebook. Individuals express their moral concerns such as purity, fairness, and other value-based positions using specific language. The authors observed that individuals expressed their moral concerns using language that was social and emotional. Such studies show that moral positions in our social life are expressed with the type of language we prefer to use. Therefore, language's role in moral decision making is very foundational.

4. Empathy, morality, and the brain

Although moral decision making is understood in terms of its general welfare-related attributes, the role of empathy remains unclear. In spite of the many neuroimaging studies, it remains very difficult to define morality as a unique behavioural or cognitive process. In this section my focus is to explore if empathy and morality are dissociable entities. Empathy has played a fundamental role in the evolution of our social cognition. Its evolutionary origin in our species may be very recent compared to the evolution of sophisticated cognitive systems. Being empathetic towards anything also means being able to experience subjective emotions beyond the facts. Situations that make us emotional or strongly evoke our empathy receive different moral treatment compared to those that are notable.

It is possible that when we refer to something as a moral decision it may actually be an expression of empathy. Many early authors who studied morality using sentences or pictures and constructed their theories may have confounded them. Empathy has been studied along with theory of the mind as critical attributes of our cognitive system (Schurz et al., 2021). Individuals, being social agents, use empathy to understand other agents' mental states and more particularly, the effects of their decisions on them. This subjective awareness of the effects of moral judgments on other agents implicitly includes an empathetic component (Gallagher & Frith, 2003). It is often observed that individuals are more emotional about moral judgments when the topic is personal than when it is impersonal. Similarly, they are much more emotional when the decision is related to their own people than to strangers. Empathy plays an important role in such scenarios (Woodward, 2016). A study comparing intentional versus accidental harm, caused by agents, found that young people consider all agents equally malign irrespective of the agents' intentions. But older adults behave differently in this task (Decety et al., 2012). Evolution of empathy, moral decision making, and their interaction follows a definite trajectory over the lifespan (Saxe, 2013). The role of empathy in moral decision making may be dependent on age and maturity. There could also be some amount of exaggeration about the role of empathy in moral decision making. Partly because empathy is not very well understood in psychological terms and is also not clear how it is controlled by higher cognition. While some psychologists think that even children under the age of three can read others' minds and display the contextually appropriate emotional response, others think this is an overestimation (Burge, 2018). The most widely held consensus is that the social mind takes a very long time to get fully formed since it depends on the maturity and sophistication of many other cognitive systems including language (Lavelle, 2018). It's also being debated if human empathy is an automatic reflex or is a controlled behaviour guided by rational cognition (Szuster & Jarymowicz, 2020). Similarly, the question of intelligence and its relation to morality is also problematic. Some scholars think that intelligence may not predict moral behaviour (Bostyn et al., 2020).

Moral positions are influenced by how we view the world and other actions from the point of view of who we are. Human moral decision making is not only restricted to other humans but also extends to inanimate objects. Objects are judged as good or bad based on our knowledge of the socio-economic positions of the individuals they are associated with. If objects belong to people with higher economic standing, then they are considered to be of greater worth. Emotion regulation directly intervenes with moral positions by modifying our rational thoughts. This give and take between the rational and the emotional parts of the brain with regard to moral decision making is culture governed (Greene & Haidt, 2002). In one brain imaging study, participants were told stories in which either they or someone else committed a moral violation either intentionally or unintentionally. Amygdala activation was higher when the transgression was intentional and linked to the participants (Berthoz et al., 2006). Thus, moral positions generate a higher emotional response and probably stronger guilt when they are our intentional actions. Neuroimaging studies have found that in criminals there is a structural impairment in important areas such as the prefrontal cortex, amygdala, and dorsal and ventral prefrontal cortices (Raine & Yang, 2006). The self-regulation of thoughts and actions applying the executive control machinery is critical for everyday life. An inability to see how one's actions impact larger social norms leads to reprehensible actions (Heatherton, 2011).

Meta-analysis of neural data across studies indicates that there are probably specialised networks in the brain for each moral domain (Eres et al., 2018). For instance, those who have higher moral competence also show higher connectivity between the medial orbito-frontal cortex and the amygdala (Jung et al., 2016). This indicates a dynamic interaction between rational decision making and emotional sensitivity. In individuals with high moral competence, rational decision making and emotion work rather independently. Depending on contextual demands, such individuals may take a non-emotional rational decision and at other times opt for emotional decisions. Such dissociations could be a result of the functional connectivity of medial prefrontal cortex with emotion areas such as the amygdala and orbital prefrontal cortex that control moral decision making (Jung et al., 2016). The connectivity of the medial prefrontal cortex with other critical regions governs such behaviour (Liu et al., 2019). There are books now that provide training manuals for enhancing moral competence based on these neuroscience findings (Lind, 2019). Apart from the activity of specific brain regions during specific moral decision making, the default mode network of the brain can indicate the moral competence of people (Beni, 2019). For instance, spontaneous activity in the dorsomedial prefrontal cortex is linked to the tendency to forgive in individuals (Li & Lu, 2017).

5. Summary

The origin of morality in our species remains one of the last frontiers in our quest for the holistic understanding of our minds and selves. The chapter has merely scratched the surface of this important question and much remains to be unearthed. Research reviewed in this chapter suggests that cognitive psychology has made successful attempts to understand the basic mechanisms of feelings associated with moral decision making. Since morality includes both emotional and rational attitudes it has not been easy to explore the fundamentals with experimental techniques. It gets complicated also because morality is a philosophical question as well. Data suggest the involvement of fundamental cognitive processes behind moral actions. The chapter shows that both emotional and rational understanding of facts help in finding the right moral response. Research with brain imaging has revealed important mechanisms that govern moral decision making. Additionally, language influences the moral concerns of people in different contexts. Cognitive psychologists have developed models that may explain how we can make different moral decisions depending on different considerations.

References

Avise, J. C., & Ayala, F. J. (2010). In the light of evolution IV: The human condition. *Proceedings of the National Academy of Sciences, 107*(Supplement 2), 8897–8901.

Ayala, F. J. (2010). The difference of being human: Morality. *Proceedings of the National Academy of Sciences, 107*(Supplement 2), 9015–9022.

Ayala, F. J. (2014). Evolution and value. *Expositions, 8*(1), 50–58.

Bandura, A. (1977). Self-efficacy: Toward a unifying theory of behavioral change. *Psychological Review, 84*(2), 191.

Bandura, A. (2014). Social cognitive theory of moral thought and action. In *Handbook of moral behavior and development* (pp. 69–128). Psychology Press.

Beni, M. D. (2019). Social and moral aspects of the self. In *Structuring the self* (pp. 211–239). Palgrave Macmillan.

Bekoff, M. (2001). Social play behaviour: Cooperation, fairness, trust, and the evolution of morality. *Journal of Consciousness Studies, 8*(2), 81–90.

Bekoff, M., & Pierce, J. (2009). *Wild justice: The moral lives of animals.* University of Chicago Press.

Berthoz, S., Grèzes, J., Armony, J. L., Passingham, R. E., & Dolan, R. J. (2006). Affective response to one's own moral violations. *Neuroimage, 31*(2), 945–950.

Brandt, M. J., Reyna, C., Chambers, J. R., Crawford, J. T., & Wetherell, G. (2014). The ideological-conflict hypothesis: Intolerance among both liberals and conservatives. *Current Directions in Psychological Science, 23*(1), 27–34.

Braver, T. S. (2012). The variable nature of cognitive control: A dual mechanisms framework. *Trends in Cognitive Sciences, 16*(2), 106–113.

Bostyn, D. H., De Keersmaecker, J., Van Assche, J., & Roets, A. (2020). Bright mind, moral mind? Intelligence is unrelated to consequentialist moral judgment in sacrificial moral dilemmas. *Psychonomic Bulletin & Review*, 1–6.

Burge, T. (2018). Do infants and nonhuman animals attribute mental states?. *Psychological Review, 125*(3), 409.

Chafe, W. L. (1974). Language and consciousness. *Language*, 111–133.

Clark, A. (1999). An embodied cognitive science?. *Trends in Cognitive Sciences, 3*(9), 345–351.

Cosmides, L., Barrett, H. C., & Tooby, J. (2010). Adaptive specializations, social exchange, and the evolution of human intelligence. *Proceedings of the National Academy of Sciences, 107*(Supplement 2), 9007–9014.

Costa, A., Foucart, A., Hayakawa, S., Aparici, M., Apesteguia, J., Heafner, J., & Keysar, B. (2014). Your morals depend on language. *PloS One, 9*(4), e94842.

Darwin, C. (1871). *The descent of man and selection in relation to sex.* Appleton.

Decety, J., Michalska, K. J., & Kinzler, K. D. (2012). The contribution of emotion and cognition to moral sensitivity: A neurodevelopmental study. *Cerebral Cortex, 22*(1), 209–220.

De Waal, F., Macedo, S. E., & Ober, J. E. (2006). *Primates and philosophers: How morality evolved.* Princeton University Press.

Eres, R., Louis, W. R., & Molenberghs, P. (2018). Common and distinct neural networks involved in fMRI studies investigating morality: An ALE meta-analysis. *Social Neuroscience, 13*(4), 384–398.

Foot, P. (1967). The problem of abortion and the doctrine of the double effect. *Oxford Review, 5.*

Gallagher, H. L., & Frith, C. D. (2003). Functional imaging of "theory of mind". *Trends in Cognitive Sciences*, 7(2), 77–83.

Geipel, J., Hadjichristidis, C., & Surian, L. (2016). Foreign language affects the contribution of intentions and outcomes to moral judgment. *Cognition*, *154*, 34–39.

Gigerenzer, G., & Gaissmaier, W. (2011). Heuristic decision making. *Annual Review of Psychology*, *62*, 451–482.

Greene, J. D. (2015). The rise of moral cognition. *Cognition*, *135*, 39–42.

Greene, J. D., & Haidt, J. (2002). How (and where) does moral judgment work?. *Trends in Cognitive Sciences*, 6(12), 517–523.

Haidt, J. (2007). The new synthesis in moral psychology. *Science*, *316*(5827), 998–1002.

Hamlin, J. K. (2013). Moral judgment and action in preverbal infants and toddlers: Evidence for an innate moral core. *Current Directions in Psychological Science*, 22(3), 186–193.

Hargreaves, J. (2000). *Freedom for Catalonia?: Catalan nationalism, Spanish identity and the Barcelona olympic games*. Cambridge University Press.

Heatherton, T. F. (2011). Neuroscience of self and self-regulation. *Annual Review of Psychology*, *62*, 363–390.

James, W. (1890/1950). *The principles of psychology* (Vol. I). Henry Holt and Co.

Joyce, R. (2007). *The evolution of morality*. MIT Press.

Jung, W. H., Prehn, K., Fang, Z., Korczykowski, M., Kable, J. W., Rao, H., & Robertson, D. C. (2016). Moral competence and brain connectivity: A resting-state fMRI study. *Neuroimage*, *141*, 408–415.

Kahneman, D. (2011). *Thinking, fast and slow*. Macmillan.

Kennedy, B., Atari, M., Davani, A. M., Hoover, J., Omrani, A., Graham, J., & Dehghani, M. (2021). Moral concerns are differentially observable in language. *Cognition*, *212*, 104696.

Lavelle, J. S. (2018). *The social mind: A philosophical introduction*. Routledge.

Li, H., & Lu, J. (2017). The neural association between tendency to forgive and spontaneous brain activity in healthy young adults. *Frontiers in Human Neuroscience*, *11*, 561.

Li, L., & Tomasello, M. (2021). On the moral functions of language. *Social Cognition*, *39*(1), 99–116.

Lind, G. (2019). *How to teach moral competence*. Logos Verlag Berlin GmbH.

Liu, J., Yuan, B., Luo, Y. J., & Cui, F. (2019). Intrinsic functional connectivity of medial prefrontal cortex predicts the individual moral bias in economic valuation partially through the moral sensitivity trait. *Brain Imaging and Behavior*, 1–13.

Milgram, S., & Gudehus, C. (1978). *Obedience to authority*. Ziff- Davis.

Mishra, R. K. (2015). *Interaction between attention and language systems in humans*. Springer.

Mishra, R. K., & Marmolejo-Ramos, F. (2010). On the mental representations originating during the interaction between language and vision. *Cognitive Processing*, *11*(4), 295–305.

Moll, J., & de Oliveira-Souza, R. (2007). Moral judgments, emotions and the utilitarian brain. *Trends in Cognitive Sciences*, *11*(8), 319–321.

Moll, J., Zahn, R., de Oliveira-Souza, R., Krueger, F., & Grafman, J. (2005). The neural basis of human moral cognition. *Nature Reviews Neuroscience*, 6(10), 799–809.

Overing, J. (Ed.). (2013). *Reason and morality*. Routledge.

Pinker, S. (2017). The moral instinct. In *Understanding Moral Sentiments* (pp. 59–80). Routledge.

Pratt, N. L., & Kelly, S. D. (2008). Emotional states influence the neural processing of affective language. *Social Neuroscience, 3*(3–4), 434–442.

Raine, A., & Yang, Y. (2006). Neural foundations to moral reasoning and antisocial behavior. *Social Cognitive and Affective Neuroscience, 1*(3), 203–213.

Redlawsk, D. P. (2002). Hot cognition or cool consideration? Testing the effects of motivated reasoning on political decision making. *The Journal of Politics, 64*(4), 1021–1044.

Ruse, M. (1984). Evolution and morality. *Philosophic Exchange, 15*(1), 1.

Saxe, R. (2013). The new puzzle of theory of mind development. *Navigating the Social World: What Infants, Children, and Other Species Can Teach Us,* 107–112.

Schurz, M., Radua, J., Tholen, M. G., Maliske, L., Margulies, D. S., Mars, R. B., Sallet, J., & Kanske, P. (2021). Toward a hierarchical model of social cognition: A neuroimaging meta-analysis and integrative review of empathy and theory of mind. *Psychological Bulletin, 147*(3), 293.

Schwartz, B. (1987). *The battle for human nature: Science, morality and modern life.* W. W. Norton & Company.

Sloane, S., Baillargeon, R., & Premack, D. (2012). Do infants have a sense of fairness?. *Psychological Science, 23*(2), 196–204.

Streib, V. L. (1983). Death penalty for children: The American experience with capital punishment for crimes committed while under age eighteen. *Oklahoma Law Review, 36,* 613.

Strohminger, N., & Nichols, S. (2014). The essential moral self. *Cognition, 131*(1), 159–171.

Sunar, D. (2009). Suggestions for a new integration in the psychology of morality. *Social and Personality Psychology Compass, 3*(4), 447–474.

Szuster, A., & Jarymowicz, M. (2020). Human empathy of automatic vs. reflective origin: Diverse attributes and regulative consequences. *New Ideas in Psychology, 56,* 100748.

Van de Vondervoort, J. W., & Hamlin, J. K. (2016). Evidence for intuitive morality: Preverbal infants make sociomoral evaluations. *Child Development Perspectives, 10*(3), 143–148.

Woodward, J. (2016). Emotion versus cognition in moral decision-making: A dubious dichotomy. *Moral Brains: The Neuroscience of Morality,* 87–116.

Woumans, E., Van der Cruyssen, I., & Duyck, W. (2020). Crime and punishment: Morality judgment in a foreign language. *Journal of Experimental Psychology: General, 149*(8), 1597.

9 Gender and Cognition

1. Gender and cognition

The word "cognition" refers to mental activities by an agent. Importantly, human agents have well-defined genders. Although much research has gone into the role of gender in cognition, in recent years, many complicated issues have surfaced. For example, some individuals do not categorise themselves into traditionally fixed genders, or gender is perceived as fluid and dynamic. Cognitive psychologists often analyse their experimental data without focusing much on such issues and arrive at general interpretations. However, considering the rise of gender rights and awareness this may not be what future research will look like. One's gender identity enters into the debate on cognition, as a serious factor related to individual differences and socio-cultural identity. The focus of this chapter is to review research on individuals that do not conform to traditional gender roles and their cognition. The major debate surrounds the conflict between biological gender vs perceived gender and their influence on different aspects of everyday cognition. These issues are controversial but when it comes to understanding the cognition and mind of agents, the perceived gender becomes important for theory. The most interesting cases are of those individuals who refer to themselves as transgender and defy traditional bracketing and descriptions.

One of the most controversial topics currently in the mind and brain sciences is that of gender and how it influences cognition. Although individual difference research in cognitive science has been on a rise, gender differences have not been looked at carefully. This is primarily because this variable has social, political, and cultural connotations – which quickly becomes controversial. In the age of massive social changes and growing socio-political consciousness, all are interested in gender equality but not much in gender differences. However, for cognitive scientists, how people view themselves gender-wise matters. Although the phrase "gender equality" is popular, it is time to understand the biological, social, and cognitive aspects of gender. Biological sciences and social sciences have pursued the question of gender from different vantage points resulting in conflicting notions. Is the gender of a person socially constructed or biologically hardwired? Science does not

DOI: 10.4324/9781003316053-9

believe in social construction. According to most scientific views, individuals are born belonging to a certain gender and that stays that way till they die. They are not allowed to talk differently or describe their genders. But we will see in this chapter that this is indeed possible and can be met with wider acceptance.

The problematisation of gender began in the eighteenth century with the rise in democracy and religion (Foucault, 1990). In antiquity, gender transformation was common and was less attached to social stigma. The Roman emperor Elagabalus liked to dress like a female and used to refer to himself by feminine names. In the ancient Greco-Roman world, many influential personalities identified themselves as transgender or indulged in cross-dressing (Campanile et al., 2017). There were priests in the ancient Roman city of Cybele who were eunuchs. The Roman poet Ovid in his story of Iphis and Ianthe tells that Iphis was born a female but her father wanted a son and so she was dressed as a boy. Later, when she married a girl named ianthe, a miracle happened through the mother's prayers. She transformed into a boy indeed. In the Indian mythological story "Mahabharata," Shikandi was a transgender. In the Hindu religious tradition, Lord Shiva has been depicted as a union of both male and female forms (Ardhanareeshwara). These examples suggest that individuals have held the right to the public identification of their gender and their social roles. In that respect, it becomes a serious matter for cognition and its theories of such individuals.

The question I pursue is what happens to cognition when the biological gender conflicts with the experienced gender. I won't get into the question of human, political, and social rights connected with this issue, but the mind-brain aspects of it. With the worldwide rise in people who identify themselves as transgender, with increasing political and legal rights being conferred to them, it has become important to look at its interaction with cognition. The issue of rights to transgender persons and all others centres on their uniqueness. They are not more or less like males or females. They experience a very different gender and sexual identity which needs explanations. The chapter will consider views from disparate fields such as neuropharmacology, brain sciences, and cognitive sciences on the issue of gender and cognition.

2. Gender and the brain

Does our biological gender or our own perceived gender influence our brains and hence our minds? Experimental data in cognitive psychology or cognitive neuroscience is presented without gender differences. It is assumed that there is not much of a difference between men and women if they are cis-gendered. However, men and women differ on multiple tasks and in the way their brains work (Adenzato et al., 2017). The focus in this section is on those individuals and their brain functions who identify themselves as transgender. These individuals do not accept their biological gender assigned at birth. Their agency, sense of self, and psychological attributes belong to the gender they identify with (Ku et al., 2013). Some individuals also claim that they are gender-fluid or simply queer. It is not often easy to track down when a person starts to consciously feel that he/she belongs to the other gender. Therefore, there have been no longitudinal studies on the changes in the brain as a function of maturation in transgender individuals over time. Most research with brain mapping has been on transgender adults who have been on hormone therapy. This therapy is widely prevalent in both transgender men and women. Apart from this, there is also speech therapy, psychological counselling, and behavioural therapy that assists such persons into full transition. As we will see in the following, it has been seen in many studies that the brain activities of transgender people resemble brain activities of their perceived but not biological gender. That is, a trans woman's brain activity will resemble that of a woman and not a man.

Resting-state functional connectivity analysis using graph theory is a popular method in brain mapping. This allows researchers to explore which critical brain cortical areas are functionally connected when the participant is not doing any particular task. This state has been linked to ongoing transient cognition which controls psychological states. Research comparing transgender and cis-gender people suggests that the resting-state functional connectivity is different in trans individuals (Lin et al., 2014). A high degree of centrality is observed in the bilateral superior parietal lobule and primary somatosensory cortex in the trans individuals. Brain imaging data also show a difference in structural connectivity in male-to-female and female-to-male transgenders (Hutchison et al., 2013). Structural connectivity refers to how different brain areas are connected. Functional connectivity is a term used in brain imaging that refers to dynamic collaboration among brain areas that are not connected. Functional connectivity in the executive control areas is also found to be weaker in transgendered men and women compared to the cis-gender men and women (Uribe et al., 2020). One brain mapping study found that the inter-hemispheric connectivity differs between transgender and cis-gender individuals (Hahn et al., 2015). These studies indicate that both structural and functional connectivity differs among the transgender and cis-gender individuals. However, these studies do not show to what extent such neural variables correlate with their cognition or changing sense of self.

Gender incongruence in childhood is designated as gender dysphoria, a diagnostic label in the DSM 5. Individuals who experience emotional conflict because of the incongruence between their biological gender and their perceived gender are diagnosed with it. The treatment often involves hormone therapy and surgery in a wide range of cases (Unger, 2016). Specific male and female hormones are known to influence brain functioning and behaviour in individuals. Transgender male and female brains show similarity with the brains of control subjects of their preferred gender even before they have taken any hormone therapy (Nguyen et al., 2019). This fact is puzzling and has not been explained well. How could this happen if there has not been any external biological intervention? Variables such as cortical thickness, grey matter volume, structural connectivity, etc. reflect this. Investigations suggest that the brains of transgender individuals do not resemble the brains of their preferred gender completely but only to some extent (Kranz et al., 2014). However, much of these data cannot tell why and because what kind of biological changes a person becomes transgender. An excessive surge in male hormone production has been linked to behavioural changes in females. There have been no systematic longitudinal studies that have tracked hormone production and brain changes during maturation.

Only properly controlled longitudinal studies can reveal the dynamic changes in cognition in individuals who perceive their gender identities differently than what has been assigned biologically. Very few individuals show medically diagnosed gender dysphoria since childhood. Estimates suggest that less than 1 in 10,000 males and fewer than 1 in 30,000 females present this scenario post-natal (Zucker et al., 2016). Given such few numbers, it has not been easy to do large-scale longitudinal studies. One study tracked changes in cortical thickness in male-to-female and female-to-male transsexuals (Figure 9.1, Zubiaurre-Elorza et al., 2014) as a function of treatment with the male hormone testosterone. Female-to-male transsexuals

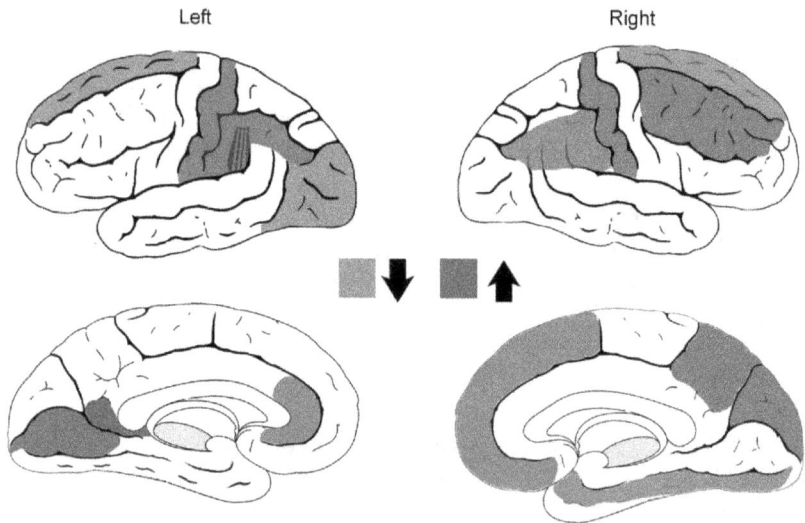

Figure 9.1 Effects of hormone treatment on cortical thickness in transsexuals. Blue: cortical regions in which estradiol + antiandrogens thinned the cortex in male-to-females. Red: cortical regions in which testosterone thickened the cortex in female-to-males.

Source: Guillamon et al. (2016)

showed increased thickness bilaterally, particularly in the postcentral gyrus and few other areas. Important to note is that brain volume studies with cis-gendered individuals show that males, in general, have higher cortical thickness and volume than females. In sum, sex hormone therapy can make the brains of female transexuals more like cis-gender males in the long run. It is widely believed that testosterone therapy does change both the body and behaviour of transgender individuals; however, it may also have some negative consequences. There have not been many randomised control trials that clearly show what changes to expect as a function of such therapy (Irwig, 2017).

From the discussion so far it is clear that most researchers assume that the transgender brain gradually approaches the brain of its preferred gender. As soon as the transgender feels like somebody else, the structural and functional connectivity changes and approximates what one would find in a heterosexual brain of the perceived gender. What happens when the brain networks of a transgender do not show evidence of their preferred gender? This may lead to confusion and discrimination. Secondly, there is a big difference between the brains of female-to-male and male-to-female transgenders as they progress. So far we have little understanding of even the psychologies of such people. The percentage of male-to-female transgenders is much larger than female-to-male. This difference, of course, will impact any neuroscience research on them. Finally, as in many other fields, brain data is not absolute evidence of psychological and mental states. Neuroscience research on the trans individual views them as an approximation of another gender. The trans-self in itself does not have any essence but only with regard to what they are trying to be. Of course, intuitively it is acceptable that a male transgender is trying to be a female in their behaviour, cognition, and many other domains including emotions and sexuality. Given this, a more fundamental question arises on the links between gender, brain, and cognition. Furthermore, the social constructionist theories of gender and sexuality complicates the matter. Critical theories on the transgender self by humanistic scholars do not take into account neuroscientific findings (Drabinski, 2014). Neuroscience data as of now does not show that the transgender has a unique neuronal self that is distinct from the male or female brain. It shows the transgender individuals are merely trying their best to change towards either of the two fixed genders. Their psychological conflicts are directly proportional to this degree of conformity.

It is widely known that the sense of gender identity can be different from sexual orientations (Kuper et al., 2012). Many individuals have different sexual orientations than what their biology would indicate. Thus, sexual orientation is experienced and realised differently by many individuals irrespective of their gender (Iantaffi & Bockting, 2011). Some people are bisexuals – those who entertain the sexuality of both genders. They are not classified as transgender. These individuals primarily identify themselves as of one gender but also shift their sexual preferences without any confusion.

It has not always been possible to exactly differentiate to what extent a transgender could also be bisexual (Lucal, 2008).

3. Sexuality and cognition

Cognitive and psychological science's explorations into gender and sexuality have not been only focused on transgender individuals. Many studies have explored cognitive and behavioural differences in homosexual individuals compared to heterosexuals. In such individuals, the biological sex remains stable during lifespan while the sexual preferences are different. There are also groups who describe themselves as gender-fluid and queer with specific cognitive and social profiles (LeVay, 1996). There is now growing attention to psychological profiling of such individuals keeping in mind the tremendous growth in theoretical advancements in multiple fields (Thorne et al., 2019).

Homosexuality was common among the ancient Greeks (Dover, 2016). Michel Foucault's penetrative studies have revealed how homosexuality came to disrepute. Massive criminalisation and bureaucratisation of any deviant behaviour brought stigma to those who wished to go against their biological gender (Foucault, 1990). Homosexuality is today viewed just as a matter of personal sexual preference that is out of the state's interference and control in most countries except a few where religious beliefs prohibit homosexuality.

How do homosexuals and heterosexuals differ on some core dimensions of their cognition? There is some evidence that suggests that homosexuals have unique cognitive profiles. D. F. Reuter coined a word called "gaydar" to describe a sort of metaphorical sixth sense in homosexuals (Reuter, 2002). Homosexual individuals gaze and find out other homosexuals using very intense attention. Looking and evaluation of personality including prediction of cognition remains the most ancient pillars of social cognition in humans. Reuter suggested that in any crowd, one gay man can find another gay man easily. It could be a matter of just statistics since the percentage of homosexuals is far less than heterosexuals in any culture. They have to make a greater effort at finding a mate and consolidation of social relations compared to heterosexuals. Dr. Scott G. Shelp presented videotapes of unfamiliar people to homosexual and heterosexual individuals and proposed a new phrase based on the evidence that homosexual individuals have a very high accuracy level in identifying the sexual orientation of these strangers (Shelp, 2003). The author used the phrase "adaptive gaydar" to define this ability. This is possible since many researchers have believed that sexual orientation indeed modifies how one samples information available in the environment (Rule & Alaei, 2016). Such studies indicate that the individuals whose gender identity conflicts with their biological gender try to adapt to the society using various strategies. Thus, sexual identities can influence how one looks at the world, and deploys attention for instance.

Colzato and colleagues (Colzato et al., 2010) investigated the underlying basis of gaydar. It is assumed that homosexuals are good at finding out cultural cues that indicate sexual orientation. They are likely to pay very intense local selective attention compared to heterosexual individuals. Further, the authors speculated that if this way of attention control is unique to gay people, then this must translate into other tasks over time. The authors recruited gay and straight individuals in the Netherlands and presented them with the popular local-global task. This task measures attention to global and local features (Navon, 1977). The global precedence effect suggests that we perceive global features of any visual object preferentially over its local features, which seems to be a natural tendency of our visual system. However, in contrast to this assumption, the study found that homosexual individuals were worse at global attention than heterosexual individuals, and better at location attention instead (Figure 9.2). The authors speculated that mate-finding difficulty has led to neuroplasticity in such individuals over some time in the domain of visual selective attention.

Spatial memory and verbal fluency are cognitive tasks that show interesting differences between genders. One study found that homosexual men were poorer in a spatial memory task than heterosexual men. However, they were better on the verbal fluency task. Their overall performance fell between heterosexual men and women (McCormick & Witelson, 1991).

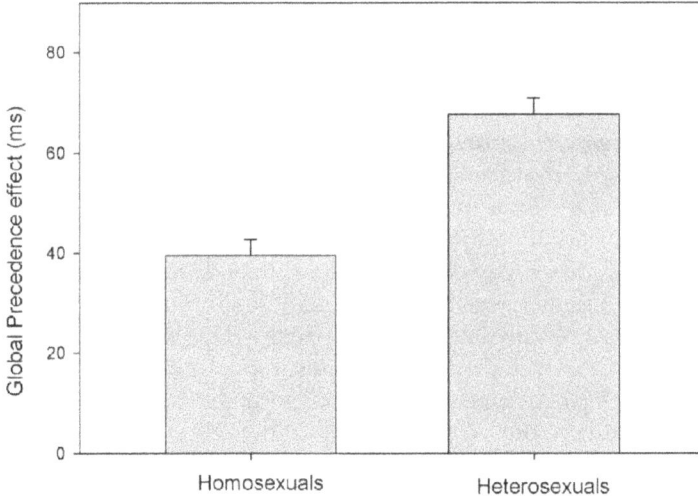

Figure 9.2 Global precedence effect (GPE) in homosexual and heterosexual individuals. GPE indexes the ability of an individual to process global features of a stimulus better than local features. Homosexuals show lesser GPE indicating lesser preference for global features (and greater relative processing of local features) compared to heterosexuals.

Source: From Colzato et al. (2010)

However, not many have found such differences among different gendered groups. One early study administered intelligence tests and questionnaires on perceived femininity to heterosexual and homosexual individuals. No difference was found in this study on any of the measures between the groups (Tuttle & Pillard, 1991). More recently several meta-analyses have been performed that show subtle differences between homosexuals and heterosexuals in specific domains of cognition. For instance, homosexual men may show some difference in mental rotation but not in spatial memory tasks compared to heterosexuals (Xu et al., 2020). These pieces of evidence point towards the fact that sexual inclination influences some aspects of cognition. These data suggest that, while homosexuals or bisexuals do not have identity conflict regarding gender, their sexual orientation plays an important role in their cognition. Homosexual men also have greater suicidal tendencies compared to heterosexual men (Friedman, 1999). Many studies have found that in everyday life homosexual men endure huge stress and anxiety (Derryberry & Reed, 1998). Stimuli with negative emotions narrow down the scope of attentional engagement (Harmon-Jones et al., 2013).

The connection between attention and sexual preference is complicated since there are many other variables that have been shown to influence attention in individuals. Cultural theorists such as Nisbett and others have long observed that specific cultures shape our cognition in a specific manner (Nisbett & Miyamoto, 2005). Practitioners of different religions could develop a different kind of attention control (Hommel & Colzato, 2010). It is likely that specific type of attention is an outcome of everyday practice of smaller groups that are homogeneous in themselves. Attention develops as a cognitive strategy in communities for social cognition (Posner, 2011). Viewed in this way, homosexual individuals as members of a specific group have developed narrow attentional processing since this is what is rewarded in their community. By using attention in this manner, they enhance their social communication and the ability to find a mate. Attentional modulations as a result of sensory deprivation in specific communities such as the deaf have also been shown (Bavelier et al., 2006). Attention control in the deaf is a result of compensatory neuroplasticity (Dye & Bavelier, 2013). Of course, the aim, through these comparisons, is not to suggest that homosexual individuals have suffered sensory deprivation that has led to changes and consequently, adaptation in their attention. But life experience can induce neuroplasticity in cognitive systems that are helpful for the individual for survival in specific communities and cultures. As individuals of a certain specific group with unique identities, they may end up adopting specific cognitive styles. This argument may seem problematic to universal theories of cognition that aim to be valid for all kinds of people. However, this may not be valid since cultural considerations penetrate down to the individual who lives in a certain situation and uses certain types of cognition. Viewed in this way, the cognition of the homosexual is conceptualised as the type of cognition that serves the homosexual. If localised and narrower attention is what is required, then the brain adapts to it. Unfortunately, there are not many studies to know the developmental and maturational aspects of these claims.

4. Development, gender, cognition

Gender is both a biological and an experiential phenomenon. While biologists may be interested in the material basis of it, cognitive scientists are more concerned with the personal and experiential basis of gender. How are gender and sexuality experienced during childhood? For normally developing children who conform to their genders there is not much problem. However, when the child expresses a non-conforming gender status that eventually leads to a different type of sexuality, the concerns of parents and can caregivers grow. Uncertainty of medical diagnosis and societal stigma complicates the matter and such children face severe personal trauma (Olson et al., 2011). Correct diagnosis, management of mental issues, and societal integration become a problem (Burnes et al., 2016). Much research attention has been given to the development and transition of young children through their gender identities. Many parents seek out the help of therapists to enforce conformity on children that report gender dysphoria. A glance at the research on this issue shows an obvious conflict. While some studies have shown that the transgender child resembles the experienced gender since childhood, others think that it's only a later outcome. Parents generally discuss the emerging gender awareness of their children and any instance of non-conformity with their primary health care providers (Reilly et al., 2019). When the child is very young, it is often not possible to diagnose if the child is indeed experiencing any shifts in gender identity. The child's social and larger environment merely views this as some kind of oddity that must be quickly treated. Changes in patterns of daily living and counselling begin with the aim to convince the child that it could be just an illusion. While much studies in the last several decades have examined the cognitive development of normal children with many journals devoted to such a cause, very little is known about the developmental issues of the gender non-conforming child (Pyne, 2014). Naturally then, the gender non-conforming child who soon becomes an adolescent faces several cognitive and societal challenges that must be examined.

The biology and the psychology of the gender non-conforming child remains mysterious. It is around puberty that the biological gender is fully actualised in behaviour and the individual accepts it. However, for the child who has been experiencing gender issues, puberty could be the beginning of bigger psychological trauma. Medical practitioners often suggest puberty suppression mechanisms to such children. This is primarily an externally induced hormone therapy that halts the natural secretion of the hormones of the biological gender of the child. This approach is widely popular yet also controversial (Lambrese, 2010). This therapy extends the natural time-line of puberty by a few years. Puberty suppression has been shown to provide some benefits on the psychological front. With increasing age and gender incongruency, the transgender children face serious psychological conflicts. Suicidal ideation is very high at this age in this group of children. Puberty suppression provides a prolongation of the expected gender and thus has been linked to less psychological trauma. One study found that adolescents who underwent puberty suppression also experienced less suicidal ideation (Turban et al., 2020). Puberty suppression with hormones has been shown to also influence the brain actuary during this critical period. Brain activity related to executive functioning does not change between adolescents treated with puberty suppression and normal controls (Staphorsius et al., 2015). This is consistent with the observation that brains of normal cis-gendered adolescents and those who are experiencing gender dysphoria do not differ a lot even without any hormone therapy (Nota et al., 2017). However, interestingly, by this age the transgender adolescent differs from the cis-gendered on a range of social and psychological attributes. In sum, the puberty suppression method widely practised has not been studied for its psychological and cognitive effects.

Those who recommend this treatment argue that it helps the transgender child to achieve a degree of congruency between the biological and psychological selves. The child need not wait further and suffer the everyday trauma of gender imbalance. During the period of puberty suppression, the child can undergo more behavioural therapy and training to see if the projected psychological gender is permanent. If that is so, then both hormone therapy and gender reassignment surgeries can be done eventually. However, puberty suppression as a potential intervention method has raised serious ethical issues. Many argue that since children and pre-puberty adolescents are minors they can't provide consent for such a procedure which could prove to be fatal. It's also possible that many who have been experiencing gender non-conformity in due course of time may stabilise more naturally. Therefore, it's unethical to induce hormones to stop the natural course of puberty. While leading psychiatrists recommend puberty suppression, many think that the true evidence-based efficacy of these methods is still to be uncovered (Costa et al., 2016; Mahfouda, 2017).

Gender diversity issues have always posed both theoretical and methodological problems for developmental research. Most empirical studies are on children that are so-called cis-gendered. Therefore, our current knowledge about gender non-conforming cognition remains limited. Treating them as a special population can always go against the zeitgeist of social inclusion. However, because their psychological and emotional awareness could be different, cognitive theories should deal with them separately. One can, of course, study many domains of cognition wherein the transgender child differs both quantitatively and qualitatively from the cis-gender child. The most important domains could be attention, emotion, executive functions, and social cognition. One of the greatest challenges for the therapist is their social integration. This is linked to the fact that such children may view themselves differently from their surroundings. One study examined how such children categorise gender (Fast & Olson, 2018). The assumption was that since these children have some kind of gender conflict this should show up in any gender categorisation task. The study examined how such children perceive others' gender. It was found that transgender children perceive others' gender as more fluid compared to the controls. Further, they also think that others may be similarly confused with their claimed gender and their biological gender. The results can be interpreted in many different ways. Such children possibly view others to be like them given their inherent conflict. There is evidence that when such children violate gender stereotypes there is a wider social stigma against them (Sullivan et al., 2018). Since society operates on accepted norms with regard to gender, any incongruency in its perception is taken as abnormal cognition.

Very early evidence of gender preference has been linked to later social transition in the transgender children (Rae et al., 2019). This is not merely a linguistic question of pronoun use by these children but their perception of gender as a fluid entity. Very early on, transgender children show resistance towards their natural gender. They do not accept their natural gender which is normal for the cis-children. One study found that this shows up in tasks that measure gender identity more implicitly (Olson et al., 2015). Given this data, it is interesting to note that despite their consistency in accepting their preferred gender they suffer psychological trauma. Here comes the wider role of society and caregivers. While the individual child has accepted another gender more at a psychological level, society does not accept it and considers it abnormal. Multiple studies have documented abuse and harassment of such children at home by parents when they first express their gender incongruency (Grossman et al., 2005). As of now, there is a wider movement to repeal gender binary concepts within psychology (Hyde et al., 2019). However, neuroscience approaches in general look at gender as binary.

The developmental stages of the transgender child through adolescence and adulthood are not very well understood. Psychological and societal stigma starts early, at home and school. The issue of puberty suppression remains very controversial as described earlier. Further, it's not clear how cognition changes post puberty suppression. Although the biological interventions and their more overt physical manifestations are relatively well understood, the psychology of it is not that clear. How does the transgender individual continue to develop self and others' perception and cognition? The therapeutic angle has been popular as an applied science since it provides clinical support. Few studies that have been on the perception and categorisation of gender assume prototypical effects. Going by common sense one would assume that the transgender individual identifies and perceives himself or herself more of the desired gender than the biological. They bring

206 Gender and Cognition

the same perception to others. Such perceptual changes and their exact point of change remains intractable. Many studies have shown that hormone therapy does influence perception and cognition. But the studies that have been done so far to examine this have been limited on many counts. There are other avenues to examine this than just gender identification and perception. We know almost nothing about their attention, emotion regulation, executive functioning, and social cognition. These mechanisms have been well-studied in the more general cis-gendered population. The transgender population have been excluded for very obvious reasons. There have been two opposite waves of theoretical assumptions in this issue. While one group of theoreticians tend to view them as similar to anyone else, others believe that there is a sharp difference. This is problematic for many reasons. It's not just for theorisation within the mind-brain sciences but in wider fields that deal with policy. The "uniqueness" of the transgender's personality and psychology as many identity theorists like to claim is not supported by hard science often. When differences in neural functioning and cognition have been found, they tend to be of very small effect size or sample size. Almost no longitudinal study exists that shows development of such individuals given their problematic lives. In sum, the transgender child is a new concept for developmental and cognitive scientists.

5. Minority stress and future directions

The great homogenising forces of science look at individual differences with scepticism. Since scientific theories aim to propose general theories that could answer most problems. Even though theories of the mind and cognition are sensitive to individual differences, they have not been incorporated into theory building. The case of the transgender's cognition, even though it is unique, cannot be taken to be beyond the approach of general theories. The cognitive and behavioural issues of the gender non-conforming person as we saw deserves unique approaches because they form a distinct group of individuals whose gender identity shapes their everyday cognition. Cultural and societal forces induce different cognitive strategies in them than in the so-called normal individual. Individual difference research at the moment aims to uncover how the brain and behaviour are an outcome of the individual's typical life experiences. I will briefly summarise them, and speculate what newer dimensions can be integrated into this very important research domain within the broad disciplines of mind and brain sciences.

"Minority stress" is a phrase that has been coined to describe the many emotional and psychological problems that gender non-conforming individuals undergo daily (Meyer, 1995). Minority stress is an outcome of the individual's inability to deal with religious and cultural forces that fix norms of behaviour. Therefore, there is no "normal" development of such individuals during the lifespan. Given this scenario, it has been found that minority stress differs again between transgenders and bisexuals and is linked to the degree to which they depend on substances to alleviate such pain (Lehavot & Simoni, 2011). Interestingly, homosexuals are less dependent on substances and have probably lower minority stress. Therefore, the psychopathological attributes of such individuals interact with cognitive attributes. Societal pressure that causes stress and a deformed social cognition in transgender individuals is linked to their brain abnormalities. Few studies have tracked longitudinal life coping strategies of such individuals. Minority stress is not similar for children who are newly discovering their gender identity and adults who have already found a way to deal with it. Studies with normal development are inadequate to throw light on this since they are on gender-conforming heterosexual children or adults.

The brain-based studies with neuroscience approaches stand at a cross-roads because of both conceptual and methodological problems. The popular assumption that the transgender brain should resemble the preferred heterosexuals' brain is problematic. It takes away the unique attributes of the gender non-conforming individual and forces a homogeneous measurement of brain and cognitive functions. Further, validity of any structure-function correlation claims remains debated since brain-based data do not predict performance on behavioural tasks. The changes that are seen as the transgender slowly starts to accept the non-natal gender arise from a range of environmental and social factors. These factors are not often well integrated into studies. Cross-cultural comparative studies of cognitive neuroscience are the need of the hour. That would reveal the intricate nature-nurture interactions that shape the transgender self in different contexts.

Brain functions are influenced by social and cultural variables. While structural changes have been found in individuals experiencing gender dysphoria, it is not clear how one can account for these changes. There is an emerging concept in cultural neuroscience called the culture – behaviour – brain (CBB) loop model (Figure 9.3; Han & Ma, 2015; Mohammadi & Khaleghi, 2018). In this framework, neural changes are understood as an outcome of sustained interaction and adaptation on the part of the individual to a different set of beliefs. Transgenders believe that their perceived gender and sexual orientation is not what is given to them biologically – while the larger society around them is not inclined to accept this belief. Therefore, the transgender individual struggles to adapt to a different set of belief structures from what is acceptable. This incongruity shapes the brain changes in the transgender individual leading to experience-dependent neuroplasticity. The stronger the belief, more changes will be noticed. The biological basis of transsexuality and sexual orientation are independent mechanisms. One can be transsexual without a corresponding change in sexual orientation. It's very intriguing to think that the sexual orientation of the transgender remains congruent with that of the given biological gender while psychologically there is a shift towards another gender. Many such facts are not currently part of the neuroscience approaches to the gender-sex-mind triad.

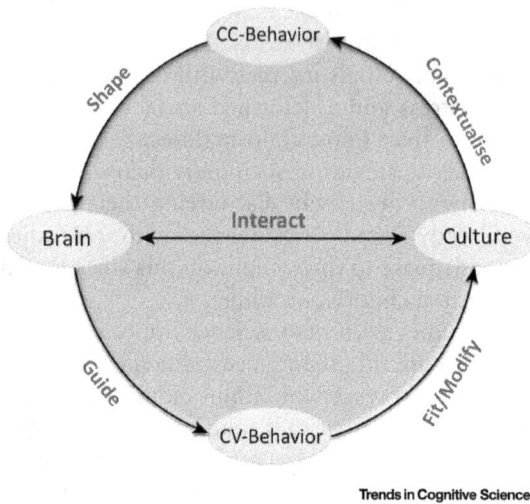

Figure 9.3 The CCB model. A model of human development based on cultural factors. There can be direct or indirect interactions between brain and culture. Cultural context can induce brain changes without any overt behavioural changes (direct). Culture can also induce novel beliefs which modify behaviour which in turn shapes the brain resulting in culturally appropriate behaviour.

Source: Reprinted from *Trends in Cognitive Sciences*, Vol. 19, Shihui Han, Yina Ma, A Culture – Behavior – Brain Loop Model of Human Development, 666–676, 2015, with permission from Elsevier

Until some time ago, the most dominant theory from neurobiology explaining gender dysphoria, the clinical condition that many transgender individuals manifest, was explained as the different brain sex theory. That is, such individuals' brains manifest the sexual self differently than the given biological self. More recently the neurobiological approaches have embraced other dimensions to the structural classifications. They target the transgender individual experiencing distress or dysfunction in three specific neural networks such as the social behavioural network, distress, anxiety, and fear network, and the body ownership network. It's widely taken that individuals with gender conflict do not own their biological assigned gender and self. Further, they entertain fear and anxiety in an excessive magnitude compared to heterosexual individuals. Each of these networks evolves and changes as a function of experience. Culture and environmental triggers can create more perceptual ambiguity in the transgender individual while dealing with everyday anxiety. Such theories propose a new outlook on the more medical side of the problem that includes traditional surgical intervention and hormone therapy. It has been shown that such therapy can reduce body ownership problems.

The incongruence between a body given at birth and a gender that is based on one's own conscious choices leads to psychological distress. Many have examined such distress which transgender individuals go through (Lemma & Savulescu, 2021). It is of importance to theories of the mind since the problem is psychic and existential and involves the mind. It is not yet clear from research if there is ever mind-body harmony with regard to both self, gender, and sexual identity in such individuals. We do not yet know which conscious and unconscious forces work on the cognition of such individuals. The cognitive psychologists could but study the cognitive systems such as attention networks, memory, perception, decision making, and emotion and arrive at some understanding of the mind when the body is not congruent with it. Psychological attributes of transitioning from one gender to another has to be understood in general terms. The transgender individual's problems are not just problems of gender confusion or non-acceptance but more of a cognitive transition. It's not even necessary to posit a binary cognitive model for this since we do not know how over-all cognition is affected because of gender non-conformity. An area of research that needs a boost with regard to the question of gender, identity, and sexuality is how the control systems of the brain work in such cases. Since individuals with gender identity issues inevitably face difficulties, it may be critical that they exert greater cognitive control in coping with daily demands. Currently we know little about executive functioning and behavioural control in this group of individuals. Our everyday social cognition is linked to our executive control. Many studies have shown that faulty cognitive control networks can lead to different pathologies. Concepts such as proactive and reactive modes of control help us understand how different individuals prevail in the face of demanding situations. Studies that target the executive control networks and their changes over time in such individuals will be helpful along with the traditional observations. Finally, while we know something about the biology of gender dysphoria and the effects of hormones on some aspects of behaviour, we know little on higher cognition. Neurobiological studies tell little about cognitive consequences.

6. Summary

Mental health issues that transgender and other such individuals face are largely cognitive, because gender identity influences both self-awareness and cognitive responses. The chapter focused on some themes that are of great contemporary relevance in this domain. The chapter also explored the differences between social and biological investigations of gender. The case of transgenders in particular has attracted much research attention in different fields given its complexity. Brain imaging data reveals how these individuals process different stimuli and how their brains react to the question of gender in general. The current scientific approaches show that gender is a dynamic concept from the individual's point of view and therefore poses specific problems for complete exploration. One's gender is what one thinks of. The chapter was limited in many ways given the paucity of research on this topic at least from the mind-brain point of view. We also discussed the case of equality in relation to gender since it has such a massive influence on social structures and bureaucracy. The ultimate question remains to what extent these are biologically determined and socially constrained. For the cognitive psychologist, gender creates the psychological profile of the individual and thus influences cognition in many ways. Although experimental researchers have not been very cautious about gender differences, this correction in research methodology is in the cards now.

References

Adenzato, M., Brambilla, M., Manenti, R., De Lucia, L., Trojano, L., Garofalo, S., Enrici, I., & Cotelli, M. (2017). Gender differences in cognitive theory of mind revealed by transcranial direct current stimulation on medial prefrontal cortex. *Scientific Reports, 7*(1), 1–9.

Bavelier, D., Dye, M. W., & Hauser, P. C. (2006). Do deaf individuals see better?. *Trends in Cognitive Sciences, 10*(11), 512–518.

Burnes, T. R., Dexter, M. M., Richmond, K., Singh, A. A., & Cherrington, A. (2016). The experiences of transgender survivors of trauma who undergo social and medical transition. *Traumatology, 22*(1), 75.

Campanile, D., Carlà-Uhink, F., & Facella, M. (Eds.). (2017). *TransAntiquity: Cross-dressing and transgender dynamics in the ancient world*. Taylor & Francis.

Colzato, L. S., Van Hooidonk, L., Van Den Wildenberg, W., Harinck, F., & Hommel, B. (2010). Sexual orientation biases attentional control: A possible gaydar mechanism. *Frontiers in Psychology, 1*, 13.

Costa, R., Carmichael, P., & Colizzi, M. (2016). To treat or not to treat: Puberty suppression in childhood-onset gender dysphoria. *Nature Reviews Urology, 13*(8), 456–462.

Derryberry, D., & Reed, M. A. (1998). Anxiety and attentional focusing: Trait, state and hemispheric influences. *Personality and Individual Differences, 25*(4), 745–761.

Dover, K. J. (2016). *Greek homosexuality* (S. Halliwell, M. Masterson, & J. Robson, Foreword). Bloomsbury Publishing.

Drabinski, K. (2014). Incarnate possibilities: Female to male transgender narratives and the making of the self. *Journal of Narrative Theory, 44*(2), 304–329.

Dye, M. W., & Bavelier, D. (2013). Visual attention in deaf humans: A neuroplasticity perspective. In *Deafness* (pp. 237–263). Springer.

Fast, A. A., & Olson, K. R. (2018). Gender development in transgender preschool children. *Child Development, 89*(2), 620–637.

Foucault, M. (1990). *The history of sexuality: An introduction*. Vintage.

Friedman, R. C. (1999). Homosexuality, psychopathology, and suicidality. *Archives of General Psychiatry, 56*(10), 887–888.

Grossman, A. H., D'Augelli, A. R., Howell, T. J., & Hubbard, S. (2005). Parent'reactions to transgender youth'gender nonconforming expression and identity. *Journal of Gay & Lesbian Social Services, 18*(1), 3–16.

Guillamon, A., Junque, C., & Gómez-Gil, E. (2016). A review of the status of brain structure research in transsexualism. *Archives of Sexual Behavior, 45*(7), 1615–1648.

Hahn, A., Kranz, G. S., Küblböck, M., Kaufmann, U., Ganger, S., Hummer, A., Seiger, R., Spies, M., Winkler, D., Kasper, S., & Windischberger, C. (2015). Structural connectivity networks of transgender people. *Cerebral Cortex, 25*(10), 3527–3534.

Han, S., & Ma, Y. (2015). A culture – behavior – brain loop model of human development. *Trends in Cognitive Sciences, 19*(11), 666–676.

Harmon-Jones, E., Gable, P. A., & Price, T. F. (2013). Does negative affect always narrow and positive affect always broaden the mind? Considering the influence of motivational intensity on cognitive scope. *Current Directions in Psychological Science, 22*(4), 301–307.

Hommel, B., & Colzato, L. S. (2010). Religion as a control guide: On the impact of religion on cognition. *Zygon®, 45*(3), 596–604.

Hutchison, R. M., Womelsdorf, T., Allen, E. A., Bandettini, P. A., Calhoun, V. D., Corbetta, M., Della Penna, S., Duyn, J. H., Glover, G. H., Gonzalez-Castillo, J., & Handwerker, D. A. (2013). Dynamic functional connectivity: Promise, issues, and interpretations. *Neuroimage, 80*, 360–378.

Hyde, J. S., Bigler, R. S., Joel, D., Tate, C. C., & van Anders, S. M. (2019). The future of sex and gender in psychology: Five challenges to the gender binary. *American Psychologist, 74*(2), 171.

Iantaffi, A., & Bockting, W. O. (2011). Views from both sides of the bridge? Gender, sexual legitimacy and transgender people's experiences of relationships. *Culture, Health & Sexuality, 13*(3), 355–370.

Irwig, M. S. (2017). Testosterone therapy for transgender men. *The Lancet Diabetes & Endocrinology, 5*(4), 301–311.

Kranz, G. S., Hahn, A., Kaufmann, U., Küblböck, M., Hummer, A., Ganger, S., Seiger, R., Winkler, D., Swaab, D. F., Windischberger, C., & Kasper, S. (2014). White matter microstructure in transsexuals and controls investigated by diffusion tensor imaging. *Journal of Neuroscience, 34*(46), 15466–15475.

Ku, H. L., Lin, C. S., Chao, H. T., Tu, P. C., Li, C. T., Cheng, C. M., Su, T. P., Lee, Y. C., & Hsieh, J. C. (2013). Brain signature characterizing the body-brain-mind axis of transsexuals. *PLoS One, 8*(7), e70808.

Kuper, L. E., Nussbaum, R., & Mustanski, B. (2012). Exploring the diversity of gender and sexual orientation identities in an online sample of transgender individuals. *Journal of Sex Research, 49*(2–3), 244–254.

Lambrese, J. (2010). Suppression of puberty in transgender children. *AMA Journal of Ethics, 12*(8), 645–649.

Lehavot, K., & Simoni, J. M. (2011). The impact of minority stress on mental health and substance use among sexual minority women. *Journal of Consulting and Clinical Psychology, 79*(2), 159.

Lemma, A., & Savulescu, J. (2021). To be, or not to be? The role of the unconscious in transgender transitioning: Identity, autonomy and well-being. *Journal of Medical Ethics*, 1–8.

LeVay, S. (1996). *Queer science: The use and abuse of research into homosexuality.* MIT Press.

Lin, C. S., Ku, H. L., Chao, H. T., Tu, P. C., Li, C. T., Cheng, C. M., Su, T. P., Lee, Y. C., & Hsieh, J. C. (2014). Neural network of body representation differs between transsexuals and cissexuals. *PLoS One*, *9*(1).

Lucal, B. (2008). Building boxes and policing boundaries:(De) constructing intersexuality, transgender and bisexuality. *Sociology Compass*, *2*(2), 519–536.

Mahfouda, S., Moore, J. K., Siafarikas, A., Zepf, F. D., & Lin, A. (2017). Puberty suppression in transgender children and adolescents. *The Lancet Diabetes & Endocrinology*, *5*(10), 816–826.

McCormick, C. M., & Witelson, S. F. (1991). A cognitive profile of homosexual men compared to heterosexual men and women. *Psychoneuroendocrinology*, *16*(6), 459–473.

Meyer, I. H. (1995). Minority stress and mental health in gay men. *Journal of Health and Social Behavior*, 38–56.

Mohammadi, M. R., & Khaleghi, A. (2018). Transsexualism: A different viewpoint to brain changes. *Clinical Psychopharmacology and Neuroscience*, *16*(2), 136.

Navon, D. (1977). Forest before trees: The precedence of global features in visual perception. *Cognitive Psychology*, *9*(3), 353–383.

Nguyen, H. B., Loughead, J., Lipner, E., Hantsoo, L., Kornfield, S. L., & Epperson, C. N. (2019). What has sex got to do with it? The role of hormones in the transgender brain. *Neuropsychopharmacology*, *44*(1), 22–37.

Nisbett, R. E., & Miyamoto, Y. (2005). The influence of culture: Holistic versus analytic perception. *Trends in Cognitive Sciences*, *9*(10), 467–473.

Nota, N. M., Kreukels, B. P., den Heijer, M., Veltman, D. J., Cohen-Kettenis, P. T., Burke, S. M., & Bakker, J. (2017). Brain functional connectivity patterns in children and adolescents with gender dysphoria: Sex-atypical or not?. *Psychoneuroendocrinology*, *86*, 187–195.

Olson, J., Forbes, C., & Belzer, M. (2011). Management of the transgender adolescent. *Archives of Pediatrics & Adolescent Medicine*, *165*(2), 171–176.

Olson, K. R., Key, A. C., & Eaton, N. R. (2015). Gender cognition in transgender children. *Psychological Science*, *26*(4), 467–474.

Posner, M. I. (2011). *Attention in a social world.* Oxford University Press.

Pyne, J. (2014). The governance of gender non-conforming children: A dangerous enclosure. *Annual Review of Critical Psychology*, *11*, 79–96.

Rae, J. R., Gülgöz, S., Durwood, L., DeMeules, M., Lowe, R., Lindquist, G., & Olson, K. R. (2019). Predicting early-childhood gender transitions. *Psychological Science*, *30*(5), 669–681.

Reilly, M., Desousa, V., Garza-Flores, A., & Perrin, E. C. (2019). Young children with gender nonconforming behaviors and preferences. *Journal of Developmental & Behavioral Pediatrics*, *40*(1), 60–71.

Reuter, D. F. (2002). *Gaydar: The ultimate insider guide to the gay sixth sense.* Crown.

Rule, N. O., & Alaei, R. (2016). "Gaydar" the perception of sexual orientation from subtle cues. *Current Directions in Psychological Science*, *25*(6), 444–448.

Shelp, S. G. (2003). Gaydar: Gaydar. *Journal of Homosexuality*, *44*(1), 1–14.

Staphorsius, A. S., Kreukels, B. P., Cohen-Kettenis, P. T., Veltman, D. J., Burke, S. M., Schagen, S. E., Wouters, F. M., Delemarre-van De Waal, H. A., & Bakker, J.

(2015). Puberty suppression and executive functioning: An fMRI-study in adolescents with gender dysphoria. *Psychoneuroendocrinology*, *56*, 190–199.

Sullivan, J., Moss-Racusin, C., Lopez, M., & Williams, K. (2018). Backlash against gender stereotype-violating preschool children. *PloS One*, *13*(4).

Thorne, N., Yip, A. K. T., Bouman, W. P., Marshall, E., & Arcelus, J. (2019). The terminology of identities between, outside and beyond the gender binary–A systematic review. *International Journal of Transgenderism*, *20*(2–3), 138–154.

Turban, J. L., King, D., Carswell, J. M., & Keuroghlian, A. S. (2020). Pubertal suppression for transgender youth and risk of suicidal ideation. *Pediatrics*, *145*(2).

Tuttle, G. E., & Pillard, R. C. (1991). Sexual orientation and cognitive abilities. *Archives of Sexual Behavior*, *20*(3), 307–318.

Unger, C. A. (2016). Hormone therapy for transgender patients. *Translational Andrology and Urology*, *5*(6), 877.

Uribe, C., Junque, C., Gómez-Gil, E., Abos, A., Mueller, S. C., & Guillamon, A. (2020). Brain network interactions in transgender individuals with gender incongruence. *NeuroImage*, *211*, 116613.

Xu, Y., Norton, S., & Rahman, Q. (2020). Sexual orientation and cognitive ability: A multivariate meta-analytic follow-up. *Archives of Sexual Behavior*, *49*(2), 413–420.

Zubiaurre-Elorza, L., Junque, C., Gómez-Gil, E., & Guillamon, A. (2014). Effects of cross-sex hormone treatment on cortical thickness in transsexual individuals. *The Journal of Sexual Medicine*, *11*(5), 1248–1261.

Zucker, K. J., Lawrence, A. A., & Kreukels, B. P. (2016). Gender dysphoria in adults. *Annual Review of Clinical Psychology*, *12*, 217–247.

10 Future Directions

1. Multidisciplinarity and cognitive science

Starting with the great European plague, the Renaissance, the scientific revolution, the industrial revolution, and the great social and cultural changes following the Second World War, collective human cognition has periodically changed. I refer to the plague since we are under the cloud of the coronavirus pandemic which has almost paused life for millions, indicating a decisive change to human behaviour for times to come. However, the most enduring aspect of human cognition has remained its ability to adapt quickly to any challenge. Any revolution leads to gradual stratification and evolution of solid structures that ensure its continuance. Often, however, the central motives of that revolution may get revised or completely modified depending on circumstances and demands of the times. In the same spirit, over the decades, the central aims of cognitive science enterprise have undergone notable changes. In this section, I will again go back to some history before sketching the present scenarios of this field in a few domains that are thematic. What the field may likely deliver in the future will be covered thereafter.

Johnson and Erneling (1997) edited a volume gathering the scholars who had participated in the cognitive revolution. In their introductory remarks, the editors made an interesting argument. They questioned if the so-called cognitive revolution were a true revolution. They argued that a true revolution dismantles the old tradition and, in its place, erects something new. For example, behaviourism dismantled the introspective structuralist psychology and brought in very radical ideas. It rejected the notion that organisms have anything as inner mental states. In contrast to this, functionalism, which was and is the de facto conceptual framework of cognitive science, brought nothing new (Johnson & Erneling, 1997). Functionalism tried to keep the essences of methodological behaviourism and physicalism and created a compromise. It additionally brought in the computational framework developed by Turing and others. This patchwork, therefore, can't be called a true revolution. Functionalists such as Chomsky, Miller, and Brunner and others who represented the cognitive revolution and wrote chapters for the

DOI: 10.4324/9781003316053-10

volume by Johnson and Erneling (1997) did work that explained much of the mechanism in different fields from language to visual perception, but remained non-committal to what the "mind" is. Thus, the "mind" as a metaphysical concept was replaced by the "mind" as a computer algorithm. The question is whether the revolution which led to this shift in characterisation of the mind indeed can be called "mentalist."

Aptly named "cognitivism," this movement after the cognitive revolution led the study of the mind. It replaced behaviourism in the sense that mental functions of the brain were examined as computational processes. However, even this movement left out a very critical ingredient of the mind or mental states; that is its affective and phenomenological attributes. After all, minds belong to agents and agents feel, experience, and act in the world in unique ways. Cognitivism examined psychological processes such as attention, memory, perception, and decision making in an amodal and disembodied void. This has now been recognised by many in the field as one of the major drawbacks of the movement that should be corrected (Chemero, 2011). Some researchers who have studied the cognitive systems for decades using psychological, computational, and neurobiological methods have come to recognise that one can't define the mind without taking into account the dynamic influence of affective modules (Dukes et al., 2021). Multiple experiments show that affective states that include emotions, mood, desire, and motivational states modulate core processes such as attention, memory, and perception. Thus, after behaviourism and cognitivism, cognitive science has now entered into activism. This shift in paradigm will change how we view and explain mental functions in the future.

What is the current assessment of the cognitive science enterprise? Rafael Núñez more recently has written a very strong critique of the cognitive science enterprise. Núñez and colleagues have questioned that we don't have any cognitive science at all (Núñez et al., 2019). All that has happened is a very confusing amalgamation of different disciplines that have progressed in different directions. There are no coherent concepts that define cognitive science today. For example, within cognitive psychology, there are multiple frameworks and concepts like attention and memory that are confusing, given their resemblance at a mechanistic level. Explanatory levels between the so-called behavioural and neural paradigms remain heterogeneous.

One of the foundational aims of the cognitive science agenda was to map well-defined psychological/mental functions onto the brain's neurobiological strata and create computational models. However, we still can't accurately explain how mental states map onto brain activity. Cognitive neuroscience which was created to objectively study the subjective within the brain imaging methods has not delivered the results. Many of its activities and colourful brain images have been dubbed merely "new phrenology" (Uttal, 2001). Brain activity does not tell anything about mental states. Núñez is right in suggesting that there are wide discrepancies between psychology and neuroscience today. These fields have independently flourished but the common project of cognitive science has not been realised. Psychological and neuro-biological approaches do not converge on definitions, leading to confusions. One example from cognitive psychology is relevant here. Anderson wrote a very scathing paper (Anderson, 2011) called "There is no Such Thing as Attention." He wanted to point out that even though there are many paradigms, tests, and models to study different aspects of attention, we still don't know what exactly attention is. We still don't know how to clearly define those information processing modules that make up the mind and how to pinpoint their neurobiological status.

One main argument of Núñez et al. was that cognitive science did not materialise into a coherent field with a definite research program over the decade. Some scholars think that the evaluation of cognitive science by Núñez is too pessimistic and misguided (Cooper, 2019). It is a fact that, although about five disciplines started the revolution, in due course of time, only cognitive psychology and computer science seem to have driven the field. This has led to the under-representation of some fields like linguistics and anthropology. But one can also ask if cognitive science when it began was designed to have a coherent research program. Was it designed to be interdisciplinary or multidisciplinary? These words are often used so interchangeably that one does not get their meanings. Núñez et al. (2019) analysed the papers published in the flagship journals of the society of cognitive sciences as an indicator of the fields that the journal always has tried to foster and also the affiliations of researchers in cognitive science. The analysis also included the doctoral training backgrounds of researchers who call themselves cognitive scientists now. The entire exercise suggests that the fields did not develop into a cohesive multidisciplinary field as was envisaged by the founding fathers, and has lost diversity. It's dominated by psychology and important disciplines such as anthropology from which many important concepts in cognitive science have come such as embodied cognition and cross-cultural cognition, which have been overlooked. Many authors agree with this assessment of under-representation of anthropology in the field and think that it should play an important role in the future (Bender, 2019). Gentner (2010) has predicted that by 2038, all of cognitive science will be mostly psychology. Cognitive science today is largely defined by progress in cognitive psychology and its neural version, cognitive neuroscience. It has well adopted the original goals of studying intelligent behaviour and mental representations using computational tools (Simon & Kaplan, 1993). This framework specifically includes functionalism (Hommel, 2020) and mechanistic theories of the mind.

In contrast to Núñez, Cooper (2019) argues that cognitive science was not designed to be interdisciplinary since it was impossible. Interdisciplinary success has worked where very few disciplines are involved such as biochemistry or psycholinguistics. And the central thrust of the cognitive revolution was to propose a radical alternative to behaviourism which was about the mind. Therefore, psychology was to play a key role compared to, say, anthropology. Similarly, with the computer revolution, computer science started playing a key role in cognitive science. Therefore, the disbalance with regard to the prominence of different founding disciplines is well justified and not too surprising. Cooper further adds that if we follow the foundational work of Gardner on the history of cognitive science, it will be clear that the founding fathers' aim was explicitly to develop a framework to study the mind without much regard to its neurobiological or social-cultural dimensions. Therefore, cognitive science had to evolve without neuroscience or anthropology. Data from journal articles submitted with the label of cognitive science shows this disbalance (Figure 10.1).

Schunn et al. (1998) did a meta-analysis taking actual data from departments and journal articles to explore to what extent cognitive science was indeed multidisciplinary. They noted that the research work and what is valued within the broad tag of cognitive science is dominated by cognitive psychology and computer science. Other disciplines have been relegated to a minority. They concluded that this could mean under the banner of cognitive science some disciplines are essentially practising disciplinarity. They are doing the same kind of research that they otherwise could have done without the cognitive science tag. There has not been any interface with

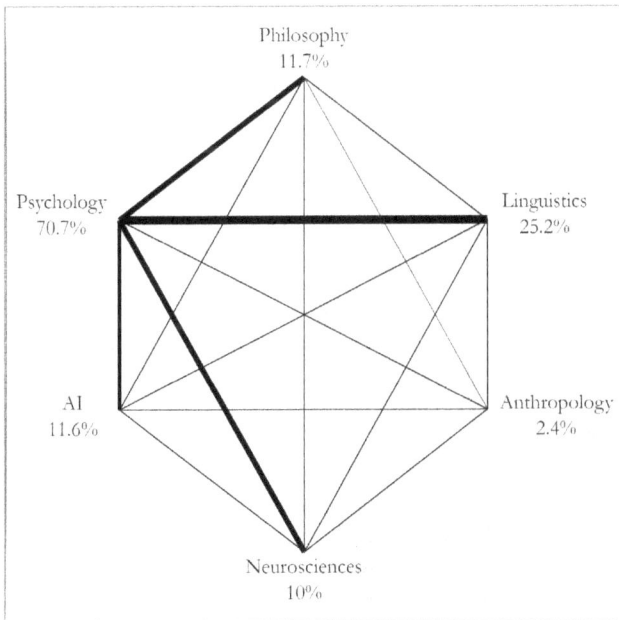

Figure 10.1 Percentage of submissions by field to the journal *Cognitive Science.* Most of the submissions come from psychology. Other fields like philosophy, AI, or anthropology are severely under-represented.

Source: Adapted from Cooper (2019)

other disciplines. Von Eckardt (2001) wrote that when the journal *Cognitive Science* began, its editor-in-chief mentioned that the main objective is to study the mind in a multidisciplinary manner. To this end, different disciplines could contribute from their perspectives. However, the overall aim was to study intelligence as a key feature of cognition; this feature both bound together and also sharply differentiated how animals, humans, and machines function. Now, if that were the ambition, it's likely that disciplines such as anthropology and linguistics could not fare well within these criteria since they did not directly study any intelligence or mental processes in any of these categories or employed qualitative methods. Von Eckardt proposed two ways of looking at the problem. One is the localist way, which Schunn et al. have pursued in their verdict against the multidisciplinarity of cognitive science. This view puts the responsibility on each discipline to contribute on its own for the larger cause of the field to which they are contributing. If they fail in their contribution, then it can't be called multidisciplinary. On the contrary, the holistic view proposes that individual disciplines are free to pursue whatever they deem fit as long as their entire research programmes contribute towards the lofty goals of the field. In that case, we have to see if cognitive psychology, computer science, linguistics, and anthropology have contributed towards the overall aims of the cognitive science field in the last decades. It appears that both the views to evaluate the status of cognitive science pose contradictory challenges. What has happened is that these disciplines further developed into many sub-disciplines because of their internal conflicts. Only a few of the sub-disciplines remained relevant to cognitive science and kept contributing. Nevertheless, this historical analysis is important to understand what is in store for cognitive science in future.

2. Embodied cognition

One of the most decisive developments in the past few decades in the study of the mind has been the acceptance of the context and the environment. The mind is not anymore looked at as some computer program that decides about perception and presents reality, but it is an act of nature. This holistic view that links mind, brain, and environment has been dubbed the embodied cognition enterprise with its many variants (Shapiro, 2019). The embodied cognitive view has extended the way the mind's rationalism and unique attributes have been viewed for centuries. Is the mind independent of body and nature? Raymond Gibbs in his important introduction to embodiment and cognitive science traces the neglect of the body with regard to the theories of the mind (Gibbs, 2005). He cites Plato, who in his *Phaedo* says that mind is the theatre where reality emerged and the body merely followed commands. The body did not give any feedback to the mind which it obeyed. Thus, since Plato, the disembodied mind has remained the metaphor to study cognition, self, consciousness, etc. Descartes took the extreme step in delinking it from anything material thus influencing all later theories.

Embodism has questioned the central tenet of classical cognitive science that the mind itself is powerful enough to extract meaning from the world. The external world plays no role except presenting sensory stimulation. The mind therefore transforms such presentation of sensory stimulation into cognition following computational processes (Pylyshyn, 1980). Given this legacy, it was thought that the body and the environment are secondary for a theory of cognition. However, given the current state of research, this view has been revised and the future tilts towards more integrative theories of cognition that link mind, brain, and environment together. The idea of embodiment is a philosophical idea (Nikkel, 2010). The concept of embodiment in cognitive science is not new. In this vision, the mind does not exercise the role of the disinterested computational machine. Computation may be the mechanism that explains workings of mental states more formally but this can't be the *a priori* view of what the mind is. The concept of the embodiment has both philosophical and psychological attributes (Glenberg, 2010).

The body is central to cognition in any organism (Figure 10.2). By body, one means the whole body with all its parts and not just the brain.

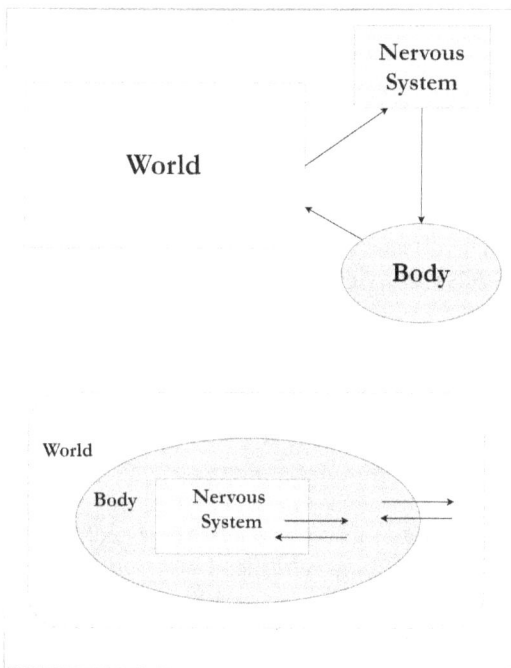

Figure 10.2 Illustration of embodied cognition framework (Thelen, 2000). Traditional perspectives treat the world, the body, and the brain as independent systems with unidirectional interactions. But the embodied view suggests that cognition is shaped by the bodily experiences of the human embedded in the world.

Organisms are capable of cognition to the extent their bodies allow them to do so (Shapiro, 2019). Bodies have evolved to interact dynamically with the environment taking into account contingencies. The computational mind plays a minor role in cognition, if at all. However, beyond the rhetoric, how does one explain the emergence of the mind in such a framework? Shapiro proposes that the dynamic system approach is better suited as a computational framework for embodied cognition than the usual representational theories (Shapiro, 2019) in which the body becomes central to cognition and the organism gets its cognition by enacting out in the world. Embodism rejects the view of the mind as a passive, tricky, all-knowing computational system that has no connection to reality in the material universe.

Embodiment concepts have wide applications. The use of virtual technology either for everyday life requirements or for entertainment is a growing area. Embodied robotics uses concepts from embodiment and cognitive science to make robots more contextually sensitive. Affective computing tackles the issue of emotion recognition and expression in the artificial. The iCub baby robot developed by the scientists at the Italian Institute of Technology is an example of what we can expect from embodied robotics (Metta et al., 2008). This robot was trained to learn from its interactions with its environment. Sensors provided data input to its system and acted as an interface with the outside environment. Central to any cognitive behaviour is the dynamic adaptation to environmental demands. Any fixed computer program that can't take into account situations and contingencies will not be of much value. They may use the stored knowledge in any emerging situation or update it as it demands. This makes this paradigm extremely different from traditional robotics (Lara et al., 2018). Given the lofty ideals of this movement, neuroscience theories have also started to match up to the expectations. The classical view is that neurons process information fed by sensors using representations. The body plays no role in it. For successful embodied robotics, the brain and its activities have to be integrated with the actions that the body performs in the environment. Therefore, there is dynamic interaction among the body, brain, and environment. More recent approaches within the brain-based theories have proposed dynamic interactions among the computational systems, brains, and environment. This holistic approach to cognition is a radical theory and it's the future of robotics since it has the potential to resurrect AI research from the accusation of not having any phenomenology. Artificial systems that are integrated into the environment through their bodies and actions may end up having experiential phenomenology that has been missing (Senden et al., 2020).

3. Cross cultural cognitive psychology

The future will see more and more culturally constrained theories of human cognition than what exists now. This is because of the overwhelming evidence that human cognition is culturally rooted and may be geographically localised. Gone are the days when psychological theories were constructed on mostly white participants assuming they will be applied to all humans (Barrett, 2020). We may not have general theories that apply to all humans irrespective of the cultures they come from. Historically, other scholars in human sciences, such as cultural anthropologists, have studied the expression of psychological states in different cultures. In contrast to this, cognitive psychology has not traditionally valued the influence of unique cultures on psychological processing. This may explain why anthropology could not play a key role in the progress of mainstream cognitive science (Rigoli et al., 2020). Cultural differences in cognition have been well documented, for instance in the processing of visual stimuli (Nisbett & Miyamoto, 2005). Easterners process pictures more holistically and the Westerners process them more objectively. The argument is that Easterners process visual and emotional stimuli differently than Westerners. Both computationalism and neural approaches being behaviouristic and materialistic disregard cultural and individual differences. That is because the functionalist programme in current cognitive science aspires for objective status and natural science type models. But cross-cultural cognitive psychology and cognitive neuroscience would predict that constructs used in cognitive psychology such as attention, memory, perception, and emotion would vary across cultures. For example, participants from different cultures perform similarly on Stroop or flanker tasks (Ktaiche et al., 2021). Such data suggest that culturally and ethnically different groups bring with them different strategies of selective attention and inhibitory control which such tasks measure.

The challenge for the future lies in objectively measuring task variance in different populations and explaining the reasons in a holistic way. The reasons could be biological, social, economic, or cultural. Further, different tasks may have to be developed that accurately map the cognitive functions of different populations in diverse cultural settings. It is time that we give up this general idea that one task measures a certain cognitive ability in everyone. The reasons are obvious and belong to long histories of adoptive cognitive evolution in different humans who have inhabited different regions (Sperber & Hirschfeld, 2004). It makes sense at a practical level since we see strong variations in human cognition as a function of culture across the globe (Machery & Faucher, 2017). Cognitive functions have evolved to help people survive and adapt in different circumstances. For example, the type of selective attention which people in the Amazon basin need is not the same for those who stay in New York. If this evolutionary adaptive view is taken, then it makes sense to assume that not only brains and their networking have evolved to support specific types of cognition in specific populations, even the cognitive strategies are different. The population-level differences in colour perception in the famous Berlin and Kay studies can offer critical insights into this (Berlin & Kay, 1969). Of course, about a century ago Sapir and Whorf had first suggested this with regards to language and meaning and both strong and light versions of that hypothesis have remained relevant even now (Kay & Kempton, 1984). If cognitive psychology has to remain relevant and speak for all groups, it has to be more sensitive to cultural and individual variations. There is no problem using one or the other variation of the tasks but their interpretations have to be specific to the groups measured. One must ask what type of attention or memory or emotion regulation these specific sets of people have evolved and how to measure and compare them objectively.

Michel Posner has written that attentional mechanisms may be fundamentally different in people belonging to different cultures (Posner & Rothbart, 2017). That's because the functional links between genes and brain networks that they help form are shaped by culture. The requirements of attention may vary from culture to culture and therefore there is no need to assume that people from two different cultures will perform similarly on any task. Even subcomponents of attention may differ from one cultural group to another. A recent study that compared Canadian and Japanese children on flanker tasks found noticeable differences in distractor suppression (Senzaki et al., 2018). That is because Japanese process things holistically considering the whole context while Westerners process the focal objects prominently. Even brain-imaging techniques such as ERP have shown such differences in attentional strategies linked to cognitive styles in different cultures (Hsieh et al., 2020). Therefore, the key point here is to find out the cognitive styles that people from any particular culture use to deal with everyday life and develop suitable tasks to measure them. This raises a very important question concerning cross-cultural measurements of cognitive processes. If tasks are central to cognitive psychology, then they must be culture-bound to some extent.

There are also other indicators of why culture should influence task performance in everyday laboratory situations. This has been precisely either avoided or overlooked in almost all cognitive psychological experiments so far. Needless to mention, most studies have also considered a specific type

National Location of Samples Published in *Psychological Science* in 2014								
Region	United States	Non-English Speaking Countries	Europe	Israel	Asia	Africa	Latin America	Unknown
No. of Samples	227 (50.8%)	53 (11.9%)	70 (15.7%)	20 (4.4%)	17 (3.9%)	6 (1.3%)	3 (0.6%)	51 (11.4%)

Figure 10.3 Example illustrating the lack of representation of non-US, non-English-speaking countries in articles published in psychological journals. Almost half of the articles involved studies based on a sample living in the United States. This reflects the lack of diversity in papers published in top scientific journals and calls for more non-WEIRD research.

Source: Adapted from Rad et al. (2018, *PNAS*)

of population, i.e., college-educated, white, and upper-middle-class dubbed the WEIRD population (Henrich et al., 2010). More recent studies have shown that traditional practices such as specific religions, and mind control techniques such as meditations influence brain networks significantly. For example, the practice of meditation in Eastern civilisations has shaped their cultures for thousands of years which is not the case with the West, although in the Western traditions within the Judeo-Christianity traditions, prayers and other devotional rituals have performed the same functions. The Indian tradition of yoga and its influence on the mental processes such as attention and awareness are being swiftly recognised globally. How does one take this into account while developing theories of attention and consciousness? Specific differences in attention and inhibitory control have been found by practitioners of different believers (Colzato et al., 2008). It would be difficult to answer the question here why certain cultures developed such specific practices and attached great significance for the mind while others did not. As I noted in the chapter on religion, the field called cognitive science of religion is now a growing field as well as cognitive archaeology. Both these fields are unearthing how both evolution and adaptations have shaped our cognition. It's time that the laboratory-based cognitive psychologist wakes up to this reality and considers them in both research design and data analysis and interpretation.

Language is a key indicator of culture. The norms of language and its use are embedded within the larger cultural context of any society. There has been a growing interest in studying how language use influences core executive functions such as attention and working memory (Mishra, 2015). Particularly the study of how bilingualism and multilingualism affect cognition has been very popular for some time. There are many reasons for this since most people today in the world speak multiple languages. Bilingualism has been shown to influence the executive control networks of the brain in a very significant way and it confers some cognitive advantages to the speakers (Mishra, 2018). The sociolinguistic realities and cognitive demands of bilingualism or for that matter everyday language use vary tremendously across cultures.

Mishra et al. (2012) found that Indian bilinguals with superior second language proficiency had a greater ability to disengage their attention from irrelevant stimuli than those who did not have very good fluency in the second language. When the study was conducted in Canada these effects were not found (Saint-Aubin et al., 2018). In both the studies the participants were university-level students who lived in a bilingual community. There are many different ways to reflect on the results of both the studies. For example, India is more massively bi- and multilingual than Canada where bilingualism is prevalent only in one or two provinces. Importantly the nature and demands of bilingualism in India are far different than what one may experience in Canada. The nature of adaptive control settings that any bilingual speaker requires in India probably is greater than Canada. Therefore, the environmental demands set constraints on the nature of executive control that the language user may set up. In an earlier study in this area on children, Bialystok had found that children who are bilingual both in India and Canada show superior cognitive advantage compared to monolinguals (Bialystok et al., 2004). Therefore, it's not a question of using standardised tasks across cultural groups but to precisely identify which variables influence the nature of bilingualism in certain cultures. This shows that unless we understand cultural variables deeply, we won't know how linguistic and non-linguistic behaviours emerge in different cultures.

The question of cross-cultural cognition can't be understood without taking into account the ever-changing nature of the international world order. Globalisation led to dynamic acculturation in many societies shaping their cultures (Chen et al., 2008). There have also been some cross-cultural investigations in cognitive neuroscience on the effect of globalisation on brain networks in bilinguals (Abutalebi & Weekes, 2014). Bilingualism brought in many social advantages in a globalised world (Ramírez-Esparza et al., 2020). Economic globalisation has defined the living and working conditions of people in the last three decades. This led to a massive influx of immigrants from less advanced countries to the more advanced. The immigrants had to learn the language and culture of the host for survival and prosperity. This movement of human cultural capital worked well for a decade until most countries fell into the grip of growing nationalism. Those countries that are rich could afford a closed homogeneous culture mostly speaking one language and abiding by one religion which unites them. But the poor have to look for greener pastures at all times willing to accommodate new languages and new cultures sometimes at the expense of their own. Therefore the question of bilingualism and its effect on cognition as a specific example becomes the question of who has migrated where and what have been the terms and conditions of cultural amalgamation (Vaccarino & Walker, 2011). Its degree and magnitude are different for different cultures. For example, the extent to which the Chinese have established themselves in the United States is not similar to the way Indians have – both economically and culturally. Viewed from this broad angle, the issue of cross-cultural cognition assumes new complexity which should be the focus of future research.

In sum, cross-cultural studies of cognition are the future. The effort will be to find cultural invariants that specific tasks could tap into and attributes that vary across cultures. The question should be what kind of cognition a specific people need who have evolved in a specific historical context than to view all as homogeneously sensitive to all tasks. There is currently increasing effort towards the replication of tasks across cultures and this seems to be a fine way to go forward. The differences should not surprise us since that is how evolution has shaped cognition in specific people who embody specific cultures. And this includes all dimensions of cognition including much higher mechanisms such as consciousness and awareness which are also under cultural pressure.

4. Social cognition

Humans are social animals who have a long evolutionary history. That history, full of intriguing cultures, art facts, religions, habits, food, and personal lives, indicates the evolution of a strong and unique social mind (Donald, 1991). Humans are social primates that live in a certain way forging deep bonds and they suffer when these bonds erode. Psychological suffering as a member of the species or a group is also ensured when one does not belong to a group or can't act altruistically (Van Slyke, 2010). Although the structure of a social organisation has been studied in disciplines like sociology and anthropology for decades, the study of the social mind is new. Cognitive scientists are now interested in understanding how the mind became social and what its attributes are. Classical cognitive science visualised the mind as a computer algorithm that uses the information to interpret what's out there. But why did such a mathematical program become social? Why do we crave social relationships with other fellow humans without which we become mentally disordered? Even psychiatrists and clinical psychologists have not fully answered such questions although they have developed many methods and therapy programmes to alleviate the pains of individuals. A new discipline has emerged now called social cognitive neuroscience which attempts to understand why the brain craves to be social (Lieberman, 2007). In the following we will see some aspects of this research and its potential future.

Experimental cognitive psychologists study individual people and their behaviour on well-controlled tasks. For example, we theorise about someone's attention by asking him to do a flanker task. However, such measures do not tell us how individuals bring their attention capacities into the real world when they are in a specific environment and with other agents. Attention as a cognitive mechanism is different from how it is exercised by agents in the world (Kingstone et al., 2003). Individualistic psychological data has helped us understand both behavioural and neural bases of task performance but it has not revealed how people use them during everyday life. Social cognition studies have proposed "interactional" methods to study how humans perform tasks in the presence of other individuals, something that is ecologically valid and relevant to real life. These "interactional" studies have used different paradigms and methods to examine how performance changes when people perform tasks with other people, for example in joint tasks (De Jaegher et al., 2010). Results from such studies show that an interactional environment with other agents directly influences how participants perform their tasks. Other agents affect our attention, even if they happen to be Chinese toy cats (Dolk et al., 2013). What is important here is to note that in the presence of other agents, an individual mind becomes something different; it starts to adapt and accommodate the intentions of the others. Therefore, social cognition is not merely about how individuals go about interacting with other agents in different environments permuting different tasks but how their psychology and goals change rapidly as a function of this.

A fundamental assumption in the philosophy of the mind is that humans are capable of decoding the mental states of other humans. This was dubbed "theory of mind" and has greatly influenced cognitive science (Frith & Frith, 2005). Reading the mental states of others has helped us in our survival and evolution. Theory of mind evolved since it was required for humans to be able to understand one another and prepare their actions. This ability allows us to work collaboratively by sharing intentions (Roth,2010). Shared intentions and the capacity for joint action indicate that we might not have evolved to hold only individual perception and cognition (Gallotti & Frith, 2013). Therefore, while cognitive theories are about individuals and their cognition, they may not explain how we can read the mental states of others and organise our actions around other people. This is the new theory of social cognition in which there is no individual cognition but only collective, as a network (Stephenson et al., 2021). All our collective achievements and ideas are a reflection of this network of shared intentions and a biological need to be with others (Schaller et al., 2007).

The human brain has also evolved to interpret others' mental states and modify its mechanisms according to the situation. For example, there is currently much discussion on the different brain networks that are active during social cognition tasks, such as the frontal areas and the many subcortical areas (Adolphs, 1999). When participants see others doing the same actions or they guess other agents' intentions, their brain activations change (Varela et al., 2020). It has been argued in evolutionary psychology that the human brain, particularly the frontal cortex, many parts of the parietal cortex, and their connectivity expanded to support the growing demands on social cognition (Schaller et al., 2017). This expansion of the brain made sure that humans achieved greater competence in their social relations and could cooperate widely among themselves for greater benefit. While current cognitive science aims to explain individual variability in cognitive capacity, it also has to explain how diverse types of humans with their very different intentions come together to accomplish common projects that have much higher utility. Selective pressure for the survival of the species through mutual understanding and cooperation could have led to such adaptive changes in biology (Emery, 2004).

Current research in social cognition has opened up several applied possibilities. For example, there is experimental evidence that humans manifest social cognition through joint attention. For example, when people gaze at the same object in the environment and also at each other, they access the mental states of one another (Stephenson et al., 2021). This mapping of mental states plays a key role in reinforcing both affective harmony and social cognition. Attention through eye gaze, therefore, is the glue between agents. Training in social cognition has been shown to improve the functioning of people with schizophrenia (d'Arma et al., 2021). How patients interact with the therapists and with each other in a certain environment plays a key role in their recovery or at least management of their core symptoms. Thus, minds that are malfunctioning can't be treated in isolation but only through active interaction with other minds. Social cognition is impaired in neurodegenerative diseases even though they may have some cognitive functioning intact (Alonso-Recio et al., 2021). It is then apparent that these individuals have not lost their cognitive functions but can do simple tasks and recognise objects. However, they become impaired in forging positive and constructive social relationships with other humans, which is key to a good life. Social cognition itself likely depends on the fine orchestra of several cognitive systems such as attention, memory, and perception. Training in social cognition as well as in cognitive therapy jointly play a facilitative role in the management of such diseases of cognition.

Social cognition and the activities that humans do together being in the presence of one another suffered during COVID-19. Humans are social primates that need to see the faces and bodies of others to grasp their mental states; this feeds back into their mental health. During COVID-19, when mask-wearing became mandatory, people did not have access to others' faces. Patients with dementia showed reduced social cognition when they had no full access to the faces of others when they were masked (Schroeter et al., 2021). Other studies have shown that COVID-19 isolation, particularly social distancing and mask-wearing, impaired social cognition (Bland et al., 2022). Social cognition also diminished, affecting learning during online classes (Latheef et al., 2021). These data indicate that humans have evolved to live an embodied and interactive life with fellow humans. Any absence of that or its mere artificial simulation will impair social cognition.

5. Individual differences and cognition

It is gradually being recognised that one's specific biological and psychological attributes decide one's cognition. One important future aim of cognitive science is to be of some help to the individual. This is possible when individual-level differences are considered in research. Every individual's brain structure and networks are different. The cognition each brain produces is also different. Some major markers of individual difference could be sexual orientation, gender, cognitive capacity, and levels of literacy. It's expected that the next decades of research are to be more sensitive to individual difference factors just like the cultural factors. Of course, at some level, individual difference factors and cultural factors do interact, influencing cognition.

In this book, I wrote on cognition in people with different gender preferences. Needless to say, so far cognitive psychology research has mostly considered the usual stereotypes. Sexual orientation is an important individual difference factor. Very little experimental work on the cognition of individuals with non-conforming sexuality is currently available. It's likely that from many mainstream studies they are excluded. It is possible that people who don't identify themselves within the binary gender system may have unique attributes to their everyday cognition. How they view their gender identity is not a socio-political question. It's a cognitive question given that a majority of them undergo hormone therapy which has the potential to bring about changes to the mind and brain. Similarly, we have long studied the cognition of people who do not have much literacy. In spite of rapid technological progress in many pockets of the world, many people still do not have formal literacy. In longitudinal brain imaging studies, while we trained them on literacy, we found significant changes in brain networks over time (Skeide et al., 2017; Mishra et al. 2012; Huettig & Mishra, 2014). Many individuals in countries like India, China, and many Latin American countries have remained illiterate. In the absence of literacy, they live a cognitively and socially inferior life, since the modern world treats literacy as the most significant indicator of social and cultural currency. Therefore, these individuals need to be studied differently since they can't be grouped with literate individuals in experiments. Such cognitive and individual difference factors directly influence both data analysis and interpretation as well as theory construction.

Another group that was long excluded from any experimentation was the geriatric population since most studies have been on young, healthy, college-going populations. Of course, the rationale for this choice has been that the young have the optimal cognition at that life stage before it starts to slow down. It's now well recognised that with ageing, the structure and functions of the brain change and along with it the cognition. Attention, working memory, and language production decrease rapidly when we age (Roberts & Allen, 2016). If additionally there is a neurodegenerative disease, their decline is even more rapid and serious. The concept of cognitive reserve has been popular in this context. The idea is to explain why some individuals cope better with their cognitive functions as they age while others face a stiff decline. Cognitive reserve is known to be boosted by critical practices such as literacy, bilingualism, and other hobbies. Since the human life span has increased many folds in many countries it's important to investigate how cognition remains stable over time. Future studies will likely be more intense on the question of ageing and cognition.

Individual difference factors also include any specific abilities or disabilities that individuals may have. For example, children with different types of developmental and cognitive disorders have often been neglected by mainstream cognitive psychologists and psycholinguistics. In comparison to normal healthy individuals, they perform differently on standard tasks. For example, in many studies on adults with hearing loss, we have found that they have superior visual attention. But the advantage appears in some key attributes of attention (Prasad et al., 2015). They can process some stimulus at the extreme periphery unlike us or can track subtle changes in motion. We also have demonstrated that they are sensitive to stimuli presented subliminally or show more awareness of the visual dimension (Prasad et al., 2017). This sets them apart from those who have normal hearing. Therefore, these findings have very serious consequences for their training and integration into society. It's well known that children with autism show impairment in emotion processing. But we also have to be careful in how we measure emotion in the laboratory set-up with such children. It's possible that the way they process emotion is not captured by the traditional tasks. On the other extreme, some children have superior gifts in some components of cognition and show extreme talent early on. This list can go on to include different types of individuals whose cognitive processing strategies are different from many of us. The future of experimental cognitive psychology is to investigate these variations and then create a different model of cognition if that's possible. The exclusion model of theorising has to be replaced by an inclusion model.

Individual difference factors include structural aspects of the brain, functional uniqueness, and control of cognitive functions. Participants bring these variables to any task that is administered. One can use an individual difference approach to almost all types of questions while investigating cognition. Individual difference factors can be stable and floating, that change with time. For example, weight, body type, and gender are stable factors. However, most cognitive mechanisms are floating and change dynamically over time. Both stable and floating variables influence experimental results. For example, cognitive control settings are dynamically adapted considering environmental demands. Stable factors do not influence them a lot since they don't change. However, cognitive mechanisms can adapt themselves dynamically to decide on the proper action. A recent study showed this in the case of social and non-social cognitive control processes (Darda et al., 2020). People with different levels of anxiety profile experience social behaviour differently (Czekóová et al., 2020). Sometimes individual difference factors don't predict cognitive behaviour. For example, it's well known that infants immediately learn how to mimic human behaviour that they see around them very early on. This mimicking behaviour plays an important role in later developments of social behaviour. One can link this phenomenon to the mirror neuron system. One study did not find any correlation between early mimicking and the later development of prosocial behaviour (Redshaw et al., 2020). It's to be noted that individual difference studies use correlational approaches often to analyse data. The aim is to see if any individual difference factors will predict some key cognitive functions. At times the number of individual difference factors to consider can be very overwhelming. That's why researchers may seek only a few factors that have shown previous correlations to the anticipated cognitive variable. A recent study used the factor analytic method to explore why individuals differ in their creative cognition. For instance, traditionally, studies on creativity have used factors such as divergent thinking and problem solving. Creative people use these skills to bring novelty to their work in any domain. However, so far, from a cognitive science point of view, it has not been clear which mechanisms help people in problem solving or divergent thinking first of all. It appears that working memory capacity and fluency impact these basic skills on which creativity depends (Dygert, & Jarosz, 2020). Specific tasks show specific utilisation of brain mechanisms in individuals that differ widely from person to person (Jiang et al., 2020). Individual difference factors can impart their effects from basic skills such as using language to higher functions such as conflict detection and structuring belief systems. For example, studies show that individuals may differ with regard to their sensitivity to rational reasoning depending on their strategies of cognitive processing (Šrol & De Neys, 2020).

6. Artificial agents and virtual reality

Virtual reality and artificial intelligence will dominate future research in cognitive and allied sciences. In this book, I dealt with the question of artificial intelligence in depth. While most think the future of AI is a question of technical sophistication, to me it's the ethical and embodied dimension that seems critical. Humans will never respect AI unless they grant them the status of agency and they will never fully enjoy their presence unless they overcome their embodiment constraints. Importantly both these things are also linked to our understanding of our higher mental lives, particularly phenomenal consciousness – the sort of consciousness that gives us qualia beyond objective knowledge, since it's pretty much clear that this is what matters to us. This is clearly what the artificial lacks despite its tremendous and ever-increasing computational power. The question of ethics in AI is a historically debated issue. While some agree that it's important for us to extend ethical and moral behaviour to AI, others think that it's meaningless since they are not moral agents. They don't feel pain, they can't think for themselves, and they are simply not like us. However, more recently many corporations that use AI in different formats have been developing guidelines to make ethical treatment legally binding (Jobin et al., 2019).

The future of AI is to develop generalised intelligence. This is the type of intelligence we have that is domain-general and easily transferable. At the moment, the intelligence of the AI is limited to the domains for which they are programmed. For example, Deep Blue was programmed to win at chess but not to make coffee well using that intelligence. A human being can do both easily. This sort of intelligence also will be self-regulated. Deep learning algorithms are aiming for this as the future of AI. However, if the AI will have generalised behaviour then it's known what their behaviour towards humans will be. That's the future that is linked to the future of AI (Dignum, 2018). Generalised intelligence may open up a territory that we don't know yet. The question of morality and ethics will assume new dimensions since the AI will start knowing us. At the moment they are brute computational algorithms. And generalised intelligence may also make them more phe-nomenally aware. If that happens then we have no choice but to bring in necessary modifications to our theory-of-mind requirements and show ethi-cal behaviour towards them.

Another application closely related to the question of AI is the embodi-ment in the virtual reality arena. The growth in virtual reality so far has not been very impressive. It's a question of technological sophistication. However, the real future lies in the embodiment. Just as humans are not capable of accepting AI as moral agents, they feel very superficial in VR environments. It's because getting into VR does not fulfil the requirements of embodiment. Our sense of embodiment consists of our sense of agency, our awareness of our own body, with regard to the environment and other bodies (Kilteni et al., 2012). At the moment these components are missing from the available VR systems. The keyword in the context that defines our experience is immersiveness. Immersiveness can be defined as an experience without boundaries. It's the total and extendable experience in any environ-ment given appropriate feedback with a two-way channel. It's possible that VR systems can be made very immersive and they can then generate appro-priate feelings and emotions in us. It's important to note that the extent to which one experiences immersiveness is dependent on many personal traits (Shin, 2018). The new concept is a progressive embodiment which has now been implemented in many VR technologies (Biocca, 1997). Virtual reality does not appear real to us since we don't recognise the capabilities of the body. Following the ground-breaking ideas of psychologist J. J. Gibson, it's possible to get out of this Cartesian trap. The VR world is an animated world where what we see influences how we feel. The entire body works as a giant sensor that gives us feedback regarding objects, depth, our position, and other such things. Therefore, the embodiment depends on the way the environment is structured and the quality of the immersive feedback. The key to a successful virtual reality experience lies within the extent to which the user can experience the avatars as real. Users must not think of the ava-tars as mere shadows with no selves or agency. Newer concepts like "medi-ated embodiment" shows that at some level of sophistication some users can feel the avatars as real and have an immersive experience (Aymerich-Franch, 2018). At times they even feel that the bodies of the avatars are their own. If this happens then VR would be sufficiently realistic for all our purposes.

Thus, both AI and embodiment in virtual reality are related questions. These technologies have massive applications in all walks of human life and they will grow very rapidly. However, technological and allied growth does not mean that we have sorted out our conceptual problems, such as the question of consciousness in the AI or the question of true immersiveness in the VR. They are for cognitive scientists to debate and understand; however, this may not stop the progress in applications in the real world. Therefore, the true multidisciplinary future of cognitive science lies in embracing these ideas and exploring them with some freshness. We can't use those old-world dichotomies such as mind and body for all such projects. It's of course quite possible that humans are designed to view an experience and the world from certain vantage points only. Come what may, humans will bring these dichotomies to understand consciousness or immersiveness. They will have any system that's not natural to have consciousness just like them. They will want the VR to be as real as the reality they experience; they are rigid with regard to modulating these constraints for other systems. It's not just a matter of philosophical discussion but that's how we are. It's also possible that these systems will change us forever and in total. It's a matter of time.

7. Looking ahead

In this last section of the last chapter, I will speculate on some themes that are going to receive the most attention in future times within the mind and the brain sciences. Núñez et al.'s (2019) article lamented about cognitive science's lack of coherence and focus. Cognitive science, being a human science, will be influenced by the changing nature of cognition in humans. It is not a static science played around by few disciplines but will look at the ever-changing adaptive strategies of humans. The study of the mind and cognition will take place in very different environments than what we know so far. This will also require more interface between the natural sciences and human sciences.

The focus of the study of cognition will change from the brain to other systems. The last decades saw very rapid and extensive growth of brain-based models. At the moment researchers have started focusing on biological systems that may offer clues to those shades of cognition previously unknown. For example, the vestibular system is traditionally known to be a reflex system that kind of maintains the posture of the body and does other basic processing. It appears that this system also influences cognition in significant ways (Ferrè & Haggard, 2020). The vestibular neurocognitive network can offer clues to many neuropsychological conditions. This may change our current views of higher cognitive functions associated with the frontoparietal brain networks and some other subcritical structures.

Future studies will explore more fundamentally how environmental factors give rise to unexpected patterns in cognition. Let's consider the issue of material deprivation and cognition. Traditionally it is believed that deprivation affects cognitive growth more generally. One study examined children who had seen early stress and deprivation and those who had more or less a normal upbringing (Nweze et al., 2021). The study found that children who faced early deprivation showed greater ability at working memory capacity later. Evolutionarily speaking, deprivation has always challenged the cognitive systems to adapt and remain prepared for uncertainties. Such results may also explain why often the immigrants' children who migrate to more advanced countries do well academically. It's the nature of evolution that forces the system to adapt that function which is critical for its success and survival. While many children from well-to-do homes may do computer-based working memory tasks to improve this aspect of cognition, children from poverty and deprived homes are boosting the same system simply by adapting to the ever-present uncertainties and contingencies. This is not just about culture variation or individual differences which we have dealt with before. It's about how evolution sculpts brains and behaviour in different environmental circumstances.

Future research on cognition will include more studies on religion and different belief structures than what has been seen so far. Current approaches indicate that the practice of religion engages cognitive control, reasoning, and the social brain in individuals (Grafman et al., 2020). It's another thing that the same processes also produce religious fanatics. Religion and other such ritualistic behaviour are a rich source to study cognition in an evolutionary sense. Humans are prisoners of habits and rituals. These are transmitted from one generation to another and form the fabric of cultures. Future directions in the study of the mind will consist of studying human rituals in all their dimensions in many cultures to understand the underlying thread (Boyer & Liénard, 2020). This also fits well with the aspirations of an emerging framework called cultural neuroscience. This is about how the brain evolves and gets its functions in different cultures. Religious and all such culture-specific practices train the mind to bring its fullest potentials to work. Just like the computational mind, neuroscience won't remain merely about the nervous system and its working. It has to explain why particular types of brain networks evolve with their specific functions in specific cultures that we see (Chiao, 2020).

The new frontiers in cognitive science will also see more and more evolutionary approaches. Work in fields like cognitive archaeology and its interface with cognitive psychology and cognitive neuroscience holds the key (Bruner et al., 2018). More recent discoveries have shifted the dates of the evolution of *Homo sapiens* even backwards. Of course, it won't be easy to answer if the evolution of mental functions has proceeded parallel to the evolution of the brain. But this track of research will reveal how brains are adapting and evolving now under current constraints. This has significant insights to offer to those problems that we see around why some people can cope and do well in the modern world with its complexity and others cannot. Why do some individuals get diseases of the brain and others do not? The vast disparity in human conditions in different pockets of the world is not just a socio-political or anthropological question. Cognitive scientists can't shy away from explaining this because it has to do with brains and what they can do. The evolutionary angle also will help create predictive models of collective human cognition for the future (Laland & Seed, 2021).

The future will also see rapid growth in the use of cognitive science techniques in understanding many diseases that plague humankind. Once cognitive psychologists have charged their tools and have a grip on the individual and cultural variables, it will be easy to explain the symptoms through the core mechanisms, as is the case now with many developmental and acquired disorders of cognition. Research on working memory, attention, and executive control are valuable tools in explaining deficits that stretch from language and emotion to social cognition. The traditional boundary between sensory and motor will disappear since much of the current data don't show such effects precisely. Listening to language activates motor areas as well as seeing things and mental imagery. On the other hand, motor actions influence cognition in many ways. At the moment the interface of cognitive science with medical science is weak. Many neurologists and neurophysiologists are not well aware of the massive developments in cognitive neuropsychology. The use of animal models remains with the usual constraints and can't be rapidly adopted to the human condition when it comes to something as abstract and fundamental as cognition. The use of artificial intelligence techniques and simulations will come in handy in integrating these disciplines and making them work together. A newly emerging field called cultural computational neuroscience should encourage us in this direction. Thus, philosophical speculations apart from cognitive science will assume a key role in extending practical help to people where they need it most. Ultimately, the question becomes how to live well and find meaning in an ever-changing world. Cognitive science has to explain and also empower us in understudying this adaptation. While we debate the future of cognitive, mind, and brain sciences as scientific and academic disciplines, the question of the mind's presence in a material universe will remain central. Along with this, the discipline itself will be further diversified as human nature itself changes.

References

Abutalebi, J., & Weekes, B. S. (2014). The cognitive neurology of bilingualism in the age of globalization. *Behavioural Neurology.* https://doi.org/10.1155/2014/536727

Adolphs, R. (1999). Social cognition and the human brain. *Trends in Cognitive Sciences, 3*(12), 469–479.

Alonso-Recio, L., Carvajal, F., Merino, C., & Serrano, J. M. (2021). Social cognition and cognitive decline in patients with Parkinson's disease. *Journal of the International Neuropsychological Society, 27*(7), 744–755.

Anderson, B. (2011). There is no such thing as attention. *Frontiers in Psychology, 2,* 246.

Aymerich-Franch, L. (2018). Is mediated embodiment the response to embodied cognition?. *New Ideas in Psychology, 50,* 1–5.

Barrett, H. C. (2020). Towards a cognitive science of the human: Cross-cultural approaches and their urgency. *Trends in Cognitive Sciences, 24*(8), 620–638.

Bender, A. (2019). The value of diversity in cognitive science. *Topics in Cognitive Science, 11*(4), 853–863.

Berlin, B., & Kay, P. (1969). *Basic color terms: Their universality and evolution.* University of California Press.

Bialystok, E., Craik, F. I., Klein, R., & Viswanathan, M. (2004). Bilingualism, aging, and cognitive control: Evidence from the Simon task. *Psychology and Aging, 19*(2), 290.

Biocca, F. (1997). The cyborg's dilemma: Progressive embodiment in virtual environments. *Journal of Computer-Mediated Communication*, 3(2).

Bland, A. R., Roiser, J. P., Mehta, M. A., Sahakian, B. J., Robbins, T. W., & Elliott, R. (2022). The impact of COVID-19 social isolation on aspects of emotional and social cognition. *Cognition and Emotion*, 36(1), 49–58.

Boyer, P., & Liénard, P. (2020). Ingredients of "rituals" and their cognitive underpinnings. *Philosophical Transactions of the Royal Society B*, 375(1805).

Bruner, E., Fedato, A., Silva-Gago, M., Alonso-Alcalde, R., Terradillos-Bernal, M., Fernández-Durantes, M. Á., & Martín-Guerra, E. (2018). Cognitive archeology, body cognition, and hand – tool interaction. *Progress in Brain Research*, 238, 325–345.

Chemero, A. (2011). *Radical embodied cognitive science*. MIT Press.

Chen, S. X., Benet-Martínez, V., & Harris Bond, M. (2008). Bicultural Identity, bilingualism, and psychological adjustment in multicultural societies: Immigration-based and globalization-based acculturation. *Journal of Personality*, 76(4), 803–838.

Chiao, J. Y. (2020). *Philosophy of computational cultural neuroscience*. Routledge.

Colzato, L. S., van den Wildenberg, W. P., & Hommel, B. (2008). Losing the big picture: How religion may control visual attention. *PLoS One*, 3(11), e3679.

Cooper, R. P. (2019). Multidisciplinary flux and multiple research traditions within cognitive science. *Topics in Cognitive Science*, 11(4), 869–879.

Czekóová, K., Shaw, D. J., Pokorná, Z., & Brázdil, M. (2020). Dissociating profiles of social cognitive disturbances between mixed personality and anxiety disorder. *Frontiers in Psychology*, 11.

Darda, K. M., Butler, E. E., & Ramsey, R. (2020). Individual differences in social and non-social cognitive control. *Cognition*, 202, 104317.

d'Arma, A., Isernia, S., Di Tella, S., Rovaris, M., Valle, A., Baglio, F., & Marchetti, A. (2021). Social cognition training for enhancing affective and cognitive theory of mind in schizophrenia: A systematic review and a meta-analysis. *The Journal of Psychology*, 155(1), 26–58.

De Jaegher, H., Di Paolo, E., & Gallagher, S. (2010). Can social interaction constitute social cognition?. *Trends in Cognitive Sciences*, 14(10), 441–447.

Dignum, V. (2018). Ethics in artificial intelligence: Introduction to the special issue. *Ethics and. Information Technology*, 20(1).

Dolk, T., Hommel, B., Prinz, W., & Liepelt, R. (2013). The (not so) social Simon effect: A referential coding account. *Journal of Experimental Psychology: Human Perception and Performance*, 39(5), 1248.

Donald, M. (1991). *Origins of the modern mind: Three stages in the evolution of culture and cognition*. Harvard University Press.

Dukes, D., Abrams, K., Adolphs, R., Ahmed, M. E., Beatty, A., Berridge, K. C., Broomhall, S., Brosch, T., Campos, J. J., Clay, Z., Clément, F., Cunningham, W. A., Damasio, A., Damasio, H., D'Arms, J., Davidson, J. W., de Gelder, B., Deonna, J., de Sousa, R. . . . Sander, D. (2021). The rise of affectivism. *Nature Human Behaviour*, 1–5.

Dygert, S. K., & Jarosz, A. F. (2020). Individual differences in creative cognition. *Journal of Experimental Psychology: General*, 149(7), 1249.

Emery, N. J. (2004). The evolution of social cognition. In *The cognitive neuroscience of social behaviour* (pp. 127–168). Psychology Press.

Ferrè, E. R., & Haggard, P. (2020). Vestibular cognition: State-of-the-art and future directions. *Cognitive Neuropsychology*, 1–8.

Frith, C., & Frith, U. (2005). Theory of mind. *Current Biology, 15*(17), R644–R645.

Gallotti, M., & Frith, C. D. (2013). Social cognition in the we-mode. *Trends in Cognitive Sciences, 17*(4), 160–165.

Gentner, D. (2010). Psychology in cognitive science: 1978–2038. *Topics in Cognitive Science, 2*(3), 328–344.

Gibbs Jr., R. W. (2005). *Embodiment and cognitive science.* Cambridge University Press.

Glenberg, A. M. (2010). Embodiment as a unifying perspective for psychology. *Wiley Interdisciplinary Reviews: Cognitive Science, 1*(4), 586–596.

Grafman, J., Cristofori, I., Zhong, W., & Bulbulia, J. (2020). The neural basis of religious cognition. *Current Directions in Psychological Science, 29*(2), 126–133.

Henrich, J., Heine, S. J., & Norenzayan, A. (2010). Most people are not WEIRD. *Nature, 466*(7302), 29.

Hommel, B. (2020). Pseudo-mechanistic explanations in psychology and cognitive neuroscience. *Topics in Cognitive Science, 12*(4), 1294–1305.

Hsieh, S., Yu, Y. T., Chen, E. H., Yang, C. T., & Wang, C. H. (2020). ERP correlates of a flanker task with varying levels of analytic-holistic cognitive style. *Personality and Individual Differences, 153*, 109673.

Huettig, F., & Mishra, R. K. (2014). How literacy acquisition affects the illiterate mind – A critical examination of theories and evidence. *Language and Linguistics Compass, 8*(10), 401–427.

Jiang, R., Zuo, N., Ford, J. M., Qi, S., Zhi, D., Zhuo, C., Xu, Y., Fu, Z., Bustillo, J., Turner, J. A., Calhoun, V. D., & Calhoun, V. D. (2020). Task-induced brain connectivity promotes the detection of individual differences in brain-behavior relationships. *NeuroImage, 207*, 116370.

Jobin, A., Ienca, M., & Vayena, E. (2019). The global landscape of AI ethics guidelines. *Nature Machine Intelligence, 1*(9), 389–399.

Johnson, D., & Erneling, C. (Eds.). (1997). *The future of the cognitive revolution.* Oxford University Press.

Kay, P., & Kempton, W. (1984). What is the Sapir-Whorf hypothesis?. *American Anthropologist, 86*(1), 65–79.

Kilteni, K., Groten, R., & Slater, M. (2012). The sense of embodiment in virtual reality. *Presence: Teleoperators and Virtual Environments, 21*(4), 373–387.

Kingstone, A., Smilek, D., Ristic, J., Kelland Friesen, C., & Eastwood, J. D. (2003). Attention, researchers! It is time to take a look at the real world. *Current Directions in Psychological Science, 12*(5), 176–180.

Ktaiche, M., Fares, Y., & Abou-Abbas, L. (2021). Stroop color and word test (SCWT): Normative data for the Lebanese adult population. *Applied Neuropsychology: Adult*, 1–9.

Laland, K., & Seed, A. (2021). Understanding human cognitive uniqueness. *Annual Review of Psychology, 72*, 689–716.

Latheef, A., Ali, M. F. L., Bhardwaj, A. B., & Shukla, V. K. (2021). Structuring learning analytics through visual media and online classrooms on social cognition during COVID-19 pandemic. In *Journal of physics: Conference series* (Vol. 1714, No. 1, p. 012019). IOP Publishing.

Lara, B., Astorga, D., Mendoza-Bock, E., Pardo, M., Escobar, E., & Ciria, A. (2018). Embodied cognitive robotics and the learning of sensorimotor schemes. *Adaptive Behavior, 26*(5), 225–238.

Lieberman, M. D. (2007). Social cognitive neuroscience: A review of core processes. *Annual Review of Psychology*, *58*, 259–289.

Machery, E., & Faucher, L. (2017). Why do we think racially? Culture, evolution, and cognition. *Handbook of Categorization in Cognitive Science*, 1135–1175.

Metta, G., Sandini, G., Vernon, D., Natale, L., & Nori, F. (2008, August). *The iCub humanoid robot: An open platform for research in embodied cognition* (pp. 50–56). Proceedings of the 8th Workshop on Performance Metrics for Intelligent Systems.

Mishra, R. K. (2015). *Interaction between attention and language systems in humans*. Springer.

Mishra, R. K. (2018). *Bilingualism and cognitive control* (Vol. 6). Springer.

Mishra, R. K., Hilchey, M. D., Singh, N., & Klein, R. M. (2012). On the time course of exogenous cueing effects in bilinguals: Higher proficiency in a second language is associated with more rapid endogenous disengagement. *Quarterly Journal of Experimental Psychology*, *65*(8), 1502–1510.

Nikkel, D. H. (2010). *Radical embodiment* (Vol. 125). Wipf and Stock Publishers.

Nisbett, R. E., & Miyamoto, Y. (2005). The influence of culture: Holistic versus analytic perception. *Trends in Cognitive Sciences*, *9*(10), 467–473.

Núñez, R., Allen, M., Gao, R., Rigoli, C. M., Relaford-Doyle, J., & Semenuks, A. (2019). What happened to cognitive science?. *Nature Human Bhaviour*, *3*(8), 782–791.

Nweze, T., Nwoke, M. B., Nwufo, J. I., Aniekwu, R. I., & Lange, F. (2021). Working for the future: Parentally deprived Nigerian Children have enhanced working memory ability. *Journal of Child Psychology and Psychiatry*, *62*(3), 280–288.

Posner, M. I., & Rothbart, M. K. (2017). Integrating brain, cognition and culture. *Journal of Cultural Cognitive Science*, *1*(1), 3–15.

Prasad, S. G., Patil, G. S., & Mishra, R. K. (2015). Effect of exogenous cues on covert spatial orienting in deaf and normal hearing individuals. *PloS One*, *10*(10), e0141324.

Prasad, S. G., Patil, G. S., & Mishra, R. K. (2017). Cross-modal plasticity in the deaf enhances processing of masked stimuli in the visual modality. *Scientific Reports*, *7*(1), 1–11.

Pylyshyn, Z. W. (1980). Computation and cognition: Issues in the foundations of cognitive science. *Behavioral and Brain Sciences*, *3*(1), 111–132.

Rad, M. S., Martingano, A. J., & Ginges, J. (2018). Toward a psychology of *Homo sapiens*: Making psychological science more representative of the human population. *Proceedings of the National Academy of Sciences*, *115*(45), 11401–11405.

Ramírez-Esparza, N., García-Sierra, A., & Jiang, S. (2020). The current standing of bilingualism in today's globalized world: A socio-ecological perspective. *Current Opinion in Psychology*, *32*, 124–128.

Redshaw, J., Nielsen, M., Slaughter, V., Kennedy-Costantini, S., Oostenbroek, J., Crimston, J., & Suddendorf, T. (2020). Individual differences in neonatal "imitation" fail to predict early social cognitive behaviour. *Developmental Science*, *23*(2), e12892.

Rigoli, C. M., Goel, A. K., Bender, A., Goldstone, R. L., & Núñez, R. E. (2020). Where is cognitive science now? *CogSci*, 873–874.

Roberts, K. L., & Allen, H. A. (2016). Perception and cognition in the ageing brain: A brief review of the short-and long-term links between perceptual and cognitive decline. *Frontiers in Aging Neuroscience*, *8*, 39.

Roth, A. S. (2021). Shared agency. *The Stanford Encyclopedia of Philosophy* (Summer edn), Edward N. Zalta (Ed.), URL = https://plato.stanford.edu/archives/sum2021/entries/shared-agency/.

Saint-Aubin, J., Hilchey, M. D., Mishra, R., Singh, N., Savoie, D., Guitard, D., & Klein, R. M. (2018). Does the relation between the control of attention and second language proficiency generalize from India to Canada?. *Canadian Journal of Experimental Psychology/Revue canadienne de psychologie expérimentale*, 72(3), 208.

Schaller, M., Kenrick, D. T., Neel, R., & Neuberg, S. L. (2017). Evolution and human motivation: A fundamental motives framework. *Social and Personality Psychology Compass*, 11(6), e12319.

Schaller, M., Park, J. H., & Kenrick, D. T. (2007). Human evolution and social cognition. *Oxford Handbook of Evolutionary Psychology*, 491–504.

Schroeter, M. L., Kynast, J., Villringer, A., & Baron-Cohen, S. (2021). Face masks protect from infection but may impair social cognition in older adults and people with dementia. *Frontiers in Psychology*, 12.

Schunn, C. D., Crowley, K., & Okada, T. (1998). The growth of multidisciplinarity in the cognitive science society. *Cognitive Science*, 22(1), 107–130.

Senden, M., Peters, J., Röhrbein, F., Deco, G., & Goebel, R. (2020). The embodied brain: Computational mechanisms of integrated sensorimotor interactions with a dynamic environment. *Frontiers in Computational Neuroscience*, 14.

Senzaki, S., Wiebe, S. A., Masuda, T., & Shimizu, Y. (2018). A cross-cultural examination of selective attention in Canada and Japan: The role of social context. *Cognitive Development*, 48, 32–41.

Shapiro, L. (2019). *Embodied cognition*. Routledge.

Shin, D. (2018). Empathy and embodied experience in virtual environment: To what extent can virtual reality stimulate empathy and embodied experience?. *Computers in Human Behavior*, 78, 64–73.

Simon, H. A., & Kaplan, C. A. (1993, January). Foundations of cognitive science. In *Foundations of cognitive neuroscience* (pp. 1–47). MIT Press.

Skeide, M. A., Kumar, U., Mishra, R. K., Tripathi, V. N., Guleria, A., Singh, J. P., Eisner, F., & Huettig, F. (2017). Learning to read alters cortico-subcortical crosstalk in the visual system of illiterates. *Science Advances*, 3(5), e1602612.

Sperber, D., & Hirschfeld, L. A. (2004). The cognitive foundations of cultural stability and diversity. *Trends in Cognitive Sciences*, 8(1), 40–46.

Šrol, J., & De Neys, W. (2020). Predicting individual differences in conflict detection and bias susceptibility during reasoning. *Thinking & Reasoning*, 1–31.

Stephenson, L. J., Edwards, S. G., & Bayliss, A. P. (2021). From gaze perception to social cognition: The shared-attention system. *Perspectives on Psychological Science*, 16(3), 553–576.

Thelen, E. (2000). Grounded in the world: Developmental origins of the embodied mind. *Infancy*, 1(1), 3–28.

Uttal, W. R. (2001). *The new phrenology: The limits of localizing cognitive processes in the brain*. The MIT Press.

Vaccarino, F., & Walker, U. (2011). Responding to the globalisation challenge: A project for migrant families to maintain their language and culture. *International Journal of Diversity in Organisations, Communities & Nations*, 11(2).

Van Slyke, J. A. (2010). Cognitive and evolutionary factors in the emergence of human altruism. *Zygon®*, *45*(4), 841–859.

Varela, S. A., Teles, M. C., & Oliveira, R. F. (2020). The correlated evolution of social competence and social cognition. *Functional Ecology*, *34*(2), 332–343.

Von Eckardt, B. (2001). Multidisciplinarity and cognitive science. *Cognitive Science*, *25*(3), 453–470.

Index

For Product Safety Concerns and Information please contact our EU
representative GPSR@taylorandfrancis.com
Taylor & Francis Verlag GmbH, Kaufingerstraße 24, 80331 München, Germany

www.ingramcontent.com/pod-product-compliance
Lightning Source LLC
Chambersburg PA
CBHW050638280326
41932CB00015B/2696

9 7 8 1 0 3 2 3 2 6 5 6 6